THEOI MEGALOI:
THE CULT OF THE GREAT GODS
AT SAMOTHRACE

ÉTUDES PRÉLIMINAIRES
AUX RELIGIONS ORIENTALES
DANS L'EMPIRE ROMAIN

PUBLIÉES PAR

M. J. VERMASEREN

TOME QUATRE-VINGT-SEIZIÈME

SUSAN GUETTEL COLE

THEOI MEGALOI:
THE CULT OF THE GREAT GODS
AT SAMOTHRACE

LEIDEN
E. J. BRILL
1984

Artemidoros of Perge, relief cut into rock face at Thera.
Inscription: Μνημόσυνον Θήραι, καὶ ἕως πόλου ἄστρ' ἐπιτέλλει
γῆς ἔδαφός τε μένει, ὄνομ' οὐ λίπεν Ἀρτεμιδώρου.

SUSAN GUETTEL COLE

THEOI MEGALOI:
THE CULT OF THE GREAT GODS
AT SAMOTHRACE

WITH A FRONTISPIECE, 5 PLATES, 1 FIGURE AND 3 MAPS

LEIDEN
E. J. BRILL
1984

ISBN 90 04 06885 6

PRINTED IN THE NETHERLANDS BY E. J. BRILL

TABLE OF CONTENTS

PREFACE

I began to study the Samothracian mysteries many years ago in a seminar conducted by John Ferguson. Eventually I chose the clientele of the mysteries as a subject for a doctoral dissertation, completed under the direction of A. Thomas Kraabel and accepted at the University of Minnesota in 1975. Since that time I have been able to visit Samothrace, Thera, Delos, and other sites to examine buildings and inscriptions discussed in the text.

Over the years many people have offered advice and encouragement. I would like to thank here Charles Edson, John Ferguson, A. Thomas Kraabel, and Friedrich Solmsen. I am endebted to James McCredie for permission to examine material in the storerooms of the Samothrace Museum in 1976.

Many read the book in early drafts or manuscript form. I would like to thank for their comments and suggestions Michael Alexander, Jack Davis, Albert Henrichs, Michael Jameson, Eugene Lane, James McCredie, and M. J. Vermaseren.

I gratefully acknowledge support from the Graduate College of the University of Illinois at Chicago for a fellowship in 1976 to travel to Greece and the American Council of Learned Societies for a Grant-in-Aid in 1977 to prepare the final manuscript for the book.

I wish to record my thanks to Helen Hay and Susan Chiasson for typing various versions of a complicated manuscript, to Jack Davis for preparing a plan of the sanctuary, to Frank Williams for drawing the maps, to Renee Schwartz for proofreading, to Anni Gregor for support and hospitality, and to the Photography Laboratory at the University of Illinois at Chicago for preparing negatives from my slides.

Finally, I would like to dedicate this book to my family: Brock, Joshua, and Toby Cole, experienced travellers and patient comrades.

ABBREVIATIONS

Abbreviations for journals follow the system of *L'année philologique*. Other abbreviations are as follows:

AEMÖ	*Archäologisch-epigraphische Mitteilungen aus Österreich.*
Antike Denkmäler	E. Kalinka. *Antike Denkmäler in Bulgarien* (Schriften der Balkankommission, Antiquarische Abteilung, 4). Vienna 1906.
ATL	B. D. Meritt, H. T. Wade-Gery, and M. F. McGregor. *The Athenian Tribute Lists.* Princeton 1939-53.
BerlBer	Preussische Akademie der Wissenschaften, Berlin. *Monatsberichte.*
BMI	*Collection of Ancient Greek Inscriptions in the British Museum.* London 1874-1916.
Chapouthier	F. Chapouthier. *Les Dioscures au service d'une déesse* (Bibliothèque des Écoles françaises d'Athènes et de Rome 137). Paris 1935.
CIG	*Corpus Inscriptionum Graecarum.*
CIL	*Corpus Inscriptionum Latinarum.*
CIMRM	M. J. Vermaseren. *Corpus Inscriptionum et Monumentorum Religionis Mithriacae.* The Hague I-II, 1956-60.
CIRB	*Corpus Inscriptionum Regni Bosporani.* Leningrad 1965.
Denkmäler	H. Swoboda, J. Keil, and F. Knoll. *Denkmäler aus Lykaonien, Pamphylien und Isaurien.* Prague 1935.
EAD	T. Homolle, etc. *Exploration archéologique de Délos.* École française d'Athènes. Paris 1909-.
Études thasiennes	*Études thasiennes.* École française d'Athènes. Paris 1944-.
FGrHist	F. Jacoby. *Die Fragmente der griechischen Historiker.* Berlin and Leiden 1923-.
GGR	M. Nilsson. *Geschichte der Griechischen Religion.* Munich I[3], 1967; I[2], 1961.
Guide[4]	K. Lehmann. *Samothrace. A Guide to the Excavations and the Museum.* Locust Valley, New York 1975[4].
Hemberg	B. Hemberg. *Die Kabiren.* Uppsala 1950.
Holleaux, *Études*	M. Holleaux. *Études d'epigraphie et d'histoire grecques.* Paris 1938-68.
HRR	H. W. G. Peter. *Historicorum Romanorum Reliquiae.* Leipzig 1906-14.
IAOSPE	B. Latyšev. *Inscriptiones Antiquae Orae Septentrionalis Ponti Euxini Graecae.* Petersburg I[2], 1916; II-IV, 1890-1901.
ID	*Inscriptiones de Délos.* Paris 1926-.
IG	*Inscriptiones Graecae.*
IGBR	G. Mihailov. *Inscriptiones Graecae in Bulgaria Repertae.* Sophia I-IV, 1956-68; I[2], 1970.

ILind	C. Blinkenberg. *Lindos. Fouilles de l'acropole II: Inscriptions.* Berlin and Copenhagen 1941.
ILS	H. Dessau, *Inscriptiones Latinae Selectae.* 1892-1916.
IOlb	*Inscriptiones Olbiae, 1917-65.* Leningrad 1968.
IPerg	M. Fränkel. *Die Inschriften von Pergamon (Altertümer von Pergamon VIII).* Berlin 1890-95.
IPrien	F. Hiller von Gaertringen. *Die Inschriften von Priene.* Berlin 1906.
LeBas and Waddington	P. LeBas and W. H. Waddington. *Inscriptions grecques et latines recueillies en Asie mineure.* Hildesheim 1972 (reprint of P. LeBas and W. H. Waddington. *Voyage archéologique en Grèce et en Asie mineure.* Inscriptions III, première partie. Paris 1870).
LGS	J. von Prott and L. Ziehen. *Leges Graecorum Sacrae.* Leipzig I, 1896; II, 1906.
LSAM	F. Sokolowski. *Lois sacrées de l'Asie mineure* (École française d'Athènes, Travaux et mémoires, 9). Paris 1955.
LSCG	F. Sokolowski. *Lois sacrées des cités grecques* (École française d'Athènes, Travaux et mémoires 18). Paris 1969.
LSCG Suppl.	F. Sokolowski. *Lois sacrées des cités grecques. Supplément* (École française d'Athènes, Travaux et mémoires 11). Paris 1962.
MP	D. Kanatsoules. Μακεδονικὴ Προσωπογραφία. Thessalonike 1955.
MRR	T. R. S. Broughton, *The Magistrates of the Roman Republic.* New York 1951.
Nock, *Essays*	A. D. Nock. *Essays on Religion and the Ancient World.* ed. Z. Stewart. Cambridge, Massachusetts 1972.
OGIS	W. Dittenberger. *Orientis Graeci Inscriptiones Selectae.* Leipzig 1903-05.
Opera Minora Selecta	L. Robert. *Opera Minora Selecta.* Amsterdam 1969.
PIR[1]	E. Klebs, H. Dessau, and P. von Rohden. *Prosopographia Imperii Romani.* Berlin 1897.
PIR[2]	E. Groag and A. Stein. *Prosopographia Imperii Romani.* Berlin 1933-.
POxy	B. Grenfell and A. S. Hunt. *The Oxyrhynchus Papiri.* London 1898-.
PSI	*Papyri greci e latini* (Pubblicazioni della Società italiana per la ricerca dei papiri greci e latini in Egitto). Florence 1912-.
RAEM	Th. Sarikakes. Ῥωμαῖοι Ἄρχοντες τῆς Ἐπαρχίας Μακεδονίας. Thessalonike 1971.
RE	G. Wissowa, etc. *Paulys Real-Encyclopädie der classischen Altertumswissenschaft.* Stuttgart 1894-.
Recueil	C. Michel. *Recueil d'inscriptions grecques.* Brussels 1900.
Samothrace 1	N. Lewis. *Samothrace 1, The Ancient Literary Sources.* New York 1958.
Samothrace 2.1	P. M. Fraser. *Samothrace 2.1, The Inscriptions on Stone.* New York 1960.
Samothrace 2.2	K. Lehmann, Samothrace 2.2, *The Inscriptions on Ceramics and Minor Objects.* New York 1960.

Samothrace 3	P. W. Lehmann, *Samothrace* 3.1-3, *The Hieron*. Princeton 1969.
Samothrace 4.1	K. Lehmann. *Samothrace* 4.1, *The Hall of Votive Gifts*. New York 1962.
Samothrace 4.2	K. Lehmann and Denys Spittle. *Samothrace* 4.2, *The Altar Court*. New York 1964.
Samothrake I	A. Conze, A. Hauser, and G. Niemann. *Archäologische Untersuchungen auf Samothrake*. Vienna 1875.
Samothrake II	A. Conze, A. Hauser, and O. Benndorf. *Neue archäologische Untersuchungen auf Samothrake*. Vienna 1880.
SEG	*Supplementum Epigraphicum Graecum*.
SGDI	H. Collitz and F. Bechtel. *Sammlung der griechischen Dialekt-Inschriften*. Göttingen 1884-1915.
SIG	W. Dittenberger. *Sylloge Inscriptionum Graecarum*. Leipzig 1883¹; 1898²; 1915-1924³ (reprint 1960).
SP III	D. L. Page. *Select Papyri III: Literary Papyri, Poetry*. London and Cambridge, Massachusetts 1962.
Staatsverträge	H. H. Schmitt. *Die Staatsverträge des Altertums*. Munich 1969.
Thera	F. Hiller von Gaertringen and P. Wilski. *Stadtgeschichte von Thera*. Berlin 1904.
TAM	*Tituli Asiae Minoris*. Vienna 1920-.
TitCam	M. Serge and I. Pugliese Carratelli. "Tituli Camirenses," *ASAA* 11-13 (1949-50) 141-318; 15-17 (1952-54) 211-46.
TMMM	F. Cumont. *Textes et monuments figures relatifs aux mystères de Mithra*. Brussels I-II, 1886-98.
Vidman, *Sylloge*	L. Vidman, *Sylloge Inscriptionum Religionis Isiacae et Sarapiacae* (*RGVV* 28). Berlin 1969.

BIBLIOGRAPHY

Abbott, G. F. "A Greek Inscription from Dedeagatch," *CR* 15 (1901) 84-85.

Accame, S. "Iscrizioni del Cabirio di Lemno," *ASAA* n.s. 3-5 (1941-1943) 75-105.

Accame, S. "Una lettera di Filippo V," *RFIC* 69 (1941) 179-93.

Applebaum, S. *Jews and Greeks in Ancient Cyrene* (Leiden 1979).

Andreades, A. M. "Les finances de guerre d'Alexandre le grand," *Annales d'histoire économique et sociale* 1 (1929) 321-33.

Arbesmann, R. *Das Fasten bei den Griechen und Römern* (*RGVV* 21; Giesen 1929).

Badian, E. "A King's Notebooks," *HSPh* 72 (1968) 183-204.

Baege, W. *De Macedonum Sacris* (*Dissertationes Philologicae Halenses* 22 1913).

Bakalakis, A. and Scranton, R. L. "An Inscription from Samothrace," *AJPh* 60 (1939) 452-58.

Barbritsas, A. Κ. "Σχέσεις τῆς Μακεδονίας μὲ τὴν Θράκην καὶ τῆς ἰδιῶς τὴν Σαμοθράκην κατὰ τὴν Ἑλληνιστικὴν ἐποχήν," (*Ancient Macedonia* I; Thessalonike 1970) 109-14.

Barth, K. *Die Kabiren in Deutschland* (Erlangen 1832).

Bartoletti, V. "Frammenti di un rituale d'iniziazione ai misteri," *ASNP* 6 (1937) 143-52.

Belin de Ballu, E. *Olbia. Cité antique du littoral nord de la Mer Noire* (Leiden 1972).

Bell, H. I. *Cults and Creeds in Greco-Roman Egypt* (Liverpool 1953).

Bell, H. I. "Popular Religion in Graeco-Roman Egypt," *JEA* 24 (1948) 82-97.

Bellinger, A. R. *Essays on the Coinage of Alexander the Great* (New York 1963).

Beloch, K. J. *Griechische Geschichte* (Strassburg 1912-1927²).

Bernand, A. *Le Paneion d'El-Kanaïs: Les inscriptions grecques* (Leiden 1972).

Bernand, E. *Inscriptions métriques de l'Égypte gréco-romain* (Paris 1969).

Bernand, E. *Recueil des inscriptions grecques du Fayoum I* (Leiden 1975).

Bianchi, U. *The Greek Mysteries* (Leiden 1976).

Bieber, M. *The Sculpture of the Hellenistic Age* (New York 1961).

Blau, O. and Schlottmann, K. "Mittheilung über die Altertümer der von ihnen im Sommer 1854 besuchten Inseln Samothrake und Imbros," *BerlBer* (1855) 601-36.

Blegen, C. "The Coming of the Greeks," *AJA* 32 (1928) 141-54.

Bloch, H. "L. Calpurnius Piso Caesoninus in Samothrace and Herculaneum," *AJA* 44 (1940) 485-93.

Bodnar, E. W. *Cyriacus of Ancona's Journeys in the Propontis and Northern Aegean, 1441-1445* (Philadelphia 1976).

Boehlau, J. and Schefold, K. *Larisa am Hermos* (Berlin 1940).

Boesch, P. Θεωρός (Berlin 1908).

Bonfante, G. "A Note on the Samothracian Language," *Hesperia* 24 (1955) 101-109.

Bonner, C. *Studies in Magical Amulets* (Ann Arbor 1950).

Bordenache, G., and Pippidi, D. M. "Le temple du Θεὸς Μέγας à Istros," *BCH* 83 (1959) 455-65.

Bosworth, A. R. "Alexander and Ammon," *Greece and the Ancient Mediterranean in Ancient History and Prehistory*, ed. K. Kinzl (Berlin 1977) 1-75.

Bousquet, J. "Callimaque, Hérodote, et le thrône de l'Hermès de Samothrace," *RA* 29-30 (1948) 105-31.

Brady, T. A. *The Reception of Egyptian Cults by Greeks during the Last Three Centuries before Christ* (The University of Missouri Studies 10.1; Columbia 1935) 1-88.

Broneer, O. Review of *Samothrace 4.2, The Altar Court*, by Karl Lehmann and Denys Spittle (New York 1964), *AJA* 71 (1967) 96-98.

Broughton, T. R. S. *The Magistrates of the Roman Republic* (New York 1951-1952).

Brown, R. F. *Schelling's Treatise on "The Deities of Samothrace"* (AAR Studies in Religion 12; Missoula, Montana 1974).

Bruneau, P. and Ducat, J. *Guide de Délos* (Paris 1966).

Bruneau, P. *Recherches sur les cultes de Délos à l'époque hellénistique et l'époque impériale* (Paris 1970).

Bruns, G. "Kabirenheiligtum bei Theben," *AA* (1964) 231-65 and (1967) 228-73.
Burkert, W. *Griechische Religion der archaischen und klassischen Epoche* (Stuttgart 1977).
Burkert, W. "Jason, Hypsipyle, and New Fire at Lemnos," *CQ* 20 (1970) 9-10.
Burton, A. *Diodorus Siculus Book I, A Commentary* (Leiden 1972).
Champoiseau, M. "Note sur des antiquités trouvées dans l'île de Samothrace," *CRAI* 20 (1892) 22-25.
Chapouthier, F. "Kabire béotien et Kabires de Samothrace," *REA* 44 (1942) 329-30.
Chapouthier, F. "La prétendue initiation de Pythagore à Délos," *REG* 48 (1935) 414-23.
Chapouthier, F. *Le sanctuaire des dieux de Samothrace* (*EAD* XVI; Paris 1935).
Collart, P. and Devambez, P. "Voyage dans le région du Strymon," *BCH* 55 (1931) 171-206.
Conze, A. *Reise auf den Inseln des Thrakischen Meeres* (Hanover 1860).
Cook, J. M. Review of *Samothrace 4.2, The Altar Court*, by Karl Lehmann and Denys Spittle (New York 1964), *CR* 15 (1965) 130-131.
Coquart, E. "Note explicative accompagnée de plans et dessins au rapport de M. Gustave Deville," *Archives des missions scientifiques et littéraires* ser. 2, 4 (1867) 267-78.
Corbett, P. E. "Greek Temples and Greek Worshippers," *BICS* 17 (1970) 149-58.
Cormack, J. M. R. "L. Calpurnius Piso," *AJA* 48 (1944) 76-77.
Cosi, D. M. "Adamma: un problema e qualche proposta," *AAPat* n.s. 88 (1975-1976) 149-56.
Creuzer, F. *Symbolik und Mythologie der alten Völker* (Leipzig 1810-1812).
Cumont, F. *Catalogus Codicum Astrologorum* (Brussels 1898-1921).
Cumont, F. "Un fragment de rituel d'initiation aux mystères," *HThR* 26 (1933) 151-60.
Cumont, F. "Les mystères de Samothrace et l'année caniculaire," *RHR* 127 (1944), 55-60.
D'Arms, J. *Commerce and Social Standing at Rome* (Cambridge, Mass. 1981).
Daux, G. "Théores et théarodoques," *REG* 80 (1967) 292-300.
Daux, G. "Trois inscriptions de la Grèce du Nord," *CRAI* (1972) 478-93.
Deville, G. "Rapport sur une mission dans l'île de Samothrace," *Archives des missions scientifiques et littéraires*, ser. 2, 4 (1867) 253-65.
Dieterich, A. *Eine Mithrasliturgie* (Leipzig and Berlin 1923³).
Dieterich, A. "Ueber eine Scene der aristophanishen Wolken," *RhM* 48 (1893) 275-83 = *Kleine Schriften* (Leipzig and Berlin 1911) 117-24.
Dimitrov, D. P. "Neuentdeckte epigraphische Denkmäler über die Religion der Thraker in der frühhellenistischen Epoche," *Latomus* 28 (1957) 181-93.
Dimitrov, D. P. "Seuthopolis, ville thrace, près du village Koprinka de la région Kazanluk," *SA* (1957) 199-216.
Dimitrov, D. P. and Čičikova, M. *The Thracian City of Seuthopolis* (BAR Supplementary Series 38; London 1978).
Dörpfeld, W. *Troja und Ilion* (Athens 1902, reprint 1968).
Dohrn, T. *Die Tyche von Antiochia* (Berlin 1960).
Düll, S. *Die Götterkulte Nordmakedoniens in römischer Zeit* (Munich 1977).
Dunand, F. *Le culte d'Isis dans le bassin oriental de la Méditerranée* (Leiden 1973).
Dusenbery, E. B. "Two Attic Red-figured Kraters in Samothrace," *Hesperia* 47 (1978) 211-43.
Duthoy, R. *The Taurobolium* (Leiden 1969).
Edson, C. "Cults of Thessalonica," *HThR* 41 (1948) 153-204.
Eckstein, F. "Review of *Samothrace 4.2, The Altar Court*, by Karl Lehmann and Denys Spittle," *Gnomon* 38 (1966) 817-23.
Ellis, J. R. *Philip II and Macedonian Imperialism* (London 1976).
Farber, G. S. *A Dissertation on the Mysteries of the Cabiri* (Oxford 1803).
Farnell, L. R. *Cults of the Greek States* (Oxford 1896-1909).
Ferguson, J. *The Religions of the Roman Empire* (London 1970).
Ferguson, W. S. "Orgeonika," *Hesperia* Suppl. 8 (1949) 130-63.
Firatli, N. and Robert, L. *Les stèles funéraires de Byzance gréco-romaine* (Paris 1964).
Fleischer, R. *Artemis von Ephesos und verwandte Kultstatuen aus Anatolien und Syrien* (Leiden 1973).
Foucart, P. "Inscriptions du Pirée," *BCH* 6 (1882) 278-82.
Foucart, P. "Στρατηγὸς Ὕπατος, Στρατηγὸς Ἀνθύπατος," *RPh* 23 (1899) 254-73.
Fraser, P. M. and McDonald, A. H. "Philip V and Lemnos," *JRS* 42 (1952) 81-83.

Fraser, P. M. *Ptolemaic Alexandria* (Oxford 1972).
Fraser, P. M. and Bean, E. G. *The Rhodian Peraea and Islands* (Oxford 1954).
Fraser, P. M. "Two Dedications from Cyrenaica," *ABSA* 57 (1962) 25-27.
Fraser, P. M. "Two Studies on the Cult of Sarapis in the Hellenistic World," *OAth* 1 (1960) 1-54.
Fredricksmeyer, E. A. *The Religion of Alexander the Great* (Diss: University of Wisconsin 1958).
Frisch, P. *Die Inschriften von Ilion* (*IGSK* 3; Bonn 1975).
Frisch, P. *Die Inschriften von Lampsakos* (*IGSK* 6; Bonn 1978).
Gardiner, E. N. *Olympia; Its History and Remains* (Oxford 1925).
Ginouvès, R. *Balaneutikè, Recherches sur le bain dans l'antiquité grecque* (Paris 1962).
Goldstein, M. *The Setting of the Ritual Meal in Greek Sanctuaries* (Diss: Univ. of California 1978).
Gow, A. S. F. and Page, D. L. *The Greek Anthology* (Cambridge 1965).
Graillot, H. *Le culte de Cybèle, mère des dieux, à Rome et dans l'Empire romain* (Paris 1912).
Griffith, G. T. "The Macedonian Background," *G & R* 12 (1965) 125-39.
Griffiths, J. G. *Apuleius, The Isis-Book* (Leiden 1976).
Grimm, G. *Kunst der Ptolemäer- und Römerzeit im Ägyptischen Museum Kairo* (Mainz 1975).
Guarducci, M. "Le offerte dei conquistatori Romani ai santuari della Grecia," *RPAA* 13 (1937) 41-58.
Habicht, C. *Gottmenschentum und griechische Städte* (Munich 1970²).
Hadzisteliou-Price, T. "An Enigma in Pella: the Tholos and Herakles Phylakos," *AJA* 77 (1973) 66-71.
Hahn, L. *Rom und Romanismus im griechisch-römischen Osten* (Leipzig 1906).
Hamilton, J. R. *Plutarch. Alexander, A Commentary* (Oxford 1969).
Hampl, F. "Alexanders des Grossen *Hypomnemata* und letzte Pläne," *Studies Presented to D. M. Robinson* (St. Louis 1953) II, 816-29.
Hasluck, F. *Cyzicus* (Cambridge 1910).
Hatzfeld, J. "Les Italiens résidant à Délos," *BCH* 36 (1912) 5-218.
Hatzfeld, J. *Les trafiquants italiens dans l'Orient hellénique* (Paris 1919).
Heisserer, A. J. *Alexander the Great and the Greeks. The Epigraphic Evidence* (Norman, Oklahoma 1980).
Henderson, B. W. *Life and Principate of the Emperor Hadrian* (London 1923).
Hepding, H. *Attis, seine Mythen und sein Kult* (*RGVV* 1, Giessen 1903).
Herbrecht, H. *De sacerdotii apud Graecos emptione venditione* (Dissertationes Philologicae Argentoratenses 10; 1885).
Herter, H. *De Priapo* (*RGVV* 23, Giessen 1932).
Hiller von Gaertringen, F. "Die samothrakischen Götter in Rhodos und Karpathos," *MDAI* (*A*) 18 (1893) 391-94.
Hirst, G. M. "The Cults of Olbia," *JHS* 23 (1903) 24-53.
Jeanmaire, H. *Couroi et courètes* (Lille 1939).
Kane, J. P. "The Mithraic Cult Meal in its Greek and Roman Environment," *Mithraic Studies*, ed. J. R. Hinnells (Manchester 1975).
Kerényi, K. "The Mysteries of the Kabeiroi," *The Mysteries* (Papers from the Eranos Yearbooks 33.2, New York 1955) 32-63.
Kerényi, K. "Nach einem Besuch auf Samothrake," *Auf Spuren des Mythos* (Munich 1967) 201-08.
Kerényi, K. "Das Θ von Samothrake," *Geist und Werk aus der Werkstatt unserer Autoren zum 75. Geburtstag von Dr. Daniel Brody* (Zurich 1958) 125-37.
Kerényi, K. "Varro über Samothrake und Ambrakia," *Studi in onore di G. Funaioli* (Rome 1955) 157-62.
Kern, O. "Aus Samothrake," *MDAI* (*A*) 18 (1893) 337-84.
Kern, O. "Kabeiros und Kabeiroi," *RE* X, cols. 1399-1450.
Kern, O. "Zu dem neuen Mysterieneide," *APF* 12 (1937) 66-67.
Klauser, T. *Reallexikon für Antike und Christentum* (Stuttgart 1950-).
Kleywegt, A. J. *Varro über die Penaten und die „Grossen Götter"* (Mededelingen der Koninklijke Nederlandse Akademie van Wetenschappen. Afd. Letterkunde N.R. 35, no. 7, Amsterdam 1972).

Kontorini, V. "L'autonomie de Ptolémaïs-Akko," *RN* ser. 6, 21 (1979) 30-41.
Körte, A. "Literarische Texte mit Ausschluss," *APF* 10 (1931-1932) 56-61.
Kornemann, E. *Kaiser Hadrian* (Leipzig 1905).
Kourouniotes, K. "Εἰς τὸ Ἀνάκτορον τῆς Ἐλευσίνος," *AD* 10 (1926) 145-49.
Kourouniotes, K. Ἐλευσινιακά (Athens 1932).
Kraabel, A. T. "Ὕψιστος and the Synagogue at Sardis," *GRBS* 10 (1969) 87-93.
Kraus, T. *Hekate. Studien zu Wesen und Bild der Göttin in Kleinasien* (Heidelberg 1960).
Laidlaw, W. A. *A History of Delos* (Oxford 1933).
Lambrino, S. "Les tribus ioniénnes d'Histria," *Istros* 1 (1934) 117-26.
Lazarides, D. Ὁδηγὸς Μουσείου Καβάλας (Athens 1969).
Lazarides, D. Σαμοθράκη καὶ ἡ Περαία (Ancient Greek Cities, no. 7; Athens 1971).
Lehmann-Hartleben, K. "Cyriacus, Aristotle, and Teiresias in Samothrace," *Hesperia* 12 (1943) 118-34.
Lehmann, K. "Documents of the Samothracian Language," *Hesperia* 24 (1955) 93-100.
Lehmann-Hartleben, K. "Excavations in Samothrace," *AJA* 43 (1939) 133-45.
Lehmann, K. "Excavations in Samothrace, Summer 1948," *Archaeology* 2 (1949) 40-41.
Lehmann, K. "From the Bulletin on the 1949 Campaign in Samothrace," *AJA* 54 (1950) 128-29.
Lehmann, K. "Kallistratos Meets a Centaur," *AJA* 61 (1957) 124-27.
Lehmann, K. "The Mystery Cult of Samothrace, Excavations in 1953," *Archaeology* 7 (1954) 91-95.
Lehmann-Hartleben, K. "Observations in Samothrace," *AJA* 42 (1938) 126.
Lehmann-Hartleben, K. "Preliminary Report on the Second Campaign of Excavation in Samothrace," *AJA* 44 (1940) 328-58.
Lehmann, K. "Samothrace: Fifth Preliminary Report," *Hesperia* 21 (1952) 19-43.
Lehmann, K. "Samothrace: Fourth Preliminary Report," *Hesperia* 20 (1951) 1-30.
Lehmann, K. "Samothrace: Seventh Campaign of Excavations, 1952," *Archaeology* 6 (1953) 30-35.
Lehmann, K. "Samothrace: Sixth Preliminary Report," *Hesperia* 22 (1953) 1-24.
Lehmann, K. "Samothrace: Third Preliminary Report," *Hesperia* 29 (1950) 1-20.
Lehmann, K. "The State of Antiquities in Samothrace," *Archaeology* 1 (1948) 44-49.
Lehmann, P. W. "Addendum to *Samothrace*, Volume 3: The Lateral Akroteria," *Hesperia* 41 (1972) 463-65.
Lehmann, P. W. "Excavations at Samothrace," *AD* 16 (1960) 231-35.
Lehmann, P. W. "Excavations at Samothrace," *AD* 18 (1963) 261-64.
Lehmann, P. W. "The Floral Akroteria of the Hieron in Samothrace," *AJA* 67 (1963) 214.
Lehmann, P. W. "New Light on Skopas," *BASP* 15 (1978) 67-71.
Lehmann, P. W. *The Pedimental Sculptures of the Hieron in Samothrace* (New York 1962).
Lehmann, P. W. "Report on Samothrace," *Archaeology* 15 (1962) 129-30.
Lehmann, P. W. and Lehmann, K. *Samothracian Reflections: Aspects of the Revival of the Antique* (Princeton 1973).
Lehmann, P. W. *Skopas in Samothrace* (Northampton, Massachusetts 1973).
Lehmann, P. W. "The Wall Decoration of the Hieron in Samothrace," *Balkan Studies* 5 (1964) 277-86.
Levi, D. "Il Cabirio di Lemno," Χαριστήριον εἰς Ἀναστάσιον Κ. Ὀρλάνδον (Athens 1966) III, 110-32.
Linforth, I. M. "Greek Gods and Foreign Gods in Herodotus," *Univ. Cal. Publ. Class. Phil.* 9 (1926) 1-25.
Lobeck, C. A. *Aglaophamus, sive de theologiae mysticae Graecorum causis* (Königsberg 1829).
Lolling, H. G. "Altar aus Sestos," *MDAI (A)* 6 (1881) 210-14.
Longega, G. *Arsinoe II* (Rome 1968).
McCredie, J. R. "Excavations in Samothrace," *AD* 24 (1969) 365.
McCredie, J. R. "Excavations on Samothrace," *AJA* 69 (1965) 171; 71 (1967) 191; 73 (1969) 42; 75 (1971) 209.
McCredie, J. R. "Investigations in Samothrace 1971-1972," *AJA* 77 (1973) 221.
McCredie, J. R. "Recent Investigations in Samothrace," *Neue Forschungen in griechischen Heiligtümern*, ed. U. Jantzen (Tübingen 1976).

McCredie, J. R. "Samothrace: Preliminary Report of the Campaigns of 1962-1964," *Hesperia* 34 (1965) 100-24.

McCredie, J. R. "Samothrace: Preliminary Report on the Campaigns of 1965-1967," *Hesperia* 37 (1968) 200-34.

McCredie, J. R. "Samothrace: Supplementary Investigations, 1968-1977," *Hesperia* 48 (1979) 1-44.

McCredie, J. R. "A Samothracian Enigma," *Hesperia* 43 (1974) 454-69.

McCredie, J. R. "The Stoa on Samothrace: Preliminary Report," *AJA* 67 (1963) 214.

Maiuri, A. *Nuova silloge epigrafica di Rodi e Cos* (Florence 1925).

Marconi, P. *Agrigento arcaia* (Rome 1933).

Mason, H. J. *Greek Names for Roman Institutions. A Lexicon and Analysis* (American Studies in Papyrology 13; Toronto 1974).

Meiggs, R. *The Athenian Empire* (Oxford 1972).

Merkelbach, R. "Der Eid der Isismysten," *ZPE* 1 (1967) 55-73.

Metzger, B. M. "Methodology in the Study of the Mystery Religions and Early Christianity," *Historical and Literary Studies: Pagan, Jewish, and Christian* (Grand Rapids, Michigan 1968) 1-24.

Miller, S. G. "The Philippeion and Macedonian Hellenistic Architecture," *MDAI (A)* 88 (1973) 189-218.

Momigliano, A. *Filippo il Macedoni, saggio sulla storia greca del IV secolo a.e.* (Florence 1934).

Moore, M. B. "Attic Black Figure From Samothrace," *Hesperia* 44 (1975) 234-50.

Mueller, B. Μεγὰς Θεός (Dissertationes Philologicae Halenses 21.3; 1913).

Myers, J. L. *Herodotus, The Father of History* (Oxford 1953).

Mylonas, G. *Eleusis and the Eleusinian Mysteries* (Princeton 1961).

Nock, A. D. "A Cabiric Rite," *AJA* 45 (1941) 577-81.

Oberleitner, W. *Funde aus Ephesos und Samothrake* (Vienna 1978).

Oikonomides, A. N. "Misread Greek Inscriptions as Documents of the 'Samothracian,' 'Tarentine,' 'Gallic,' and 'Illyrian' Languages," *The Ancient World* 1 (1978) 159-66.

Oikonomos, G. Ἐπιγραφαὶ τῆς Μακεδονίας (Athens 1915).

Oliver, J. H. "Latin Inscription from Samothrace," *AJA* 43 (1939) 464-66.

Onurkan, S. "Artemis Pergaia," *MDAI (I)* 19-20 (1969-70) 290-96.

Papakonstantinou-Diamantourou, D. Πέλλα I (Athens 1971).

Parke, H. W. *The Oracles of Zeus* (Oxford 1967).

Perret, J. *Les origines de la légende troyenne de Rome* (Paris 1942).

Petsas, P. M. "A Few Examples of Epigraphy from Pella," *Balkan Studies* 4 (1963) 157-70.

Pettazzoni, R. *Essays on the History of Religions* trans. H. J. Rose (Leiden 1954).

Pettazzoni, R. "Una rappresentazione romana dei Kabiri di Samotracia," *Ausonia* 3 (1908) 79-90.

Picard, C. "L'entrée de la salle absidale a l'Attideion d'Ostie," *RHR* 135 (1949) 129-42.

Pick, B. *Die antiken Münzen Nord-Griechenlands* (Berlin 1898).

Pick, B. "Thrakische Münzbilder," *JDAI* 13 (1898) 134-74.

Piganiol, A. "Les Dionysies d'Alexandre," *REA* 42 (1940) 285-92.

Pippidi, D. M. *Conţributii la Istoria Veche a Romîniei* (Bucharest 1958).

Pippidi, D. M. *Epigraphische Beiträge zur Geschichte Histrias in hellenistischer und römischer Zeit (Berlin 1962).*

Pippidi, D. M. "*Inscriptions d'Istros. Décret inedit du IIᵉ siècle*," *Dacia* n.s. 5 (1961) 305-16.

Pippidi, D. M. "Monumente Epigrafice Inedite," *Histria* I (1954) 473-564.

Plassart, A. *Les sanctuaires et les cultes du Mont Cynthe* (*EAD* XI; Paris 1928).

Poland, F. *Geschichte des griechischen Vereinswesens* (Leipzig 1909).

Preller, L. and Robert, C. *Griechische Mythologie* (Berlin 1887-1926, reprint 1964).

Prinz, F. *Gründungsmythen und Sagenchronologie* (Zetemata 72; Munich 1979).

Ramsay, W. M. *The Cities and Bishoprics of Phrygia* (Oxford 1895-1897).

Reitzenstein, R. *Die hellenistischen Mysterienreligionen* (Berlin 1927).

Richardson, N. J. *The Homeric Hymn to Demeter* (Oxford 1974).

Robert, F. "Inscription métrique trouvée au Dioscurion délien," *BCH* 58 (1934) 184-202.

Robert, F. *Thymélè* (Paris 1939).

Robert, F. *Trois sanctuaires sur le rivage occidental* (*EAD* XX; Paris 1952).
Robert, L. "Arsinoè de Kéos," *Hellenica* 11-12 (1960) 146-60.
Robert, L. *Collection Froehner I* (Paris 1936).
Robert, L. "Décrets de Samothrace," *RA* 24 (1926) II, 174-87 (= *Opera Minora Selecta* 232-35).
Robert, L. *Études anatoliennes; recherches sur les inscriptions grecques de l'Asie mineure* (Paris 1937).
Robert, L. "Hellenica," *RPh* 65 (1939) 152-53.
Robert, L. "Inscriptions de Lesbos et de Samos," *BCH* 59 (1935) 471-88.
Robert, L. *Monnaies antiques en Troade* (Geneva and Paris 1966).
Robert, L. "Monument de Lysimacheia," *Hellenica* 10 (1955) 266-71.
Robert, L. "Un mot nouveau dans une inscription de Samothrace," *StudClas* 16 (1974) 85-88.
Robert, L. Review of *Samothrace* 2.1, by P. M. Fraser (New York 1960), *Gnomon* 35 (1963) 50-79.
Robert, L. *Le sanctuaire de Sinuri près de Mylasa* (Paris 1945).
Robert, L. *Villes d'Asie mineure* (Paris 1935).
Roebuck, C. *Ionian Trade and Colonization* (New York 1959).
Rönne, T. and Fraser, P. M. "A Hadra-vase in the Ashmolean Museum," *JEA* 39 (1953) 84-94.
Roscher, W. H. *Ausführliches Lexikon der griechischen und römischen Mythologie* (Leipzig 1884-1937, reprint Hildesheim 1965).
Ross, L. *Archäologische Aufsätze* II (Leipzig 1861).
Rostovtzeff, M., and Welles, C. B. "A Note on the New Inscription from Samothrace," *AJPh* 61 (1940) 207-208.
Roussel, P. "A propos d'un nouveau décret de Samothrace," *BCH* 63 (1939) 133-41.
Roussel, P. *Les cultes égyptiens à Délos du IIIe au Ier siècle av. J.-C.* (Nancy and Paris 1916).
Roussel, P. *Délos, colonie athénienne* (Paris 1916).
Roussel, P. "L'initiation préalable et le symbole éleusinien," *BCH* 54 (1930) 49-54.
Roussel, P. "La pérée samothracienne au IIIe siècle avant J.-C.," *BCH* 63 (1939) 133-41.
Roussel, P. "Remarques sur quelques règlements religieux," *BCH* 50 (1926) 305-18.
Roux, G. "Salles de banquets à Délos," *BCH* Supplement I (1973) 525-54.
Rubensohn, O. *Die Mysterienheiligtümer in Eleusis und Samothrake* (Berlin 1892).
Salač, A. "La dédicace du Nouveau Temple des Grands Dieux à Samothrace," *BCH* 70 (1946) 537-39.
Salač, A. "Le grand dieu d'Odessos-Varna et les mystères de Samothrace," *BCH* 52 (1928) 395-98.
Salač, A. "Inscriptions inédites de Samothrace," *BCH* 49 (1925) 245-53.
Salač, A. "Z Malé Asie, Samothraky a Thrakie," *Niederlův Sbornik* (Prague 1925) 158-59.
Salviat, F. "Addenda samothraciens," *BCH* 86 (1962) 268-304.
Salviat, F., Chapouthier, F., and Salač, A. "Le théâtre de Samothrace," *BCH* 80 (1956) 118-46.
Samuel, A. E. *Greek and Roman Chronology* (Munich 1972).
Schachermeyer, F. "Die letzten Pläne Alexanders des Grossen," *JÖAI* 41 (1954) 118-40 (= *Forschungen und Betrachtungen zur griechischen und römischen Geschichte* [Vienna 1974] 292-314).
Schachermeyer, F. "Prähistorische Kulturen Griechenlands," *RE* XLIV, cols. 1498-1548.
von Schelling, F. W. J. *Ueber die Gottheiten von Samothrake* (Stuttgart 1815, reprint 1968).
Schutz, O. "Ein neuer orphischer Papyrustext," *APF* 13 (1939) 210-12.
Schwyzer, E. *Griechische Grammatik* (Munich 1963²).
Seyrig, H. "Un édifice et un rite de Samothrace," *CRAI* (1965) 105-10.
Shofman, A. S. "The Religious Policy of Alexander the Great," *VDI* 140 (1970) 111-20.
Simon, M. "Theos Hypsistos," *Ex Orbe Religionum, Studia Geo Widengren* (Leiden 1972).
Smith, D. R. *The Functions and Origins of Hieropoioi* (Diss: Univ. of Pennsylvania 1968).
Smith, D. R. "Hieropoioi and Hierothytai on Rhodes," *AC* 41 (1972) 532-39.
Smith, D. R. "The Hieropoioi on Kos," *Numen* 20 (1973) 38-47.
Steinleitner, F. *Die Beicht im Zusammenhange mit der sakralen Rechtspflege in der Antike* (Leipzig 1913).
Stewart, A. *Skopas of Paros* (Park Ridge, N. J. 1977).
Stoian, I. *Tomitana, Contribuții epigrafice la istoria cețatii Tomis* (Bucharest 1962).

Tarn, W. W. *Alexander the Great* (Cambridge 1948).

Tarn, W. W. "Alexander's ὑπομνήματα and the 'World-Kingdom'," *JHS* 21 (1921) 1-17.

Taşliklioğlu, Z. and Frisch, P. "New Inscriptions from the Troad," *ZPE* 17 (1975) 101-14.

Teixidor, J. *The Pagan God* (Princeton 1977).

Točilescu, G. "Neue Inschriften aus der Dobrudscha," *AEMÖ* 14 (1891) 10-37.

Vermaseren, M. J. *Corpus Cultus Cybelae Attidisque* (Leiden 1977).

Vermaseren, M. J. *Cybele and Attis. The Myth and the Cult* (London 1977).

Vermaseren, M. J. and van Essen, C. C. *The Excavations in the Mithraeum of the Church of Santa Prisca* (Leiden 1965).

Versnel, H. S. "Mercurius amongst the *Magni Dei*," *Mnemosyne* 27 (1974) 144-51.

Visser, E. *Götter und Kulte im Ptolemäischen Alexandrien* (Amsterdam 1938).

Vitelli, G. "Frammenti della ,,Commedia Nuova" in un papiro della Società italiana," *SIFC* n.s. 7 (1929) 235-42.

Wächter, T. *Reinheitsvorschriften im griechischen Kultus* (*RGVV* 9.1; Giessen 1910).

Walbank, F. W. *A Historical Commentary on Polybius* (Oxford 1967-1979).

Walbank, F. W. *Philip V of Macedon* (Cambridge 1940, reprint 1967).

Weinreich, O. "Θεοὶ Ἐπήχοοι," *MDAI* (*A*) 37 (1912) 1-68.

Welles, C. B. *Royal Correspondence in the Hellenistic Period* (New Haven 1934).

von Wilamowitz-Moellendorf, U. *Der Glaube der Hellenen* (Berlin 1932).

Wilhelm, A. *Beiträge zur griechischen Inschriftenkunde* (Vienna 1909).

Witt, R. "The Kabeiroi in Ancient Macedonia," *Ancient Macedonia* 2 (1977) 67-80.

Wolters, P. and Bruns, G. *Das Kabirenheiligtum bei Theben* I (Berlin 1940).

Yavis, C. G. *Greek Altars* (St. Louis 1949).

Ziebarth, E. "Cyriacus von Ancona in Samothrake," *MDAI* (*A*) 31 (1906) 405-14.

Zijderveld, C. Τελετή, *Bijdrage tot de Kennis der religieuze Terminologie in het Grieksch* (Purmerend 1934).

CHAPTER ONE

INTRODUCTION

The Samothracian Gods

The Samothracian mysteries, celebrated on the island of Samothrace for perhaps as many as a thousand years, were the focus of a cult which attracted worshippers from the entire Greek and Roman world. After the decline of the mysteries in the fourth century A.D., the island and its rites were almost forgotten. A Byzantine writer of uncertain date may have visited the island; he described the sanctuary and some of its features.[1] Cyriacus of Ancona visited the island in 1444 and recorded several important Samothracian inscriptions, some of which have since disappeared.[2] Until the nineteenth century, however, the only information generally available about the island and its religion was found in ancient literary sources. Consequently, the only issues scholars discussed were the identity of the Samothracian gods and the meaning of their mysteries.

Scholars of the eighteenth and nineteenth centuries, concerned with discovering the origin of religion, believed that by explaining the enigmatic identity of the Samothracian gods, they would understand Greek and Roman religion as an early form of Christianity. Preoccupied with the question of origin, they tried to establish the etymology of the word Kabeiroi, a name which ancient writers often associated with the Samothracian gods.[3] Creuzer[4] and Schelling[5] constructed various arguments to show that the Samothracian gods were a triad whose nature prefigured the Christian trinity. Barth, attempting to show a Teutonic substratum, argued for parallels between the Samothracian gods and a pair of male divinities located by Tacitus in Germany.[6] Faber associated legends of the Kabeiroi with the flood story in the Bible.[7] Lobeck was the first to show that we cannot learn who or what the Samothracian gods were simply by an examination of the literary sources.[8]

Because ancient writers often knew of the Samothracian gods only by hearsay, and because the identity and nature of these gods were part of the secret of the mysteries, the evidence we have is confusing and often contradictory. Ancient writers did not know the sex of these gods, or their individual powers and attributes. They did not even know for certain how many gods there were although they always refer to them in the plural. Some writers call them Kabeiroi. Because of the use of this name, many argue that the Samothracian gods were identical with the Kabeiroi associated with mysteries elsewhere, specifically on Lemnos and at Thebes on the Greek mainland.[9] The term Kabeiroi, however, never appears at Samothrace where on inscriptions the gods are called either simply Theoi or Theoi Megaloi.[10] When the Samothracian gods are mentioned at other sites, they are called Theoi Samothrakes, never Kabeiroi Samothrakes.[11]

Herodotus[12] and Stesimbrotos of Thasos[13] are the earliest writers to call the gods worshipped on Samothrace Kabeiroi. The term is not used by others writing on Samothrace until Mnaseas in the Hellenistic period.[14] Hemberg argues that Herodotus is almost certainly, as is his propensity, using a familiar name for newly encountered gods on the basis of superficial similarities, and that the term Kabeiroi need not be taken as the Samothracian name for these gods.[15] Stesimbrotos is likely to be doing the same thing. Stesimbrotos' statement is preserved by Strabo.[16] Strabo also quotes an objection by Demetrios of Skepsis who does not think the term Kabeiroi was used at Samothrace because no *mystikos logos* was told there about the Kabeiroi. Clearly Demetrios, at least, did not believe that the Samothracian gods were called Kabeiroi.

Whatever the case, the Samothracian gods appear to be different in function from the Kabeiroi worshipped elsewhere. Initiation into the mysteries of the Samothracian gods was thought to provide protection from storms at sea.[17] The Kabeiroi on Lemnos were companions of Hephaistos and associated with metalworking and wine drinking.[18] At Thebes there was only one Kabeiros, associated with a younger male figure called Pais. Kabeiros was similar in appearance to Dionysos.[19] Demeter Kabeiraia was worshipped nearby.[20] There were some similarities between the Theban and Lemnian Kabeiroi cults and the cult at Samothrace. Mysteries were practiced at all three sites, and in all three cults there was a concern for explaining the origins of life.[21] The sanctuary at Thebes even shared some characteristics with the sanctuary at Samothrace. Both were located in valleys near streams and had apsidal buildings, but clearly the deities associated with each place were not identical.[22] It is possible that certain external similarities contributed to the identification of the Theban Kabeiros, the Lemnian Kabeiroi, and the Samothracian Theoi Megaloi, but there is no good evidence that these divinities were in origin the same or that the Samothracian gods were ever called Kabeiroi at Samothrace.

Mnaseas preserves a series of names which seem to be authentic Samothracian cult titles. His list includes four names: Axieros, Axiokersa, Axiokersos, and Kasmilos.[23] The first three, beginning with the same prefix, are interpreted in various ways. Because the scholiast who reports what Mnaseas said associates these names with the Eleusinian triad of Demeter, Persephone, and Hades, Karl Lehmann maintains that the central group of Samothracian deities consisted of two females and one male.[24] Burkert, attesting Varro's identification of the Great Gods with Jupiter, Juno, and Minerva, concurs.[25] Two objections can be raised. While the scholiast does seem to have had knowledge of special information in that he preserves titles known from no other source, there is no reason to believe that he actually knew what they meant, and it is even possible that he invented the identification with the Eleusinian divinities himself. Second, Varro is not concerned with identifying the Samothracian gods, but, as St. Augustine says, with improving upon Samothracian theology.[26] As Kleywegt points out, Varro is not influenced by any experience at Samothrace, but is concerned to show that the Capitoline triad of Jupiter, Juno, and Minerva are the Roman *dei magni* who because of similar titles must be the same as the Samothracian Theoi Megaloi.[27] Varro himself admits that the Samothracian Theoi Megaloi included a male pair.[28]

Mnaseas says that Kasmilos is added to the other three gods. If this is so, then Kasmilos, who may have been similar to Hermes with whom he is sometimes compared, is not one of the central group, but only an attendant.[29] The central group would still be a triad. Chapouthier[30] and Hemberg[31] interpret Mnaseas along these lines and argue that the triad was composed of a central female figure (Axiokersa) accompanied by two male divinities (Axieros and Axiokersos). Their interpretation is consistent with the fact that the Samothracian gods were identified with the Dioskouroi on Delos in the second century B.C., an identification which would be puzzling unless two of the Samothracian gods were male. In the same way, comparison in the literary sources of these gods to the Dioskouroi, Kouretes, and Korybantes, male divinities often associated with a female divinity, strongly suggests that the Samothracian gods were a triad consisting of two male deities attendant upon a goddess.[32] The goddess with attributes similar to those of Kybele who appears on Samothracian coins is likely to represent that female divinity.[33]

The same triadic structure appears in the legendary heroes associated with the mythical foundation of the mysteries. The story is told that Eetion (also Aetion or Iasion) and Dardanos, sons of Elektra, came to Samothrace where Eetion founded the mysteries[34] and Dardanos remained a short time before eventually going on to Troy to establish mysteries there.[35] The earliest reference to the figures of this myth is found in a papyrus fragment believed to record part of a Hesiodic catalogue.[36] The fragment mentions Elektra, Dardanos, and Eetion, but not Samothrace; it is therefore not established that this particular collection of these traditional characters actually originated at Samothrace. In fact it is unlikely that a Samothracian version of this story could already have been in general circulation at the time of Hesiod, because there is no evidence for Greek contact with Samothrace before 700 B.C.[37] Prinz in fact has shown that the Samothracian foundation myth is a compilation of various traditional elements put together sometime between the time of Hesiod and Hellanikos and that by the fifth century the Theban myth of Kadmos and Harmonia had become part of the story with Harmonia becoming the third child of Elektra.[38] The marriage of Kadmos and Harmonia was supposed to have taken place on Samothrace. Apparently the story of Kadmos and Harmonia figured in the celebrations associated with the annual festival because a scholiast says of Harmonia καὶ νῦν ἔτι ἐν τῇ Σαμοθράκῃ ζητοῦσιν αὐτὴν ἐν ταῖς ἑορταῖς.[39] The story of Kadmos and Harmonia was well established in Samothracian tradition by the Hellenistic period when the Samothracians conferred an award on the poet Herodes of Priene for a play about the deeds of Aetion and Dardanos and the deeds of Kadmos and Harmonia.[40]

Exploration and Excavation of the Samothracian Sanctuary

In the second half of the nineteenth century, Samothrace attracted the attention of European travellers and archaeologists, and the results of their investigations marked a new period in the development of Samothracian studies. The emphasis of this period was primarily on describing the buildings and sculpture of the sanctuary, but there was also an interest in collecting and publishing the Samothracian inscriptions. During this period, German, French, and Austrian explorers and archaeologists made important finds in the sanctuary. The early excavations were not extensive, but, because the site has been subject to vandalism during the last hundred years, the reports of these excavations are still of value for their record of finds which are now lost or destroyed.

In 1854 Blau and Schlottman visited the island and drew the first plan of the visible ruins.[41] In 1867 Alexander Conze made his first visit to the island and published a record of that visit.[42] In 1863, Champoiseau, French consul at Adrianople, discovered the now famous statue of the Nike of Samothrace.[43] In the same decade two French explorers, Deville and Coquart, visited the island and dug exploratory trenches in the sanctuary and charted seven of the main buildings.[44] Conze returned to Samothrace in 1873 and under his direction the first systematic excavations of the sanctuary began. He spent a second season at Samothrace in 1875. The photographs published with his excavation reports provide important evidence for buildings whose interior installations have been disturbed since this original excavation.[45]

No new work, except for the collecting and publishing of Samothracian inscriptions, was undertaken at Samothrace until after World War I. In 1923 A. Salač and F. Chapouthier made some excavations in the area of the Samothracian theater and in the area of two of the major buildings.[46] Nevertheless comprehensive excavation did not begin until 1938 when Karl Lehmann began to excavate in the northern area of the sanctuary. Interrupted by World War II, these excavations were resumed in 1948 and continue to the present day.[47] The project is now directed by James R. McCredie. Most of the main buildings of the sanctuary have been excavated, and although this latest series of excavations has not solved the problem of the identity of the

Samothracian gods or revealed the secrets of their rites, it has contributed much new evidence for the character of the cult and the nature of the buildings which housed the mysteries. Further, the discovery of many new inscriptions listing initiates of the mysteries and visitors to the sanctuary has greatly improved our understanding of the cult's clientele.[48]

The literary record indicates that the Samothracian mysteries were well known by the fifth century B.C., but the archaeological record shows that most of the important buildings of the sanctuary were not constructed until after the middle of the fourth century B.C. Dedicatory inscriptions found in the sanctuary itself indicate an interest in Samothrace on the part of the Macedonian aristocracy, and it is therefore very likely that the impetus for the expansion of the sanctuary in the early Hellenistic period came from the family of Alexander the Great. The initiate lists, however, give the impression of a wider clientele. During the Hellenistic and Roman periods Greek initiates came from Macedonia, Thrace, Asia Minor, and the Aegean islands. These areas are also the source of the *theoroi* sent by Greek cities as official delegates to the annual public festival at Samothrace.

The Hellenistic period was an important period of growth for the Samothracian mysteries. One reflection of this growth and an indication of the reputation of the cult is the existence of many Greek inscriptions mentioning the Theoi Samothrakes found at other sites. Most of them are dated to the Hellenistic and early Roman periods. Comparison of these inscriptions with the initiate and *theoroi* lists at Samothrace shows that their geographical distribution is similar to that of the sites mentioned in the inscriptions found on the island. Further, in spite of the appearance of many Romans as initiates at Samothrace itself, it was the Greek initiates who maintained an enduring religious interest in the Samothracian gods after leaving the island by making dedications, establishing priesthoods and festivals, and by building temples to these gods in their home cities.

Roman involvement at Samothrace was considerable, and records of Roman participation span the entire history of the extant initiate lists. One of the earliest lists records a Roman initiate, and the last dated list from the sanctuary records a Roman governor of Macedonia and his staff. However, there are no Romans listed among the *theoroi* sent to Samothrace, and there are no records found in Italy of dedications by Romans to the Samothracian gods. Clearly, the Roman initiates did not have the same ties with Samothrace as did their Greek counterparts.

A Description of the Island and the Sanctuary

No history of the Samothracian mysteries can ignore the way in which geography shaped the character and development of the cult. Samothrace is an island west of the Thracian Chersonesos, accessible both from Thrace and from the coast of Asia Minor. It is rocky and mountainous, and its physical characteristics determined in part its attraction for people from nearby islands and coastal areas. The Samothracian Mt. Phengari is the highest point in the Aegean between Mt. Athos and Mt. Ida, and is at times visible from as far away as Troy. By its very size this mountain seems to dominate the surrounding sea. It is no accident that the divinities associated with this island and its mountain were believed to have power over wind, sea, and storm. The island itself, difficult of access, was threatening and awesome, but it was also a haven. There was a legend that in the time of a great ancient storm, Samothrace was the only place to be saved, and that great stone altars were set up by the survivors in thanks for their preservation.[49] This story may be only a crude explanation for altars located in the sanctuary in historical times, but it does show that one of the important concerns of worshippers was protection at sea. The same concern motivated worshippers in the Hellenistic period when they made dedications to the Samothracian gods when saved from shipwreck. Initiation at Samothrace offered protection at sea,[50] aid in battle, safety in danger, and most certainly, protection after death.[51]

The town of Samothrace was located on the north coast of the island, near one of the island's few harbors, facing Thrace. The sanctuary was located just outside the gates of the city in a valley between two hills. In antiquity two streams cut through the valley and flowed through the sacred area to the sea, only a few hundred meters away. The central buildings where religious activities took place were located in a narrow gully between the two streams and bounded by the two hills. The limited area of the sanctuary required that the large stone buildings of the Hellenistic period be closely crowded together. On the hill to the east were the Propylaia, the formal entrance to the sanctuary, and on the hill to the west was the stoa, possibly the place where candidates for initiation stayed when visiting the sanctuary.[52]

The sacred area was entered from the north by a path leading out of the gate of the ancient town, running south to the Propylaia, a building dedicated by Ptolemy II (plan, no. 26). From the Propylaia, in the Hellenistic and Roman periods, the only structures immediately visible would have been a small Doric building opposite, on the eastern hill, a building dedicated by Philip III and Alexander IV (no. 24), a circular paved area next to it,[53] the Hieron (no. 15)[54], the Rotunda of Arsinoë (no. 20)[55], and the Hellenistic stoa on the far western hill (no. 11). The Anaktoron (no. 23) and the other buildings would have been hidden from view.

From the eastern hill the path descended to the main area of the sanctuary. The unusual form of the buildings in the central precinct suggests that they were unusual in function. There was no building whose specific purpose was simply to house a cult statue.[56] The Arsinoeion (no. 20) was round, and the

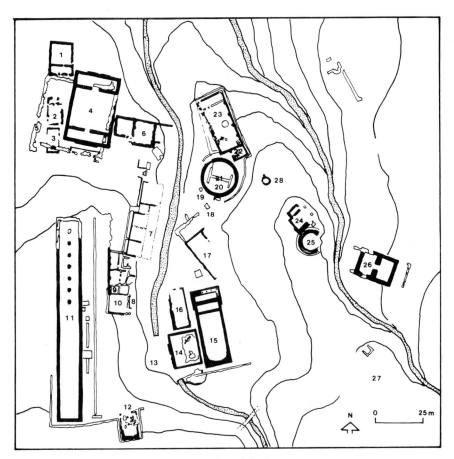

Samothrace: Plan of the Sanctuary
From a plan by John Kurtich, Guide⁴, plan II

1-3 Unidentified late Hellenistic buildings; 4 Unidentified early Hellenistic building; 5 Byzantine fort; 6 Milesian dedication; 7 Dining rooms; 8, 10 Unidentified rooms; 9 Archaistic niche; 11 Stoa; 12 Nike Fountain; 13 Theater; 14 Altar Court; 15 Hieron; 16 Hall of Votive Gifts; 17 Temenos; 18 "Altar of Hekate"; 19 Paved area with "rock altar"; 20 Arsinocion; 21 Orthostate Structure; 22 Southern chamber of Anaktoron; 23 Anaktoron; 24 Dedication of Philip III and Alexander IV; 25 Paved circular area; 26 Propylon of Ptolemy II; 27 Southern Nekropolis; 28 Round Doric building.

Hieron (no. 15) had an enclosed circular apse on its southern end. Four of the rectangular buildings had their main entrance on the side (nos. 14, 16, 17, 23). These side entrances may have been in part necessitated by the exigencies of the site, but this feature may also have been a consequence of specific cult needs. Several of the buildings had interior altars, and two of the large buildings, the Hieron and the Anaktoron, were equipped with benches for the seating of worshippers. These two buildings were designed to contain the activities associated with initiation. Like the Telesterion at Eleusis, they were intended for large groups of people.

Proceeding from north to south on the eastern bank of the stream to the west, the first building a visitor would have encountered was the Anaktoron (no. 23), a rectangular building with three divisions, the central one furnished with benches.[57] It is generally agreed that *myesis*, the first of the two stages of Samothracian initiation took place in the central area. Immediately to the south of the Anaktoron was the Arsinoeion, one of the largest known round buildings from antiquity, dedicated by Arsinoë II.[58] On the hill to the east of the Anaktoron and the Arsinoeion, a small round building of the early Hellenistic period has recently been discovered and excavated (no. 28). The function of this building is not known, but it may be the same small building depicted in relief on several Samothracian inscriptions.[59]

To the south of the Arsinoeion was a building named by its excavators the Temenos (no. 17). At its entrance on its eastern side was an Ionic propylon decorated with a sculptured frieze of dancing girls. The main section of this structure was an unroofed precinct containing two altars: a *bothros*, or pit, and an *eschara*, or hearth altar.[60] The Temenos may have served some purpose for ceremonies preliminary to initiation, but it has also been conjectured that this structure served for sacrifices and dancing ceremonies believed to have been part of an annual festival held at Samothrace.[61]

Directly to the south of the Temenos were three buildings, the largest of which was the Hieron (no. 15).[62] Like the Anaktoron, this building was equipped with benches. It has been identified as the site where *epopteia*, the second stage of Samothracian initiation, took place. Flanking the western side of the Hieron were buildings no. 14 and 16. No. 14 was called by Karl Lehmann the Altar Court, because he believed that it had originally contained a monumental altar.[63] However there are certain problems with the reconstruction of this building,[64] and other uses for the building have been suggested.[65] The facade of the building faced the *cavea* of the theater almost directly, and may have served as part of the *skene* when plays were performed there. The building numbered 16 on the plan has been called the Hall of Votive Gifts because Karl Lehmann believed that it was a repository for personal dedications and gifts donated by initiates and worshippers.[66]

North of the theater and built into the lower bank of the western hill was a series of small square rooms (no. 7), identified by their excavator, James McCredie, as dining rooms.[67] Between the theater and the series of dining rooms were two other rooms (nos. 10 and 8) of uncertain function, and immediately to the south of these was a curious construction of Hellenistic date, apparently a Hellenistic imitation of the entrance to a Mycenaean tholos tomb.[68]

Of the buildings in the northwest corner of the area the largest (no. 4) was never completed. The three smallest buildings (nos. 1-3) may have been treasury buildings.[69] The larger three chambered building (no. 6) was donated by a woman from Miletos in the Hellenistic period, but its function is unknown.[70] The stoa on the western hill (no. 11) probably provided shelter and refreshment for visitors to the sanctuary. Initiate lists were recorded on its walls, and the building commanded a view of the entire sacred area.[71] To the south and east of the stoa is the Nike Fountain (no. 12), the original site of the famous statue of Nike, or Victory, found at Samothrace in 1863.[72]

CHAPTER TWO

HISTORY OF THE SAMOTHRACIAN SANCTUARY

Early History

The early history of worship on Samothrace is obscure. The island seems to have been inhabited in the Neolithic period, but the earliest sites of inhabitation have not been excavated.[73] Diodoros, who preserves stories about an ancient storm at Samothrace, says that the original inhabitants of the island were autochthonous, but this is only his way of explaining the belief that certain arcane words, preserved in the Samothracian ritual, were remnants of an ancient dialect spoken on Samothrace by its original inhabitants.[74] Herodotus is conscious of a pre-Greek past because he says that the Pelasgians once lived on Samothrace, and that it was from these people that the Samothracians learned the rites which they practiced.[75]

Legends about the island suggest incursions by several groups.[76] The term zerinthian, associated with Samothrace by a late scholiast,[77] because of its -nth- suffix, could indicate ties with a pre-Greek Anatolian culture, but the evidence is not strong.[78] There may have been a migration from Thrace sometime during the Bronze Age or later. The Samothracians were known to have preserved in their later dialect words which may be Thracian, and the tradition of an ancient language, as related by Diodoros, may have its source in them.[79]

There is no evidence at Samothrace for contacts with Greeks before about 700 B.C. Karl Lehmann argues that Greek settlers came to the island at that time from settlements in the northern Aeolic islands or the coast of the Troad.[80] This hypothesis would mean that the first Greek influence on the Samothracian religion originated not in mainland Greece, but in the distinctive culture of the eastern Aegean and Asia Minor. From inscriptions found at Samothrace it is clear that the Aeolic dialect was still used there in the fourth century B.C.[81] Little is known, however, about the first Greeks at Samothrace. Karl Lehmann believes that the earliest indication of their presence is a deposit of pottery containing Greek vessels and local handmade cups and bowls.[82] This pottery was found in a sacrificial deposit which was later enclosed in the fourth century walled precinct known as the Temenos, indicating to Lehmann that already in the seventh century B.C. the Samothracian sanctuary was considered a sacred area. Lehmann also believes that a nearby rock formation was the site of early sacrifices by both Greeks and non-Greek Samothracians.[83] However new excavation in 1974 in the area of the rock formation has not confirmed Lehmann's early dating.[84] The date of the earliest religious activity therefore remains uncertain. Until the complete results of recent excavations are published, the issue of the earliest Greek settlement of the island remains an open question as well.

Excavation at Samothrace has not established the date of the earliest initiation ceremonies. The literary tradition associated with the island tells that the hero Iasion, also called Aetion or Eetion, the legendary founder of the mysteries, was the first to initiate strangers.[85] This story implies only that the mysteries never excluded outsiders, and gives no evidence for the date of their establishment. Herodotus uses the verb μυεῖν for the Samothracian ceremony when he mentions a secret story told only to initiates, a story which he is not permitted to tell. The fact that Herodotus claims to know a secret Samothracian story has been taken as evidence that he himself was an initiate, but at present one can only speculate about the nature of the rites in Herodotus' day.[86] It is not even clear that there were permanent buildings in the sanctuary in the fifth century B.C. Aristophanes refers to the Samothracian mysteries in a context which suggests that by the end of the fifth century, many Athenians were already acquainted with them, and that some were even initiates,[87] but such a suggestion is not clearly confirmed by the few Classical remains from the Samothracian sanctuary itself. The earliest inscribed ceramic dedications date from the second half of the fifth century B.C. They are all of local manufacture.[88] There are scattered finds of Athenian Black and Red Figure pottery in the sanctuary,[89] but these few examples are likely to be the result of trade rather than an indication of actual Athenian participation in the cult. One can infer that although the Samothracian ceremonies were open to foreigners from an early period, the operations of the sanctuary remained small, concentrated around open air altars[90] and perhaps carried on in small wooden structures throughout the Classical period, a time of relative poverty for the island.

The limited financial means of the Samothracian *polis* in the fifth century are one indication that religious activity at the Sanctuary was not yet an important source of income. The only external evidence for the financial status of Samothrace in the fifth century comes from a speech of Antiphon and from the Athenian tribute lists. When the island was suffering under the burden of paying tribute to Athens, Antiphon wrote a speech for a Samothracian delegation requesting that their assessment be reduced. Only fragments of the speech survive, but one of them describes the plight of the island: ἡ γὰρ νῆσος ἣν ἔχομεν δήλη μὲν καὶ πόρρωθεν ὅτι ἐστὶν ὑψηλὴ καὶ τραχεῖα· καὶ τὰ μὲν χρήσιμα καὶ ἐργάσιμα μικρὰ αὐτῆς ἐστι, τὰ δ' ἀργὰ πολλά, μικρᾶς αὐτῆς οὔσης.[91] Allowing for rhetorical exaggeration, Antiphon's remarks show that the Samothracians did not consider their island to be especially prosperous, and it therefore seems likely that the Samothracian mysteries were still a local affair, not generating enough income to affect the Samothracian economy.

The evidence from the Athenian tribute lists is difficult to assess because until the end of the century, the towns of the Samothracian *peraia* on the Thracian mainland were included in the Samothracian assessment. The Samothracian tribute from 452 until the 420's was six talents, but there is not a record for every year.[92] Meiggs suggests that Antiphon's speech may have been delivered in 425 in protest against a raise in the assessment,[93] explaining a low payment of two talents in 429 as an incomplete payment,[94] but it may reflect the fact that the towns on the mainland were then making payments on their own. Three of these towns, Drus, Zone, and Sale, appear on the tribute lists for the first time in 422/21.[95] If the Samothracian tribute was only two talents during this period, it would reflect a low standard of living for the only *polis* on an island of its size. Even six talents for Samothrace and the Samothracian *peraia* together is not excessive. The tribute for Thasos, for instance, was at this time thirty talents, the tribute for Lemnos was nine talents, and the tribute for Paros ranged from sixteen to eighteen talents.

Two things become clear from the fifth century evidence. Religious activity at Samothrace had attracted outside attention by the end of the fifth century, but the island had not yet achieved remarkable prosperity. The next step is to relate this picture with the archaeological evidence. At one time it was seriously argued that there were substantial stone structures in the sanctuary as early as the Archaic period. Karl Lehmann believed that the Orthostate Structure, a predecessor to the Anaktoron, was a double precinct built in the latter part of the seventh century B.C.,[96] and that the first version of the Anaktoron was built to the north in the late sixth century. In line with this development, Phyllis Lehmann has argued that the Hellenistic Hieron had two predecessors, the first built in the Archaic period, and the second in the Classical period. However excavations by James McCredie in 1974 have raised new questions about the dating of the Anaktoron and its predecessors. The most recent examination and excavation in the area of these two buildings suggest radically different dates for the Orthostate Structure and the Anaktoron and have necessitated a re-evaluation of the state of development of the mysteries in the Archaic and Classical periods.

McCredie's excavations have shown that Lehmann's Double Precinct had three rather than two divisions and that it was built in the first half of the fourth century B.C. instead of in the latter part of the seventh.[97] The date of the Anaktoron itself has also been considerably revised. Instead of dating from the end of the sixth century, the Anaktoron has been shown to date from the early Imperial period.[98] The Orthostate Structure, now dated to the first half of the fourth century B.C. is one of the earliest known stone structures in the sanctuary.[99] In dimension (30.5 m. × 12 m.) and design (three parallel divisions), it is almost identical to the later Anaktoron. Remains of a proto-Anaktoron on the same site as the Anaktoron date from the early third century B.C.[100] McCredie has now shown that the Orthostate Structure was the earliest of these, most likely the site of the celebration of *myesis*, the first stage of initiation at Samothrace, and that when the Arsinoeion was built in the early third century, a new building, similar in size and shape (the proto-Anaktoron) was built to the north of the Arsinoeion to replace the Orthostate Structure which had been covered over by the construction of the Arsinoeion. The third century proto-Anaktoron was apparently destroyed by earthquake in the first century B.C., and replaced soon after by the Anaktoron, of almost identical size.[101]

The new dating of the Anaktoron has serious consequences for claims of the Lehmanns that the Hellenistic Hieron had two predecessors, one Archaic and the other Classical.[102] On the basis of an inscription found at the door to the Hieron, it has been generally agreed that this building was the site of the Samothracian *epopteia*, the second stage of initiation.[103] Because there is now no evidence for a large stone building for *myesis* earlier than the fourth century, it is important to examine in detail Phyllis Lehmann's claim that a special building of monumental size for the celebration of *epopteia* existed as early as the Archaic period. Because *myesis* was a necessary prerequisite for *epopteia*, it is unlikely that a building would have existed for the celebration of *epopteia* if one did not exist for *myesis*.

The Date of the Samothracian Hieron

It is difficult to reconcile the character of the pottery found in the foundation trenches of the Hieron with the idea that there were two earlier buildings on the site. This pottery, except for one small piece from the late fifth century B.C.,[104] is no earlier than the fourth century B.C., a date consistent with that for the Hellenistic Hieron established on architectural grounds.[105] If there had been a large stone building on this site in the Archaic period, it is surprising that not a trace of Archaic pottery turned up in the excavation of the Hieron. The few Attic fragments of the late fifth century B.C., found in the fill of the Hellenistic pronaos,[106] could have been brought from an earlier dump. The inscribed sherds of Samothracian manufacture found in the same fill are of uncertain date, but most seem to be of the fourth century.[107]

The evidence upon which Phyllis Lehmann bases the reconstruction of the two predecessors of the Hieron consists in four things: several limestone blocks in the lowest foundation courses of the Hellenistic apse, some apsidal roof tiles, three separate levels in two stepping stones located to the east of the building, and an isolated Doric geison block of uncertain date.

There are serious problems in accepting these items as evidence for two predecessors of the Hellenistic building. The Doric geison block can be disposed of first. Although Phyllis Lehmann admits that it is too badly damaged to be dated accurately, she believes that it is Archaic and attributes it to a hypothetical Archaic predecessor of the Hieron only because she has no other available building to which she can assign it.[108] The geison block does present a puzzle, but this is not the only possible explanation. The block was found by the Austrian excavators beneath the Temenos (which they called "The Old Temple"). The location of the find does not require that it be associated with the Hieron; there may yet be found at Samothrace another building whose remains provide a fuller context for this isolated block.[109]

Another argument depends on the identification of a group of foundation stones lying at the lowest level of the apse of the Hieron.[110] In the apse of the Hieron are three different kinds of foundation stones, a course of crystalline porphyry field stones, a course of porous limestone blinders, and the first course of wall blocks of a finer limestone. Because the first course of wall blocks differs from the upper courses, Phyllis Lehmann claims that they come from two different periods and that the inner foundations of the apse are from a third and earlier version of the building. However, the porphyry field stones which she interprets as the foundations of an Archaic apse and the porous limestone blocks which she believes to be the foundation of a Classical apse adjacent to and enclosing the porphyry field stones may simply be the lowest subterranean foundations of the Hellenistic apse itself. It is significant that although the foundation trenches on other sides of the building were examined, no similar inconsistencies in the foundation stones appeared elsewhere. Rather than assuming that the variety of building material in the foundation of the apse indicates three different building periods, it would perhaps be preferable to consider that this variety had something to do with the nature of the apse itself. In view of the fact that the pottery from the foundation trenches dates from the fourth century, it seems necessary to accept the foundation stones of the apse as belonging to a single building dating from that time.

The significance of a series of rounded roof tiles is also open to debate. At issue are five red tiles and three black ones.[111] Because no early structures with a curved roof are known, Phyllis Lehmann postulates two consecutive roofed apses, one for an Archaic building and the other for a Classical building, with the black tiles from the former and the red ones from the latter. None of these tiles can have come from the Hellenistic apse as it has been reconstructed, since it is believed to have been enclosed beneath the pitched roof which covered the entire building.[112]

Phyllis Lehmann's assumption that these tiles must come from earlier versions of the apse is not indisputable. First, one of the black tiles is inscribed with an epsilon the style of which seems to date it roughly anywhere between the fifth and third centuries B.C. Although she does not make this difficulty explicit, she is apparently aware of it, attempting to dispose of it by suggesting that some of the tiles were from a fifth century repair. Second, there seems no good reason to associate all of these tiles with a single building. Although it is unfortunately impossible from the published reports to determine where all the tiles were found,[113] five at least were widely scattered.[114] If these rounded tiles were from earlier apsidal buildings on the site of the Hellenistic Hieron, it is curious that no similar tiles were found in the foundation fill of the Hellenistic apse. It is likely that the roof tiles in question came from a roof of the Arsinoeion, and it is not impossible that this building was roofed simultaneously with tiles of both colors.[115]

Phyllis Lehmann also argues that three distinct levels in a set of stepping stones along the outside eastern wall of the Hieron are to be associated with three different building periods, assuming that the height of the foundation of the building was raised each time the building was rebuilt. This picture is not consistent with the excavation of the interior of the building, where it is clear that in some places the Hellenistic floor goes down to bedrock.[116] It is hard to believe that the floor would not have been raised if the foundations had been raised.

It is more plausible to assume that the stepping stones had to be renewed because of hard use over a period of several hundred years. The two lowest levels of the stepping stones were of marble, but the top layer was made of rough cement framed by terracotta tiles. It seems unlikely that the final phase of the stepping stones, corresponding in Phyllis Lehmann's reconstruction to the most elaborate phase of the building, would be composed of such poor stuff. Phyllis Lehmann prefers to assume that the cement was originally topped with a marble slab, now lost. It would be simpler to explain the top layer as a rough repair installed during the period of crude remodelling of the Hieron known to have taken place in the second century.[117]

The inevitable conclusion, after considering the arguments for the two earlier versions of the Hieron, is that these buildings never existed. McCredie has shown that there was no building in the area of the Anaktoron before the fourth century.[118] Moreover, the only evidence for buildings elsewhere in the sanctuary before the fourth century is not conclusive. It consists of pottery used as fill in rubble walls of structures built in the stoa terrace in the Hellenistic period.[119] Fine examples of Attic Black and Red Figure pottery dating from the late sixth and fifth centuries B.C., found together with debris from a building believed to have been burned, indicate that there may have been some sort of a modest structure in the area as early as the late sixth century or the fifth century, but that structure may not have been contemporary with the earliest pottery associated with it. Another indication of fifth century activity is found on the eastern hill of the sanctuary. Clamps used in the construction of a series of steps in the open circular paved area suggest a date of the late fifth or early fourth century B.C. A small building adjoining the circular area was built later, sometime in the fourth century, before 323 B.C.[120] Karl Lehmann had dated the building which he called the Hall of Votive Gifts to the sixth century B.C.[121] This date, however, was suggested solely on the basis of stylistic considerations in spite of admitted difficulties in establishing the stratigraphy of the site, and by assuming that any fifth century pottery in the foundation ditches was the result of later intrusion. The structure, then, cannot be earlier than the fifth century B.C.

The only other evidence for early activity at Samothrace is problematical. There were two deposits of seventh century pottery beneath the Temenos. Whether these are from "sacrificial meals," as has been suggested, is not clear. What is clear is that there was no seventh century building associated with them. At one time, K. Lehmann maintained that sacrifices were conducted in the Archaic period in the area of the Orthostate Structure around two "rock altars" and in two deep shafts dug into the ground.[122] Given the revised dates of the Anaktoron and the Orthostate Structure by McCredie, it is no longer possible to assume that any of these items is as early as previously thought. One of the shafts is now described as "contemporary with" the foundation of the third century Arsinoeion, and the other may be considerably later.[123] It is possible that there was religious activity in the area of the two rock formations before the building of the Orthostate Structure in the fourth century B.C., but without further evidence, it seems premature to speculate about the nature of that possible activity.

The Development of the Samothracian Sanctuary in the Fourth Century B.C.

If the Hellenistic Hieron was the first building on its site, the date of its construction has important consequences for the history of the sanctuary. Fifth century Samothrace did not have the wealth to support large building projects. The fourth century, however, was a period of extensive building at Samothrace, and it is clear that this period of building had to be the result of outside interest and investment.

The first substantial building in the sanctuary, the Orthostate Structure, was built at about the time that Philip II came to power in Macedonia, and the Hieron, larger, grander, and more ornate, was begun while Alexander still ruled. During Alexander's reign three other buildings were constructed. First, sometime after 340 B.C. the precinct of the Temenos was enclosed by walls, and an Ionic propylon was constructed at its entrance, marking the earliest use of marble in the sanctuary.[124] Phyllis Lehmann suggests that it was Philip II himself who contributed the original donation which made this project possible.[125] Second, the building which Karl Lehmann calls the Altar Court was begun sometime between 340 and 320 B.C. Third, the Doric building on the eastern hill was dedicated by Philip III and Alexander IV between 323 and 317

B.C.[126] With these buildings and the Hieron, all begun within a period of about twenty-five years, it is clear that the development of the sanctuary was the result of a deliberate policy. The expenditure of what must have been a considerable amount of capital could have taken place at Samothrace only as the result of outside interest, and it now seems likely that this interest was generated by successful Macedonian military expansion. The questions we must ask are: who initiated this interest, and who was responsible for supporting the continuing expansion of the Samothracian sanctuary?

Plutarch tells of a tradition that Philip II met Olympias for the first time when they were being initiated at Samothrace. This story is almost certainly a romantic fiction,[127] but the association of Philip with Samothrace may well be fact. Curtius Rufus says that Alexander criticized his father for spending so much time at Samothrace when he could have been conquering Asia,[128] a criticism which implies a special interest in Samothrace on the part of Philip. As Phyllis Lehmann points out, Philip dedicated a building at Olympia to enhance Macedonian prestige.[129] It is not impossible that Philip also hoped to extend that prestige by contributing to the development of a sanctuary in the north, one well within the Macedonian orbit. Philip, together with his son Alexander, apparently donated a *hiera chora* on the Thracian coast to the Samothracian sanctuary.[130] The *hiera chora* was considered a possession of the gods of the sanctuary, as indicated by a boundary stone found on the mainland designating the territory as ἱερὰ χώρα Θεῶν ἐν Σαμοθρᾴκῃ.[131] The dedication of this territory shows a concern with establishing ties between the mainland and Samothrace. The city of Samothrace, as opposed to the sanctuary, had long had an interest in the Thracian mainland opposite the island, but the previous association had been political rather than religious.[132] Taken together with the dedications of the fourth century in the sanctuary itself, the consecration of the *hiera chora* on the Samothracian peraia indicates a desire on the part of the Macedonian dynasty to foster the sanctuary as a religious center.

It is important to notice, however, that the expansion of the Samothracian sanctuary continued and even gained momentum after Philip's death. Alexander, who apparently wasted no time himself in dallying at Samothrace, nevertheless is said to have included the Samothracian gods in a dedication left in India,[133] an indication that he may have had an interest in Samothrace himself. Although he is known to have donated 150 gold philippics for the rebuilding of the temple at Delphi,[134] it is believed that he was otherwise short of funds before he started east.[135] The picture changes considerably after the capture of Persian treasury funds at Gaugamela in 331; the continued building program at Samothrace seems to have been a direct result of this new wealth.

Can this activity be attributed to Alexander himself? His religious interests were varied,[136] sometimes apparently motivated more by political than theological concerns. He promoted Dionysos,[137] went out of his way to obtain recognition from Zeus Ammon,[138] claimed to have been a descendant of Herakles,[139] may have offered sacrifices at Jerusalem,[140] and even sponsored oriental cults before his death.[141] He was also interested in individual temple projects. The Ephesians refused his donation and offer to dedicate their new temple of Artemis,[142] but at Priene a contribution to defray the cost of completion of a new temple for Athena Polias gained for Alexander the right to dedicate that building,[143] and he won popularity in Babylon for having the temple of Bel rebuilt.[144] Diodoros says that at the time of his death, Alexander planned to construct temples at a cost of 1500 talents each at six Greek sites: Delos, Delphi, Dodona, Dion (to Zeus), Amphipolis (to Artemis Tauropolos), and Kyrrhos (to Athena), and a seventh to Athena at Ilion.[145] Of these seven only the temple at Ilion is known to have been built.[146] The list of projected temples occurs in a much deputed passage, a speech of Perdiccas to the army at Babylon in 323 B.C. purporting to contain Alexander's posthumous memoranda. Whether or not the memoranda as a whole are indeed Alexander's own is not the issue here.[147] What is important is that there was a tradition that Alexander planned temple foundations in Greece and that the details of this tradition actually correspond to the situation at the time of his death. Of the six Greek sites on Perdiccas' list, three are major cult centers. Only Olympia is absent, and Alexander would not have needed to build a building there to enhance Macedonian prestige because his father had already provided one. The other three sites are located in Macedonia, an area which shows considerable building activity in the fourth century.

Samothrace, like the second group, was a site located near Macedonia, and like the first group, was a site of international reputation. Unlike Delphi, Delos, and Olympia, however, Samothrace was relatively undeveloped and therefore attractive to Macedonian interests. The island was conveniently situated between Macedonia and the nearest of Alexander's conquests in the east. If it was not Alexander himself who chose to contribute temples at Samothrace, it is likely to have been someone close to him or someone in his immediate family.

From inscriptions found at Samothrace the likely individual responsible for the execution, if not the inspiration, of his plan was Philip III (Arrhidaios), eldest son of Philip II and half-brother and immediate successor to Alexander himself. As Philip III he appears in one dedication at Samothrace and may possibly have been the dedicant in a second. With his co-regent Alexander IV he dedicated the Doric building on the eastern hill,[148] and may have been the dedicant of the building known as the Altar Court.

The interpretation of the Altar Court inscription, however, presents several problems. Karl Lehmann's original reconstruction of this inscription reads: ['Ἀρρ]ιδαῖος ἱ[δρύσατο ἀπὸ λαφύρ]ων Θεο[ῖς] Μ[εγάλοις -]ρρᾶι.[149] Fraser restores the inscription in this way: Ἀδαῖος χ[ο]ρράγ[ου Μακεδ]ὼν Θεο[ῖς Μεγάλοις].[150] Fraser's reading, although usually preferred,[151] does not preserve the order which the blocks exhibited when they were found. With this criticism in mind Karl Lehmann offers a third reading which, although incorporating some of Fraser's suggestions regarding individual letters, still gives the donor of the building as Arrhidaios: [Ἀρρ]αδαῖος χ[οίης Μακεδόν]ων Θεο[ῖς τὰ κάτο]ρρα...[152] This reading does preserve the order in which the blocks were found, but it depends on some rather daring assumptions. Not only is Arrhidaios' name spelled in an unusual way, but two of the restored words, *koies* and *katorrha*, are unattested anywhere except in Hesychius, where *koies* is defined as a priest of the Kabeiroi who purifies murderers, and *katorrha* as an altar by the road-side.[153] It would be an extraordinary coincidence to find that Hesychius preserved two words used only here, words for which there is no epigraphical precedent. Further, Hesychius does not say in either case that the terms were used at Samothrace; although the Kabeiroi are often identified with the Samothracian gods in the literary sources, their name never appears at Samothrace itself. Moreover Karl Lehmann's restoration of the building as an altar court has been challenged.[154] If the building were not actually an altar court, there is no justification for the term *katorrha* in the inscription.[155] Lehmann objects to Fraser's restoration because it upsets the order in which the blocks were found, but as Broneer points out, the earthquake which brought the building down in the sixth century A.D. would certainly have disarranged the blocks of the architrave, blocks which fell from a considerable height.[156]

The many objections to Karl Lehmann's second reading of the inscription do not override its most attractive feature, the fact that it can be associated with a historical figure.[157] However, although the involvement of Arrhidaios in the affairs of the sanctuary is already attested by the inscription from the eastern hill, on the basis of the present evidence it is unlikely that Arrhidaios was named in the dedication of the Altar Court. If Fraser is right about the donor of the building, the name Adaios itself is of Macedonian origin, and the donor would therefore have to be someone from Macedonia,[158] not impossible if we consider the general Macedonian interest at Samothrace at this time and later.

Whether we follow Lehmann's or Fraser's reading of the dedicatory inscription from the Altar Court, the fact remains that the other inscription shows that Philip III (Arrhidaios) was closely involved in the affairs of the sanctuary. Curtius Rufus says that Arrhidaios had accompanied Alexander and had served as "consort of sacred and religious ceremonies."[159] If it was a member of Alexander's family who carried out the building program at Samothrace, it may have been he. Olympias is a less likely choice. Although notorious for her interest in Dionysos,[160] known to have contributed money toward the building of the new temple at Delphi,[161] and closely identified with religious matters at Dodona,[162] there is no reason to assume that she took a special interest in Samothrace, except for the tradition that she was a Samothracian initiate.

If it was Arrhidaios who actually carried out the plan to develop the sanctuary at Samothrace, this development should not be viewed as a result of an eccentric desire on his part to promote an obscure cult. Rather, the motivation for the development of the sanctuary is more likely to have issued from a desire to legitimize Macedonian military supremacy by creating in the north a religious center to rival those of Olympia, Delphi, and Delos. The success of this plan can be measured by the continuing popularity and influence of Samothrace in the next century.

Dodona offers an obvious parallel to Samothrace. Like Samothrace, Dodona is mentioned in Homer, where association with Zeus and with an oracle is already well established.[163] Dodona is also mentioned several times before and during the fifth century, but, as in the case of Samothrace, the earliest writer to have actually visited the site is Herodotus.[164] Excavation in the area of the temple at Dodona shows that it was occupied in the Neolithic period, had almost no contact with Mycenaean Greece, and remained isolated from the rest of Greece until the eighth century B. C. Archaic bronzes found in the area indicate a Greek presence during that period, but although lead tablets recording enquiries to the oracle date from the beginning of the fifth through the middle of the third century, there is no evidence, as there is none at Samothrace, of a permanent stone building until the fourth century B.C., and even this building was very small, only 6.5×2.8 meters.[165] The enclosed precinct at Dodona dates from the end of that century, and a second small temple may be contemporary. The temple mentioned in the memoranda of Alexander was never built. It was only under the stimulus of a local successful and ambitious leader, Pyrrhos of Epiros, that the temple court was remodelled and an impressive theater built in the third century B.C.[166] The sanctuaries at Dodona and Samothrace were famous and even popular long before extensive building projects were carried out at either site. Both sites were on the fringes of the Greek world and both were relatively inaccessible, Dodona because of mountains, and Samothrace because of difficult seas. In both cases eventual development of the site can be related to political events. It was the substantial contributions of powerful neighboring monarchs which made the new building projects possible.

Samothrace in the Hellenistic Period

The Hellenistic period marks a time of continued building activity in the Samothracian sanctuary. After the death of Alexander, the Hieron, the Altar

Court, and the Doric building on the eastern hill were built. They were followed in the third century B.C. by the Arsinoeion and the Propylaia. To the Hellenistic period also belong the large three-chambered building dedicated by a woman from Miletos,[167] the stoa on the western hill,[168] permanent installations in the theater,[169] construction of a fountain crowned by the famous Nike of Samothrace,[170] and the elaborate porch and pedimental sculpture of the Hieron.[171]

The Hellenistic period is also a period of expanded activity associated with the Samothracian gods at sites far from Samothrace itself, something which is a direct consequence of the growing popularity of the mysteries. Before the middle of the third century B.C., the only reference to the Samothracian gods in a foreign inscription occurs at Seuthopolis, an inland Thracian town.[172] After the middle of the third century B.C., the Theoi Samothrakes are mentioned often in inscriptions at other cities far from Samothrace, as the fame of the mysteries grew, and worshippers and initiates carried back to their home cities ceremonies associated with these gods. Inscriptions that refer to the Samothracian gods, found at sites other than Samothrace, confirm that the period of greatest activity associated with their mysteries began in the third century B.C. and continued well into the Roman period.

Sometime before the third century a public festival attended by *theoroi* from other cities became a regular feature of the cult at Samothrace. The date of the origin of the public festival is not clear from the available evidence, but the fact that official *theoroi* lists were already being compiled and recorded by the middle of the third century B.C. indicates that the public festival was by then well established.[173] This festival, which eventually included processions, sacrifices, theatrical performances, and probably banquets, seems almost certainly to have been the result of Macedonian patronage. One curious feature of Samothracian *theoroi* lists is that cities represented on the lists are concentrated in Asia Minor and the Aegean islands, with central Greece generally excluded. If the Samothracian public festival had originally been strongly identified with Macedonia, the absence of *theoroi* from central Greece may be explained in part by the traditional hostility of the cities of that area to Macedonia.

During the third century, Alexander's successors took a special interest in Samothrace, and the mysteries continued to be important to Macedonian leaders. Lysimachos is the subject of two decrees found at Samothrace, and it is likely that he was an initiate. Both decrees show that he was involved in the affairs of the sanctuary. The earlier one honors him for the protection which he exercised when he captured and turned over to the administrators of the sanctuary certain "sacrilegious people" who had broken in and stolen dedications made by the kings and other Greeks.[174] The mention of the kings emphasizes the Macedonian involvement at Samothrace in the late fourth and early third centuries B.C.

Lysimachos is praised for his piety and the city declares that an altar will be set up and an annual sacrifice performed in his honor.[175] The main theme of the inscription is the contrast between the piety of Lysimachos and the impiety of the intruders. Lysimachos is congratulated for putting his reverence (*eusebeia*) for the gods in first place. In the second decree Lysimachos is commended for some service performed in connection with the *hiera chora* on the mainland, but what these services were is not clear from the remaining piece of the text.[176]

The interest of Lysimachos in Samothrace is underscored by the spectacular dedication of his wife Arsinoë. Arsinoë dedicated the unusual round building in the central area of the sanctuary while she was still wife of Lysimachos, during the years of his reign as king (299-281 B.C.).[177] After the death of Lysimachos, in flight from Ptolemy Keraunos, Arsinoë fled to Samothrace where she sought asylum.[178] Initiation was probably not a condition for asylum,[179] but Arsinoë must have been an initiate when she dedicated the round building in the sanctuary.

At about the same time, Ptolemy II Philadelphos dedicated the great Propylaia to the east of the sanctuary,[180] while Ptolemy Soter, father of Arsinoë and Philadelphos, was still alive.[181] Beloch argues that this dedication must have been made after Samothrace came into the Ptolemaic political orbit, assuming that this happened through Arsinoë's marriage to Philadelphos,[182] ignoring the fact that Philadelphos, as a member of a prominent family originally from Macedonia, would have had an interest in Samothrace because of this connection. If the interest of Arsinoë and Philadelphos in Samothrace stems from the Macedonian origin of their family, it is not difficult to reconcile their dedications with the scant evidence for interest in the Samothracian gods in Egypt.[183] The formula of the dedicatory inscription of the Propylaia, indicating that Ptolemy I was still alive at the time of the dedication, confirms that it must have been made during Lysimachos' reign.[184]

In the latter part of the third century, Samothrace had dealings with delegates of Ptolemy III Euergetes concerning the territory on the mainland. The evidence for this association comes from two decrees, one in honor of the Ptolemaic general Hippomedon, and the other honoring Epinikos, Ptolemaic governor of Thrace.[185] Hippomedon is the earliest Samothracian initiate whose initiation is actually established by an inscription. Lines 5-7 of the decree in his honor state that he not only made dedications to the gods, but that he made an effort to be present at the island to take part in the mysteries. Hippomedon himself was originally from Sparta, cousin of the Spartan king Agis IV.[186] His initiation at Samothrace should be seen, however, as representative of neither Spartan nor Egyptian interest in Samothrace, but as the act of an individual who found it convenient to be initiated because he was stationed in the area. Bengtson has suggested that Hippomedon may have had a political motive for seeking initiation at Samothrace,[187] and this may be true, but the favors for which the Samothracians thank him in the decree are associated with the Samothracian *peraia* on the mainland, and not the island itself.[188] Hippomedon was certainly in control of the Thracian coast, but it is not clear that he was in control of the island.

Hippomedon was probably initiated sometime about 240 B.C., a period for which there is little epigraphical evidence about individual worshippers.[189] Consequently this decree is an important record for the history of the Samothracian clientele. It records the earliest surviving example of what may already have been, and was certainly to become, an established practice—the initiation of a political or military figure on temporary duty in the northern Aegean.

Between the decree in honor of Hippomedon (middle of the third century B.C.) and the capture of Perseus in 168, Samothrace continued to attract Macedonian interest. The recent discovery of the base of a monumental bronze statue of Philip V in the center of the sanctuary[190] confirms, as Fraser had suspected, that Philip took Samothrace when he assumed control of Ptolemaic territory in Thrace in 200-199 B.C.[191] Any statue of Philip would indicate ties between the sanctuary and the king, but since the statue is dedicated by the Macedonians,[192] it is evidence as well of ties with the people of Macedonia. The statue itself was an impressive monument, prominently located in front of the stoa on the western hill.

Although there is no record of the initiation of Philip V at Samothrace, the dedication of his statue to the Theoi Megaloi implies that he himself was an initiate.[193] Another piece of evidence for Philip's interest in the Samothracian gods comes from the treaty between Philip and Lysimacheia, where the Theoi Samothrakes are included in the oath sworn by the Lysimacheians.[194] It seems unlikely that these divinities would be introduced into such an oath unless they were recognized by both parties.

The display of a statue of Philip V at Samothrace establishes a connection between this monarch and the sanctuary. The ties between Macedonia and Samothrace in this and the next generation would have given Philip's son Perseus a natural reason for seeking asylum at Samothrace after his disastrous defeat at Pydna in 168 B.C. In seeking asylum at Samothrace, Perseus may have been motivated by desperation, and if an initiate, he would have had a special reason for seeking protection from those gods whose very function it was to preserve their initiates in times of danger.[195] However, Perseus may also have counted on the support of the administrators of a sanctuary whose very buildings had been financed by Macedonian funds.

In addition to the inscriptions found on the island, there are two inscriptions from Seleucid territory which indicate that the dynasts of that kingdom also had a certain interest in the Samothracian sanctuary. The earliest of the two documents is a letter giving the conditions of the purchase of a piece of property by Laodike from her husband Antiochos II, dated 254/3 B.C.[196] After considering the date of the inscription, the nominal price paid, and the fact that the land was not to be subject to taxes, Welles suggests that the sale was part of the divorce settlement negotiated between Antiochos II and his wife when he intended to marry the daughter of Ptolemy II Philadelphos.[197] The letter closes with the injunction that it is to be inscribed and displayed in five places: at Ilion in the temple of Athena, in the sanctuary at Samothrace, in the temple of Artemis at Ephesos, in the temple of Apollo at Didyma (this is the copy which has survived), and in the temple of Artemis at Sardis. All of these sites except Samothrace were clearly in the Seleucid orbit at that time; consequently Fredrich uses this inscription as evidence that Samothrace became a Seleucid dependency as a result of the battle of Kos in 265.[198] Fraser, although he apparently at one time agreed with Fredrich,[199] has since argued that the inclusion of Samothrace in such a list is more an indication of the importance of the Samothracian sanctuary than evidence for its political status.[200] Antiochos may have had other reasons for choosing Samothrace. As Welles points out, four of the sites were great religious centers, and Sardis was a Seleucid capital.[201] However Antiochos may have been bound to Samothrace by the religious traditions of his family. Samothrace, as neutral territory where *theoroi* of the Aegean area met to worship together, may have enjoyed special recognition by all of the three major Hellenistic dynasties because of their common Macedonian past.

Seleucid recognition of Samothrace continued into the early second century B.C., as attested by a treaty between the Ilians and Antiochos III. This treaty stipulates that copies be erected at Lysimacheia at the altar of Zeus Soter and in Samothrace in the sanctuary of the Theoi Megaloi.[202] Samothrace continued to maintain its position as a place for display of international documents even after Macedonia became a Roman province in the second century. In about 100 B.C. an inscription recording an agreement of *sympoliteia* between the Ilians and the Skamandrians was set up at Ilion.[203] A copy of that agreement was also set up at Samothrace at the same time; fragments of the Samothracian copy have recently been found.[204] Like the letter of Antiochos II, these inscriptions confirm the international prestige of the Samothracian sanctuary.

This brief summary of Macedonian involvement with Samothrace in the Hellenistic period has been limited to those few famous people who, although their names do not actually appear on Samothracian initiate lists, seem to have taken a special interest in the sanctuary. Many may have been Samothracian initiates. There are no surviving initiate lists from before the second century B.C., but after that time initiates are recorded from Aigai, Amphipolis,

Beroia, Kassandreia, Thessalonike, and Philippi, testifying to the interest of ordinary Macedonian citizens in Samothrace. In Macedonian territory on the mainland there is evidence for local interest in the Samothracian gods. An inscription at Philippi lists four Samothracian initiates,[205] and another from near Amphipolis records a man who claims to have been an initiate of both the Samothracian and Eleusinian mysteries.[206] Finally, there has been found at Pella a dedication to the Theoi Megaloi, possibly the Samothracian gods and perhaps even from a temple to those gods in that Macedonian capital.[207]

CHAPTER THREE

THE MYSTERIES

Myesis at Samothrace

Candidates for initiation at Samothrace would have entered the sanctuary from the east, through the Propylaia, and proceeded first to the circular, paved area in front of the building dedicated by Philip III and Alexander IV (no. 24). This area, about nine meters in diameter, is surrounded by five rows of steps which rise gradually from the floor below.[208] These steps are too narrow to have been seats, but it is likely that worshippers stood on them to face some event performed in the center of the circular area, probably a sacrifice, if, as McCredie speculates, a circular altar found on the eastern hill originally stood in the center of this area.[209] It is likely as well that the *praefatio sacrorum* mentioned by Livy was delivered here by a priest to the assembled candidates before they proceeded to the secluded main area of the sanctuary on the other side of the eastern hill. In the *praefatio*, where candidates would have learned the requirements for the initiation ceremonies, it was announced that those who were unclean of hand were forbidden to take part.[210] A similar proscription is known to have been included at Athens as part of the *prorrhesis* delivered on the first day of the ceremonies preliminary to the Eleusinian mysteries.[211] The circular paved area on the eastern hill of the Samothracian sanctuary is the likely spot for such a proclamation, since the more sacred precincts of the sanctuary would not yet have been reached. It was probably at this place as well that the procedures for the ceremonies were explained.

From the eastern hill a path descended to the main area of the sanctuary. Presumably those who were qualified would have taken this path to the buildings in the hollow below where the initiation ceremonies took place. In order to understand what a prospective initiate might encounter, it is necessary to examine the evidence of the buildings in the central area of the sanctuary.

Samothracian inscriptions distinguish between *mystai* and *epoptai*, indicating that there were two separate stages of initiation. The largest buildings in the central area, the Anaktoron and the Hieron, had interior seats and interior altars, suggesting that these buildings were the location of the initiation ceremonies. It seems likely, then, that the two stages, *myesis* and *epopteia*, took place in separate buildings. An inscription found at the door of the Hieron prohibits entry to those who had not undergone *myesis*,[212] an indication that this building was the site of *epopteia* and that *myesis*, or the first stage, took place in the Anaktoron. This suggestion is in some measure confirmed by a second inscription found at an interior door to the northern chamber of the Anaktoron.[213] A bilingual inscription in Greek and Latin, it too forbids entrance to those who have not yet achieved *myesis*. It seems likely that the entire Anaktoron was given over to the first stage of the initiation, and that a candidate had to achieve *myesis* in the large central hall before being able to proceed to an inner sanctum in the northern chamber.

This second inscription, however, has been taken to have a different significance. Because the northern chamber of the Anaktoron was reserved for those who had already taken part in *myesis*, Karl Lehmann argues that this higher stage is to be understood as *telete* and that there were three separate rites in the Samothracian initiation ceremonies: *myesis* in the large central hall of the Anaktoron, *telete* in the small northern chamber of the same building, and for those who were eligible, *epopteia* in the large hall of the Hieron.[214] There are several problems with this hypothesis. Lehmann relies in his argument on analogies with the Eleusinian mysteries where there appear to have been three distinct stages: *myesis* at Agrai in the spring, followed by *telete* at Eleusis in the fall, and *epopteia* at Eleusis one year later.[215] The Samothracian situation is, however, different from that of Eleusis. As far as we know all of the ceremonies associated with initiation at Samothrace took place in the sanctuary itself, and from an inscription of the Roman period it is clear that a person could become a *mystes* and *epoptes* in a single night.[216] Further, if some intermediate stage of initiation called *telete* were required for entrance into the Hieron, it is strange that the inscription at the door of that building did not use the word *ateleston*,[217] a term which appears neither here nor anywhere else at Samothrace. Further, writers who use *telete* and its related terms to refer to the Samothracian mysteries do not use *telete* in the specific sense required by Lehmann, but only in the general sense of "a religious festival" or "the religious ceremonies associated with the mysteries."[218] Lehmann argues that Samothracian initiates were called *teleioi* because Hippolytos uses this term for them. Hippolytos, however, refers not to an intermediate stage of initiation, but only to initiation in general. If we had to rely on the literary sources for specific Samothracian procedures, we would have no reason to suppose that there was a rite of *epopteia* at Samothrace, for it is mentioned in no extant source. The best source for Samothracian usage is the inscriptions from the sanctuary itself. These inscriptions mention only *mystai* and *epoptai*. Consequently these are likely to have been the only distinct classifications at Samothrace.

Other features of the Anaktoron may have been included in its predecessors. In the southeast corner of the Anaktoron is a structure which Lehmann calls a *bothros*, a round structure surrounding a circular pit with a threshold at the entrance large enough to accommodate a person, but too small to allow entry into the pit itself. There is a shallow recess at the top, apparently for a cover, and at the time of excavation by Karl Lehmann, there was a stone at the bottom of the pit.[219] Lehmann conjectures that the structure was used for libations. A similar structure may have been part of the fourth century Orthostate Structure. Located in the southern chamber of that building, this circular domed construction, 2.5 meters in height, has an opening at the top. Beneath ground level a shaft extends for five meters into the earth.[220] Apparently libations were poured into the dome and through the shaft below. The very limited remains of the proto-Anaktoron do not preserve any similar structure, but there are good reasons to believe that this building, otherwise so similar in size and shape to its immediate predecessor and immediate successor, was also similar to them in this respect. The nature of the *bothros* in the southeast corner of the Anaktoron and the deep shaft in the Orthostate structure suggest that the pouring of libations to chthonic deities was an important part of the initiation ceremonies in the late Classical and Roman periods, and presumably in the Hellenistic period as well.

Another feature which may have been part of the Anaktoron and its predecessors are two ithyphallic bronze statues which Varro says stood *ante portas*.[221] These seem to be the same statues mentioned by Hippolytos when he says, ἕστηκε δὲ ἀγάλματα δύο ἐν τῷ Σαμοθράκων ἀνακτόρῳ ἀνθρώπων γυμνῶν ἄνω τε<τα>μένας ἐχόντων τὰς χεῖρας ἀμφοτέρας ἐς οὐρανὸν καὶ τὰς αἰσχύνας ἄνω ἐστραμμένας.[222] The entrance to the northern chamber of the Anaktoron has a double doorway, and such statues may very well have stood there. Varro, however, who may have visited Samothrace in 66 B.C.,[223] would not have seen the Anaktoron, but its predecessor, the proto-Anaktoron. Herodotus knew of ithyphallic statues at Samothrace, and says that there was a *hieros logos* about them which was revealed in the mysteries.[224] If such statues played an important part in the mysteries, they may have stood in each of the three successive buildings associated with *myesis*.

It is impossible to reconstruct in detail the procedures for *myesis*, but the remains of the Anaktoron give some indication of the possible activities. The small chamber on the southern end of the Anaktoron was entered only from the outside and was not connected with the large central chamber. Karl Lehmann suggests that candidates went first to the small outer chamber where they changed their clothing[225] and perhaps received a lamp.[226] If so, candidates would have left the building to proceed to the western side of the building where they could have entered one of the three doors which opened on the large central chamber.

The procedures inside the building probably included revelation of certain secret or sacred objects. If such sacred objects were normally kept in the northern chamber of the building, it would be natural to exclude from that chamber those who had not undergone *myesis*. This would explain the prohibition expressed by the inscription at the door.

Candidates would have observed the ceremonies from benches along the eastern and northern walls of the central chamber. The stone supports for wooden benches have been found. Karl Lehmann found in the central area of the chamber traces of carbon, suggesting to him that a large wooden platform once stood in that area.[227] McCredie has not commented on this possibility, but it has been suggested that such a platform could have been used for the rite of *thronosis*,[228] associated by Plato with Korybantic rites, where dancers circled around a seated initiate.[229] Until the final report on the recent excavations of the Anaktoron are published, it is impossible to decide whether such a platform actually existed. Finds from within the building which may have played a part in the ritual include a large bronze shield, cone-shaped bronze objects, plain pottery, and iron knives.[230] Karl Lehmann suggested that triangular clay objects found in the Anaktoron are the pyramids or cones said to have been used in the mysteries, but these objects have now been shown to be kiln supports used in the firing of pottery and therefore have no religious significance.[231]

The ithyphallic statues which are said to have stood in the Samothracian Anaktoron must have symbolized something important for the mysteries. Herodotus connects the Samothracian *hieros logos* with ithyphallic statues, indicating that the mysteries were concerned with the meaning of sexual activity. A concern for sexual activity and the origin of human life is also reflected in an account of Hippolytos who says: τοῦτ' ἔστι, φησί, τὸ μέγα καὶ ἄρρητον Σαμοθράκων μυστήριον, ὃ μόνοις ἔξεστιν εἰδέναι τοῖς τελείοις, φησίν, ἡμῖν. διαρρήδην γὰρ οἱ Σαμόθρακες τὸν Ἀδὰμ ἐκεῖνον παραδιδόασιν ἐν τοῖς μυστηρίοις τοῖς ἐπιτελουμένοις παρ' αὐτοῖς ἀρχάνθρωπον; and describing the statues in the Anaktoron, εἰκόνες δέ εἰσι τὰ προειρημένα ἀγάλματα τοῦ ἀρχανθρώπου καὶ τοῦ ἀναγεννωμένου πνευματικοῦ κατὰ πάνθ' ὁμοουσίου ἐκείνῳ τῷ ἀνθρώπῳ.[232] If the two bronze statues stood in or near the small northern chamber of the building, the secret which they symbolized and the story told about it may have been part of the message communicated to initiates in the central chamber.

A shield found in the building may have been used in a dance like a dance which Nonnos says Kadmos saw at Samothrace. He describes a dance of the Korybantes, where they lept about and beat oxhide shields with their spears to the tune of the double flute.[233] Armed dancers are associated with Samothrace by several authors.

Two items were possibly given to the initiate at some time during the ceremony of *myesis* as signs of the protection which that rite guaranteed. The first of these was a purple sash or belt. A scholiast, commenting on Samothracian initiation says, μυεῖσθαί τε φασι τοὺς μυομένους περιεζωσμένους ταινίας πορφυρᾶς, καὶ τοὺς μυηθέντας ἐν τοῖς κατὰ θάλασσαν κινδύνοις διασώζεσθαι.[234] Karl Lehmann, on the basis of a decorated initiate list found in the sanctuary, associates the purple sash or *porphyris*[235] with *epopteia*,[236] but because he misinterprets the inscription,[237] it seems simpler to follow the evidence of the scholiast.

The second item which may have been given to the initiate during the ceremony was a ring of magnetized iron. One iron ring was found in the Samothracian sanctuary and another in a Samothracian grave.[238] The meaning of these rings becomes clear after an examination of the literary sources. There is a tradition that there was a loadstone at Samothrace,[239] and Lucretius describes Samothracian iron in a way which indicates that it was magnetized.[240] Further, Pliny says that iron rings coated with gold were called Samothracian rings.[241] Karl Lehmann suggests that iron rings were made at Samothrace and were worn by worshippers who connected them with the goddess.[242] The identification, however, may have been stronger than this. Loadstones were believed to be endowed with magic or divine power.[243] The stone found at the bottom of the *bothros* in the Anaktoron may have been meant to represent a loadstone, symbolizing the power of the divinity whose strength was transmitted to initiates by the iron rings which they wore. In fact, a demonstration of magnetism may have formed one of the secret rites of *myesis* when the initiate acquired an iron ring. Plato uses a metaphor which could have had its source in just such a demonstration.[244] If a loadstone had been discovered at Samothrace in early times, its apparently magic power could be explained only by assuming that it was divine.[245] If the rock itself were considered to be inhabited by a divine power, this might explain why the whole island was considered sacred,[246] and it would also explain why certain rocks, placed at the bottom of the various *bothroi*, one of them located in the southeast corner of the Anaktoron itself, were the objects of special libations. An iron ring, magnetized by the force of the divine loadstone, symbolized the power of the divinity. The initiate who wore the ring, possibly coating it with gold as Pliny describes, maintained direct contact with the power of the goddess after leaving Samothrace, and the ring became a token of the protection conferred on the initiate by his initiation.

Epopteia at Samothrace

There is no evidence in the literary sources for a second, advanced stage of initiation at Samothrace, and only since 1892, when Champoiseau found an inscription in the sanctuary which mentioned *epoptai*, has such a stage been recognized.[247] The word *epopteia* was known to have been used to designate the highest state of initiation at Eleusis, and it has been assumed that it must have served a similar function at Samothrace. Such an assumption seems reasonable, although the lists of *epoptai* at Samothrace are few in number and reveal nothing of the nature of the ceremony. Indeed, it was not until 1951, when Karl Lehmann succeeded in identifying the Hieron as the site of *epopteia*,[248] that any attempt could be made to describe the Samothracian rite. There are a number of structural features of this building which were apparently determined by the nature of the ceremonies performed within.

Karl Lehmann isolates several features of the building, two stepping stones or *bathra* flanking a torch support to the east of the building, a drain in the northwest corner of the cella, an *eschara* in the central aisle, and the apse at the far end of the building, all of which he believes played a part in the ritual.[249] He suggests that the preliminary ceremonies began with a moral examination of the candidate at the *bathra* or stepping stones outside the building, followed inside by a lustration rite at the drain, and a sacrifice accompanied by an oath of secrecy at the *eschara* in the center aisle. From what follows, it will become clear that it was an oath of secrecy which was administered at the *bathra* outside the building and that Lehmann has exaggerated the significance of the moral examination of the candidate and the lustration rite by calling them "confession of sins" and "baptism."[250]

The first element to be considered is the two stepping stones or *bathra* which flanked a marble torch outside the building along the eastern wall of the cella.[251] To Lehmann these suggest a passage from Plutarch where a candidate for initiation at Samothrace is required to testify to any past crimes, and he concludes that such a testimony was a preliminary to *epopteia*.[252] Lehmann conjectures that a priest stood on one of these stones and the candidate on the other while the priest questioned him about his past life. He calls the response of the candidate a "confession of sin" and suggests that it was stringent moral qualifications which severely limited the number of initiates to achieve the second stage. Diodoros does say that those who are initiated at Samothrace become more pious, more just, and better in general, but he says nothing about confession and nothing about *epopteia*.[253] The word "confession" is unfortunate because it leads to a comparison between the inquisition of the candidate before initiation and the Christian act of confession. There is no evidence that the priests at Samothrace were interested in the moral character of the initiate, but there is reason to believe that they were concerned with protecting their sanctuary from the unclean. What is at issue when the priest asks the candidate to name the worst deed ever committed is not confession, but a judgement on the part of the priest about the candidate's state of purity. The concern for purity at Samothrace was great enough to exclude certain offenders from the mysteries, and the *praefatio sacrorum* described by Livy[254] certainly applied to the Samothracian *epopteia* as well as to *myesis*. The priest is not concerned with the moral state of the candidate except insofar as the sanctuary might be polluted. It is not a matter of guilt and atonement, as Karl Lehmann's "confession of sins" may suggest, but the traditional Greek concern for contamination of a sacred place.[255] There seems to have been a special concern for purity at Samothrace. Livy mentions trials (*iudicia*) for those who pollute the sacred precincts, and there is some evidence that a special priest purified murderers, but there is no reason to assume that either of these was connected specifically with *epopteia*.[256]

Karl Lehmann believes that a candidate, while still standing on the stepping stone, swore an oath to tell the truth about his greatest sin. If any oath was administered at this point, it was probably not an oath about sin, but an oath of secrecy. Oaths of secrecy were part of any mystery ceremony.[257] The stepping stones or *bathra* would have been an appropriate place for such an oath, and it is suggestive that there were Athenian legal procedures where stepping on a stone was associated with the swearing of oaths.[258] More importantly, the stones are *outside* the Hieron. It would make sense for the candidate to swear here not to reveal any of the secrets which would be shown within the building's doors.[259] In Plato's *Symposium* doors are a metaphor for secrecy, and at Eleusis an inscription refers to an official taking an oath between two altars, probably the altars of Demeter and Kore, which stood outside the Telesterion.[260] In addition, Firmicus Maternus describes an orphic oath as taking place *in primo vestibulo*.[261]

In spite of these analogies, Karl Lehmann prefers to assume that the oath of secrecy for the Samothracian *epopteia* was sworn inside the building and that the oath sworn at the *bathra* was an oath pertaining to the candidate's moral qualifications, a type of oath with no known precedent.

After confronting the priest at the *bathra* outside the building, the candidate proceeded to the porch to wait to enter the Hieron. The unusually deep porch and pronaos of the Hieron seem to be part of a deliberate design worked out to accommodate a large group of *mystai*.[262] Each person would have had to wait before passing through the narrow door because another individual ceremony may have taken place immediately after entering the cella. Inside the cella, to the right of the door, a drain is set into the floor in the corner.[263] Karl Lehmann suggests that this drain provided the outlet for a lustration rite.[264] He believes that the candidate disrobed, stood over the drain, and was washed with water. Ritual purity was a requirement in many cults,[265] and installations for bathing or washing in temples or sanctuaries are not uncommon,[266] but it seems that there was a special emphasis on purity in the mysteries.[267] Actual basins or outlets for water have been found in other temples used for initiation.[268] The evidence for a lustration rite in the Hieron is another indication of this concern for purity, but it is misleading to call this rite, as Lehmann does, "a kind of baptismal rite."[269] To draw analogies with Christian practices is here again more likely to distort than illuminate.

Karl Lehmann believes that an allusion to nudity by Aristophanes[270] refers to just this moment of the Samothracian *epopteia*.[271] The incident in Aristophanes occurs just before Strepsiades is about to enter the Phrontisterion, when Socrates tells him to take off his outer garment because he must be naked to enter. This request, together with the indication a few lines later that Strepsiades must "step down" to enter the building, leads Lehmann to believe that Aristophanes is referring to the Samothracian *epopteia*. He does not think that Aristophanes would have dared to make fun of the Eleusinian mysteries in this way, and because of a humorous reference to the Samothracian mysteries in another play,[272] he considers it possible that Aristophanes knew enough about them to make an explicit joke about the Samothracian *epopteia*. This is unlikely. Even though Aristophanes and his audience had heard of the Samothracian mysteries, there is no evidence that *epopteia* was part of the cult at that time. Further, Aristophanes could not have known about the step down into the building because it is a feature of a Hellenistic building. Dieterich was the first to point out that the *Clouds* contains an elaborate parody of the mysteries, but he believed that Aristophanes had "Orphic" rites in mind.[273]

There is no other evidence that candidates for Samothracian *epopteia* completely disrobed for the lustration rite, but the outlet for the drain is certainly large enough to accommodate a fair amount of water.[274] Even so, it should be remembered that the rite may have consisted of nothing more than the washing of hands.[275] Nevertheless, arguing that the lustration rite involved the entire body, Karl Lehmann claims that the candidate for *epopteia* completely disrobed, and after bathing put on another garment. He believes that the robe donned by the candidate for *epopteia* was the *porphyris* or purple belt described as a band worn by Samothracian initiates around the waist.[276] It seems unlikely, in spite of Lehmann's assertions, that candidates for *epopteia* would have spent the rest of the ceremony clothed only in a belt or sash. The *porphyris* may have been only part of the costume worn by initiates, and there is no reason to believe that its use was restricted solely to the rite of *epopteia*.

The only evidence which Karl Lehmann has to connect the *porphyris* with *epopteia* is a fragmentary initiate list decorated with two circular wreaths which he identifies as the *porphyris*.[277] Because the name of an *epoptes* is inscribed inside one of the wreaths, he argues that the *porphyris* is to be associated with *epopteia*. However, names were added at various times to the list which originally recorded only *mystai* from Kyzikos. The wreaths and other decorations belong to the original inscription, but the names inside the wreaths, including the name of the only *epoptes*, are later additions.[278] Although it is possible that the circular items on the original inscription were in fact meant to represent the *porphyris*, there is no reason to believe from this inscription that such a garment was reserved for *epopteia*. In the accounts of the Samothracian *porphyris* as preserved by the scholiasts there is no mention of *epopteia*. If Samothracian *epoptai* did put on a garment symbolizing the *epopteia* at this point in the ceremony, it was likely a robe associated with that rite or perhaps a robe with a special decoration.[279] There is, however, no evidence for such a garment, and it would perhaps be safer not to offer a specific suggestion.

After the lustration rite each initiate would presumably take a seat on one of the marble benches along the sides of the cella. It is at this point in the proceedings that Karl Lehmann places the oath of secrecy, adducing as evidence not any structural feature of the building, but a papyrus fragment of the first century A.D., thought to preserve an oath of silence from an unspecified Egyptian mystery cult.[280] Upon Lehmann's reading, this oath would have been administered before a congregation of other initiates, and he conjectures that a similar procedure might have been observed at Samothrace. Each initiate, he suggests, would have stepped up to the *eschara* in the center aisle and, after performing a sacrifice, sworn an oath of secrecy while companions and other initiates observed the ritual from the benches placed around the hall.

This conjecture is certainly problematic, not least because of the evidence mentioned earlier pointing to the *bathra* outside the Hieron as a more suitable place for such an oath. Moreover, Lehmann bases his reading of the crucial fragment upon a hypothesis which may be wrong, and it may be that even the practices of the Egyptian cult have been misinterpreted. The fragment preserves the introduction to an oath of silence, describing the events leading up to the oath itself. This part of the fragment is incomplete, owing to the deterioration of the margins, and it is difficult to restore. Lehmann translates part of this introduction as "...the father shall lead the initiate to and make him stand in the middle of the congregation, and he shall swear an oath administered by the herald...."[281] He does not show in either his transcription or his translation that there is a gap of two and a half lines between "initiate" and "make him stand." He also nowhere acknowledges the problem with the translation of the word which he takes to mean "congregation." That word is διάθεμα, for which no such meaning is cited. Lehmann translated this word as "congregation" because of a reading suggested by Oscar Schütz,[282] but if "congregation" was meant, one would expect a word like σύνοδος. Διάθεμα, on the other hand, is always used in an astrological context to refer to the position of the stars at a person's birth.[283] For this reason, Bartoletti, who originally published the fragment, took it to refer to an object which symbolized in some way the stars of the heavens, an object by which the initiate swore when he took his oath of secrecy.[284] He offered as a possible example the design in the floor of a Mithraeum at Ostia. This particular mosaic floor is decorated with seven semi-circles, representing the seven spheres of the planets, and twelve signs of the zodiac.[285] Bartoletti's reconstruction is based on the assumption that the initiate stood on something like this floor when he uttered his oath [ἐπὶ (?) τοῦ] διαθέματος.[286] Oscar Schütz, who believed that the fragment referred to an "Orphic" cult, proposed the reconstruction followed by Lehmann: μέσ[ον ἐντὸς] διαθέματος.²⁸⁷ Bartoletti, however, in his final publication of the papyrus, retained his previous interpretation, unwilling to deny the textual evidence.²⁸⁸

In spite of the confusion about the restoration of the preposition preceding διαθέματος, the astrological context of the word in each of its known uses is hard to deny. The cosmic nature of the oath itself, on both the papyrus documents, together with the appearance of the word ἀστερῶν in the fragmentary last section of a similar third century fragment render it more likely that the cult from which this oath came was an astral cult of some sort. Although there is scanty evidence for the penetration of the Mithraic cult into Egypt,²⁸⁹ Mithraic influences cannot be ruled out.²⁹⁰ It is also possible that the oath is from the mysteries of Isis.²⁹¹ Lehmann's translation is then not supportable, and there seems to be no reason to believe that at Samothrace the oath of silence was sworn inside the Hieron.

Although the *eschara* was not the site for the oath of silence, its focal position indicates that it was the location of an important ritual, perhaps a final sacrifice preliminary to the rite of *epopteia*.²⁹² The size of the *eschara* and the fact that fragments of bones were found inside, suggest to Lehmann that the sacrificial victims were birds and that the figure to whom the sacrifices were directed was Aetion, the Samothracian hero and legendary founder of the mysteries.²⁹³ These suggestions, however, must be considered tentative.

The procedures considered up to this point are only preliminaries to the actual rite of *epopteia*. The ceremonies central to that rite must have taken place in the apse of the building. Except for a central marble platform which Karl Lehmann calls a *bema*, the apse was probably cut off from the seated audience by curtains.²⁹⁴ It is likely that some part of the ceremony was delivered by a priest standing on the platform or *bema*,²⁹⁵ but it is impossible to determine the nature of the ceremonies located in the apse. The apse itself was considerably disturbed by remodelling in about A.D. 200 and again by Austrian excavation in the last century. Karl Lehmann believes that there was originally a *bothros* located in the apse, but the only trace of such an installation is a large hole cut in the *bema* at the time of alterations to the apse in the late second century A.D. A shallow lip was left in the stone so that it could be fitted with a cover, probably of wood, and to allow the *bema* to be used for its original purpose.²⁹⁶ Presumably the hole in the *bema* replaced an earlier *bothros* located elsewhere in the apse, now covered over so that the interior of the apse could be used for some other ceremony.

The changes in the apse were accompanied by changes elsewhere in the building. These changes included the enlarging of the main door, building of parapets on either side of the central aisle, a decrease in the number of seats, the covering over of the *eschara* in the central aisle, as well as the recutting of the *bema* near the apse. Karl and Phyllis Lehmann believe that these changes in the building accompanied a drastic change in the ceremonies associated with *epopteia*, and arguing that the changes would allow for the introduction of large animals into the cella itself, suggest that these changes included the introduction of *taurobolium* or *criobolium*.[297] One of the goddesses worshipped at Samothrace, by her representation on coins, can be compared with Kybele, the divinity with whom *taurobolium* is most often associated.[298] There is evidence for *taurobolium* in connection with the cult of the Kabeiroi at Pergamon.[299] However, there is no reason to assume that the alterations to the Hieron in the late second century necessarily imply the practice of *taurobolium* in that building. There is no mention of *taurobolium* on any Samothracian inscription, and there is no evidence for a *fossa sanguinis* in the Hieron.[300]

Ritual Dining in the Samothracian Sanctuary

It has long been assumed that ritual eating and drinking played a part in the Samothracian mysteries.[301] Many cups and bowls have been found in the course of excavation of the sanctuary,[302] but it was not until the most recent series of excavations that the significance of these finds could be assessed. In the process of excavating the terraces in the hill below the stoa, McCredie has found a series of small rooms, several of which are definitely dining rooms or *hestiatoria*.[303] Dating in part from the late Classical period through the third or fourth century A.D., these rooms, with their close proximity to the halls of initiation, present strong evidence for the practice of ritual eating in connection with the mysteries. The rooms are situated across the stream from the Anaktoron and the Hieron, but they are located below the hill on which the stoa stood, and therefore are on the same level as the halls of initiation.

The rooms as excavated represent the latest phase of development, belonging to the third or fourth century A.D., and it is difficult to reconstruct their history. Evidence for such rooms before the late Classical period is not conclusive,[304] but at least one group of three rooms belongs to the second half of the fourth century B.C. (plan, no. 7).[305] The floor of one of these rooms was paved with a pebble mosaic, and the floors of the other two were paved with mosiac made of marble chips. Both of these last two rooms had platforms about one meter in width around all four walls, platforms suitable for movable dining benches.[306] Floors of mosaic, which could be easily washed, were common in dining rooms.[307]

The literary sources are almost silent on the subject of eating at Samothrace, but Nonnos, who knew that there was a round building in the sanctuary, also knew that there was a banqueting area nearby. He mentions the two streams in the sanctuary and describes statues holding torches near the streams. He says that the light of the torches fell on those who banqueted there in the evening.[308] The description of diners in conjuction with his reference to the streams in the sanctuary suggests the location of the dining rooms on the bank of the western stream beneath the western hill.

Samothrace is not unique in having installations for dining located in a sacred *temenos*. Such installations are well known and are found throughout the Greek world.[309] The central act of Greek ritual was animal sacrifice, and the act of sacrifice often resulted in a communal meal. It is unlikely that any eating connected with the mysteries was sacramental in nature.[310] It is possible, however, that initiates at Samothrace were required to fast during the ceremonies of *myesis* and *epopteia*.[311] It is equally likely that a communal meal after the ceremony of initiation provided the means for the breaking of that fast.

CHAPTER FOUR

GREEK INITIATES AND *THEOROI* AT SAMOTHRACE

Samothracian Initiate Lists

There are three ways to trace the people who were initiated at Samothrace: the literary sources, the dedications and decrees found in the sanctuary, and the Samothracian initiate lists. Of these, the first is the least productive. We learn that mythological figures like Herakles, Jason, Orpheus, Kadmos, and the Dioskouroi were supposed to have been initiated at Samothrace,[312] but when it comes to tracing historical figures, the literary sources are not very instructive. The only Greek figures for whom a literary source actually claims initiation are Philip II and Olympias, but we can infer from his own remarks that Herodotus was an initiate,[313] from Plutarch that Antalkidas, Lysander, or some other Spartan king was an initiate,[314] and from Strabo that Demetrios of Skepsis was also an initiate.[315]

From the dedications and decrees we can infer that people like Philip III (Arrhidaios), Lysimachos, Ptolemy II, Arsinoë II, and Philip V were Samothracian initiates, but nowhere is it explicitly stated that any of these people were initiates. Only the decree honoring Hippomedon actually states that he came to the island for the mysteries.[316]

The most important evidence for Samothracian initiates are the inscriptions recording lists of *mystai* and *epoptai*. Over one hundred such inscriptions have been found, and they provide a catalogue, incomplete though it may be, of the clientele of the mysteries. They record more than six hundred legible names, and have traces of over one hundred others. Lists are recorded in both Greek and Latin. The earliest lists are from the second century B.C. and the latest may be as late as the early third century A.D. For the most part they record the names of ordinary citizens and slaves. Few initiates have had their names preserved elsewhere.

Because the initiate inscriptions have been found scattered throughout the sanctuary and the rest of the island, it is difficult to speculate about their original location and means of display. Some of the stones were free standing stelae,[317] but others were apparently fitted into the walls of buildings.[318] Some of these were found in the chamber on the southern end of the Anaktoron where people would have gathered before the first stage of initiation. This room would certainly have been an appropriate place for the display of initiate inscriptions, but it is not large enough to have contained many. More inscriptions were probably displayed in the larger and grander Arsinoeion;

two stones have been found whose slightly concave shape seems to indicate that they were made to fit the curved walls of that building.[319]

Most of the initiate inscriptions exhibit the same form. The date is usually given at the top of the stone, followed by the names of the initiates, often with their city of origin indicated. However, although certain conventions are followed, there were apparently no exact rules. The stones themselves are usually less than a meter in height and the uniformity of the inscriptions seems to indicate that they were carved by resident stonecutters, probably under the jurisdiction of the sanctuary.

The Greek inscriptions are dated according to the eponymous magistrate, the Samothracian *basileus*, whose name is used to date decrees of the city as well as the initiate lists of the sanctuary.[320] Like the Athenian archon *basileus* who had jurisdiction over the Eleusinian mysteries, the Samothracian *basileus* appears to have been an official of the city whose authority extended to the affairs of the sanctuary. Livy describes Theondas, the Samothracian official who delivered the decision of the *boule* to Perseus, as *summus magistratus apud eos*, and says that the Samothracians call him "king" (*regem ipsi appellant*).[321]

After the local Samothracian date, the Latin initiate lists give the Roman consular date. Eighteen of these still preserve the year date, and fifteen the name of the month. The dates mentioned on the initiate lists occur in the months from April through November, indicating that at Samothrace initiation was available whenever visitors came to the island,[322] and that both stages of initiation could, at some time of the year at least, be available in the same night.[323] This flexibility is not characteristic of the procedures at Eleusis where not only the times for the three stages of initiation were fixed, but candidates had to wait at least one year between the rite of *telete* and the rite of *epopteia*.

The dates on the *mystai* lists coincide, as Hemberg points out, with the sailing season.[324] The months mentioned are April (once), May (three times), June (five times), July (once), August (once), September (twice), October (once), and November (once).[325] The available sample is of course only a fraction of the original lists, but the fact that five of the inscriptions fall in the month of June may be more than a coincidence. If June were the month of the annual festival, it would be natural to expect that more people would be initiated at this time than at other times. Further, the only two dated inscriptions to list *epoptai* both happen to carry June dates.[326] Karl Lehmann, who thinks that three of the *epoptai* lists were dated to June, does not believe that this is significant.[327] If, however, *epopteia* was available only at a certain time of year or only during a specific month, that there are relatively few *epoptai* on the inscriptions could be explained without claiming that it was a moral requirement which greatly restricted their number. It is possible that if there were a requirement, it was a temporal one. The evidence for June as the month for the annual festival and as the month during which *epopteia* was available is extremely fragile, but the fact that one third of the inscriptions which show Latin month names are dated to that month cannot be completely disregarded.

Some of the Greek inscriptions are dated according to local systems of the home city of the initiate. A Rhodian list is dated according to the Rhodian *hiereus*,[328] a Kyzikene list according to the Kyzikene *hipparchos*,[329] and an unknown Greek city according to the local *hieromnamon*.[330] Two other lists are dated according to the Macedonian era, but this seems to reflect the usage of the home city rather than that of Samothrace.[331] Only two inscriptions give the name of a Greek month. One records a month called Artemisios, a month name used in the Macedonian calendar, but not everywhere to refer to the same part of the year.[332] The second records the local calendar month Mounychion which, because it occurs on an inscription bearing the Roman date as well as the Greek, shows that Mounychion corresponded to Roman May.[333]

Some of the initiate lists include a second eponymous official. The official is the Samothracian *agoranomos* whose name and title occasionally occurs on the top of the stone after that of the *basileus* or, less often, at the bottom of the stone after the list of initiates.[334] The *agoranomos* is almost certainly an official of the city, but the frequent appearance of the title on the initiate inscriptions indicates that the official probably played some role in the business of the sanctuary. L. Robert suggests that the *agoranomos* was the official who was in charge of the Samothracian public festival. This suggestion cannot be confirmed by the evidence at Samothrace, but the appearance of this title to designate officials of religious festivals at other cities is well documented.[335] The extant Samothracian inscriptions, in contrast with the records from Eleusis, do not reveal the titles of hierophants, priests, or other cult officials. Information about the personnel, the actual procedures of the sanctuary, and the duties of the people who administered the mysteries and the festival are consequently not available from the inscriptions.

The initiate lists usually indicate the stage of initiation achieved by the initiate. Those who achieve the first stage are called *mystai eusebeis* on the Greek inscriptions and *mystae pii* on the Latin inscriptions.[336] Initiates proceeding to the higher stage of initiation are called *epoptai* or *epoptae*. People were often initiated in groups: a group of *theoroi* from the same city, a family group, a group of people from the same town, a group of people travelling on the same boat, or an official and his retinue. The government officials who appear on the inscriptions are usually Romans, but at least one list gives a Greek general and his associates.[337] If *mystai* and *epoptai* appear on the same stone, the *mystai* are usually mentioned first and the *epoptai* second although there are exceptions to this practice.[338]

The use of the singular on a few inscriptions shows that some people were recorded alone. This need not indicate that they were initiated alone. In commenting on one of these inscriptions, the inscription which records the initiation of Iuventius Thalna, *mystes pius*, Fraser says, "Such single records—which presumably correspond to single ceremonies of initiation—are rare as compared with lists inscribed after a collective ceremony."[339] Fraser assumes that the names on an inscription reflect the number of people initiated in a single ceremony, and that if only one name appears, this person must have been initiated alone, but this is not necessarily the case. A new list which lists the officers of a ship by name states that those who sailed with them (who are not named individually) also became *mystai* and *epoptai* too.[340] Further, although most of the groups who appear on the inscriptions seem to have an inherent unity, there is no indication that any one group was initiated alone. The buildings where the ceremonies took place could accommodate a fair sized audience (the seating capacity of the Hieron is estimated at 150), and it seems possible that for any given ceremony several small groups could be accommodated at one time. It would therefore be possible for an individual travelling alone to be initiated along with others. The possibility also remains that occasionally those who had taken part in a group ceremony did not choose to inscribe their names. It is important to remember that it is impossible to know just what percentage of the initiates actually had their names inscribed and likewise important to recall that the extant lists record only a mere fraction of the original total.

Some of the inscriptions contain names of initiates added after the original list was inscribed. If stones with multiple, but separate inscriptions are considered, the practice of recording a single initiate appears more common than it would if only stones with a single name are taken into account. Stones were used and re-used often many times. Names are added at the top, in the middle, or at the end of other lists. On some occasions it is several names which are added, on others it is only one. For example, in the Imperial period about four Roman names were added at the top of a stone which originally recorded an inscription from the late Republican period.[341] In another case three Romans are added to an inscription which had been used previously on three separate occasions to record three different groups of Greeks.[342] Most often extra names are added at the end of another inscription. On one stone a Roman group is added to a Greek list,[343] and on another a Greek *epoptes* is added to a stone which had already been used four times for both Greek and Roman groups. Single Greek initiates are also added to the end of earlier lists at least twice.[344] Because a single name can be easily incorporated into earlier lists, they are sometimes found in odd places. In one case a name is added later in a different style of lettering between two syllables of another name.[345] And on another stone a Roman name is cut vertically along the narrow edge of a stele which had already been carved on the front and the back with Greek lists.[346] Sometimes names are incorporated into the empty spaces of decorative elements on the stone. This may be the case where the name Hilarus Prim[us] is carved into the pediment of a pedimental stele in what seem to be more irregular letters than those of the rest of the stone.[347] On another inscription names were added in empty spaces of circles carved on the stone.[348]

There are also occasions when through error on the part of the stonecutter, the singular is used when the plural title would seem warranted. For instance, the singular form *mystis* (fem.) occurs twice where more than one initiate seems to be designated. In both cases it is a Greek woman and her female slave or companion who are named.[349] It seems unlikely that the slaves' names would have been listed at all unless they were initiated, but it seems odd not to have included them with their respective mistresses by a plural title. In both cases the initiate happens to be a woman initiated alone without male companions. Although it is not usual for women to be travelling alone, there are two other instances of unaccompanied Greek women seeking initiation at Samothrace.[350] A similar misuse of the singular seems to occur on a Roman inscription where M. Paccius P. f., Fal. Rufus, is called *musta pius* while the status of the freedman and two slaves listed after him is left unspecified.[351] As in the two preceding cases it seems unlikely that the slaves would even be named on a stone which is so obviously an initiate list if they had not been initiated. Slaves and freedmen appear often on other lists, and the simplest solution is to assume an error on the part of the stonecutter.[352]

Greek Mystai at Samothrace

Twice as many Greeks as Romans are recorded on the extant lists.[353] Although the lists record citizens, freedmen, and slaves, there are very few women on either the Greek or the Latin lists. It is not surprising to find that so many of the Samothracian initiates are men. The nature of Greek society was such that few women would have had the opportunity to seek initiation. The inconvenience of the site meant that many of the people who came to Samothrace were sailors, and there is some indication that soldiers made a special effort to be initiated. Further, all of the *theoroi* recorded at Samothrace are men. Nevertheless, although so few women appear on the initiate lists, it should be remembered that two of the major buildings in the sanctuary were donated by women and that Olympias was one of the traditional initiates.

One of the most important pieces of information available from the initiate lists is the home city of the initiate. The ethnic origin of the initiate was given on almost half of the inscriptions, and it is possible to reconstruct a tentative picture of the area from which the initiates came. The Samothracian mysteries were never restricted to only the local population, and after the fourth century B.C., when the sanctuary was expanded and a large public festival developed, the Samothracian mysteries took their place among the major Greek cults of the Hellenistic world. The success of this development is reflected in the initiate inscriptions which show that people travelled to Samothrace from a considerable area. Like the *theoroi* lists, however, the initiate lists show a certain limitation. The sites mentioned are confined for the most part to northern Greece (Thrace and Macedonia) and the west coast of Asia Minor. Athens does appear on the inscriptions, but only once and not until the second century A.D.[354] Although the extant lists are not a complete record, the almost total lack of reference to the cities of central Greece must have some significance. Taken together with a similar picture from the *theoroi* lists, it would seem that the Samothracian mysteries appealed far more to the people living in Macedonia, Thrace, Asia Minor, and the Aegean islands. A comparison of the sites from which *theoroi* and *mystai* came with the sites where inscriptions mentioning the Samothracian gods have been found will show that the Samothracian clientele does seem, except for the Roman initiates, to have been limited to a certain defined area.[355]

A survey of the Samothracian *mystai* lists shows that Greek initiates came from the following sites:[356]

Abydos	*IG* XII (8), no. 183, 14 names
Aigai[357]	*IG* XII (8), no. 206, 1 name
Ainos	*IG* XII (8), no. 217, 2 names
	no. 218, 6 names (women)
	no. 221.6, 1 name
	Samothrace 2.1, no. 42, 3 names
Alexandria[358]	*IG* XII (8), no. 206, 4 names
Alexandria Troas[359]	*IG* XII (8), no. 223, 1 name
Alopekonnesos	*IG* XII (8), no. 190a, 1 name
Amphipolis[360]	*IG* XII (8), no. 195, 7 names
Antioch[361]	*IG* XII (8), no. 184.3-4, 2 names
Arsinoe[362]	*IG* XII (8), no. 184.12-13, 1 name
Athens	*IG* XII (8), no. 216, 11 names
Azoros	*IG* XII (8), no. 178, 1 name
Beroia	*IG* XII (8), no. 195, 1 name
	Samothrace 2.1, no. 47, 6 names
Byzantion[363]	*IG* XII (8), no. 206.5-8, 2 names
Chios	*IG* XII (8), no. 209, 2 names
	Samothrace 2.1, no. 36.12, 1 name
Dardanos	*IG* XII (8), no. 173, 9 names (2 are *theoroi*)
	no. 174, 4 names (3 are *theoroi*)
Elis	*IG* XII (8), no. 176, 2 names
Ephesos	*IG* XII (8), no. 186b, 2 names
Epidamnos	*IG* XII (8), no. 196, 4 names
Herakleia apo Strymonos[364]	*Samothrace* 2.1, no. 58, 1 name

Ilion	*IG* XII (8), no. 206.4-5, 2 names
Kassandreia	*IG* XII (8), no. 178, 2 names
Kaunos	*IG* XII (8), no. 222, 4 names
Keramos	*IG* XII (8), no. 160b, 2 names
Knidos	*Hesperia* 48 (1979) 17, 6 names plus a group
(Kos)[365]	*BCH* 86 (1962) 276-8, no. 4
Kyzikos	*IG* XII (8), no. 189
	no. 190 (?)
	no. 194, 3 (?) names
	Samothrace 2.1, no. 29, 5 names
	Samothrace 2.1, App. IV
Magnesia	*IG* XII (8), no. 206.9, 1 name
Maroneia	*IG* XII (8), no. 215.12-17, 4 names
	no. 220a.13-15, 3 names
Parion	*IG* XII (8), no. 175, 2 names (*theoroi*)
Pergamon	*Samothrace* 2.1, no. 36.11, 1 name
Perinthos[366]	*IG* XII (8), no. 186b, 1 name
	no. 197
	no. 203 (?)
Philippi	*Samothrace* 2.1, no. 59, 1 name
	Appendix I, no. 16, 4 names
Priapos	*IG* XII (8), no. 184.5, 1 name
Rhodes	*IG* XII (8), no. 184.2, 1 name
	no. 186a, 9 names
	no. 186b, 5 names
Serrhai[367]	*IG* XII (8), no. 206.8, 1 name
	Samothrace 2.1, no. 46, 1 name
Styberra	*IG* XII (8), no. 206.11-12, 1 name
Thasos	*IG* XII (8), no. 184.11, 1 name
	no. 206.4, 1 name
	no. 220a, 2 names
	Samothrace 2.1, no. 59, 7 names
Thessalonike	*IG* XII (8), no. 195.8-9, 2 names
	Samothrace 2.1, no. 58, 2 names
Tomis	Appendix I, no. 6
Tralles[368]	*IG* XII (8), no. 190b.38-48, 1 name

The initiates are usually listed in groups and often, on the Greek inscriptions, the initiates are all from the same city. Some of the inscriptions of this type list *theoroi* or *hieropoioi*. Those which list *theoroi* do not seem to include other citizens, but inscriptions listing *hieropoioi* from Rhodes and Kyzikos also list other people who travelled with them.[369] One of the Rhodian inscriptions calls these attendants συνέγδαμοι, a denotation which is probably not an official title.

On some of the inscriptions the captain or sailors of the ship which brought the initiates to Samothrace are also listed. For instance, on one occasion a sailor from Perinthos and two other sailors from Ephesos came with a Rhodian delegation and all are listed together.[370] One of the inscriptions which lists a group of Kyzikene officials is headed by a man who is called τριήραρχος;[371] he was apparently the captain of the ship on which they sailed. A group of Romans on another occasion is accompanied by Λεωνίδης, who is described as [ἄρχων] ὑπηρετιχοῦ [πλοίου δη]μοσίου.[372]

The two cities which appear on the initiate inscriptions the most often are Rhodes and Kyzikos. It is not surprising to find Rhodes so prominently represented; the island was throughout the Hellenistic period an active commercial center. It is natural to expect that Rhodian sailors would have taken an interest in a ceremony which promised protection at sea. The activity of Rhodians at Samothrace, both as *theoroi* and initiates, is supplemented by a corresponding activity connected with the Samothracian gods on Rhodes itself, one of the places where there is considerable epigraphical evidence for local worship of the Samothracian gods.[373]

Kyzikos is the second city which appears often on Samothracian lists. Kyzikene *theoroi* are listed on four occasions and Kyzikene initiates appear several times. In fact, two of the Kyzikene *theoroi* appear once on an official *theoroi* list, and again on an initiate list. Presumably they were initiated on the same visit when they came as official delegates from Kyzikos.[374] Kyzikos is mentioned on five initiate lists, three of which are decorated with the same relief. The relief pictures a round building flanked by snake-entwined torches; figures are shown standing on top of the building.[375] A fourth inscription which does not refer to Kyzikos on the extant part of the list seems also to belong to this group because it depicts the same building.[376] The inscriptions are badly weathered, but Cyriacus of Ancona saw the stone in the fifteenth century and three manuscripts reproducing his drawings survive. From them the building can be reconstructed. Phyllis Lehmann has discussed these decorated inscriptions in some detail and has argued that the building originally pictured on these inscriptions was a round building associated with the Samothracian gods and located at Kyzikos.[377] The recent discovery of a small round Doric building at Samothrace, however, provides an example of such a building within the sanctuary itself.[378] It is possible that the Kyzikene worshippers of the Samothracian gods provided at Samothrace a building similar in design to a Samothrakion at home, a· building whose shape may have been influenced by the other round building at Samothrace, the Arsinoeion. A Kyzikene initiate who appears twice on Samothracian inscriptions, Asklepiades Attalou, is called *architecton*,[379] a title which means that he served an official function connected with buildings.[380] The inscription records special services performed at Samothrace by Asklepiades, who seems to have been involved in the making of sacrifices and perhaps in setting up sacred images (*eikones*). It is possible that Asklepiades, already a *mystes* and *epoptes* at Samothrace, returned a third time as an official representative of Kyzikos at Samothrace to set up either paintings or sculpture in the round

Doric building. The *Theoi Samothrakes* as such do not appear on Kyzikene inscriptions but mysteries of Kore were a feature of that city's cults.[381]

Epoptai at Samothrace

Out of over one hundred initiate inscriptions, only eighteen mention *epoptai*.[382] Of the eighteen, twelve list Greek names,[383] and seven list Romans.[384] Among the Greeks there are 33 names, seven fragmentary or broken names, and traces of a few more names. All of the Greek *epoptai* are men. On the Latin inscriptions there are nine names and two fragmentary names. Of those whose names are complete, eight are men and one is a women.[385] The fact that more Greeks than Romans are listed as *epoptai* is consistent with the greater number of Greeks mentioned on the inscriptions as a whole. When compared with the number of initiates who received only *myesis*, the total number of *epoptai* is very small; it is clear that not even ten percent of the initiates advanced to the higher degree.[386] There may be several reasons for this limitation. Karl Lehmann believes that certain moral requirements restricted the number of those who achieved *epopteia*, but some initiates may not have chosen the second stage for other reasons. It is not impossible that *epopteia* was available at only a certain time of year, and it is in addition extremely likely that there was a fee charged for the rite. There is no evidence from the inscriptions at Samothrace that a fee was charged for initiation, but fees for initiation are recorded at Eleusis,[387] and it is likely that fees were charged at Samothrace as well. If so, it is possible that the fee for *epopteia* was a factor in restricting the number of *epoptai*.

The procedure for indicating *epoptai* on the inscriptions is not the same in every case. The comparative infrequency of *epoptai* in general may obscure or distort the evidence, but since *myesis* was apparently a requirement for *epopteia*, and since both stages may have been obtainable on the same day (at least in the Imperial period), it is curious that many of the inscriptions do not state that those achieving *epopteia* had also achieved *myesis*. Of the eighteen *epoptai* inscriptions, only five definitely indicate that the persons who attained *epopteia* had also obtained *myesis*.[388] There seems, then, to have been no general rule about indicating the *myesis* of an *epoptes*. Four of these inscriptions state that the initiate was μύστης καὶ ἐπόπτης, which could be taken as evidence that both stages were achieved on the same day.[389] However, the same formula is used to describe the only initiate who is known to have undergone the two sets of ritual on separate occasions.[390] The fifth inscription, one of the most complete of the entire corpus, lists the *epoptai* twice, once as *mystai* in the list of other *mystai*, and again at the end of the inscription in a separate, but special section reserved for the three people of the group who had achieved *epopteia*.[391]

On some of the inscriptions which list *epoptai*, the term *epoptes* can probably be understood as an inclusive term referring to both stages of the mysteries. When the *epoptes* heads a group of *mystai*, it is possible to assume that the *epoptes* underwent *myesis* with his friends and then went on to *epopteia* alone or with a select few of the large group. This is clear where Schinas, his wife Rupilia, and their companion Marius Fructus are listed first among a large group of *mystai* and then a second time as *epoptai*.[392] Although none of the other *epoptai* inscriptions are as explicit as this one, it seem likely that the procedure was similar even where the *epoptai* are not actually stated to be *mystai* as well.

There are eight Greek inscriptions and five Roman inscriptions which mention *epoptai* without referring to their *myesis*.[393] Three of these clearly mention the *epoptai* first and the other *mystai* second.[394] Four list the *epoptai* at the end of the group.[395] On two and perhaps even three occasions the *epoptes* is inserted on a stone which has already been used to list other *mystai*.[396] Finally, although the other three inscriptions are too fragmentary from which to generalize, the *epoptai* seem to be mentioned first.

In spite of the fragmentary nature of the evidence, there are a few facts which become apparent from examination of individual texts. First of all, while in some cases it seems that it is only the more prominent members of the groups who achieve *epopteia*, in other cases it appears that the opposite is true. Social status does not seem to be a sufficient or even a necessary requirement for *epopteia*. Karl Lehmann points out that on one of the inscriptions Schinas and his wife become *epoptai*, but the third *epoptes* of the group is only a freedman, and another freeborn Roman citizen is only a *mystes*.[397] Another inscription presents a similar case. In this case the Roman citizen Lucius Sicinius and his slave Seleucus achieve *epopteia*, while two other freedmen (one of which had originally belonged to the *epoptes* Sicinius) are only *mystai*.[398] To take a third example, on an inscription listing official delegates from Rhodes, the delegates listed on one side of the stone achieved *epopteia*,[399] while the delegates on the other side of the stone, presumably sent in another year, were only *mystai*.[400] On the only complete Greek inscription where a large group of Greeks in the retinue of a public official are initiated together, three of the initiates are called *epoptai*, but the leader of the group, an Athenian general stationed on Imbros, is only a *mystes*.[401] Whatever the restriction was, it is clear that *epopteia* was either not available to all or not desired by all.

Among the *epoptai* inscriptions there are three Greek lists which differ from all the others in that they were originally long lists which included several *epoptai*.[402] It is possible that the people on each list were from one city.[403] All three of the lists are fragmentary and two of them are badly defaced, but it is clear that originally they recorded many *epoptai*. Although there are other long lists of Greek names on inscriptions which are undoubtedly initiate lists,[404] these three are the only inscriptions where a large group of *epoptai* is recorded. It is significant to notice that there are no comparable Latin lists of this type, not surprising considering that on the whole far fewer Romans than Greeks proceeded to *epopteia*.

Greek Theoroi at Samothrace

It was an established custom for Greek cities to send to Samothrace special delegates called *theoroi*. The word *theoros* is thought to be related to the verb ὁράω.[405] A *theoros* is a person whose function it is to observe. The word is used in Greek in five different senses: for a spectator, an official who visits festivals, an official who announces festivals, a person sent to make inquiries of an oracle, and, in some cities, for a local civic official.[406] The *theoroi* who visited Samothrace, and whose names are recorded on official lists from the sanctuary, were *theoroi* in the second sense. They were delegates, sent by their home cities to take part in a special festival at Samothrace.

The date and the exact nature of this festival is not known, but Plutarch calls it a *panegyris*, and his account of Voconius' initiation implies that people made a special effort to seek initiation at the time of the festival.[407] The only evidence for the length of the festival is a late initiate list which happens to record three day dates (20, 21, and 22), but the inscription is only a fragment and the name of the month is missing. The claim that this month was July is, as Karl Lehmann says, merely conjecture.[408] The only other reference to a Samothracian festival is the statement of a scholiast that "even now they search for her (Harmonia) in the festivals,"[409] a statement which has been taken as evidence for the presentation of dramas or plays in the Samothracian theater as part of the public festival.[410] Other activities which the *theoroi* would have participated in must have included processions and public sacrifices. Only two of the Samothracian buildings were restricted to initiation ceremonies, and some of the others were probably designed for activities related to the public festival. One important and central structure which probably played a part in this festival was the Temenos in the center of the sanctuary, used for public sacrifices and the display of cult statues. This building is the one which Phyllis Lehmann believes was donated by Philip II. If so, he may have been responsible for the original development of the festival as a regular feature of the Samothracian cult.

The earliest of the surviving *theoroi* inscriptions dates from the middle of the third century B.C.,[411] and the latest possibly from the first century A.D.[412] The importance of Samothrace as a cult center during this period is nowhere so clearly defined as by these lists of *theoroi*, lists which imply not only the participation of individuals in the ceremonies, but also the official recognition and sponsorship of the sanctuary by city governments throughout the Aegean. These *theoroi* came primarily from the Greek cities of the west coast of Asia Minor and the islands. Fraser points out that the geographical area covered by the later lists is much the same as that of the earlier lists, suggesting that the clientele was already well established by the third century B.C.[413] The earliest list, for instance, gives *theoroi* from Teos, Knidos, Melos, Methymna, Samos, Kolophon, Klazomenai, Kaunos, Abdera, Parion, Kalchedon, and Rhodes.[414] Fraser thinks that the absence of earlier lists is due either to accident or to the fact that earlier records may not have been on stone. Another explanation, perhaps more plausible given the history of the sanctuary in the fourth century B.C., is that the public festival, before that time only a fairly local festival, did not attract official visitors from distant cities until after the elaborate dedications of the Macedonian kings in the late fourth and early third centuries B.C.

The most striking thing about the *theoroi* lists, when compared with *mystai* inscriptions, is that the people represented as *theoroi* are exclusively Greek. Though the *theoroi* lists chronologically overlap the initiate lists where many Romans appear, there are no Romans mentioned as *theoroi*.[415] In addition, even the Greek cities named on the lists are restricted to a definite geographic area, an area concentrated along the west coast of Asia Minor and throughout the islands, with Thrace, Macedonia, and northern Greece only marginally represented. This may be due to the fact that so few lists are preserved, but it does seem that the cities of the *theoroi* lists are more heavily concentrated in the east than the cities mentioned on the initiate inscriptions.

There are a total of forty-six cities which appear on the *theoroi* lists at Samothrace.[416] Many of these cities appear more than once, testifying to a traditional interest in Samothrace and to continuing support of the sanctuary. Most of the cities sent two *theoroi* at a time, but often the larger cities sent as many as three, four, or even more. The following list is a summary of the cities which appear on inscriptions found at Samothrace, with references to the inscriptions where the *theoroi* are named.

Abdera	*IG* XII (8), no. 161.15-16
	no. 170d.52-54
	Samothrace 2.1, no. 22.45-50
Aigai (Aeolis)	*IG* XII (8), no. 162.7-10
Alabanda	*IG* XII (8), no. 160a.10-11
	no. 168.8
	no. 170b.20-23
	Samothrace 2.1, no. 24b.9-11
Astypalaia	*IG* XII (8), no. 168b.4-7
Bargylia	*IG* XII (8), no. 170b.31-33
Chios	*IG* XII (8), no. 162.24-27

Dardanos	*IG* XII (8), no. 160a.12-13
	no. 162.4-6
	no. 173.10-12
	no. 174.2-7
Elis	*IG* XII (8), no. 176.1-4
Ephesos	*IG* XII (8), no. 164.10-12
	no. 170f.85-88
	no. 172.12-15
	Samothrace 2.1, no. 23.12-15
	BCH 86 (1962), 274-5, no. 3
Eresos	*IG* XII (8), no. 162.36-39
	no. 163.19-21
Erythrai	*Samothrace* 2.1, App. IIIAc. 3-7
Halikarnassos	*IG* XII (8), no. 160a.5-6
	no. 162.17-23
	no. 164.3-6
Iasos	*IG* XII (8), no. 170e.70-71
Kalchedon	*Samothrace* 2.1, no. 22.65-69
Kaunos	*IG* XII (8), no. 160.7-9
	no. 170.45-49
	Samothrace 2.1, no. 22.42-44
	App. IIIAb.7-8 (restored)
Keramos	*IG* XII (8), no. 160b.16-21
Klazomenai	*IG* XII (8), no. 161.9-10
	no. 168.4-6
	Samothrace 2.1, no. 22.38-41
(Knidos)[417]	*Samothrace* 2.1, no. 22.5-8 (and 71?)
Kolophon	*IG* XII (8), no. 163.24-26
	no. 164.7-9
	no. 166.1
	Samothrace 2.1, no. 22.24-26
Kos	*IG* XII (8), no. 168.8-9
	no. 170.59-62
	no. 171b.27-29
Kyme	*IG* XII (8), no. 163.27-29
	no. 170b.24-27
	Samothrace 2.1, no. 23.8-12
Kyzikos	*IG* XII (8), no. 160a.3-4
	no. 162b.14-16
	no. 163b.16-18
	no. 169.9
Lampsakos	*IG* XII (8), no. 172.5-7
Larisa	*Samothrace* 2.1, no. 23.3-7
Maroneia	*IG* XII (8), no. 161.13-14
	no. 170c.39-41
Melos	*Samothrace* 2.1, no. 22.9-12
Methymna	*Samothrace* 2.1, no. 22.13-19
Mylasa	*IG* XII (8), no. 169.6
Myra	*IG* XII (8), no. 172.8-11

Myrina[418]	*IG* XII (8), no. 162.11-13
	Samothrace 2.1, App. IIIAb.4-6
Myrina[419]	*IG* XII (8), no. 171a.3-5
Mytilene	*IG* XII (8), no. 170b.28-30
Naxos	*IG* XII (8), no. 170b.34-36
Nysa	*IG* XII (8), no. 162.40-41
Parion	*IG* XII (8), no. 170f.81-84
	no. 175.1-5
	Samothrace 2.1, no. 22.51-?
Paros	*Samothrace* 2.1, no. 13.1-7
	Hesperia 48 (1979) 26
Patara	*IG* XII (8), no. 167 (a fragment)
Pergamon	*IG* XII (8), no. 170f.79-80 (envoys of King Attalos)
Phokaia	*IG* XII (8), no. 162.1-3
Priene	*IG* XII (8), no. 161.5-6
	no. 163.33-34
	no. 165.4-7
	no. 170c.42-44
Rhodes[420]	*IG* XII (8), no. 160a.1-2 (?)
	no. 170e.65-69
	Samothrace 2.1, no. 22.27-30 and 70
Samos[421]	*IG* XII (8), no. 165.8-14
	no. 170d.55-58
	no. 171.21-26
	Samothrace 2.1, no. 22.20-23
Samothrace	*IG* XII (8), no. 172.2-4
Stratonikeia[422]	*IG* XII (8), no. 170e.72-75
	Samothrace 2.1, no. 24b.12-14 (?)
Teos	*IG* XII (8), no. 163.30-32
	no. 171b.30-31
	Samothrace 2.1, no. 22.2-4
Thasos	*IG* XII (8), no. 161.10-11
	no. 172.16-20

The cities which appear most often are Alabanda, Kaunos, Kolophon, Kyzikos, Dardanos, Ephesos, Priene, Rhodes, and Samos. This is, however, probably due only to the fragmentary nature of the evidence, and it can be expected that if the evidence were more complete, not only these but many more cities would be more fully represented.

When the *theoroi* lists are compared with the initiate inscriptions, only thirteen sites appear in both groups. They are Arsinoë, Kaunos, Keramos, Chios, Kyzikos, Dardanos, Elis, Ephesos, Maroneia, Parion, Pergamon, Rhodes, and Thasos. The *theoroi* from Pergamon are sent by King Attalos, a fact which may imply his personal interest and not that of his subjects. To the sites which appear on both groups of inscriptions should also be added Kos and Samothrace itself. Kos, a city which sent *theoroi* to Samothrace, does not actually appear on the initiate lists, but L. Robert argues that the missing ethnic on one of those lists was that of Kos.[423] Samothrace presents a curious problem. The *demos* of Samothrace sent *theoroi* to the sanctuary,[424] but none of the names on the initiate lists have the Samothracian ethnic. Local citizens must have been initiates, and consequently we might assume that some of the longer initiate lists whose titles, and therefore ethnic descriptions, are missing are lists of local Samothracian initiates.[425] Even if Kos and Samothrace are included among those sites from which initiates came, it is still surprising that so few of the cities which sent *theoroi* to Samothrace are known from the initiate lists.

There is also little correspondence between the sites which sent *theoroi* and the sites where the Samothracian gods are known from other inscriptions.[426] Of the forty-six cities which sent *theoroi* to Samothrace, only seven are represented among those which preserve any epigraphical record of interest in the Samothracian gods. These seven cities are Kalchedon, Methymna, Mylasa, Rhodes, Stratonikeia, Ephesos, and Teos. There are inscriptions which mention priests of the Samothracian gods at Kalchedon and Mylasa, and there were temples of the Samothracian gods at Stratonikea and Ephesos. Finally, at Methymna, Rhodes, and Teos there were organizations or *koina* established in honor of these gods. These organizations seem to have been composed of Samothracian initiates, but at none of these sites is there any reason to believe that it was the local organization rather than the city government which sent the *theoroi* to Samothrace.

In addition to those cities where the Samothracian gods are mentioned in inscriptions, two other cities which sent *theoroi* to Samothrace had further connections with the sanctuary. A Samothracian decree of the second century B.C., set up in the city of Iasos, honors Dymas, a tragic poet of that city.[427] He is honored by the Samothracians because he had written a tragedy about Dardanos, the Samothracian hero. A similar honor is conferred by the Samothracians on another poet, Herodes of Priene, for a poem about the deeds of Dardanos and Aetion and the deeds of Kadmos and Harmonia.[428] In both cases the Samothracians decided that a copy of the decree should be inscribed and erected in the poet's home city. The means by which this was to be accomplished were specified by the Samothracians. The decree in honor of Dymas states that the *psephisma* will be given to the first *theoroi* who arrive from Iasos.[429] A similar formula is followed in the decree in honor of Herodes when the Samothracians indicate that this decree will be entrusted to the first *theoroi* who arrive from Priene.[430] On both of these occasions the Samothracians obviously expected that *theoroi* would be arriving from these cities.

Another indication that it was customary for *theoroi* to journey to and from Samothrace is given by an inscription of the middle of the third century B.C. from the island of Kos.[431] This inscription records plans for advertising the annual festival of Asklepios celebrated on that island. Apparently the city was sending out *theoroi* to announce the date of the *Asklepieia*. In addition to sending out special *theoroi* to make this announcement, the administrators decided to make use of the *theoroi* who were making a regular trip to Samothrace. The *theoroi* who were to visit Samothrace were directed to stop off at Chios to announce the festival of the *Asklepieia* there. This inscription is evidence that for Kos, just as for Iasos and Priene, the sending of *theoroi* to Samothrace was a regular and predictable occurrence.

It seems to have been a long established and well recognized custom for the cities of Asia Minor to send *theoroi* to Samothrace. During the Third Macedonian War, when Perseus wanted to hold a secret meeting with ambassadors from the cities of Asia Minor, he chose Samothrace as the site of the meeting, presumably because these ambassadors could come disguised as *theoroi*.[432] Samothrace would not have been an appropriate choice if the presence of *theoroi* on the island were not an ordinary event.

The duties and functions of the *theoroi* are not described on the inscriptions nor specified in the literary sources. It is likely that the *theoroi* simply represented their home cities at the Samothracian festival. Part of their duty may have been the performance of special sacrifices on behalf of their home city. Special representatives from Kyzikos and Rhodes are called *hieropoioi* on Samothracian initiate lists, and they, at least, must have been in charge of such sacrifices.[433] Whether the *theoroi* also played a similar role is not clear. The matter is somewhat complicated by the fact that both Kyzikos and Rhodes sent *theoroi* as well as *hieropoioi* to Samothrace. Two men from Kyzikos who are listed as *theoroi* on one inscription set up by the Samothracians[434] are called *hieropoioi* on an initiate inscription set up by a group from Kyzikos.[435] These two men are Parmeniskos Aristeos and Philoxenos Philoxenou. The second inscription records the initiation of these two men and three other men from Kyzikos. There is no way of determining whether both inscriptions were set up on the same occasion or whether these two men made more than one trip. If both inscriptions were set up at the same time, then Parmeniskos and Philoxenos served as *hieropoioi* when they were *theoroi* and became initiated at the same time. The situation with the *hieropoioi* from Rhodes is somewhat different because none of the five *hieropoioi* recorded occur as Rhodian *theoroi*. They appear on two initiate lists, one with two and the other with three *hieropoioi*, in both instances accompanied by several other initiates.[436] There is no way of determining whether these Rhodian *hieropoioi* served simultaneously as *theoroi*.[437]

It is possible that the *theoroi* brought to Samothrace a special tribute paid by their home city. The longer *theoroi* lists seem to have been inscribed by the Samothracian administration and several of them indicate that the city has conferred *proxenia* on the *theoroi* listed. This may indicate recognition of a special service performed by the *theoroi*, and in view of the extensive operations of the sanctuary during this period, this service may well have taken the form of a financial contribution. The *theoroi* may also have been commissioned to make special dedications on behalf of their home cities, but the only surviving dedication made by *theoroi* is so insignificant that it must have been a private rather than a public dedication.[438]

Some of the *theoroi* lists record that the *theoroi* were made *proxenoi* of the Samothracian *polis*. Because the formal heading is missing from so many of the stones, it is impossible to know for certain just how many of the *theoroi* became *proxenoi* of the city,[439] and whether by a certain period this had become standard practice. Fraser apparently believes that *proxenia* was eventually granted to all *theoroi* who came to Samothrace.[440] One list which Fraser dates to the late third or early second century B.C. may say that the *theoroi* became *proxenoi*,[441] but another list, possibly later, although it preserves the eponymous date, does not mention *proxenia*.[442] If the granting of *proxenia* to *theoroi* had become standard practice, it seems strange that it was not mentioned on this particular list.

There are two distinct types of *theoroi* lists. Most of the lists are rather long, recording *theoroi* from a number of cities.[443] They begin with the Samothracian eponymous date and list, often in approximate geographic order, the names of *theoroi* from various cities. These inscriptions, many of them on stones of uniform size, seem to have been set up by the sanctuary itself to record those cities which participated in a given year. The second type of *theoroi* list records only the *theoroi* from a single city. There are only six of these.[444] On the second type of list the *theoroi* are called *mystai*. None of the second group of lists mentions *proxenia* and none of the longer official lists mentions initiation. This distinction between the two types of lists has not been noticed before.[445] The longer lists seem to have been inscribed by the sanctuary in recognition of services performed by the *theoroi*. Most of these lists are inscribed on blocks of approximately uniform size. The shorter lists, where the *theoroi* of a single city are listed as initiates, must have been erected by the *theoroi* themselves to commemorate their initiation. These are inscribed on stones of various sizes. The existence of these lists recording the initiation of *theoroi* implies that initiation was not a prior condition for becoming a *theoros*.

The shorter, informal inscriptions are of various sizes and found in various places. One of these, listing initiated *theoroi* from Keramos, was inscribed in the first century B.C. in an empty place at the end of an earlier formal list of the second century B.C.[446] Another similar list of *theoroi* who seem also to have been initiates was added to an ordinary *mystai* list.[447] On two stones Greek *theoroi* from Dardanos appear as initiates together with Roman *mystai* who may not have been part of the same group. The last two *theoroi* lists of this type are simply short initiates lists. One of them is a list of *theoroi* from

Parion which has been restored to show that they were initiates.[448] The final list gives a group of *theoroi* from Elis who are called *mystai eusebeis*.[449]

Twenty-seven *theoroi* lists are carved on twenty-four different stones. Except for one stone whose original location is not recorded,[450] all were found on the island, but several had been moved from the sanctuary and been incorporated into later buildings. Twelve of the lists are inscribed on blocks of uniform size (0.35m in height).[451] The twelve lists inscribed on blocks of uniform size must have been part of the same building. Benndorf, who originally published most of these lists, thought that the building was the Temenos, a building which he called the "Old Temple."[452] He is probably correct in assuming that these blocks came from a single building,[453] but it is likely that the building was not the Temenos. The earliest *theoroi* list, not known to Benndorf, is inscribed on a stele and dates from the middle of the third century B.C.[454] If it were the practice to inscribe official lists on the walls of the Temenos, it is odd that this list was not inscribed there, because the Temenos had been in existence since the fourth century. The lists on blocks of uniform size are all later than the third century B.C. One of the lists which led Benndorf to believe that the Doric Temenos was a likely choice is a list inscribed on a Doric architrave block.[455] This list, however, is not an official list of the Samothracians, but a short initiate list erected by *theoroi* from Elis. It need not have come from the same building as the official lists. It is possible that in the third century B.C. official *theoroi* lists were normally inscribed on stelae and that when a building associated with *theoroi* was constructed at a date later than the third century, official lists were inscribed on the walls of that building. Since Benndorf's Doric architrave block does not contain an official list, the building where the lists were inscribed need not have been Doric.

A likely possibility for display of official *theoroi* lists is the Ionic building dedicated during the Hellenistic period by a woman from Miletos.[456] This particular building (no. 6) happens to be Ionic, but the Doric architrave block inscribed with a short *theoroi* list need not have come from the same building as the official lists. The building is of Hellenistic date.[457] The earliest list inscribed on a block dates from the late third century B.C. If a building were available for official lists, the practice of inscribing *theoroi* lists on stelae may have been discontinued. The identity of the woman who dedicated the building is not known,[458] but the fact that she came from a city on the Ionian coast may be of significance if the building which she subsidized was intended for the use of the *theoroi* who visited Samothrace. Miletos itself does not appear on the known *theoroi* lists, but this omission is more likely due to accident than to fact. Certainly many of the other Ionian cities are well represented on the lists, suggesting that a good percentage of the visitors to Samothrace came from this area. As with most Samothracian issues, a final decision about the use of this particular building will have to wait until the evidence is more complete. The building was excavated in 1923, but the reports are only partially published.[459] Nevertheless there is some reason to believe that this building was the original site of the blocks inscribed with the official *theoroi* lists.

CHAPTER FIVE

THE SAMOTHRACIAN GODS AND THEIR WORSHIPPERS AT OTHER SITES

Introduction

As records of the clientele of the mysteries, the *mystai* and *theoroi* lists from the Samothracian sanctuary are incomplete. The lack of epigraphical records is especially acute for the fourth and third centuries B.C., a period of expansion and development of the sanctuary itself, but a period for which few inscriptions survive.[460] The Theoi Samothrakes, however, are mentioned on inscriptions at other sites, demonstrating that these gods were popular in Thrace as early as the late fourth or early third century and well known elsewhere after the middle of the third century B.C. Many of these inscriptions seem to have been set up by Samothracian initiates, either individually or in groups, after they had returned to their home cities. We can see that people were travelling to Samothrace from distant cities earlier than the Samothracian initiate lists show, and we find new sites to add to those already known from inscriptions found on the island.

The term Theoi Samothrakes begins to make an appearance in the literary sources at about the same time that it begins to be used in inscriptions.[461] The Samothracian mysteries are mentioned as early as Herodotus[462] and Aristophanes,[463] but the information conveyed does not help to establish the general popularity of the Samothracian cult. Herodotus is personally acquainted with such a variety of religious practices that he cannot be considered a typical sample. Aristophanes writes at a time when Samothrace was paying tribute to Athens, and although some Athenian military personnel may even have come in contact with the mysteries when on duty in the northern Aegean, the general population is likely to have been familiar with the mysteries only by reputation. In the fourth century the Athenian playwright Alexis makes a joke of Samothracian prayers,[464] but like the reference in Aristophanes, the parody makes fun of the custom of praying to the Samothracian gods when in danger and is more a record of the notoriety of the mysteries than a comment about Athenian religious practice. Herodotus, Aristophanes, and Alexis do not use the expression Theoi Samothrakes, but it does occur in a fragment of New Comedy, attributed by some to Menander. There are problems with establishing the authorship, but the fragment does give a lively account of what must have been considered a conventional situation: a storm at sea with some sailors hanging on to the ropes and others shouting prayers to the Samothracian gods to avert disaster.[465]

The earliest reference to the Theoi Samothrakes which can be confidently identified occurs in an epigram of Kallimachos. He parodies the conventional vow of thanks for being saved from a storm at sea.[466] The epigram takes the form of a dedication to the Samothracian gods, but with a play on words, thanks the gods for being saved from storms of debt rather than a storm at sea.[467] Because he parodies a traditional type of dedication well known from many places, Kallimachos would not have had to travel to Samothrace to know of such dedications.[468] The significance of the epigram lies not in its form, but in its content and in that Kallimachos calls the Samothracian gods Theoi Samothrakes, the title which appears in contemporary inscriptions.

The evidence from the literary sources, even though much of it is irreverent, demonstrates that by the early Hellenistic period, the Samothracian mysteries already enjoyed a certain reputation in the Greek world. The literary evidence corresponds to the archeological evidence from the sanctuary, which indicates a period of building and development in the fourth century B.C. The success of this building program is underscored by the record of the steady growth of the clientele of the mysteries. One measure of this growth is the inscriptions which mention the Theoi Samothrakes at other sites. The earliest of these inscriptions, from Seuthopolis in Thrace, may be as early as the late fourth century B.C.[469] In the next century similar inscriptions begin to appear at sites further from Samothrace. From the middle of the third century B.C. until the early Imperial period, the Theoi Samothrakes continue to be named on inscriptions at sites which extend as far north as Olbia on the Black Sea and as far south as Koptos on the Nile. There are a total of thirty-three sites where the Samothracian gods are referred to specifically by name,[470] but only eight appear on the Samothracian *theoroi* inscriptions,[471] only six are known from the Samothracian initiate lists,[472] and only two are known from all three sources.[473] In spite of the fact that so few of these sites correspond to sites known from the inscriptions found at Samothrace, their geographic distribution is generally consistent with the distribution already apparent from the Greek *theoroi* and initiate lists, and the inscriptions found outside Samothrace give new evidence for worshippers along the Black Sea and in Egypt, areas only barely represented on the inscriptions at Samothrace. Evidence from all three types of inscriptions reveals that the Greek worshippers and initiates of the Samothracian gods came from sites along the east coast of the Black Sea, Macedonia, and Thrace, the Aegean islands, the coast of Asia Minor, and Egypt. It is important again to recall that the central area of Greece rarely appears on any of these inscriptions. The only city of central Greece to appear on the *theoroi* lists is Elis, and even though Athenian writers mention the Samothracian mysteries and the Samothracian gods, there are no initiates from Athens recorded at Samothrace before the second century A.D.[474]

The inscriptions found outside the sanctuary complement the *theoroi* and *mystai* lists. From them it is possible not only to form a more complete idea of the clientele of the mysteries, but to describe the ways in which the Samothracian gods were worshipped at sites other than Samothrace. The following discussion is limited to those inscriptions where the gods are referred to by the title Θεοὶ Σαμόθραχες or Θεοὶ οἱ ἐν Σαμοθράχῃ.[475] The epithet Samothrakes occurs only once on Samothrace itself,[476] but the geographic reference is also used officially by the sanctuary on an inscription found off the island. On a boundary stone erected on the mainland to define territory owned by the sanctuary, the gods are called Θεοὶ οἱ ἐν Σαμοθράχῃ indicating that the Samothracian administration used this title when appropriate.[477] There are many inscriptions from other sites which mention Theoi Megaloi. However, because this title is used for many other groups of gods,[478] it would be a mistake to assume that the title at other sites refers exclusively to the Samothracian gods.

Expressions which name the gods "Samothracian" are found in over fifty inscriptions and one papyrus. The gods are called Theoi Samothrakes, their temples are called Samothrakia, and their worshippers are referred to as Samothrakiastai. In some cases the Theoi Samothrakes may have been identified with similar gods worshipped at the same site, but in only two places is this identification explicit.[479] Most of the inscriptions which mention the Samothracian gods by name seem to do so because the person or persons involved wished to acknowledge a tie with the religion of the island. It seems likely that many of the individuals who made dedications to the Samothracian gods did so because they had been initiated at Samothrace and wished to recognize a benefit which they believed that initiation had conferred or because they wished to give thanks for a benefit which they believed their initiation guaranteed.

Official Documents and the Samothracian Gods

Decrees of three cities along the west coast of the Black Sea, Istros, Kallatis, and Odessos, direct that the decree itself be inscribed and installed in a local temple of the Samothracian gods.[480] These cities were originally Greek colonies whose citizens enjoyed a culture which combined Greek influences with native Thracian elements. Another inscription, from Seuthopolis in the Thracian interior, emphasizes the early interest of these northern areas in the Samothracian gods.[481] The inscription carries an oath apparently sworn by two feuding families during the reign of Seuthes III. One of the antagonists, named Epimenes, had apparently taken refuge in the temple of the Samothracian gods at Seuthopolis, the seat of Seuthes III; one purpose of the oath was the negotiation of his release from the temple. The inscription concludes with the request that it be inscribed and erected in three places: in the nearby town of Kabyle and in Seuthopolis itself in the temple of the Theoi Megaloi and in the temple of Dionysos. The temple of the Theoi Megaloi is presumably the same temple of the Samothracian gods where Epimenes had taken refuge. This inscription, dated to the end of the fourth century B.C., is the earliest known example of an inscription mentioning the Samothracian gods and indicates that the residents of Thrace took an early interest in the Samothracian mysteries.[482] Because the inscription was found in the largest residence in the city, a building whose entrace was a propylon, Dimitrov would go so far as to say that the priest was the king.[483] But this explanation must remain only a hypothesis until further evidence is forthcoming.

It is significant that the temple of the Samothracian gods at Seuthopolis was recognized as a place of asylum, a characteristic of the sanctuary at Samothrace itself.[484] More significant evidence for the importance of this cult to the local inhabitants, however, is that the inscription was to be set up in the temple of the Samothracian gods. The use of this temple for the display of official documents shows the recognition accorded to the Samothracian gods by the local citizens and their king and parallels the later practice known from Odessos, Istros, and Kallatis of exhibiting decrees in similar temples.

The Samothracian gods appear in another inscription where an official oath plays a part. In a treaty with Philip V of Macedonia, the Lysimacheians swear an oath by the Samothracian gods.[485] Philip V is known to have taken a personal interest in Samothrace, and as king of Macedonia he would logically have had a sentimental attachment for the gods whom the Macedonian royal family had traditionally patronized, but the appearance of the Samothracian gods in the oath of the Lysimacheians indicates that these gods had also achieved a special status with the citizens of that city.

Lysimacheia, originally founded by Lysimachos, had been under Ptolemaic domination from 245 B.C. until it joined the Aetolian League, probably before 202 B.C.[486] The treaty with Philip V was made in 202 B.C. when Philip peaceably occupied Lysimacheia while making his move toward the east. This alliance, referred to by Polybios,[487] and indicated by another inscription found at Lysimacheia,[488] was apparently not of long duration because Lysimacheia is not one of the cities mentioned in Polybios' summary of the *senatus consultum* relating the terms of Philip's agreement with Rome in 196 B.C.[489]

The treaty itself is divided into two parts: the conditions to be followed by the Lysimacheians with the oath which they swear to abide by these conditions, and the terms and oath of Philip himself. The Samothracian gods are mentioned among the divinities by which the Lysimacheians swear. They are the only gods whose names are actually still preserved on the stone; the other seven names are only reconstructed from other similar oaths by the original editor. The oath of Philip is even more obscure; very little survives. It would be important to know whether the Samothracian gods also appeared in Philip's oath. Oikonomos believes that the inclusion of the Samothracian gods in the oath of the Lysimacheians meant that they were special gods of that city. Although it is not impossible that these gods enjoyed a special place among the divinities worshipped at Lysimacheia, given the special interest taken in Samothrace by the Macedonian kings, it is more likely that these gods were introduced into the agreement by Philip himself. Whatever the case, it is hardly possible that these gods would have been introduced into the treaty at all unless they were recognized by both parties. As it stands, even without the oath of Philip, this treaty is an important document testifying to the international prestige of the Samothracian gods in the late third century B.C.

Personal Dedications

Personal dedications to the Samothracian gods are found at Olbia, Amphipolis, Philippi, Gökçeören, Sestos, Delos, Thera, Lindos, Rhodes, Apameia Kibotos, Fasilar, Kyrene, and Koptos. The dedications at Sestos, Thera, and Koptos are of special interest because they were not made by local citizens. Samothracian initiates were likely to travel, especially by sea, and consequently made dedications to those gods who offered protection from shipwreck. The dedications at Apameia and Koptos in fact specifically state that the offering is being made in thanks for rescue at sea. Kallimachos' parody of this type of dedication depends upon a well established custom; presumably these dedications were far more common than the extant evidence would indicate. Not all of the dedications to the Samothracian gods are made in thanks for being saved from a storm, but since travel by sea was often a necessity, many of these dedications may have been made as a precautionary measure. There may even have been other reasons to make dedications to the Samothracian gods, but the inscriptions are not explicit.

The dedication from Thera is probably the earliest of the personal dedications.[490] Because of this, and because it occurs in a rather unusual site and under interesting circumstances, it will be discussed first. The inscription was found at Thera, carved into the rock face of a low cliff in an open air *temenos* dedicated by a Greek from Perge, Artemidoros, son of Apollonios.[491] The area, called a *temenos* by Artemidoros himself,[492] is located just outside the walls of the town, a few yards below the main road.[493] In the *temenos* were statues of Hekate, Priapos, and Tyche, reliefs dedicated to Zeus, Poseidon, and Apollo, and several altars dedicated to various deities. Each statue, relief, or altar is accompanied by an inscription. The altars, carved from the natural wall of rock, are dedicated to Homonoia, the Dioskouroi, and the Samothracian gods. The inscriptions call all of the altars *bomoi* despite the fact that they are not all of the same form.

Artemidoros seems to have made a distinction between Olympian and minor deities. He included inscriptions to Zeus Olympios, Poseidon Pelagios, and Apollo Stephanephoros, but the Olympian deities are distinguished from the other gods honored at the site by the fact that they do not have altars, but only shallow reliefs carved next to the inscription. The reliefs, an eagle for Zeus, a dolphin for Poseidon, and a lion for Apollo, are conventional symbols of these gods, used on coins.[494] The impression one gets from this rather ostentatious display is that Artemidoros, reflecting a Hellenistic trend, felt that it was more practical to offer worship to those gods who could aid him in his everyday life rather than to offer sacrifice to remote Olympian figures. By the three symbolic reliefs Artemidoros acknowledged the Olympian gods, but it seems that he reserved his more extravagant devotion for those divinities who could provide protection and encouragement to individuals threatened by the vicissitudes of ordinary life.

This Artemidoros was a curious person. He included his own portrait among the carvings in the *temenos*, in a rather prominent place, just to the right of the dolphin of Poseidon.[495] If we discount the Macedonian and Ptolemaic royal families, well known from statues and coins, this picture is the only known portrait of a worshipper of the Samothracian gods.[496] The portrait shows a heavy face in profile, the hair encircled by a wreath, an attitude which Hiller von Gaertringen compares to the representations of Ptolemy Soter on coins.[497]

Artemidoros was not originally from Thera, but, as he repeats again and again in his inscriptions, was born in Perge. He apparently spent his old age in Thera, arriving after an active career.[498] We find Artemidoros settled at Thera sometime after 246 B.C., the date of the accession of Ptolemy III. This date is established by an inscription of Artemidoros stating that he dedicated shrines to Ptolemy I and Ptolemy II and that the citizens of Thera now join him in offering a shrine to Ptolemy III.[499] On this inscription, as on the altars set up in the *temenos*, Artemidoros gives his ethnic as "Pergaios", indicating that he still considers himself a citizen of Perge. It seems likely, however, that he was already playing a prominent role in local affairs at Thera. Near the altar of Homonoia there are two inscriptions erected by the people of Thera in his honor. In the second he is called by the city "a blameless citizen".[500] Apparently the city conferred citizenship on him.

Artemidoros' altar to the Samothracian gods has three unusual features. First, there is a hole 6 cm. in diameter, cut into the top of the altar. Second, a channel cut into the front face of the rock altar extends from this hole to ground level, a distance of 1.06 m. Third, directly in front of the altar, facing the channel, a shallow oval depression, measuring 1.06 m. by 0.50 m., and .20 m. deep at its deepest point, is cut into the stone floor of the *temenos*.[501] Any liquid poured into the hole in the top of the altar would flow through the channel and into the shallow depression in the floor of the *temenos*. Artemidoros calls the altar to the Samothracian gods a *bomos*, but it seems possible that it could have functioned as a *bothros* as well. There is a space at the top of the altar for the burning of animal meat, but there is also provision for liquids to flow down from the altar into the rock below. There is no exact parallel for such an altar at Samothrace itself, but it is possible that Artemidoros was familiar with *bothroi* like the one in the later Anaktoron at Samothrace and tried to imitate it here at Thera. Artemidoros must have been a Samothracian initiate.[502]

Although the altar to the Samothracian gods is located near that of the Dioskouroi, Artemidoros distinguished between the Dioskouroi and the Samothracian gods by providing separate altars. The Dioskouroi are symbolized by their traditional *piloi*, or caps, and stars carved in relief over their altar. In a couplet in dactylic hexameter Artemidoros calls them σωτῆρες and βοηθοί, "saviors" and "helpers".[503] In a similar couplet to the Samothracian gods the epithets ἀγήρατος and ἐπήκοος are applied to their altar itself.[504] It is described as "ageless" and "listening to those who pray," characteristics which by a sort of hypallage actually refer to the gods. By identifying characteristics of the gods with their altar, Artemidoros implies that the altar is a tangible link between the worshippers and the gods. By using the expression ἐπήκοον εὐχομένοισιν, "giving ear to those who pray," Artemidoros seems to say that these gods take a personal and immediate interest in their worshippers. The fact that he included the Samothracian gods in his *temenos*, describing them in this intimate way, suggests that they had a special meaning for him.

Artemidoros took an interest in a variety of divinities, but he did not actively support the traditional gods of Thera: Dionysos, Hera, and Apollo Karneios.[505] Artemidoros was more interested in promoting new divinities which he introduced from other places. His list is impressive. He brought to Thera from his home city Artemis of Perge and apparently established at Thera the office of a priestess in her honor.[506] He contributed to the repair of a temple of the Egyptian gods on the west side of the city[507] at a time when the worship of Isis was becoming established in the Aegean.[508] Artemidoros made a dedication to Priapos, the earliest dedication known outside of Lampsakos, the town on the Hellespont where the worship of Priapos seems to have originated.[509] Artemidoros calls Priapos *Lampsakenos*.[510] Next to Priapos he set up a statue of Hekate, whom he calls *Phosphoros*, an epithet used of Hekate in literature and in inscriptions.[511] Artemidoros dedicated to Hekate a throne upon which he set a black stone, plainly intended as a representation of the goddess and reminiscent of the stone baetyls representing a goddess known from Asia Minor.[512] Artemidoros also dedicated a seated statue of Tyche, a goddess known especially from Asia Minor and the east.[513]

Artemidoros' dedication to the Samothracian gods should be considered in the context of these other dedications. He recognized Zeus, Apollo, and Poseidon and remained faithful to Artemis of Perge, goddess of his homeland, but he also provided for gods whose reputations were new in his day. Nilsson calls Artemidoros exceptional for his interest in religious matters,[514] but Artemidoros is very much a man of his time. With his origin in Perge, possible trips to Samothrace, the Hellespont, and Egypt, he represents the new mobility of the Hellenistic population. By accepting new religious experiences he has also shown his flexibility. He has not resisted the new gods with whom he has come in contact, but he has made them his own and has offered them to the citizens of his adopted home. Artemidoros envisions his *temenos* as of value not only to himself, but to the city of Thera and all resident foreigners.[515] The citizens of Thera do well to recognize the benefits he has bestowed on them, for he has made a contribution to the religious life of the city.

Artemidoros lived to a ripe old age. An inscription, found next to an *exedra* built into the rock along the road into the city and several hundred meters from the *temenos*, is dedicated to Artemis Soteria of Perge. It says that she had promised for Artemidoros a lifespan of nine decades, but that Pronoia granted three more years.[516] Above the *exedra* there is a two line inscription inscribed by the citizens of Thera after the death of Artemidoros.[517] This inscription records an oracle from Delphi declaring that Artemidoros is a divine, immortal hero. For his efforts on behalf of the gods, Artemidoros himself is recognized as a god.[518] His gifts to the city seem suitably appreciated.

Artemidoros of Perge may be the most colorful worshipper of the Samothracian gods, but he was not the only one to leave a dedication in their honor outside of Samothrace. He is also not the only worshipper to make a dedication far from his original home. There are at least two more such dedications, one by Apollonios of Thera, made in Koptos, and a similar dedication left by a Pergamene woman, found at Sestos, but probably originally made at Ilion.

The dedication at Koptos has been taken as evidence for worship of the Samothracian gods in Egypt,[519] but because it is a dedication made by a foreigner, it need not be taken in this way. Apollonios of Thera describes himself as a staff officer, and gives thanks to the Theoi Megaloi Samothrakes for having saved him from dangers on the Red Sea.[520] Apollonios could have been familiar with the Samothracian gods at Thera or he may even have been a Samothracian initiate. The inscription does not mention a temple or altar and need not have stood in a sanctuary. Apollonios' dedication testifies to his own interest in the Samothracian gods and indicates nothing about the establishment of their cult in Egypt.

The dedication found at Sestos was made by a woman, Aristarche, daughter of Mikythos, from Pergamon.[521] She made her dedication to the Samothracian gods on behalf of Ptolemy IV Philopator, his wife Arsinoë III, and their son Ptolemy V, sometime between 209 and 205 B.C. There have been several suggestions about the meaning of this inscription. Lolling suggests that it was part of an altar dedicated to the Samothracian gods at Sestos.[522] Holleaux believes the inscription originally came from Samothrace because it is the dedication of a private individual who is not a local citizen.[523] Hemberg[524] and Fraser[525] think that the inscription is evidence for a temple of the Samothracian gods at Sestos. If Robert is correct, none of these suggestions can stand. Robert has shown that the stone originally stood, not at Sestos, but in or near Ilion, and that this inscription, the first of three to be recorded on it, was cut before the stone was moved to Sestos.[526] There was a temple of the Samothracian gods at Ilion,[527] and it is possible that this inscription stood near that temple.

Aristarche is one of a very few women to appear on the inscriptions outside the sanctuary, and she is the only one to sponsor a dedication. As a woman acting independently, making a dedication in her own right, she may be compared to Arsinoë II and the unknown Milesian woman who both made dedications in the Samothracian sanctuary. Aristarche may have made the dedication at Ilion after having been initiated at Samothrace. Initiation of a woman unaccompanied by a man was not unparalleled, although it was unusual.[528] Whatever the case, Aristarche must have been a woman of some wealth.

Of the other personal dedications to the Samothracian gods, one from Lindos may be from the third century B.C., perhaps as early as the dedications of Artemidoros. This dedication was made by a group of priests to the Samothracian gods.[529] The heading is missing, but the names, or parts of names, of three priests remain. One of the priests is in the service of Apollo Pythaios, another in the service of Sarapis, and the third is designated as *archierothytes*.[530] The inscription is not of the same type as the other personal dedications since it was made by priests perhaps acting in an official capacity and not by private individuals, but the word *charisterion* in the last line indicates that it is a dedication. When compared with the many other inscriptions from Rhodes connected with the Samothracian cult, this dedication indicates an early interest in the Samothracian gods by the residents of that island.

The dedication to the Samothracian gods from Apameia Kibotos, undated, is made by a man who has been saved from dangers at sea.[531] The inscription itself is of a formulaic type, similar in style to the dedication of Apollonios at Koptos and to the dedication parodied by Kallimachos.[532] Inscriptions of this sort must have been erected at Samothrace itself. Cicero attributes to Diagoras a remark that there would have been more dedications of thanks at

Samothrace if the people who drowned at sea made dedications as well as the people who were saved.[533] The anecdote, which is almost certainly at least of Hellenistic date, tells us more about Samothrace than it does about Diagoras. Samothrace was not a prominent sanctuary in Diagoras' day, but the sort of dedication mentioned in the story is similar to these Hellenistic examples in Kallimachos and the inscriptions. Cicero's story implies that such dedications were common in the Samothracian sanctuary, and together with the dedications from Apameia and Koptos, shows that people believed that the Samothracian gods preserved the safety of those at sea.

The other personal dedications to the Samothracian gods have nothing to do with the sea. Some are found inland, far from any water. One of these is located at Fasilar, where it is carved into a rock face next to a small relief showing the Dioskouroi.[534] The inscription is of particular interest because except for a series of inscriptions on Delos, it is the only known example outside the literary sources where the Dioskouroi are associated with Samothrace. They are called "Dioskouroi of the Samothracians." The relief shows two male figures, wearing the pointed caps or *piloi* associated with the Dioskouroi, and standing on either side of a small altar.[535] Each figure carries a spear and holds a horse. Above their heads there appear to be two bunches of grapes. Phyllis Lehmann refers to this relief as evidence for a use of Bacchic imagery in the Samothracian cult,[536] but it is not clear whether the relief, with its obviously syncretistic features, is related either to the Samothracian mysteries or to the Samothracian gods. As Swoboda points out, the arrangement of the figures on the relief is characteristic of coins and sculpture of Asia Minor.[537] It is more appropriate to compare these figures with representations of the Dioskouroi from that area than to use this relief as evidence for the nature of worship at Samothrace. In fact, it is the genitive Σαμοθράκων which may be the intrusive element, perhaps added for special effect by a worshipper who had no direct acquaintance with either the Samothracian mysteries or the Samothracian gods.[538]

From Amphipolis there comes a dedication by a bronzesmith who appears to have been a freedman of Greek parentage, once associated with the famous Roman family of the Caecilii.[539] Marcus Caecilius Sotas, who has his name inscribed in Greek, says that he is making a dedication to the Samothracian gods "from his craft" (ἀπὸ τῆς τέχνης). In the stone itself there are two mounting holes, suggesting that a bronze object was part of the original dedication. On the stone a caduceus is carved in relief. Poland, assuming that Sotas' profession was relevant to the dedication, argues that Sotas may have belonged to a guild or professional organization which was connected with these gods.[540] It has even been suggested that this inscription has some connection with the Kabeiroi in their role as the protectors of metalworkers.[541] It is easy, however, to place too much emphasis upon the significance of Sotas' profession. Considered in the wider context of all the known dedications to the Samothracian gods, this inscription is unique in being dedicated by a person identifying himself as a metalworker. If these gods had a special significance for members of this profession, one would expect to find more such dedications. Hemberg is certainly correct to play down this aspect of the inscription and to point out instead the significance of the caduceus on the stone.[542] This symbol was traditionally associated with the Samothracian cult.[543] It seems safer to assume that Sotas had once visited Samothrace for initiation. Initiates from Amphipolis are in fact known from at least one Samothracian inscription.[544]

The dedication from Kyrene is unlike the rest of the dedicatory inscriptions to the Samothracian gods because it is addressed to only one god and not to a group.[545] Fraser, who has published the inscription and provided a full commentary, argues that because the god who is called "Samothracian" is addressed in the singular and is called by epithets not otherwise used for the Samothracian gods, the inscription is not to be taken as evidence for the Samothracian cult.[546] It is rather to be understood as an example of a very personal, even perhaps eccentric, dedication from an individual to his own private deity. The inscription is dated to the Imperial period, but because there is no name for the person making the dedication, there is no way to identify the individual's ethnic background. The god is addressed as Πατὴρ θεὸς Σαμόθραξ ἀθάνατος ὕψιστος, a curious combination of epithets and names usually associated with several different deities. Πατήρ, as Fraser points out, could refer to Zeus, Sarapis, or Osiris.[547] Θεὸς ἀθάνατος is a phrase used to describe the Anatolian god Men.[548] Fraser associates ὕψιστος with the Hebrew god Jahwe, but as Kraabel has pointed out, this epithet was probably originally used for a variety of gods associated with mountains and heights, and was only later picked up by Hebrew worshippers and applied to their god.[549] Of the four different epithets, the only one restricted in its use is Σαμόθραξ, a term which has a specific geographic reference and which, except for one inscription,[550] is always used of the Samothracian gods. Fraser, in analyzing the motives of the person who has applied this epithet to his god, says, "... having acquired an especial interest in the mysteries, either by initiation or by some other means, (he) chose to associate his own supreme deity with the cult in this way."[551] There is no need, however, to assume that this person was an initiate. In fact, a Samothracian initiate or someone actually acquainted with the Samothracian gods would have not been likely to address a single Samothracian deity. In all other dedications to the Samothracian gods, they are addressed in the plural. We must conclude that the person who made this dedication was borrowing epithets from several gods in order to define his own unique and personal god.

In addition to the eight inscriptions discussed above, there are three other personal dedications to the Samothracian gods. Two are fragmentary. One was found near Nikomedeia[552] and the other at Bizone.[553] Another from Kythnos consists simply of the name of the Samothracian gods in the genitive case.[554] Once thought to be of the fourth century B.C., this last inscription is now considered by Hemberg to be of a later period, on the grounds that the term Theoi Samothrakes does not occur anywhere else before the third century.[555] The purpose of the inscription is difficult to determine. The original discoverer, Ross, connected it with the remains of two nearby buildings which he assumed to be temples.[556] However, without further evidence, it would be unwise to conclude on the basis of this inscription that there was a temple to the Samothracian gods on Kythnos.

The only dedication to be erected outside the sanctuary by people who explicitly state that they are Samothracian initiates is an unpublished inscription at Philippi.[557] The text indicates that it is an initiate list set up by at least four people who describe themselves as *mystai* of the Samothracian gods.[558] At first glance, the inscription seems identical with similar initiate lists at Samothrace, but the use of the dative case for the name of the gods is unusual at Samothrace where it appears on an initiate list only once.[559] The text differs from the *mystai* lists at Samothrace in that it lacks the conventional Samothracian date. It seems likely that the four people named on the list had travelled together to Samothrace for initiation and upon returning home, made a dedication to those gods into whose mysteries they had been received. This particular stone may be the counterpart of a similar stone which the same group had already commissioned at Samothrace.

Of the thirteen inscriptions which are definitely dedications, the five from Thera, Koptos, Ilion, Apameia, and Amphipolis are each made by a single individual who for some personal reason has identified the Samothracian gods as benefactors.[560] One of these inscriptions belongs to an altar, one accompanies a gift of metal work, and two acknowledge preservation from dangers at sea. There is no way to know how many of the dedicants actually were Samothracian initiates. We know from Aristophanes and Diodoros that people prayed to the Samothracian gods when in danger, and both authors imply that if a person praying were a Samothracian initiate, the prayer would be more efficacious.[561] Initiation, however, is not a prerequisite for a vow of thanks to these gods. Diodoros, for example, after saying that Orpheus was the only Argonaut who was a Samothracian initiate,[562] says that the other Argonauts, after being saved from storms because of Orpheus' prayers, made a vow of thanks by dedicating altars to the Samothracian gods in the land of King Byzas.[563] Later, when they arrived at Samothrace, the Argonauts "again paid their vows to the Great Gods and dedicated in the sacred precinct the bowls which are preserved there even to this day."[564] Diodoros does not say that the rest of the Argonauts became initiated even though they did make dedications. If the account of Diodoros reflects actual practice, it appears that one did not have to be an initiate to make a dedication to the Samothracian gods, even a dedication of thanks for being saved from storms at sea. Still, the individuals who singled out the Samothracian gods and called them by name must have had a special reason for doing so. In many cases the most likely explanation is that they were Samothracian initiates.

Priests of the Samothracian Gods

Priests of the Samothracian gods are mentioned in inscriptions from Olbia, Tomis, Dionysopolis, Istros, Kalchedon, Delos, Rhodes, Lindos, Karpathos, and Mylasa, implying official recognition of these gods by a group of worshippers or the city where they reside. Only the inscriptions from Istros and Dionysopolis are in the form of decrees, but the two inscriptions from Mylasa, accounts of the sale of a piece of property, are dated according to the investiture of the priest of the Samothracian gods. This practice suggests that this ceremony was well known enough to be recognized as a regular feature of the city's life.

The existence of these priesthoods is evidence that there were well established groups of worshippers of the Samothracian gods in each of these towns. Because initiates and *theoroi* from several of these cities appear on Samothracian inscriptions, it seems likely that these local religious groups maintained some kind of contact with the cult center on Samothrace. Although only three of these inscriptions specify that those who participated in the local ceremonies were actually *mystai*,[565] it is likely that many of these worshippers had at one time been initiated.

The tenure of a priest of the Samothracian gods varied from place to place. At Delos, Mylasa, and Karpathos priests of the Samothracian gods served but a single year.[566] At Tomis, Dionysopolis, and Istros, on the other hand, the appointment was for life, and at Istros the priesthood was, in addition, hereditary.[567] We will begin by examining first those inscriptions from sites where the appointment of a priest was a yearly affair.

The two inscriptions from Mylasa, both of them official documents having to do with the purchase of property, are dated according to the priest of the Samothracian gods.[568] Both of them were found in the sanctuary of the local god Sinuri, who seems to be related to the Babylonian god of the moon.[569] The first inscription is the account rendered by a group of officials who have purchased a piece of property. The second document is either a pledge for a mortgage or certificate of possession. Both are dated according to the wreathing of the priest of the Samothracian gods. The day in both cases seems to be the sixth of the month *Hyperberetaios*.[570] Apparently at the time a new priest took office, he was wreathed in some sort of public ceremony, and it is this ceremony, established on a specific date, to which these inscriptions refer.[571] Hemberg believes that there was a temple of the Samothracian gods at Mylasa,[572] but if there was one it has not been found, and there is no mention of such a temple in the inscriptions. However, the use of a ceremony of the Samothracian cult to date official documents implies that the ceremony was not only an established custom, but of fixed date. The importance of the priesthood to the city is confirmed by the fact that it is one of the cities known to have sent *theoroi* to Samothrace.[573] This is one of the few sites for which there is both local evidence and also evidence recorded at Samothrace for participation by its citizens in the Samothracian rites.

Just exactly how the Samothracian gods were represented at Mylasa is not clear, but there are some indications. Robert thinks that the Dioskouroi and the Samothracian gods were worshipped separately.[574] A traditional symbol of the Dioskouroi, the pointed cap or *pilos*, is found carved on a stone in the sanctuary of Sinuri.[575] The Dioskouroi themselves were worshipped nearby at Olymos.[576] There is no evidence that the two groups of gods were considered identical at Mylasa.

The situation of the priesthood at Karpathos may have been similar to that at Mylasa. At Karpathos at least thirty-nine different people are named on a list entitled "Priests of the Samothracian Gods."[577] A new name seems to have been added whenever a new priest took office. There is considerable variation in the carving of consecutive names, and from the development in the carving of the letter sigma, if the earlier names are compared with the later ones, it seems clear that the list grew over a long period of time, during which the upper and lower hastae of sigma became progressively more parallel.[578] The number of individual names suggests that no single priest could have held office for any great length of time. Consequently, these priests, as did those at Mylasa and Delos,[579] must have served terms of one year, and the inscription must have been carved over a period of years at the very end of the third and beginning of the second century B.C. The priesthood of the Samothracian gods was therefore an important and continuing institution at Karpathos.

In contrast with the inscriptions from Mylasa, Delos and Karpathos, those from the Black Sea area which mention priests of the Samothracian gods indicate that such priesthoods were there assumed for life. The inscriptions from Dionysopolis and Tomis use the expression διὰ βίου. The inscription from Istros declares that the priesthood is to be not only for life, but hereditary.[580] These priesthoods in the cities along the east coast of the Black Sea are connected with organizations of worshippers of the Samothracian gods and the functions of the priests seems to have been tied to these organizations. At Dionysopolis and Tomis these worshippers are called *mystai*. At Tomis the inscription calls them explicitly "*mystai* of the Gods in

Samothrace." The functions of the priest at Dionysopolis are to provide sacrifices and processions for the citizens as well as for the *mystai*, indicating that the cult of the Samothracian gods played an important role in the city. The close tie between city and cult is also indicated by the fact that the inscriptions which mention priests of the Samothracian gods from Istros and Dionysopolis are in the form of decrees. It is the city which has the power to control the priesthood and to decide what particular form it will take.

The inscription from Tomis is in two columns, the first apparently set up by the city, the second thought to be the regulations of an association of *mystai*.[581] This association, called "*Mystai* of the Gods in Samothrace," sets down the conditions of the sale of the priesthood of their group. The first part describes the responsibilities of the priest, and the second the honors which he receives in return. First of all, the priest will take office for life. Each year, at the annual festival, on the seventh day of the month *Apatoureon*,[582] he is to provide the materials for the sacrifice and sponsor a procession at his own expense. In return he will be wreathed by the *mystai* on the day in which he takes office as priest. He will also join the subordinate priest in offering incense at the meetings of the association and, according to a reconstruction suggested by Roussel, he will have the right to wear his wreath forever.[583]

Because of *lacunae* at certain critical places in the text, this inscription has been interpreted in various ways. The first break in the text occurs in lines 5-6, which list the duties of the priest at the annual festival. Gomperz originally restored these lines to read: παρ[έξει τὸ πέμμ]α σχίξας καὶ ἐγχέει [τὸ ποτὸν τοῖ]ς μύσταις, believing that they referred to a sacred meal during the rites of the mysteries.[584] He wished to show a connection between the celebration of the Christian eucharist and the famous mystery formula which a scholiast quotes as: ἐκ τυμπάνου ἔφαγον, ἐκ κυμβάλου ἔπιον.[585] Roussel has convincingly shown, however, that the line should properly be restored as follows: παρ[έξει τὰ ξύλ]α σχίξας καὶ ἐγχέει [τὸν οἶνον τοῖ]ς μύσταις.[586] The inscription, then, is seen to refer not to a sacramental meal of the mysteries, but a sacrifice at the annual festival of the *mystai*, a sacrifice for which the priest supplies the wood for the fire and the wine for the *mystai*. The wine may be used for nothing more than pouring a libation to the Samothracian gods. Clearly the mysteries themselves are not celebrated at this annual festival. Lines 2-3 indicate that the celebrants have already been initiated at Samothrace. The ceremony at Tomis is a celebration involving a procession and a sacrifice, a celebration which somehow commemorates the worshipper's initiation at Samothrace, but does not repeat it.

This inscription from Tomis gives some important information in spite of the textual difficulties. We learn the date of the festival celebrated by the local organization of Samothracian initiates. We also learn that the priesthood, although it is for life rather than for a specific period of time, is purchased by the priest and not granted as an honor by the association or the city. We learn even the price paid for the priesthood (lines 16-17), seven gold coins and sixty bronze coins, paid by Timaios, son of Straton, when he assumed office. In addition to holding a public festival and procession in the fall, the association seems to have held regular meetings at which the priest and assistant priest officiated and conducted sacrifices. There is no mention of a building for these meetings, but the fact that temples of the Samothracian gods are mentioned at nearby Odessos and Istros suggests that such a building must have existed at Tomis for the meetings mentioned in line 11.

At Istros we hear about a priesthood of the Samothracian gods from a decree.[587] Dated to the second century B.C., the decree honors Dionysios, son of Strouthion, because he made a loan (interest free for one year) to the city for the purchase of grain. Dionysios is to be honored in two ways: with a statue in the agora and with recognition by the city of his right to the priesthood of the Samothracian gods forever. The priesthood is recognized as hereditary. The decree itself is to be recorded in two places: on the base of the statue of Dionysios and on a stone to be erected near the altar (or the temple) of the Samothracian gods.[588] Two other inscriptions of Istros mention a temple of the Samothracian gods.[589] However the preposition παρά in the present inscription seems to demand the word βωμόν as its object instead of ἱερόν. If the decree in honor of Dionysios was to be erected near the altar of the Samothracian gods, it may date from a period before the temple mentioned in the other two inscriptions was built.[590]

The inscription seems to date from a time at which the cult of the Samothracian gods at Istros, hitherto a private cult, became recognized by the city as a public cult. The statement that Dionysios will have the right to wear the crown, just like the other priests (line 23), indicates that the city is recognizing this cult for the first time. J. and L. Robert, following Pippidi's earlier reading for line 11, originally thought that Dionysios was the priest of a private, family cult of the Samothracian gods, and as a tribute to his generosity towards the people, the city now accords to his cult official status.[591] However, a debate about the reading of line 11 weakens this argument. If the line records Dionysios' patronymic and the name of his grandfather instead of his ethnic and the title "Priest of the Great Gods," there is no reason to assume that Dionysios was previously priest of the Samothracian gods, even priest of a private cult. He may have assumed the priesthood simultaneously with its establishment as a public institution.[592] Dionysios was probably a Samothracian initiate. The city could hardly appoint as priest a person who was unfamiliar with the cult and mysteries of these gods. The fact that there seems already to have been at least an altar of the Samothracian gods at Istros is evidence for some sort of regular worship of these gods in that city. Perhaps the altar itself had been set up by Samothracian initiates who lived at Istros. If so, then the inscription honoring Dionysios records an important moment in the development of this organization. It is clear from the inscriptions of Tomis and Dionysopolis that the priest of the Samothracian gods in those cities was responsible for processions and sacrifices for the *mystai* of these gods. The establishment of such a priesthood at Istros would indicate that at the time of this inscription there was already a sizeable group of Samothracian initiates there. The temple which was to be built sometime during the same century is evidence for the growth of this group and the success of Dionysios and his heirs in the performance of their duties as priest.

Another decree, this one from Dionysopolis, was erected by the city in about 48 B.C. in honor of Akornion, son of Dionysios.[593] Akornion, apparently a prominent citizen, is honored for his generosity toward the city both as a priest and as a diplomatic envoy. The issue of his priesthoods concerns us here. Akornion held four different priesthoods. First, he was priest of Theos Megas (line 10), for which privilege he performed sacrifices and shared meat with the citizens. When he was priest of Sarapis (line 12), he fulfilled the obligations of the priesthood generously. As priest of Dionysos, the god for whom the city was named, he took up the crown of the god, performed the sacrifices, and shared the meat with the citizens (line 14). As a fourth service, Akornion accepted the priesthood of the Samothracian gods. This priesthood, like the priesthood assumed by Dionysios at Istros, seems to have been a public office. The inscription is explicit about the duties of his office. Akornion performed sacrifices and sponsored processions for the *mystai*, and for the citizens. The *mystai* mentioned in line 21 must have been people who had been initiated at Samothrace.[594] The fact that other citizens were included in the ceremonies indicates that it was a public festival, perhaps an annual affair similar to the one known at Tomis.

Like the priesthoods of the Samothracian gods at Tomis and Istros, this priesthood at Dionysopolis was for life. In contrast, Akornion's first three priesthoods, the priesthoods of Theos Megas, Sarapis, and Dionysos, seem to have been for specific terms. The verbs used to describe Akornion's activities in these priesthoods are all in the past tense. The priesthood of the Samothracian gods, however, was a permanent position.

It is important to notice that in this inscription from Dionysopolis the priesthood of the Samothracian gods is distinct from the priesthood of Theos Megas. The fact that the duties of these priesthoods do not overlap is indicated by the use of the past tense for one and the present tense for the other. The priesthood of the Samothracian gods does not include jurisdiction over the cult of Theos Megas. Likewise, the cult of Theos Megas, in this inscription at least, does not appear to have anything to do with *mystai*. Hemberg has maintained that at Odessos worshippers identified their god, called Theos Megas on coins, with the Theoi Megaloi of Samothrace.[595] Yet, in this inscription from Dionysopolis, it is clear that the public celebrations and the priesthood associated with the Samothracian gods were kept separate from the celebration and priesthood of the local god Theos Megas.

There are several other inscriptions which mention priests of the Samothracian gods, but give no information about the term of the priests.[596] One of these, from Olbia, is an honorific inscription set up by Eubiotos, son of Ariston, in honor of his uncle Epikrates, son of Nikeratos, where the uncle is described as a person who has served as a priest of the gods in Samothrace.[597] A second is from Kalchedon,[598] concerning the sale of a priesthood of a god whose name does not survive. The inscription is in the form of a contract specifying certain sums which the purchaser is to pay to various individual priests in addition to the fee which he pays to the city. Among those who are to receive payment is the priest of the Samothracian gods. It is interesting to notice that the priest of the Samothracian gods represents a rather important group of worshippers. He is to receive a sum which, although it is less than the sum paid to the priest of Zeus Boulaios, is far more than the sum paid to the priest of Herakles. Three other inscriptions about priests of the Samothracian gods come from Rhodes, two from the city of Rhodes, and the third from Lindos.[599] The two from Rhodes, dated to either the second or first century B.C., are lists which name the priests of various gods. On one list the priest of the Samothracian gods is listed after the priest of the Dioskouroi, and on the second list, the priest of the Samothracian gods is listed after the priest of the Korybantes. It is significant that in Rhodes, at this period at least, the cults of the Dioskouroi and the Samothracian gods were maintained separately.[600] The inscription from Lindos, inscribed on the base of a votive dedication made by a group of priests of various gods, was found in the sanctuary of Athena. The priest of the Samothracian gods follows the priest of the Dioskouroi.

As a group, the inscriptions which mention priests of the Samothracian gods indicate priesthoods at ten sites. At three of these sites, Dionysopolis, Tomis, and Istros, these priests were clearly involved with groups of worshippers who engage in specific and regular acts of devotion. At Tomis, where the priesthood was purchased, it may have been the local religious association and not the city which controlled and awarded the priesthood. At Istros, however, where a similar priesthood was awarded by the city as a public honor, it seems that it was the city which assumed this responsibility. The priesthood at Dionysopolis may also have been a public one.

The matter of greatest significance in the evidence from the Black Sea sites is the relation of the worshippers of the Samothracian gods to their local cities. These people, many presumably Samothracian initiates, were either so numerous or so prominent locally that they were able to introduce the worship of these gods into their own communities, where the ceremonies performed in honor of the Samothracian gods became part of the official public worship.

The inscriptions from Tomis, of uncertain date, and Istros, second century B.C., are apparently from the period when official priesthoods associated with the Samothracian gods were first being established. The inscription from Dionysopolis, about 48 B.C., reflects a time when this priesthood and the ceremonies associated with it had become an established part of the official local worship. The priesthoods mentioned at other sites were presumably associated with groups of worshippers, but on Rhodes at least, these were private associations and not official cults.

Finally, there are many sites for which, although there is mention of a temple of the Samothracian gods or an association in their honor, no information about a priesthood survives. It is to be expected that these temples and associations also sponsored priesthoods, but the character of these offices and the ceremonies associated with them are not known. For this reason the inscriptions from Tomis and Dionysopolis, with information about cult procedure, are especially important.

Temples of the Samothracian Gods

There are indications of temples in honor of the Samothracian gods at Odessos, Kallatis, Istros, Delos, Ephesos, Stratonikeia, and possibly Philadelphia. There may also have been temples at those sites where a priesthood or association in honor of these gods is known to have been established, but this section will be limited to those places where there is either epigraphical or archaeological evidence for such a temple. Delos is the only site where a building definitely identified in inscriptions with the Samothracian gods has been excavated, but decrees from Odessos, Kallatis, and Istros specify that they are to be exhibited in buildings called *Samothrakia*, an inscription from Ephesos mentions a Samothrakion, and an inscription from Stratonikeia mentions a street called "Samothrakion Street." In addition, a papyrus from Philadelphia is assumed to give evidence for a temple of the Samothracian gods as far south as Egypt.

Taking the northern sites first, there are six decrees, two from Kallatis,[601] two from Odessos,[602] and two from Istros,[603] directing that the decree itself is to be erected in a temple of the Samothracian gods or a Samothrakion. A third decree from Istros mentions that it is to be set up next to an installation of the Samothracian gods, probably an altar.[604] No building called Samothrakion has yet been found at any of these sites, but the inscriptions of Istros, Dionysopolis, and Tomis which describe the priesthoods and activities associated with the Samothracian gods indicate a strong local interest.

The evidence for Kallatis is restricted to two tiny fragments of inscriptions, assumed to be parts of decrees, and one long fragment of a decree, restored by L. Robert to include a reference to a Samothrakion.[605] If these inscriptions are decrees once displayed in a Samothrakion, Kallatis can be compared to the neighboring cities along the coast where the Samothracian gods exercised a special appeal.

The evidence for Istros is more complete. In that city a Samothrakion is mentioned twice as the site for the display of official decrees.[606] There was also a priesthood associated with the Samothracian gods.[607] A small building dedicated to Theos Megas has been discovered at Istros, but this does not seem to be the Samothrakion mentioned in the inscriptions.[608] First, it seems too small to have served as a state archive for the display of public decrees. Second, it is not dedicated by a local citizen, but by a foreigner from Thasos, suggesting a private shrine rather than a public temple.[609]

The two decrees which mention a Samothrakion at Odessos seem to be from the Hellenistic period.[610] Close ties between the city of Odessos and Samothrace during that time are indicated by another decree of Odessos erected at Samothrace.[611] The extant fragment of this decree does not seem to be part of a *theoroi* or *mystai* list, but because it does mention the Samothracian mysteries it is at least evidence for religious ties between the city of Odessos and the Samothracian sanctuary and indicates that citizens of Odessos figured among the Samothracian initiates.[612] The importance of this religious connection between Odessos and Samothrace is underscored by the reference at Odessos to a Samothrakion, recognized by the city and used for the display of public documents.[613]

Although there are temples of the Samothracian gods mentioned in inscriptions of Odessos, Kallatis, and Istros, it is not clear whether the cults associated with these temples originated under the influence of the Samothracian mysteries or whether they had local origins. The name Theos Megas is used for an important local divinity at Odessos, Istros, and Dionysopolis, but it is not clear that he was considered identical to one of the Samothracian Theoi Megaloi. Theos Megas is traditionally represented as a bearded figure, sometimes carrying a cornucopia, and he is often compared to the Greek Hades.[614] Hemberg argues that the people of these northern cities recognized in the Samothracian Theoi Megaloi their own local Theos Megas and that they identified the Samothracian gods with this male figure coupled with a female goddess with attributes of Demeter. The only evidence for such a syncretism is based entirely on coins.[615] It is important to recall that Theos Megas is always mentioned in the singular, and except for the headband which he wears on coins, there is no reason to think that he was connected with a mystery ceremony.[616] At Dionysopolis at least, the priesthood of Theos Megas was maintained separately from the priesthood of the Samothracian gods as late as 48 B.C.[617] Although it is possible to point to similarities in title, there is as yet no reason to accept this local god as being identical with one of the Samothracian gods.

Delos is the only site where a temple associated with the Samothracian gods in inscriptions has been excavated. The evidence from Delos, however, is often confusing, and except for a dedication by a Delian at Samothrace,[618] there seems to be little connection between the Samothrakion at Delos and the mysteries at Samothrace. There are no Delians recorded on the extant *theoroi* lists, Greeks from Delos do not appear as Samothracian initiates, and the term Samothrakion is introduced at Delos only in the second century B.C. The building which the Athenians called Samothrakion after 166 B.C. had an independent history as a Kabeirion before that time, and the later name was introduced only after three separate groups, the Kabeiroi, the Dioskouroi, and the Theoi Megaloi were assimilated.

Identification of some of the minor temples on the island of Delos is based on three kinds of inscriptions: temple records from the period of Delian independence mentioning priesthoods or festivals, inventories of temple possessions from the period of Athenian domination, and dedicatory inscriptions found in the temples themselves. Among the places of worship mentioned in the temple records and Athenian inventories are a Dioskourion, a Kabeirion, a Samothrakion, and a Herakleion.[619] Excavations on the island have uncovered two buildings which have been identified at various times as one or more of these temples. One of the buildings, GD 123,[620] located on the shore, has been identified by its excavator, F. Robert, as the Dioskourion mentioned in inscriptions.[621] The second building, GD 93, located near the Inopos and away from the shore, has been identified as the Samothrakion on the basis of Athenian inventory lists and dedications found in the building itself.[622] This seems to be the same building which was earlier called Kabeirion in the third century B.C.[623]

The building known as Kabeirion or Samothrakion (GD 93), located near the Inopos just to the west of Serapeions B and C, had three separate stages.[624] The original building is dated by Chapouthier from sometime between the Archaic period and the mid-fourth century B.C.[625] This temple, with four columns *in antis*, is wider than it is deep (11.2m × 5.9m), with the porch and door on the longer side.[626] Sometime before 132/131 B.C. the building was enlarged by increasing its width, but the door and the columns were not moved. At this time a niche was installed to the left of the entrance, presumably for a cult statue. In 102/101 B.C. a small annex only 4.96m wide was added. This building, called ναός in the inscriptions, was dedicated by an Athenian priest named Helianax, in honor of Mithridates and consecrated to the deities associated with the site.[627] Besides the buildings, the most significant installation in this area is a large circular monument of the late second century B.C., a construction which Chapouthier has identified as an altar for libations to the underworld gods.[628]

On the basis of a double axe carved on a stone found in GD 93 and the pre-Greek name of Mt. Kynthos, Chapouthier and Hemberg believe that the Delian Kabeiroi cult originated with Greek settlers from Asia Minor. The image of the double axe, however, and the non-Greek name for the mountain are two separate issues. The particular double axe carving from GD 93 is not dated; it could simply be a late example of a persistent motif. The non-Greek name for Mt. Kynthos indicates early settlement of the island, but there is no evidence to tie the worship associated with GD 93 with this period. The original building on the site may be as late as the fourth century. Without further evidence it is perhaps unwise to accept these speculations about the origin of the cult. It is important to notice that none of the finds associated with the Kabeirion are dated even as early as the Archaic period.[629]

Although there is no evidence for worship of the Kabeiroi at Delos in the Archaic period, the temple of the Dioskouroi, GD 123, seems to have been built during that time, and the early activity of the cult is also indicated by Archaic pottery and sculpture found in the building.[630] The lack of any remains from the Classical period suggests that the temple was neglected at that time, the first period of Athenian control of Delos. A resurgence of activity in the Hellenistic period is indicated by Hellenistic finds from the area and the great number of references to the Dioskourion in third century inscriptions.[631] The temple is not mentioned by name in inscriptions after the establishment of the Athenian administration in 166 B.C. F. Robert suggests that the abandonment of the Dioskourion in periods of Athenian domination was politically motivated because the Athenians would have been hostile to the Dioskouroi, divinities which they would connect with Sparta.[632] This explanation is at odds with the fact that the Dioskouroi were later introduced into the worship at GD 93 (the Kabeirion-Samothrakion) precisely at a period of Athenian political control. If the Athenians were in fact predisposed to ignore the Dioskouroi because of animosity toward Sparta, it seems strange that they would have encouraged the inclusion of this pair in a cult which they seem to have especially favored on Delos.[633]

The evidence for the consolidation of the worship of the Dioskouroi with the worship of the Kabeiroi in GD 93 is a series of inscriptions mentioning priests of this building. An early inscription of the second Athenian period calls the priest ἱερεὺς Θεῶν Μεγάλων (161/160 B.C.).[634] Two years later the priest is described as ἱερεὺς Θεῶν Μεγάλων καὶ Διοσκόρων καὶ Καβείρων (159/158 B.C.).[635] In the following year the title is (ἱερεὺς) Μεγάλων Θεῶν Διοσκούρων Καβείρων,[636] and by the end of the century the epithet "Samothracian" has become part of the title: (ἱερεὺς) Θεῶν Μεγάλων Σαμοθράκων Διοσκούρων Καβείρων.[637] Robert and Hemberg see in this development evidence that the worship of the Dioskouroi was simply transferred to the Kabeirion.[638] Chapouthier, however, argues that when the word καὶ dropped out of the title, a fusion had taken place between these groups of gods and that their identities became assimilated.[639] Hemberg objects to this interpretation, questioning whether the subtle change in title could bear so great a meaning, but the persistence of the final version of that title for over fifty years indicates that some sort of syncretism had taken place between these three groups of gods.[640] It seems obvious that such a syncretism could be possible only because the three different groups were thought to be similar in appearance, number, and function. The inclusion of the Dioskouroi suggests that all of these groups were believed to contain two male deities possibly associated with a single goddess. The introduction of the epithet "Samothracian" to describe these gods means that the Samothracian gods were thought to be composed of the same three figures. This assimilation of the Kabeiroi, Dioskouroi, and the Samothracian Theoi Megaloi is attested only at Delos. At no other sites are the Samothracian gods explicitly identified with both the Kabeiroi and the Dioskouroi. There must be special reasons why this happened at Delos and only at Delos.

The name "Samothrakion" does not appear in the Delian inscriptions before the installation of the Athenian administration in 166 B.C. At this time Rome removed from Delos the local Delian inhabitants and permitted the establishment of an Athenian cleruchy on the island.[641] The priests who are named in the inscriptions associated with the Samothrakion during the rest of the second century B.C. are all from Attica,[642] and they seem to have served one year terms. These facts suggest that these priests were appointed by the Athenian administration and that the cult associated with the Samothrakion was a public cult and not a private cult associated with a particular family. It is important to notice that not only is the administration of the temple changed in 166 B.C., but also the body of local worshippers. Delos, an important cult center, attracted worshippers from the entire Greek world; these visitors to the sanctuary certainly did not change, but with the dispossession of nearly the entire local Delian population, the social composition of the community was changed. This change in the local population explains some of the developments in the nature of the traditional gods worshipped in GD 93. One of these changes was the new name for the building. Previously, as has been observed, it was known as the Kabeirion. In the earliest Athenian inventory the building is called "temple of the Megaloi Theoi",[643] and within ten years of 166 B.C., it is regularly called Samothrakion.[644] This change would seem to be an Athenian innovation. A parallel change in terminology has already been noticed in the references to priests associated with the building. It was also during this period that the building was remodelled and the second, smaller temple constructed. The Athenians took the cult which they found, and by consolidating at least three groups of gods into one group, created in a sense a new cult.

Chapouthier calls the Samothrakion at Delos a temple, but Roux has argued that it was originally a *hestiatorion* or dining chamber.[645] The original floor was covered in the center by a pebble mosaic and a platform for dining couches extended around the sides of the room. Delian inventories dating from 156/155 B.C. state that the portico of the Samothrakion contained nine couches, four of them broken.[646] Goldstein puts the original number of couches at thirteen, suggesting that at the time of the inventory some were already missing.[647] The building was used for dining before its remodelling in the second half of the second century B.C., but whether it continued to have this function after it was enlarged is not known. Finds within the building indicate that it was used for the exhibition of statues, and the inventories mention in addition to statues, articles which were probably dedications of people connected with the sea: two iron anchors, one with a ring, three wooden anchors, and a trident.[648]

Chapouthier believes that the temple and upper terrace were used for public ceremonies and that the open area near the river was used for secret rites of initiation.[649] It is unlikely, however, that secret rites would have been performed outside without the protection of a building to guarantee privacy. Chapouthier places great emphasis on evidence of burnt sacrifices near the base of an altar in the open area,[650] and he also stresses the significance of lamps found nearby and the proximity of the stream. He sees the lamps as evidence for nocturnal rites and associates the stream with purification ceremonies. These elements can certainly by associated with nocturnal purification and sacrificial rites, but there is no confirmation from any of this evidence that these ceremonies included the initiation rites of the Samothracian mystery cult.[651]

Another inscription mentioning a Samothrakion was found near the harbor at Ephesos.[652] It mentions a Samothrakion located either near or within a Fishery Customs House (τὸ τελωνῖον τῆς ἰχθυϊκῆς). The inscription lists people who had contributed money and building supplies when the Customs House was built. These people are described as fisherman and fish merchants and the building was apparently used for the collection of taxes or tolls on the fish caught in the area. Many of the people listed are Roman citizens, a fact not surprising considering the late date of the inscription. Addressed to the emperor Nero, his mother Agrippina, and his wife Octavia, the inscription must have been inscribed between A.D. 54 and A.D. 59. This date makes the inscription the latest securely dated document to refer to the cult of the Samothracian gods and is definite proof that the cult was still flourishing at sites away from Samothrace as late as the middle of the first century A.D. The existence of a Samothrakion near or inside the Customs House suggests that the temple was frequented by the fishermen who paid their tax there, and also confirms the evidence from other sources that the worshippers of the Samothracian gods were people involved with the sea.

In addition to those sites where a temple of the Samothracian gods is actually mentioned in an inscription, there are two other sites where there seem to have been such temples. One of these sites is Stratonikeia in Caria. An inscription was copied there by LeBas and Waddington mentioning the word Samothrakion, interpreted as a temple in that city.[653] Hemberg, following the reading of LeBas and Waddington, accepts the inscription as evidence for such a temple.[654] He was apparently unaware of the revised reading and commentary provided by Wilhelm, who describes the inscription as a military document defining the boundaries of a district under the protection of a certain guard tower.[655] He maintains that the term Samothrakion refers not to a building or temple but to a street. Although the inscription has been lost, it seems likely that Wilhelm is correct. Louis Robert, commenting on another similar inscription from Stratonikeia, follows Wilhelm.[656] The question remains, however, as to how the street acquired its name. Wilhelm assumes that the street was named "Samothrakion" not for a temple of the Samothracian gods, but for some people from Samothrace whom he believed were living there. Robert does not say whether he shares this assumption, but it is far more likely that the street would be named for a temple of the Samothracian gods than for a group of Samothracian immigrants. *Theoroi* from Stratonikeia are recorded at Samothrace,[657] indicating an interest of the local inhabitants in the Samothracian gods, and it is possible that there was a temple in their city after which a nearby street might have been named.

The final site to be considered is Philadelphia in Egypt. A papyrus fragment records that a payment was made there to a stone-cutter named Erieus for some items made of stone (which could have been altars) set up in some place "of the Samothracians" and for *phialai* for a libation.[658] Hemberg takes this papyrus fragment as evidence that there was a temple of the Samothracian gods at Philadelphia,[659] but it is important to notice that the extant fragment does not mention a temple, and that the word θεῶν is not included with Σαμοθραίκων. The only word which might indicate a religious context is φια[λῶν] in line 32. Because Philadelphia is named for Arsinoë and because she is known to have taken a special interest in Samothrace, this papyrus is usually taken as evidence that she established the worship of the Samothracian gods in Egypt after her marriage to Ptolemy Philadelphos.[660] The papyrus, an isolated example which does not actually mention the word "temple," may not constitute such evidence. It is well to keep in mind that Arsinoë made her great dedication at Samothrace while she was still married to Lysimachos, before she married her brother Philadelphos and moved to Egypt. The interest of her family in Samothrace and the Samothracian gods is due to Macedonian tradition, and in itself is not evidence that the Samothracian gods were popular among other Greeks in Egypt.

One of the reasons that the Samothracian gods are thought to have been popular in Egypt is the confusion of the Dioskouroi with these gods. Visser maintains that by the third century B.C., the Samothracian gods were identified with the Dioskouroi, implying that worshippers did not distinguish between the two groups.[661] This is simply not the case. Although in some writers the symbols of the Dioskouroi are associated with the Samothracian gods,[662] at only two sites are the Dioskouroi associated with the Samothracian gods in an inscription,[663] and except for Delos, the worship of the Samothracian gods seems to have been maintained separately from the worship of the Dioskouroi. Clearly Samothracian initiates would know the difference. There is more evidence for worship of the Dioskouroi in Hellenistic Egypt than for worship of the Samothracian gods, but because there is no reason to believe that the two groups were considered identical, evidence for the Dioskouroi should not be taken as evidence for the Samothracian gods.[664]

Although the papyrus fragment may testify to worship of the Samothracian gods in Philadelphia after Arsinoë's death (she died in 270 or 269, and the papyrus is dated about 250 B.C.), it is not clear whether this interest could have been long sustained. The only *mystai* recorded at Samothrace from an Egyptian city seem to be sailors on a naval campaign under Roman command.[665] Fraser thinks that a Samothracian named Theondas, whose ashes were interred in a vase found in an Alexandrian cemetery, was a *theoros* or *presbeutes* from Samothrace.[666] If so, this could mean a possible religious connection between the Samothracian sanctuary and Alexandria, but the inscription which records the name of Theondas and the date of his death does not actually say that he was a *theoros*.[667] Fraser assumes this only because the person who arranged the burial had also arranged burials of other *theoroi* and *presbeutai*. It is equally as likely that Theondas was a *presbeutes* or political representative from Samothrace and that his trip had nothing to do with the religion of the sanctuary; it would exceed the evidence to say that this inscription indicates official religious ties between Alexandria and the Samothracian sanctuary.

Otto Kern maintains that there was a strong interest in the Samothracian gods in Egypt,[668] but as Hemberg has pointed out, Kern does not distinguish between the Samothracian gods and the Kabeiroi.[669] Kern also makes no distinction between the interest of foreigners and the religious interests of the resident Greek population. If the papyrus document from Philadelphia actually mentioned the word "temple," it would testify to an established cult of the Samothracian gods at Philadelphia, but the evidence of this isolated example is not conclusive. It may only indicate that sacrifices were performed at Philadelphia to the Samothracian gods. Without further evidence, it is impossible to decide just how strong a commitment there was to these gods on the part of the Greek population in Hellenistic Egypt.

Samothrakiastai

There are eleven inscriptions which mention Samothrakiastai, or "worshippers of the Samothracian gods."[670] All of these are found on islands in the southern Aegean, especially Rhodes, or along the coast of Asia Minor, where individuals formed associations or *koina* and worshipped as a group. In all cases these seem to have been private organizations and not connected with the local government. Further, although some of these groups may have sent representatives to Samothrace, in only one of the available inscriptions are the worshippers who belong to such a *koinon* actually called *mystai*. The organizations of Samothrakiastai often seem to be associated with sailing, and in this respect, differ from the organizations of worshippers of the Samothracian gods in cities along the west coast of the Black Sea. *Mystai* are definitely mentioned in the inscriptions from Tomis and Dionysopolis, and the Samothracian gods are afforded official recognition in decrees from Istros, Kallatis, and Odessos, but none of the inscriptions from these sites mention sailors or sailing.

The earliest of the inscriptions to mention Samothrakiastai are of the second century B.C. Two of these come from Methymna on the island of Lesbos and a third from Teos. The inscription from Teos lists seven separate organizations and their leaders.[671] Four of these organizations seem to be religious in nature: the *thiasos* of Simalion, the Orgeones, the Samothrakiastai, and the Mystai. The remainder seem to be political organizations. Because the same person is the leader of the Orgeones, the Samothrakiastai, and Mystai, Hemberg has argued that the three associations all worshipped similar gods. He distinguishes between the Samothrakiastai and the Mystai, claiming that the fact that the Samothrakiastai are named separately indicates that the gods who bring aid at sea were worshipped independently of the mysteries, and that the Mystai worshipped together because they were Samothracian initiates.[672] This is, of course, simply conjecture, and the *mystai* mentioned in this inscription may have nothing to do with the Samothracian gods. The inscription gives no clue as to why these seven groups are named together. They may have joined in making a group dedication, but it is also possible that the inscription is a list of small local groups who share the same building for their meetings.

The inscriptions from Methymna give some information about the functions of a private religious association. Both inscriptions describe honors conferred upon people who have done a service to the same association. The first inscription[673] states that a bronze statue is to be erected in the *temenos* in honor of Iollas son of [ ]polis, for the favor which he has bestowed. The

Samothrakiastai propose to wreathe him and pour libations proclaiming that he is being honored because he has provided sacrifices. Certain honors are to be accorded to Iollas at each of their meetings for so long as he lives, and the *koinon* is to make arrangements for a public announcement to be made concerning the honors conferred. The second inscription,[674] much like the first, describes the honors bestowed on a group of people for their generosity toward the *koinon* and for underwriting a public chorus. The members vote to praise their benefactors for their piety to the gods and for their generosity and further, to wreathe them at each meeting of the organization for as long as they shall live. Just before the inscription breaks off, it mentions a procession of Samothrakiastai sent from the town hall to the temple. Several characteristics of this *koinon* are revealed in these two inscriptions. First of all, the association seems to have held regular meetings, and these meetings may have been held in a special building, perhaps even the *hieron* mentioned in the second inscription. Poland points out that the first inscription indicates that the group had at least a *temenos*,[675] but it is not clear that this is a *temenos* set aside specifically for the Samothracian gods. Apparently this group, like other similar groups in the Black Sea area, held regular processions in honor of the Samothracian gods, and the reference to *choregia* in the second inscription suggests that the group sponsored a ceremony where performances of singing and dancing took place. There is, however, no indication that the members were actually Samothracian initiates.

The other eight inscriptions which mention Samothrakiastai come from an area centering around the island of Rhodes. Six are from the city of Rhodes itself, another from the nearby island of Syme, and the last from the Rhodian *peraia* on the mainland.[676] Six can be dated to about the first century B.C., and another may be from the first century A.D. These are not the earliest inscriptions from this area to mention worshippers of the Samothracian gods. There are also the inscriptions mentioning priests of the Theoi Samothrakes from Lindos from the third century B.C. and priest lists from Karpathos and Rhodes of the second century B.C.[677] The priests mentioned on these inscriptions may well have been associated with the local organizations of Samothrakiastai, but as yet no evidence establishing such a connection has been found.

Poland points out that in the second and first centuries B.C. Rhodes was a center for these small private religious organizations.[678] Hemberg connects the Rhodian interest in the Samothracian gods with the fact that Rhodes was a center of trade and many people living there were involved with the sea.[679] In this he is probably correct, but it should be observed that the interest in the Samothracian gods seems to have persisted long after 166 B.C., the point at which Rhodes began to decline in importance as a commercial center. If the inscription from Aulai in the Rhodian *peraia* has been correctly dated, it appears that there was still a strong local interest in the Samothracian gods as late as the first century A.D.

The first inscription of the Rhodian group, which may have been part of the base of a statue, was erected in honor of a naval commander who served under one of the Antiochids.[680] He is honored by three separate groups: a *koinon* of his comrades, the *koinon* of the Samothrakiastai "Rowers," and the *koinon* of the Samothrakiastai-Lemniastai. Early commentators were confused by the name of the second *koinon*. The term which caused the most trouble was μεσονέων ("rowers") in line 9. Rubensohn thought that the nominative was the proper name Μεσονεῖς (pl.) instead of the noun μεσόνεοι.[681] He thought that the "Mesoneians" were a Rhodian clan or family group and not an association connected with Samothrace. Rubensohn, however, is unable to show that this proper name is otherwise used on Rhodes and this interpretation of the term does not seem appropriate to the rest of the context of the inscription. It is more natural to take the genitive μεσονέων as being from μεσόνεοι, and to understand it as referring to a local organization of Samothracian worshippers who called themselves the "Rowers."[682] The fact that they are paying honor to an individual who has successfully led a naval campaign indicates their nautical interests. The early commentators seemed also to have treated all the *koina* mentioned in this inscription as a single group,[683] but it seems clear that there are three distinct groups, each conferring a separate honor.

The nature of these small, local associations is further illuminated by the other three inscriptions from Rhodes. It seems that individuals who had a special interest in the Samothracian gods, perhaps through initiation at Samothrace, could set up a local group in their honor. Aristoboulos of Rhodes apparently established a group called the "Samothrakiastai-Soteriastai-Aristobouliastai."[684] Another group of Samothrakiastai seems to have worshipped Aphrodite together with the Samothracian gods, for they call themselves the "Samothrakiastai-Aphrodisiastai."[685]

The last inscription from the city of Rhodes is from a tombstone, listing the honors accorded by various religious associations.[686] Moschion is described as having been honored by the Samothrakiastai with a golden wreath and by the Panathenaistai and the Aphrodisiastai with blooming wreaths, indicating not a special connection between these various groups, but only the varied interests of the deceased. He probably had belonged to all three of these associations. The dues which he paid to these organizations may have paid for his tombstone.

The final two inscriptions from the Rhodian group mention organizations which call themselves Samothrakiastai. The earliest is from Syme, first century B.C., set up by the *koinon* of the Samothrakiastai-Aphrodisiastai-Borboritai in honor of a *metoikos* named Euphrosynos, son of Idymeus.[687]

The inscription mentions an earlier honor by the same group plus the honors accorded to Euphrosynos by three other associations. The Samothrakiastai on Syme seem to have worshipped Aphrodite together with the Samothracian gods, but what is meant by the third name in their title—Borboritai—is not known.

The inscription from Aulai on the Rhodian *peraia*, found on the east coast of the bay of Kyr-Vassili, records the honors bestowed by two different organizations.[688] The first organization is the Adoniastai-Aphrodeisiastai-Asklapiastai, honoring a man from Kephallenia. The second organization, the Heroeistai-Samothrakiastai, honors Epaphrodeitos of Kos. The names of the wives of each of these men are included, but because the participles in line 1 and lines 5-6 are in the singular, it seems to be only the men who are honored. There is no reason to include the names of their wives unless this is a tombstone, marking the grave of the two couples. These inscriptions illustrate one of the reasons for joining a private, local religious association. Not only did the *koinon* provide companionship, prestige, and religion for the living, but special recognition for the dead. Moschion and Epaphrodeitos had paid dues to their *koina* of Samothrakiastai in order to guarantee a proper burial. In a period when many people left their ancestral homes to live abroad, the religious association became a substitute for the family. In more stable times, people could count on their families to provide burial rites and an inscription to mark the grave, but Alexandros from Kephallenia and his wife Nysa from Kos together with Epaphrodeitos from Kos and his wife Tryphera from Ephesos, all of whom died in a little town on the Rhodian Peraia, had to rely on their religious associations to provide the services which had been at one time the duty of the family.

CHAPTER SIX

ROMANS AT SAMOTHRACE

The First Romans at Samothrace

The earliest evidence for Roman interest in the Samothracian sanctuary is the account by Plutarch that Marcellus dedicated there statues and paintings, part of his booty from his victory at Syracuse in 212/211 B.C.[689] This dedication has more political meaning than religious significance. Marcellus may have intended, by his dedications, to acknowledge the protection which he had received from the Samothracian gods in his naval victory at Syracuse, but it is more likely that these dedications, taken from the greatest Greek city of the west, were intended as a message to the Greek world of the eastern Mediterranean. It is no accident that Marcellus chose to make his dedications to the Lindian Athena on Rhodes and to the Samothracian gods. Theirs were cults recognized by all Greeks. Athena was goddess of war and protector of cities; the Samothracian gods offered protection at sea and victory in battle. While recognizing the power of these Greek gods, and perhaps even claiming their protection for himself, by choosing these particular sites for his dedications Marcellus also sent a warning to the Greek cities of the east, a warning of the potential power of Rome.

Plutarch does not say that Marcellus himself became an initiate at Samothrace, but it certainly would not have been impossible. The fact that Roman initiates do not appear on Samothracian inscriptions until the second century B.C. is no argument against Marcellus' possible initiation because there are no extant inscriptions, either Greek or Roman, from the third century B.C. Lack of this type of evidence is therefore not conclusive. The First Macedonian War was contemporary with the dedications of Marcellus, and this must have provided an opportunity for Romans to become familiar with the mysteries. Because there seems never to have been any special ethnic qualification for initiation at Samothrace, Romans may have been able to seek initiation as early as their activities extended into the eastern Mediterranean. Although the dedication of Marcellus is not usually considered significant,[690] it may be an example of the growing interest in the island on the part of the Romans. Whether Marcellus himself took a personal interest in the mysteries or not, his choice of Samothrace as a location for his dedications means that the Romans—even at this date—recognized the importance of the Samothracian sanctuary in the Greek world.

The Romans appear next at Samothrace at the time of the Third Macedonian War. In 168 B.C., after his defeat at Pydna, Perseus fled to Samothrace

for asylum in an attempt to escape capture by the Romans. He was accompanied by his family and close supporters. There is no inscriptional evidence
for Perseus' connection with Samothrace, but Livy gives a full account.[691] We
know from Polybios that as king of Macedonia, Perseus had political authority extending to Samothrace.[692] However, it had long been the custom for
Macedonian rulers to support the sanctuary financially, and presumably it
was also customary for them to be initiated there. Perseus would naturally
expect protection from the Samothracian gods if he were initiated, and with
his forces scattered or captured and the Roman fleet in control of the sea, he
had no choice but to seek refuge on the island.

Perseus was forced to seek asylum at Samothrace, but the Romans were
certainly under no obligation to recognize the authority of the sanctuary. It is
significant, however, that they did so. They did not attempt to take Perseus by
force, but appealed to the Samothracian assembly, arguing that Perseus did
not qualify for asylum because of pollution from involvement with the conspiracy to murder Eumenes at Delphi.[693] Perseus had not been the actual
culprit. The crime had been attempted by his friend Evander, who had accompanied Perseus to Samothrace. The threat of pollution to the sanctuary is of
importance. The Romans recognize that at Samothrace there was a special concern for purity. Lucius Atilius, arguing before the Samothracian assembly,
forced them to admit that the whole island was sacred and inviolate.[694]
Atilius then demanded why they permitted a homicide to defile and pollute
their sanctuary. This Roman was aware of the fact that the *praefatio
sacrorum* excluded murderers from participation.[695] The Samothracian
assembly was so impressed by this argument that the *basileus* was sent to
Perseus to insist that Evander be turned over for trial and if proven guilty, be
sent away. Four things are clear from Livy's account of this incident. First,
the Samothracian assembly and magistrates seem to have had jurisdiction
over the sanctuary, an indication of the close relationship between the civil
and religious authorities. Second, it was the *basileus*, the eponymous
magistrate of the Samothracian inscriptions, who had direct control over the
affairs of the sanctuary, acting as intermediary between the assembly and
Perseus.[696] Third, Atilius must have been right when he said that the introductory formula of the rites excluded those who were not clean of hand. Clearly,
when the purity of the sanctuary was threatened, the administration did not
feel bound to protect a Greek who might defile it. Finally, the Romans appear
to have been familiar, at least by reputation, with the requirements for initiation. The dedication by Marcellus in the previous century may not have been
quite so isolated an incident as some believe.

The capture of Perseus at Samothrace in 169 B.C. marked a turning point
in the affairs of the sanctuary. Up to this time, many of the expensive building
projects had been subsidized by Macedonian ruling families, and the

administrators of the sanctuary would have understandably felt close ties with the Macedonian king. The statue of Philip V, found near the stoa, is an indication of the close relationship between the sanctuary and Perseus' father. Because of this relationship and because of Macedonian financial support, it would not have been easy for the Samothracians to hand Perseus over to the Romans. The arbitration about the disposal of Perseus is an example of diplomacy and tact on both sides. It was important for the Romans not to offend a popular Greek sanctuary, but it was equally important that the Samothracian administrators not offend the representatives of a power with which they would have to deal in the future. The Romans did not seize Perseus while he was in the sanctuary, but waited until he panicked, tried to escape, and eventually surrendered.

Macedonia became a Roman province in 148 B.C. After this date Romans appeared regularly at Samothrace.[697] As discussed earlier, many chose to record their initiation by having their names inscribed in Latin in the sanctuary. About one third of the initiate lists record Romans, and of the total number of initiates at Samothrace, more than one fourth are Roman.

The Romans who sought initiation at Samothrace fall into three groups: military personnel, provincial administrators, and private citizens residing or travelling in the east. Of this last group several seem to have been *publicani* or *negotiatores* whose families can be traced to Italian settlements in Greece or Asia Minor.[698] It is important to recognize, however, that in both the Republican and Imperial periods the inscriptions show more official delegations than private citizens, a fact perhaps attributable to the cost of setting up an inscription. After Macedonia became a Roman province, it seems to have become customary for the provincial administrators of Macedonia to be initiated at Samothrace.[699] For this group the setting up of an inscription may well have been a matter of policy, and for them certainly, cost would have been no object.

There apparently was no requirement at Samothrace, as there was at Eleusis, that candidates for initiation speak Greek.[700] The bilingual inscription at the doorway of the northern chamber of the Anaktoron shows that the administrators of the sanctuary recognized that many candidates would not know Greek.[701] That such an inscription was even necessary indicates that by the first century A.D. there were so many Latin speaking candidates that the special proscription had to be recorded in Latin as well as in Greek in order to guarantee that it be understood. Nevertheless although a good proportion of initiates at this period were Roman, few Romans seem to have advanced to *epopteia*. Of the forty-eight known *epoptai*, only seven seem to have been Roman.

Roman Provincial Administrators from Macedonia

The Roman provincial administrators from Macedonia who appear on Samothracian initiate lists may have been following the precedent set by the Macedonian royal families who had earlier patronized and supported the sanctuary. At least eight Samothracian inscriptions explicitly name Macedonian governors or their staff members. On initiate lists the official with the highest rank is named first, followed by his assistants and often a large retinue of slaves. Inscriptions listing titled officials date from 93/92 B.C. through the middle of the second century after Christ. None of the Roman administrators from Macedonia initiated at Samothrace are designated as *epoptes*.

The earliest provincial administrator from Macedonia to be mentioned at Samothrace is L. Julius Caesar, proconsul in Macedonia in 93/92 B.C. He made a dedication at Samothrace during the year of his office,[702] and probably during the same year, perhaps at the time of his visit to the sanctuary, the Samothracian polis honored him with an official inscription which might have been set up in the city itself.[703] There is no record of his initiation, but since he made a dedication addressed to the Samothracian Theoi Megaloi, one can assume that he was an initiate.[704]

The next Roman associated with Macedonia to be mentioned at Samothrace is L. Calpurnius Piso, honored in an official dedication by the assembly and people of Samothrace.[705] This Piso has been identified by Bloch as the same Piso who was consul in 58 B.C., proconsular governor of Macedonia from 57 to 55 B.C., and father-in-law of Julius Caesar.[706] We know from Cicero that Piso did make a trip to Samothrace:

> Quid quod...cum sustentare vix posses maerorem tuum doloremque decessionis, Samothraciam te primum, post inde Thasum cum tuis teneris saltatoribus et cum Autobulo, Athamante, Timocle formosis fratribus contulisti ...?[707]

Bloch, ignoring the obvious sexual innuendo in Cicero's remarks, interprets this passage as evidence that Piso was initiated at Samothrace, suggesting that *Samothraciam te...contulisti* refers to the initiation itself and that *fratribus* refers to Piso's fellow initiates or *symmystae*.[708]

Fraser objects to Bloch's interpretation, arguing that Piso is receiving secular honors from the city of Samothrace rather than initiation at the sanctuary.[709] Further, adducing evidence from Varro which suggests that Piso was active in the suppression of the Egyptian cults at Rome,[710] he thinks it unlikely that Piso would have sought initiation in some other cult from the eastern Mediterranean. Fraser's second objection is not well founded. Cicero may be playing on a Roman prejudice against oriental cults, but he is also exaggerating for rhetorical effect. The Samothracian mysteries had a reputation at Rome very different from that of the rites of Kybele, Isis and Bacchus. Hostility to the Egyptian cults need not imply hostility to the Samothracian mysteries. Because the mysteries of Samothrace appealed on the whole to a class of Romans entirely different from the Roman clientele of the mysteries of Isis and the Magna Mater, they never presented at Rome the same social threat. Samothracian initiation seems to have been sought almost exclusively by members of the upper and middle classes. If Roman slaves or freedmen were initiated, it was only because they were in the retinue of a public official or wealthy citizen.[711] In addition, Italian initiates never imported to Rome any activities relating directly to the Samothracian mysteries.[712] Unlike the Greek initiates who made dedications to the Samothracian gods and joined with fellow initiates in celebrating sacrifices and processions in honor of the Samothracian gods in their own cities, the Italians who were initiated at Samothrace seem not to have carried back to Rome any activities relating directly to their initiation. Samothracian initiation, unlike initiation into the mysteries of Isis and the Magna Mater, was available in only one place. The only Romans who could participate in the mysteries were those who could afford to go to the island or those whose political or commercial interests took them to the eastern Aegean. Piso as a public official serving in Macedonia would certainly have had the opportunity of seeking initiation at Samothrace. As a member of the old nobility he is likely to have shared the sentimental belief of many that the Samothracian gods were in some way connected with the Roman Penates and Rome's legendary Trojan past.[713] In addition, as a man of known philhellenic tastes,[714] Piso would certainly have been interested in a famous cult so important to the Greeks whom he was administering. His initiation, then, is not an impossibility, although this particular inscription provides no conclusive proof.

Of the other Roman officials from Macedonia who appear on Samothracian inscriptions, four are definitely initiates. The earliest of these, P. Sextius Lippinus Tarquitianus, a quaestor, was initiated at Samothrace in A.D. 14, on the fifteenth of September.[715] The inscription, dated by the Samothracian *basileus* and Roman consuls of that year, is known only from a copy made by Cyriacus in the fifteenth century; the stone itself has never reappeared in modern excavations. Cyriacus' transcription may be incomplete, or, more likely, he saw only the top half of the stone, because the names of the people in the quaestor's retinue do not survive. Their presence is indicated, however, by the terms *et symmys*[*t*]*ae pii* below the quaestor's name. Of Sextius Lippinus Tarquitianus himself, we know only that his father's name was Publius and that he himself was a *decemvir stlitibus iudicandis* and probably a *legatus* of Augustus.[716] On this inscription he is called *mystes pius* and presumably did not achieve *epopteia*.[717]

The next inscription to list Roman officials at Samothrace presents several problems.[718] The heading of the inscription is missing with the result that the date, the usual designation *mystae pii*, the name of the administrator, and even that of his province, are gone. The only certain point is the official's title, that of quaestor. Only a trace of the first letter of the name of his province remains, and as it could be either M or A, the province could be either Macedonia (abbreviated *Mac.*) or Asia; there is no room for Achaea. Fraser prefers the first reading,[719] but since there is little chance of certainty, there is no reason for further comment.

Chronologically, the next Roman official to be recorded as a Samothracian initiate is a *quaestor pro praetore* by the name of L. Pomponius Maximus Flavinus Silvanus.[720] Fraser suggests that Pomponius is the son of L. Pomponius, known to have been *consul suffectus* in A.D. 121.[721] That Pomponius was accompanied by a group of fellow initiates is implied by the heading *mystae pii* at the top of the stone, but the names of his companions have been broken away.

Three years later there appeared at Samothrace a proconsular governor of Macedonia, the sixth in this series of Roman visitors. His title and province are clearly indicated on the inscription.[722] His name is given as Q. Planius Sardus Varius Ambibulus. He seems to have been the same man who was *consul suffectus* in 132 or 133, the person whose career is chronicled on another inscription.[723]

The seventh and last provincial governor of Macedonia known to have visited Samothrace came on the first day of May in perhaps either A.D. 165 or 166.[724] His name is not complete on the inscription, but he was accompanied by at least four staff members and about twenty-eight slaves. This inscription, although in places difficult and almost impossible to read, gives a more complete list of the provincial governor and his staff than other similar inscriptions. Clearly most of these officials travelled as members of a large group. The size of the retinue of such an official is suggested by this particular inscription and by another, which, since the top of the stone is broken away, lists only the retinue and not the name of the official.[725] This second inscription lists two *lictores* and approximately twenty slaves. It is likely that the groups which accompanied administrators such as P. Sextius Lippinus Tarquitianus or Q. Planius Sardus Varius Ambibulus were of similar size, although in each case the names of the slaves and companions have been lost.

Roman Initiates of the Republican Period

Many Romans visited Samothrace during the Republican period. Several are known from literary sources. We hear from Appian that Sulla was staying at Samothrace at the time of a pirate raid in 84 B.C.[726] Later in the same year Sulla was initiated into the Eleusinian mysteries before returning to Rome, and it would be of interest to know whether he had sought initiation at Samothrace as well.[727] A few years later, in 73 B.C., Voconius, a lieutenant of

Lucullus during the Third Mithridatic War, chose to stop at Samothrace to seek initiation rather than to intercept the retreating Mithridates.[728] In 67 B.C. Varro was in the area of Samothrace while a legate of Pompey in the campaign against piracy. Varro's familiarity with the statues in the Anaktoron shows that he may have had direct acquaintance with the sanctuary, and, indeed, may even have been an initiate.[729] In 44 B.C., T. Pomponius Atticus, Cicero's correspondent, had supplies brought from Epiros to Samothrace for refugees from the battle of Philippi, but there is no indication that he himself actually visited the sanctuary at that time.[730]

In addition to the public officials who left their names inscribed at Samothrace, there are many private citizens, freedmen, and slaves whose names are found on Samothracian initiate lists. Not all are from Rome itself, but many come from towns throughout Italy and Italian settlements in the east, particularly Delos[731] and Asia Minor. In addition to the titled Roman officials already mentioned, one finds groups of soldiers,[732] sailors,[733] family groups,[734] and freedmen.[735] Women and slaves are never listed alone, but are always part of a larger group. Roman women appear with their husbands; female slaves with their owners.[736]

The earliest dated Latin inscription from the sanctuary carries the consular date for 113 B.C., but the names of the initiates do not survive. There are no other dated inscriptions from the second century B.C. although one stone, whose date is broken off, may be as early as that period.[737] This inscription records the *epopteia* of Cornelius Lentulus, a *legatus pro praetore*, and the *myesis* of at least ten of his companions. Although the date of this inscription is vague (either late second or first century B.C.), it is of interest to note that at this early period a Roman would have sought *epopteia*. Lentulus is unfortunately almost impossible to identify,[738] but he is the only titled Roman known from the inscriptions to have achieved *epopteia*.

Most of the dated inscriptions of the Republican period are from the first century B.C. There are eight of these.[739] On seven the names of initiates survive; three seem to list members of a family or household and four list groups of unrelated men. This distribution differs from that of the evidence for the Imperial period where among eighteen inscriptions, ten of them dated, only one lists a family group.

The earliest of these dated inscriptions to list a family group gives an *epoptes* named Q. Luccius accompanied by a group of *mystai*.[740] Two of the *mystai* are of citizen class, apparently brothers, and the third is a freedwoman. This inscription, although in form similar to the one mentioning Cornelius Lentulus, records a different type of group. The presence of the two brothers and the woman indicates a single family or household travelling with a friend rather than a group of officials. In both groups only one member appears to have gone on to the stage of *epopteia* while the others in each group became only *mystai*.

Another similar group is the household of M. Paccius P. f., Fal. Rufus, initiated on October 18, 46 B.C.[741] Included is a second man named C. Paccius, presumably the brother or son of Marcus. One freedman and at least two slaves accompany the two men. If Fraser is right about the identification of this family, they were residents of Formiae in Italy, where one of the slaves, Philodamus, was later liberated.[742] M. Paccius seems to have made more than one trip to Greece at about this time. Cicero, in a letter to Atticus, mentions a M. Paccius who had carried a letter from Atticus in Epiros to himself in Rome.[743] Cicero's letter is dated in the summer of 54 B.C., a few years too early to coincide with Paccius' appearance at Samothrace, but if the inscription and Cicero refer to the same man, he may have had business which took him to Greece more than once. There is one peculiarity about this inscription: the title *musta pius* is given in the singular. Fraser assumes that only M. Paccius is included by this designation and prefers to leave in doubt the status of his companions. If the other members of the groups were not initiated, it seems strange that their names would have been recorded. The inscription is in all other respects similar in form to other inscriptions recording the initiation of a family group where all the individuals named are initiates. The use of the singular for the plural occurs on at least two other Samothracian inscriptions and seems more the consequence of error rather than an indication that the other members of the group were not initiates.[744]

The third dated inscription of the first century B.C. to record a family group is dated to one of the consulships of Julius Caesar, but because the name of the second consul is missing, there is no way of knowing to which of his five consulships between 59 and 44 B.C. it should be assigned.[745] The inscription lists a large group of initiates headed by T. Ofatulenus Sabinus,[746] and its most interesting feature is the inclusion of the wife of Ofatulenus as one of the initiates. Her name is Tertia, and she is called *domina*. This is the only Roman inscription of the Republican period where the wife of a Roman citizen is listed as a Samothracian initiate.[747] Besides Ofatulenus and his wife, the inscription includes six freedmen, at least four of whom had once been slaves of Ofatulenus, perhaps two Greeks (their names are written in Greek),[748] and at least two slaves. This inscription gives a clear picture of a wealthy Roman family, travelling in the Aegean accompanied by a full retinue of supporters and servants. As such it presents a Republican parallel to another inscription of the early Imperial period which records the initiation of a similar group.[749] The only difference is that none of the people on the Republican inscription advanced to *epopteia*, while three of those on the later inscription did.

There are four other dated inscriptions from the first century B.C. All of these list only male initiates. The earliest, dated July 92 B.C., lists as *mystai* one *legatus*, L. Luuceius (*sic*) M. f., and three freedmen.[750] It is possible, as Degrassi suggests, that this group was connected with a Roman campaign against Thrace in that year,[751] but the presence of a person called *legatus* need not imply connection with a military event. Hatzfeld's conjecture that the *legatus* mentioned in this inscription was on the staff of the praetor of Macedonia, while tempting, is impossible to prove.[752]

The other three groups of men whose initiation is recorded in the first century B.C. are not so easily connected with a specific event. The earliest group, initiated in 76 B.C., although suggested by Fraser to be a group of government officials from Macedonia,[753] cannot be accurately identified. The leading member of this group, Q. Minucius Thermus, could be one of three different people. There is one Q. Minucius Thermus mentioned by Cicero in 65 B.C.,[754] who, however, has no known connection with the east. A second member of this family, also named Q. Minucius Thermus, as legate of the consul L. Valerius Flaccus went to the area of the Bosporus in pursuit of Mithridates in 86 B.C., too early for this particular inscription.[755] The third person with this name was born in 100 B.C., became senator by 73 B.C., and was governor of the province of Asia in 51/50 B.C. While in Asia he corresponded with Cicero who was at the time in Cilicia.[756] He may be the same person whose grave is known from Rome.[757] The evidence suggests that the third Minucius is the most likely choice of the three. Although still a young man in 76 B.C., the date of the Samothracian inscription, he was not too young for an official appointment in some eastern area. He was already senator by the age of twenty-seven, only three years later, and presumably his selection for public office depended on some earlier political or diplomatic success.

The second person listed on the stone, P. Magulnius, may have been a relative of M. Magulnius M. f., a resident of Delos, known from a dedication there in the Italian agora.[758] After the mid-second century B.C. there was a large Italian community resident on Delos and it seems more likely that the initiates on this inscription were connected with that community than with the Roman administration of Macedonia, as Fraser suggests.

The last dated inscription from the Republican period records the initiation of two freedmen, M. Servilius M. l. Philo and [M. S]e[rvilius?] M. l. Pamp[hilus].[759] They were initiated together on June 20, 35 B.C. Because the bottom of the inscription is broken away, it is impossible to tell how many people were initiated together with these two and what their status was. This is the only initiate list from Samothrace which begins with two freedmen, and since the lists usually begin with the most prominent member of the group listed first, it seems likely that if there were originally other initiates, they were

either freedmen or slaves. There is a probable parallel situation in an inscription which records the dedication (but not the initiation) of another freedmen
earlier in the Republican period.[760] Although the top of the stone recording
the dedication of M. Aufidius M. l. is broken away, it is possible that this is a
case of a freedman making a dedication in his own right and not in conjunction with a former master. The formula *de suo* seems to indicate this. If so,
these three freedmen may be examples of wealthy and independent freedmen
who had travelled to Samothrace on their own.

One of the undated initiate inscriptions of the Republican period records
the initiation of four men who seem to have travelled to the island on the same
boat.[761] This may be a group of officials (the captain is called *archon* and the
boat is called *hyperetikon ploion* or "public dispatch boat"), but none of the
initiates has a political title. Although the initiates are Roman (three of the
names include the ethnic *Romaios*),[762] the inscription is inscribed in Greek.
The significance of this list lies in the fact that it records the *epopteia* of the
first two men, one of whom is a slave. The first person is a Roman citizen, L.
Sicinius M. f., and the second is his slave, Seleukos. This is the only example
on the extant inscriptions of a slave proceeding to the stage of *epopteia*. The
other two initiates on the list, both freedmen, are called *mystai*. Karl
Lehmann maintains that the first of these freedmen, Aulos Sikinios Leukiou
Romaios Athenion, was not a freedman, but the son of Sicinius, and finds it
remarkable that the slave of Sicinius would proceed to *epopteia* while his son
would not.[763] However, Lehmann has certainly misinterpreted the name of
this man. His cognomen is a Greek name, unusual for the son of a free Roman
citizen. Dittenberger says that without a doubt this man is the freedman of L.
Sicinius.[764] Lehmann's basic point is well taken however, because even if
Aulos Sikinius is not the son of L. Sicinius, it is still surprising that a slave of
Sikinius should become an *epoptes* while a freedman apparently in his employ
is only a *mystes*. Either there is some special requirement for *epopteia*, as
Lehmann supposes, or perhaps the slave is subsidized by his master for the
second stage, but the freedman must pay his own initiation fee.[765]

Some Roman names of Samothracian initiates of the Republican period are
known from inscriptions at other sites. The family of M. Oppius Nepos,[766] for
instance, appear at Delos in the late second or early first century B.C. where
they seem to have been merchants.[767] Another Roman from Delos, possibly a
contemporary of Oppius, is the freedman Babullius Pamphilus M. l.
Astymenos.[768] He is probably to be associated with the family of Alexandros
Babullius L. f. who appears on a Delian inscription dated 99/98 B.C.[769]
Another Roman initiate who is known elsewhere in Greece is the *epoptes* L.
Furius L. f. Crassupes.[770] He must be the Roman ambassador honored by the
Athenian council in an inscription from the Peiraieus.[771]

Another initiate can be identified because he appears in a letter and in a speech of Cicero. The name of C. Cestius is inscribed along the narrow edge of a Samothracian stele, with no indication of the date[772] or title. The usual designation, *mystes pius*, is even absent, but the fact that Cestius is a later addition to a stone which was already used twice to record initiates implies that he was also an initiate. Cestius, whom Cicero calls an *eques*,[773] and whose freedman is known from an inscription at Priene,[774] seems to have been with Cicero in Ephesos on July 26, 51 B.C.[775]

Another Samothracian initiate, like Paccius and Ofatulenus who were discussed above, has been located in Italy. The name Q. Visellius L. f. is inserted into a space on an earlier Greek *mystai* list which recorded a delegation from Kyzikos.[776] Hatzfeld thought that Visellius belonged to a family associated with Delos, but Fraser has located the name in Brundisium where an L. Visellius appears as a merchant and vintner.[777]

The Romans who travelled to Samothrace during the Republican period are part of an eastward push which developed after the wars with Carthage and Macedonia created a place for Roman economic activity and political interference in the east. Samothrace is not the only place where Romans show an interest in Greek cult,[778] but Romans do seem to have been an important part of the Samothracian clientele. Initiates like Magulnius, Babullius, Oppius, and Cestius are typical of the middle class *publicani* and *negotiatores* who made permanent homes in the east. The larger class of Roman initiates, however, seems to come from military contingents, diplomatic delegations, and provincial administrators. This is not to minimize the significance of Romans among Samothracian initiates, but only to point out that the island was conveniently located for travellers on their way to Macedonia or the Hellespont. For many of the Romans who participated in the Samothracian mysteries, initiation was probably included in a trip whose ultimate goal was not religious.

Roman Initiates of the Imperial Period

Roman interest in Samothrace continues into the early years of the Empire. Ovid stopped at Samothrace to change ships on the way to his exile in Tomis in A.D. 8.[779] Germanicus Caesar, on a trip to Asia Minor, the Bosporus, and Thrace, made an attempt to visit Samothrace ten years later, but was driven off by adverse winds.[780] Tacitus mentions the mysteries as Germanicus' specific object (*sacra Samothracum visere nitentem*), and although Germanicus never actually achieved his goal, we perhaps get a glimpse of the typical Roman traveller who tried to include in his itinerary a stop at Samothrace. Ovid does not tell us whether his visit to Samothrace left him an opportunity for initiation, but we know that another Roman exile was initiated at Samothrace because the literary account of his exile coincides, by

some good fortune, with the epigraphical evidence for his initiation. C. Julius
Augurinus was apparently exiled in A.D. 65 for involvement in an assassina-
tion plot against Nero and sent together with other conspirators to islands of
the Aegean.[781] An inscription from the Samothracian sanctuary, dated May
12, A.D. 65, has been shown to list Augurinus as an initiate.[782] The plot
against Nero, scheduled for April 19, had been discovered on April 18. If
Augurinus was exiled immediately, he would have had time to arrive at
Samothrace by May 12 to be initiated there before taking up residence in exile
presumably on some island nearby. It is therefore possible that Ovid, too, was
a Samothracian initiate.

There have been found at Samothrace at least nineteen Latin initiate lists
from the first and second centuries. Of these, eleven carry dates, six in the first
century and five in the second.[783] Two other inscriptions are thought to date
early in the Imperial period,[784] and of the undated inscriptions, three are
thought to belong to the first century and three to the second century.[785] It is
hazardous to generalize from what must be only a fraction of the original
initiate lists, but when compared to the inscriptions of the Republican period,
it does seem that there is no great increase in the number of Roman initiates at
Samothrace during a period of increased Roman activity in the area. Further,
although the sanctuary continued to be used until the fourth century, Romans
do not appear on the few initiate lists from after the second century.

The later initiate inscriptions which list Roman initiates show the same
variety as the earlier inscriptions, but government officials seem more heavily
represented among the initiates of the Imperial period than among the
initiates of the Republican period. Three of the dated Imperial inscriptions do
not preserve the names of the initiates, but among those that do, only one lists
members of a family group, while the other six list political figures and
provincial officials. In addition, two of the undated inscriptions list titled
Roman officials.

The most complete of the dated Imperial inscriptions is one which lists as
initiates C. Marius L. f. Ste. Schinas, his wife Rupilia Q. f. Quinta, their companions, and their slaves.[786] Not only is this inscription dated exactly to the
day, but it is unusual in that it records the *epopteia* of three members of the
group in addition to recording their *myesis*, and the single date implies that
both ceremonies happened on the same day.

The inscription is important because it gives some idea of the initiation of a
wealthy Roman family of the Imperial period. In this respect, it is similar to
the inscription which records the initiation of the household of Ofatulenus in
the Republican period.[787] Because the group also seems to include friends or
associates of the family, it is similar to the group of Athenians resident on
Imbros who were initiated together in the second century A.D.[788] Schinas
himself is obviously the most important member of the group, for he is listed

first, followed immediately by his wife, Rupilia. Six other men, initiated at the same time, are called *symmystae pii*, a phrase used on other initiate inscriptions. Three of these men are Roman, one of whom also advances to *epopteia* with the *paterfamilias* and his wife, and three appear to be Greek, although their names are written in Latin letters. Karl Lehmann thought that these Greek initiates were the officers on the boat on which the group had travelled to the island, suggesting that the slaves mentioned below were the crew.[789] Fraser hesitates to accept this view because he does not see why the names of the Greek initiates were inscribed in Latin or why free Greeks would be included in a group apparently consisting of members of a single family and their friends.[790] In reply to his first point, the practice of inscribing Greek names in Latin letters is paralleled in another Samothracian inscription;[791] it may have been due to a desire to keep the lettering uniform for a single group. Fraser is right, however, to question Lehmann's claim that Schinas paid for the initiation of slaves who were crew members of a ship on which he travelled. It seems unlikely that Schinas would have subsidized the initiation of so large a group of slaves unless they were members of his own household staff. It therefore seems safe to assume that these slaves (there are at least twenty listed) belonged to Schinas himself.

Another inscription from approximately the same period seems to record the initiation of a group of Roman and Greek soldiers or sailors.[792] Although the inscription was found at Samothrace, the heading is gone and it is not entirely clear that the people listed on the stone are actually initiates. The form of the inscription is somewhat unusual in that the names are not cut on separate lines, one name to a line as on other initiate inscriptions, but inscribed one after the other, running on from one line to the next. Five Romans, perhaps not originally the first names on the stone, are listed first, followed by sixteen Greeks from various Aegean and Mediterranean locations, ending with at least four freedmen who are called "freedmen of King Rhoimetalkes." Fredrich is not sure whether this is a list of crew members of a ship, attendants of King Rhoimetalkes, or a list of *mystai*. It may have been all three. One of the individuals is called *kybernetes*, indicating that he at least belonged to a ship's crew.[793] The freedmen listed after the *kybernetes* are called *apeleutheroi* of King Rhoimetalkes, and they at least seem to have been associated with one of the Thracian kings of that name.[794] There were three of these kings dating between 11 B.C and A.D. 46, giving the approximate date for this inscription.

The Greeks mentioned in this group come from a variety of cities (Ilion, Thasos, Byzantion, Alexandria, and the Macedonian towns of Serrhai and Styberra), but there is no indication of the geographic origin of the Romans mentioned with them. One of these Romans, C. Octavius Bassus, is probably the same person who erected a statue in the Agora of the Italians at Delos.[795]

If so, then he may have been part of the Italian community resident on that island and not from Italy itself.

Until recently it was usually believed that the emperor Hadrian visited Samothrace and became an initiate.[796] Hadrian made a trip to the east in A.D. 123-125,[797] and the Samothracian people honored him with a statue eight years later.[798] However, because the dedication of a statue in honor of an emperor need not imply personal contact, there may be no connection between these two events. Although Hadrian is known to have been an initiate of the Eleusinian mysteries,[799] the evidence for his participation at Samothrace is slim. The issue is somewhat confused by a longstanding misinterpretation of an important Samothracian inscription which happens to be from the year A.D. 124, the time of Hadrian's eastern journey. This inscription is dated according to the kingship of Jupiter and Minerva instead of the usual Samothracian *basileus*.[800] The fragment recording the name of Minerva was not known when the inscription was published, and because of the coincidence of the consular date with the well known date of Hadrian's trip to Greece, it was commonly assumed that the emperor himself had visited Samothrace and that it was his name which had appeared on the stone with that of Jupiter.[801] The discovery of the new fragment, recording Minerv(a) instead of Aug(usto), renders this interpretation impossible. Whether or not Hadrian himself actually visited Samothrace is uncertain.

Samothrace and the Origin of the Roman Penates

Romans had always taken an interest in Greek religion and had made dedications at Greek sanctuaries even before they became politically active in the east.[802] During the second century B.C., with increased Roman activity in Greece, Romans began to appear at Greek sanctuaries in increasing numbers.[803] As an object of Roman attention, Samothrace was no exception, but Samothrace seems to have exercised a special attraction to Roman worshippers.

One of the initial reasons for Roman interest in Samothrace seems to have been the Roman belief that the island was the original home of the Roman Penates.[804] When Perseus was captured at Samothrace, the significance of the island in the legends about Rome's origin was already well established. Hellanikos is the earliest source for the story that Dardanos, legendary founder of Dardania in the Troad and ancestor of Priam and Hektor, came originally from Samothrace.[805] Because Dardanos figures in the foundation myth of Troy, Samothrace would have been considered by the Romans to have been one of their ancestral homes.

Laters writers say that Dardanos took with him from Samothrace certain statues or objects associated by some with the Roman Penates. Dionysios of

Halikarnassos says that the sacred objects brought from Troy by Aeneas were the same as images or statues of the Theoi Megaloi previously taken from Samothrace to the Troad by Dardanos.[806] Dionysios gives as his source Kallistratos, Satyros, and Arktinos. Kallistratos wrote a history of Samothrace in the first century B.C., Satyros is otherwise unknown, and Arktinos is the epic poet of the seventh or sixth century B.C. Dionysios does not specify which of the three originally attributed to Dardanos the transportation of sacred objects from Samothrace to the Troad, but at the least the first century Kallistratos must have included this event in his account.[807] Just as there was a Greek tradition that certain sacred objects had been taken from Samothrace to the Troad, there was also an established Greek tradition that Aeneas had carried to Italy certain *hiera* which he had rescued from Troy.[808] Varro follows the established Greek tradition that it was Dardanos who took these objects from Samothrace to Troy and that is was Aeneas who took them from Troy to Rome.[809] As to what the sacred objects actually were, opinion varies. Some say they were the Penates,[810] Plutarch says it was the Palladium,[811] and Dionysios says that they were the Palladium and images of the Great Gods worshipped at Samothrace.[812] Any Roman who followed either the first or third of these traditions would have regarded Samothrace not only as the home of the Trojan ancestor Dardanos, but also as the original home of the Roman Penates, and some may even have identified their own Penates with the Samothracian gods.

There is an alternate account of the origin of the Roman Penates which appeared at Rome at least a generation before Varro.[813] Cassius Hemina, in the second century B.C., said that the Penates came to Rome directly from Samothrace.[814] Atticus in the first century followed Hemina's account, saying that Aeneas brought his father from Troy, but the Penates from Samothrace.[815] The means by which this last deed was accomplished is supplied by Servius who says that Aeneas dedicated a shield at Samothrace, implying that Samothrace was one of the places where Aeneas stopped between Troy and Italy.[816] Who actually invented this version of the myth cannot be determined, but its appearance for the first time in the middle of the second century B.C. must be the result of Roman interest in Samothrace at this time. Hemina's variation of the traditional account shows that Romans were anxious to demonstrate that their claim to Samothrace was as sanctified by tradition as the claim of the Macedonians who had for so long been associated with the site.

The identification of the Roman Penates with the Samothracian gods is characteristic of both versions of the myth, but this identification seems to be the result of external similarities rather than the result of any inherent identity between the two groups. The main reason for the identification of the Samothracian gods with the Penates is to be found in the similarity of name and title. At Samothrace the local gods were called Theoi Megaloi. At Rome the Penates were called *dei magni*.[817] As Kleywegt points out, the adjective *magni* in the second case is only an epithet and not part of the name of the Roman gods.[818] However, in the case of the Samothracian gods, the adjective is part of the name and not simply an epithet.

Another reason for confusion between the Samothracian gods and the Roman Penates is that both were at times identified with the Dioskouroi. Statues of the Dioskouroi on the Velia at Rome were inscribed *Magnis Dis*, and were believed to represent the Penates.[819] It was commonly, though mistakenly, believed that the Samothracian gods were the same as the Dioskouroi. From representations like those on the Velia came the popular Roman misconception that the Samothracian gods were equivalent to the Roman Penates. This idea is exactly the belief which Varro was criticizing when he said that the *dei magni* were not the Great Gods of whom the Samothracians had erected two bronze statues in male form, and they were not, as commonly thought to be, Castor and Pollux, but that they were Sky and Earth, gods which the Samothracians call great.[820]

Varro is the source for the tradition that the Penates were three in number.[821] According to later sources, Varro was the first to identify the gods of Roman state cult, Jupiter, Juno, and Minerva, with the Penates.[822] Later tradition, however, identifies the Penates as Jupiter, Minerva, and Mercury,[823] and some connect this group with Samothrace.[824]

This last identification, tenuous at best, has been used to interpret a Samothracian inscription, the same one which was once used to show that Hadrian had been initiated at Samothrace.[825] The new fragment, which mentions Minerva, gives the eponymous date as *Regibus Iove et Minerv(a)*. Oliver suggests that the names of the gods were substituted for the name of the customary eponymous basileus in a year when there was no individual willing or able to assume the public office.[826] Basing his interpretation on the passage from Servius which associates the Penates as Jupiter, Minerva, and Mercury with Samothrace, and Varro's statement that the gods the Samothracians call great were two, a male and a female, Oliver argues that the names on the stone are the Latin translations of the names of the Samothracian Theoi Megaloi. The Servian tradition, however, is the result of a later distortion of Varro's idiosyncratic interpretation of the Samothracian Theoi Megaloi. The gods named on the inscription are not the gods of the sanctuary, but the gods of the Samothracian polis. Athena was the principal goddess of the city, as extant decrees testify.[827] Because the ancient city has never been excavated, it is impossible to determine whether Zeus had a temple there as well as Athena, but he may nevertheless have been an important divinity in the city. It is clear from Livy's account of the capture of Perseus that the office of the Samothracian basileus was primarily civil and not religious.[828] It therefore seems likely that if the name of a god were to be used in the traditional eponymous date, it would be the name of a god from the city and not the name of a god from the sanctuary, which stood outside the city walls. Further, there are no extant inscriptions which refer to the Samothraçian gods by their Greek names, presumably because these names were part of the secret of the mysteries. If the Greek names for the Theoi Megaloi could not appear in public, it would be strange to find that their Latin names did.

As Fraser says, it is no accident that Hemina's account of the Samothracian origin of the Roman Penates appears during the initial period of active Roman involvement at Samothrace.[829] However although Roman interest in Samothrace persists throughout the Republican period, it does not increase in the Imperial period, a time of increased Roman activity in the east. Moreover in both periods official Roman delegations outnumber private Roman citizens on the inscriptions. In spite of the continuing Roman presence at Samothrace, Roman initiates never come close to outnumbering their Greek counterparts. There is no Roman equivalent to the Greek *theoroi* sent to Samothrace from Greek cities, and Romans do not appear to have remembered the Samothracian gods with dedications in Rome and Italy.[830]

Of the Romans who seek initiation at Samothrace, most belong to official delegations whose numbers are inflated by the large groups of slaves and retainers who accompany civil and military officials. As opposed to the Greek lists where slaves usually appear singly, the Latin lists can include as many as twenty slaves on a single list.[831] Some Roman slaves were certainly wealthy enough to pay for their own initiation, but there may have been reasons for owners to subsidize the initiation of a slave.[832] An indication of the relative lack of commitment on the part of Roman initiates may be seen in the fact that few Romans appear to have gone on to seek *epopteia*. Of all the dignitaries and officials mentioned on the Samothracian initiate lists, only one titled Roman is listed as an *epoptes*,[833] and none of the provincial administrators of Macedonia achieved the second stage of initiation. While Samothrace itself may have continued to provide a strong attraction for its many Roman visitors, continuing Roman interest in the mysteries may well have been the result of political necessity on the part of the provincial administrators and sentimental beliefs on the part of Romans travelling in the east rather than the result of a strong and abiding religious devotion of either group.

NOTES

CHAPTER ONE

[1] Nikostratos, who lived sometime between the sixth and twelfth centuries, either visited the island himself or had access to eyewitness accounts. See O. Rubensohn, *AA* 11 (1896) 35-36 and N. Lewis, *Samothrace* 1, 115-17.

[2] Cyriacus' own notes have been published by E. W. Bodnar and C. Mitchell, *Cyriacus of Ancona's Journeys in the Propontis and the Northern Aegean, 1444-1445* (Philadelphia 1976). See also, P. Lehmann, "Cyriacus of Ancona's Visit to Samothrace," *Samothracian Reflections* (Princeton 1973) 3-56.

[3] Scaliger sought to establish a Phoenician origin by tracing Kabeiroi to a semitic root meaning "great." Others pointed out that there were mountains in Asia Minor called Kabeiria (*schol. Lib. Or.* 16.64) and argued consequently for a Phrygian origin. For a discussion of these arguments, see Hemberg, 11-12, 27-28, 135, 259, 318-25. For other early scholarship, see Chapouthier, 5-18.

[4] F. Creuzer, *Symbolik und Mythologie der alten Völker* (Leipzig and Darmstadt 1810-1812) especially II, 296, 309.

[5] F. W. J. von Schelling, *Ueber die Gottheiten von Samothrace* (Stuttgart 1815, reprinted: Editions Rodopi, Philosophical Facsimiles, no. 2, 1968); English trans. R. F. Brown, *Schelling's Treatise on "The Deities of Samothrace"* (Missoula Montana 1977).

[6] K. Barth, *Die Kabiren in Deutschland* (Erlangen 1832).

[7] G. S. Faber, *A Dissertation on the Mysteries of the Cabiri* (Oxford 1803).

[8] C. A. Lobeck, *Aglaophamus* (Königsberg 1829).

[9] L. Preller and C. Robert, *Griechische Mythologie* (Berlin 1887-1926, reprint 1964) I.II, 848-50, 858-59, 861; L. Bloch, "Megaloi Theoi," in *Ausführliches Lexikon der griechischen und römischen Mythologie*, ed. W. H. Roscher, (Leipzig 1884-1937, reprint Hildesheim 1965) II, 2523-28, 2536-40; O, Kern, *RE* X, s.v. "Kabeiros und Kabeiroi," cols. 1399-1426; C. Edson, "The cults of Thessalonica," *HThR* 41 (1948) 188; R. E. Witt, "The Kabeiroi in Ancient Macedonia," *Ancient Macedonia* II (Thessalonike 1977) 67-70.

[10] On inscribed ceramics from the Samothracian sanctuary the gods are called Theoi from the fourth century B.C. on. K. Lehmann believes that this word translated the enigmatic ΔIN found on earlier vessels which date from the sixth and fifth centuries B.C., arguing that ΔIN means "of the gods" and is from a pre-Greek Thracian language originally spoken on Samothrace and preserved in the language of the cult. In spite of D.S. 5.47.3, where it is said that the Samothracian rites preserved many words of an ancient Samothracian language, this interpretation must remain only conjecture. For Lehmann's views, see "Documents of the Samothracian Language," *Hesperia* 24 (1955) 93-100, and *Samothrace* 2.2, 8-19, 26-36. See also G. Bonfante, "A Note on the Samothracian Language," *Hesperia* 24 (1955) 101-09. There is always the possibility that the term ΔIN is simply a secret expression from the mysteries and is from no known language. Cf. the term *Nama* from the mysteries of Mithra, *TMMM* I, 314; II, nos. 62, 63, 44, and *CIMRM* 1, nos. 54-63. See, however, A. N. Oikonomides, "Misread Greek Inscriptions," *The Ancient World* 1 (1978) 160. K. Lehmann's restoration of the Samothracian graffito -ΣKA- as [Θεοῖ]ς Κα[βείροις], *Samothrace* 2.2, 17, and no. 222, should be treated with the scepticism it deserves.

[11] The conjunction of the terms Kabeiroi and Theoi Megaloi Samothrakes on Delian inscriptions results from syncretism, for which see *infra*, note 637.

[12] 2.51.

[13] *FGrHist* 107 F 20.

[14] Mnaseas in *schol.* A.R. 1.917.

[15] Hemberg, 74-76, 78, with reference to I. M. Linforth, "Greek Gods and Foreign Gods in Herodotus," *Univ. of Calif. Publ. in Class. Phil.* 9 (1926) 1-25. Akousilaos, *FGrHist* 2 F 20 mentions Kabeiroi, but not Samothrace; Pherekydes, *FGrHist* 3 F 48, mentions Samothrace, but not in connection with Kabeiroi.

[16] 10.472. W. Burkert, *Griechische Religion der archaischen und klassischen Epoche* (Stuttgart 1977) 423 joins Hemberg in following Demetrios of Skepsis.

[17] The belief that initiation into the Samothracian mysteries preserved the initiate from storms at sea is mentioned often in the literary sources and is clearly stated by scholiasts commenting on A.R. 1.918.

[18] Hemberg, 160-70; S. Accame, "Iscrizioni del Cabirio di Lemno," *ASAA* 19-21 (1941-43) 75-105; D. Levi, "Il Cabirio di Lemno," Χαριστήριον εἰς 'Αναστάσιον Κ. 'Ορλάνδον III (Athens 1966) 110-32; W. Burkert (*supra*, note 16) 420-21 and "Jason, Hypsipyle, and New Fire at Lemnos," *CQ* 20 (1970) 9-10.

[19] P. Wolters and G. Bruns, *Das Kabirenheiligtum bei Theben* I (Berlin 1940) pls. 5 (= *GGR* I, Pl. 48.1) and 8; Hemberg, 193-95. For the suggestion that the male pair at Samothrace included a younger and an older god, see K. Kerenyi, "Das Θ von Samothrake," *Geist und Werk* (Zurich 1958) 125-37.

[20] Paus. 9.25.5.

[21] Cf. *GGR* I, pl. 48.1 with inscription: Πρατολαός (Thebes), *PMG* 985 (Lemnos), and Hippol., *Haer.* 5.8.9-10 (Samothrace).

[22] For Thebes, see G. Bruns, "Kabirenheiligtum bei Theben," *AA* (1964) 231-65 and (1967) 228-73. For alleged similarities, see F. Chapouthier, "Kabire béotien et Kabires de Samothrace," *REA* 44 (1942) 329-30.

[23] *Schol.* A.R. 1.917. Burkert (*supra*, note 16) 423 n. 40 compares Hsch., s.v. χέρσης:γάμος and χέρσαι:γαμεῖν; E. Schwyzer, *Griechische Grammatik* (Munich 1953²) I, 62, suggests that Axieros is cognate with Etruscan divine names Axuvizr, Acaviser, etc.

[24] *Samothrace* 2.2, 27-28; *Guide*⁴, 25-26.

[25] *supra*, note 16, 423-24 and n. 40.

[26] *De Civ. Dei.* 7.28.

[27] A. J. Kleywegt, *Varro über die Penaten und die "Grossen Götter"* (Mededelingen der Koninklijke Nederlandse Akademie van Wetenschappen. Afd. Letterkunde N.R. 35, no. 7, Amsterdam 1972).

[28] *De Ling. Lat.* 5.1.57-58.

[29] Hdt. 2.51; *FGrHist* 68 F 1 (Dionysodoros); see also H. S. Versnel, "Mercurius amongst the *magni dei,*" *Mnemosyne* 27 (1974) 144-51.

[30] Chapouthier, 153-84.

[31] Hemberg, 73-103.

[32] Strab. 10.466. For Kybele with two male figures, see H. Graillot, *Le culte de Cybèle* (Paris 1912) 346-411, esp. pl. IX, and 397-98. For a female figure with two male companions, see M. J. Vermaseren, *Cybele and Attis. The Myth and Cult* (London 1977) pl. 10 and *Corpus Cultus Cybelae* (Leiden 1977) III, no. 304.

[33] *Guide*⁴, 27, fig. 9.

[34] *FGrHist* 4 F 23 (Hellanikos).

[35] D.H. 1.61.2-4, 68.2-4.

[36] *Fragmenta Hesiodea*, ed. R. Merkelbach and M. L. West (Oxford 1967) 85, no. 177 (= *POxy* 1359, fr. 2). Hemberg, 64, argues that because Dionysios of Halicarnassos says that Arktinos mentioned the legends of Samothrace (1.68.2), the Samothracian myth and cult were already established in the seventh century. Dionysios, however, does not tell us what Arktinos actually said and because he mentions him together with several other writers who discussed the myth of Dardanos, it is impossible to determine which elements to attribute to Arktinos.

[37] For a discussion of the original Greek settlement of Samothrace, see *infra*, 10-13.

[38] F. Prinz, *Gründungsmythen und Sagenchronologie* (Zetemata 72, Munich 1979) 189-93. For the Theban origin of Kadmos, see A. Burton, *Diodorus Siculus Book I, A Commentary* (Leiden 1972) 101.

[39] *Schol.* Eur. *Ph.* 7.

[40] *IPrien*, nos. 68-70; L. Robert, "Décrets de Samothrace," *RA* 24 (1926) II.174-77 (= *Opera Minora Selecta* 232-35). For P. Lehmann's argument that the theme of the sculpture of the northern pediment of the Hieron was the birth of Aetion, see *Samothrace* 3.1, 288-301.

[41] O. Blau and K. Schlottmann, "Mittheilung über die Altertümer der von ihnen im Sommer 1854 besuchten Inseln Samothrake und Imbros," *BerlBer* (1855) 601-36.

[42] *Reise auf den Inseln des thrakischen Meeres* (Hanover 1860). For a brief summary of early visitors to Samothrace, see Karl Kerényi, "Nach einem Besuch auf Samothrake," *Auf Spuren des Mythos* (Munich 1967) 201-202.

[43] Champoiseau's unpublished report is in Paris in the archives of the Quai d'Orsay, according to Karl Lehmann, "The Ship-Fountain," *Samothracian Reflections* (*supra,* note 2) 183 n. 4.

[44] G. Deville and E. Coquart, "Rapport sur une mission dans l'île de Samothrace," *Archives des missions scientifiques et littéraires 2nd ser., 4 (1867)* 253-78.

[45] *Samothrake* I and *Samothrake* II. Finds from these excavations now exhibited in Vienna are described by W. Oberleitner, *Funde aus Ephesos und Samothrake* (Vienna 1978).

[46] The results of these excavations were not reported fully at the time, but have since been published by F. Salviat in "Le théâtre de Samothrace," *BCH* 80 (1956) 118-46 and "Addenda samothraciens," *BCH* 86 (1962) 268-304.

[47] For preliminary reports, see bibliography: Karl Lehmann, Phyllis Lehmann, and James R. McCredie. Final publication is still in progress, formerly under the editorship of Karl Lehmann and now under the editorship of Phyllis Lehmann. Volumes published thus far are *Samothrace* I, 2.1-2, 3.1-2, 4.1-2, 5. Volume 5 was not available when this book went to press.

[48] The only attempt to establish a complete corpus of Samothracian inscriptions was made by C. Fredrich in *IG* XII (8), nos. 150-260 (1909). Fredrich collected all the Greek inscriptions known up to that time and included the Latin inscriptions in his notes. New discoveries since the first World War have easily doubled the number of Samothracian inscriptions. P. M. Fraser brought together most of the new inscriptions in *Samothrace* 2.1, but he failed to include reference to F. Hiller von Gaertringen's supplement to Fredrich's corpus, published in *IG* XII Suppl., 148-49 (1935). Fraser also did not have full access to all of the inscriptions discovered by Salač and Chapouthier. The following list, with some unavoidable duplication, includes the most recent editions of all of the known Samothracian inscriptions: *CIL* III, nos. 713-23, 12318-23, and III Suppl., nos. 7367-77 (Mommsen); *CIL* I² (3), nos. 662-71 (Lommatzsch); *IG* XII (8), nos. 150-260 (Fredrich); *IG* XII Suppl., no. 344 (Hiller von Gaertringen); *Samothrace* 2.1, nos. 1-91 (Fraser); *BCH* 86 (1962), 270-81, nos. 1-7 (Salviat). To these may be added recent announcements of new inscriptions: P. M. Fraser, *AR* (1969) 30, with photo; James R. McCredie, *AD* 24 (1969) no. 365 and pl. 372; *Hesperia* 34 (1965) 114-15 and pl. 34; *Hesperia* 37 (1968) 220, 222, and pl. 66; *Hesperia* 48 (1979) 16, 17, 26 and pls. 8a, 8b, 12d, and 12e. A Samothracian decree found in 1935 is not included in Fraser's collection because of damage to the stone since its original publication. It was published when found by A. Bakalakis and R. L. Scranton, *AJP* 60 (1939) 452-58, and with corrections and commentary by P. Roussel, *BCH* 63 (1939) 133-41; see also L. Robert, *StudClas* 16 (1974) 85-88. For Samothracian decrees displayed and found elsewhere, see *IPrien*, nos. 68-70; *BMI*, no. 444; *Études thasiennes* V, 18-20, no. 169.

[49] One version of the story is told of Myrina and the Amazons, D.S. 3.55.8-9 (following Dionysios Skytobrachion = *FGrHist* 32 F 37), the other of the supposedly autochthonous inhabitants of Samothrace, D.S. 5.47.1-48.3.

[50] Ar. *Pax* 276-86, with scholia.

[51] A. D. Nock, "Cremation and Burial in the Roman Empire," *HThR* 25 (1932) 347 (= Nock, *Essays* I, 287).

[52] *Guide*⁴, 82-85.

[53] See pl. I(a). The numbers in the text correspond to the buildings numbered on the plan, p. 7.

[54] See pl. II(b).

[55] See pl. II(a).

[56] For the variety of uses to which Greek temples could be put, see P. E. Corbett, "Greek Temples and Greek Worshippers," *BICS* 17 (1970) 149-58; at Samothrace there was an unusual combination of cult buildings whose various designs and uses are not exactly paralleled elsewhere.

[57] See *Guide*⁴, figs. 23-25. K. Lehmann calls this building the Anaktoron after Hippol. *Haer.* 5.8.9-10, where it is said that two bronze statues stood in the Anaktoron of the Samothracians. Hippolytos, however, may have been applying to Samothrace a term from Eleusis where it is used not for an entire building, but for a small enclosed chamber inside the Telesterion. For Eleusinian use of the term on inscriptions, see K. Kourouniotes, "Εἰς τὸ 'Ανάκτορον τῆς 'Ελευσῖνος," *AD* 10 (1926) 145-49 and G. Mylonas, *Eleusis and the Eleusinian Mysteries* (Princeton 1961) 83-85. Nevertheless, to avoid confusion with the recent publications on Samothrace, I will use the term Anaktoron for the whole building.

[58] *Guide*⁴, 56; see pl. II(a).

[59] *Hesperia* 48 (1979) 35-40 and figs. 9-15.

[60] K. Lehmann, *Hesperia* 20 (1951) 12-13; 21 (1952) 30-34; *Guide*⁴, 61-66; P. Lehmann, *Skopas in Samothrace* (Northampton 1973) 2-8 and pls. 4-5.

[61] References to dancing and music at Samothrace are many, among them Stat. *Achil.* 1.830-32; Str. 10.466c; Nonn. *D.* 3.61-76, 234-42. The suggestion that a ritual drama commemorating the wedding of Kadmos and Harmonia was staged in the area of the Temenos, discussed by O. Kern, *RE* X s.v. "Kabeiros, Kabeiroi," col. 1428, K. Lehmann, *Guide*⁴, 63-64, and P. Lehmann, (*supra*, note 60) 31-32 and n. 75, remains only conjectural.

[62] *Samothrace* 3.1-2. See pl. II(b). The Hieron was called the "New Temple" by its Austrian excavators, but because the term *hieron* occurs as a substantive in an inscription found at the door (*Samothrace* 2.1, no. 62), P. Lehmann calls it simply the "Hieron." J. M. Cook, *CR* 21 (1971) 273-74, doubts that the term was meant to refer exclusively to a specific building. For the term *hieron* referring to the entire Samothracian sanctuary as used on inscriptions outside Samothrace, see *infra*, Ch. II, notes 196 and 202. Again, however, to maintain consistency with the Samothracian publications, I will use the term Hieron to refer to the building.

[63] *Samothrace* 4.2, 61; *Guide*⁴, 75-77.

[64] O. Broneer, Review of *Samothrace 4.2*, *AJA* 71 (1967) 96-98.

[65] H. Seyrig, "Un édifice et un rite de Samothrace," *CRAI* (1965) 105-10, suggests that the building was used for Theoxenia.

[66] *Samothrace* 4.1, 93-95; *Guide*⁴, 73-75.

[67] J. R. McCredie, *AJA* 77 (1973) 221; *Hesperia* 48 (1979) 12-23.

[68] J. R. McCredie, "A Samothracian Enigma," *Hesperia* 43 (1974) 454-59.

[69] *Hesperia* 48 (1979) 24-26. Cf. *Guide*⁴, 81, where the three buildings are compared to *thesauroi* of similar design at Delphi and Olympia.

[70] Part of the dedicatory inscription survives, *IG* XII (8) 229; cf. *Samothrace* 2.1, no. 72.

[71] J. R. McCredie, *AJA* 67 (1963) 214, 69 (1965) 171; *Hesperia* 34 (1965) 100-12, 37 (1968) 201-204; *Guide*⁴, 82-85. See pl. III(a).

[72] The Nike fountain is discussed by K. Lehmann (*supra*, note 43) 181-90; *Guide*⁴, 85-86.

CHAPTER TWO

[73] *Guide*⁴, 14.

[74] D.S. 5.47.2. For a discussion of pre-Greek Samothrace see Chapouthier, 160-62 and Hemberg, 120-26.

[75] 2.51.

[76] Diodoros mentions settlement from Samos and Thrace (5.47.3) Strabo alternates between settlement from Thrace and Ionia (457c). The Souda, s.v. Σαμοθράκη νῆσος, says that Antiphon claimed a Samian origin; perhaps this was the fifth century tradition. See Prinz (*supra*, note 38), 193-205 and D. Lazarides, Σαμοθράκη καὶ ἡ Περαία τῆς (Athens 1971) 32-33. There is an unwalled settlement of the early Bronze Age at Kariotes, east of the later polis, and D. Triantaphyllos, "Chronika," *AD* 27 (1972) 547, now reports a pre-historic settlement at Mikro Vouni on the southwest coast of the island.

[77] Commenting on Nikander's *Theriaka* 1.462, *Samothrace* 1, no. 153, he says: Ζηρύνθιον δὲ ἄν-τρον ἐστὶν ἐν Σαμοθράκῃ. However, a scholion on 1.460 locates the cave on the Thracian mainland.

[78] Samothrace is not included among those places with pre-Greek names as discussed by C. Blegan, "The Coming of the Greeks," *AJA* 32 (1928) 141-54 or by F. Schachermeyer, *RE* XLIV, s.v. "Prähistorische Kulturen Griechenlands," cols. 1498-1548. "Zerinthion" is not included by E. Schwyzer in his discussion of words with the -nth- suffix, *Griechische Grammatik* (Munich 1963²) I, 58.

[79] 5.47.3. The titles of the gods, as preserved by Mnaseas (Axieros, Axiokersa, Axiokersos, schol. A.P. 1.917), do not seem to be Greek. K. Lehmann maintains that they are from the same language as the puzzling inscriptions on Samothracian pottery, *Samothrace* 2.2, 4-35 (*supra*, note 10). Hesychius preserves unusual words from the Samothracian dialect (e.g., Ἄωοι, παυρακίς, Σαωκίς). For speculation about these, see *Samothrace* 4.2, 130 and n. 79. Lehmann and Fraser

believe that a Samothracian inscription, *Samothrace* 2.1, no. 64 (early or mid-fourth century B.C.), is an example of the non-Greek language, but see A. N. Oikonomides, "Misread Greek Inscriptions," *The Ancient World* 1 (1978) 159-66.

⁸⁰ The argument is based entirely on pottery. For a summary, see I. Love, *Samothrace* 4.2, 231-42. The Troad was subject to Aeolic settlement from Lesbos in the eighth and early seventh centuries; see C. Roebuck, *Ionian Trade and Colonization* (New York 1959) 110-13.

⁸¹ The inscription, possibly a decree, dated to the middle of the fourth century B.C., has several Aeolic forms, *Samothrace* 2.1, no. 1. Fraser, however, points out, page 3, that the Ionic month name *Maimakterion*, used on a later Samothracian decree (no. 5, second century B.C.), indicates Ionic influence as well.

⁸² K. Lehmann, *Hesperia* 19 (1950) 11 and 21 (1952) 34-45, pls. 8d, 9e-f, 10a-c; *Guide*⁴, 15, 110, 112-13. There is always the possibility that Greek pottery was imported by native Samothracians.

⁸³ *Hesperia* 19 (1950) 8-11.

⁸⁴ J. R. McCredie, *Hesperia* 48 (1979) 32. There is a terrace wall inside the Orthostate Structure running parallel to its eastern wall. The terrace wall has been called the "Cyclopaean Terrace," but its date is not determined. K. Lehmann dated it to the "Late Bronze Age" or "Early Iron Age" in *AJA* 44 (1940) 350 and *Hesperia* 19 (1950) 8, but in *Guide*⁴, 59, gives the date as "the first centuries of the first millennium B.C." McCredie, *ibid.*, 28-32 n. 85, says only that "it can equally well be contemporary with the Orthostate Structure or earlier."

Another item which has been used in support of building activity at Samothrace before the fifth century is an Archaic relief inscribed with the names Agamemnon, Talthybios, and Epeios (*IG* XII [8] no. 226). See K. Lehmann, *Hesperia* 12 (1943) 130-31 and 20 (1951) 5. The relief, however, may not have come originally from Samothrace. J. Bousquet, "Callimaque, Hérodote, et le thrône de l'Hermès de Samothrace," *RA* 29-30 (1948) 112-13 n. 1, describes its history. It was bought at Tenedos in 1790, and is said to have been seen at Samothrace by Cyriacus in 1444; Cyriacus himself, however, does not mention it. For Cyriacus' text, see Bodnar, *Cyriacus of Ancona's Journeys in the Propontis and the Northern Aegean*, 37-41. E. Ziebarth, "Cyriacus von Ancona im Samothrake," *MDAI (A)* 31 (1906) 405-14, does not mention the relief.

⁸⁵ D.S. 5.48.4.

⁸⁶ 2.51: ὅστις δὲ τὰ Καβείρων ὄργια μεμύηται, τὰ Σαμοθρήικες ἐπιτελέουσι παραλαβόντες παρὰ Πελασγῶν, οὗτος ὡνὴρ οἶδε τὸ λέγω· For the suggestion that Herodotus actually visited Samothrace, see J. L. Myers, *Herodotus, The Father of History* (Oxford 1953) 52. Herodotus could easily have visited Samothrace when he stopped at Thasos (2.44).

⁸⁷ *Pax* 277-78.

⁸⁸ The dating of this pottery is debated. Lehmann dates inscribed pottery from the area southwest of the Arsinoeion to the sixth century B.C., *Samothrace* 2.2, 5, admitting, page 6, that his dates must be taken "for granted for the time being." McCredie, commenting on the pottery from this area, re-examined in 1974 by G. Kopcke, says "The earliest stratum in the area, which rests directly on bedrock, was deposited no earlier than the second half of the fifth century B.C." See "Recent Investigations in Samothrace," *Neue Forschungen in griechischen Heiligtümern*, ed. U. Jantzen (Tübingen 1976) 100; *Hesperia* 48 (1979) 32.

⁸⁹ M. B. Moore, "Attic Black Figure from Samothrace," *Hesperia* 44 (1975) 234-50; E. B. Dusenbery, "Two Attic Red-Figured Kraters in Samothrace," *Hesperia* 47 (1978) 211-43. See also *Guide*⁴, 113, 115-17 and figs. 54-55.

⁹⁰ *infra*, note 122.

⁹¹ Antiphon 15, fr. 50.

⁹² R. Meiggs, *The Athenian Empire* (Oxford 1972) Table III, no. 61.

⁹³ *ibid.*, 327.

⁹⁴ *ibid.*, 532.

⁹⁵ *ibid.*, 241 and *ATL* 1, 544 and A10 *passim*; III, 195. For the separate existance of Zone, see L. Robert, *Hellenica* 1 (1940) 89-90; 2 (1946) 149; 11-12 (1960) 555 n. 3.

⁹⁶ *Hesperia* 19 (1950) 8-12; 20 (1951) 3-4; *Guide*⁴, 58-60.

⁹⁷ *Hesperia* 48 (1979) 27-32.

⁹⁸ *ibid.*, 34.

⁹⁹ For discussion of other earlier structures, see 13-16, *infra*.

¹⁰⁰ *Hesperia* 48 (1979) 32-33.

[101] *ibid.*, 34.

[102] *Samothrace* 3.1, 34-36; 3.2, 51-61.

[103] *Samothrace* 2.1, no. 62.

[104] I. C. Love, *Samothrace* 3.2, 161, no. 36, discussed by P. Lehmann, *ibid.*, 70 and 145-56.

[105] *ibid.*, 74-75.

[106] *ibid.*, 174.

[107] *ibid.*, 216-36, nos. 118-53.

[108] *ibid.*, 52-53, with fig. 364.

[109] There are still unexcavated areas within the sanctuary, and the Samothracian polis itself has never been surveyed. It is possible that the geison block comes from a building in the town and not from the sanctuary. As recently as 1975 a completely unexpected building was found to the east of the Anaktoron (no. 28), for which see McCredie, *Hesperia* 48 (1979) 35-40.

[110] *Samothrace* 3.1, 21, fig. 21 and 35, figs. 33-34.

[111] *Samothrace* 3.1, 36 and 3.2, 52, 54, 61.

Black Tiles: Inv. no. 48.723 = *Samothrace* 3.3, pl. LVIII, no. 3 (found in the fill of the pronaos of the Hieron).

Inv. no. 49.129 = *Samothrace* 2.2, no. 277 (found west of the Arsinoeion).

Inv. no. 39.275 = *Samothrace* 2.2, no. 276; 3.3, pl. LX, no. 4 (found in the river bed).

Red Tiles: Inv. no. 53.162A, B, C = *Samothrace* 3.3, pl. LX, no. 1 (found near terrace wall east of Hieron).

Inv. no. 54.155 = *Samothrace* 2.2, no. 278; 3.3, pl. LX, no. 3 (found west of the Hieron).

Inv. no. 52.599 = *Samothrace* 2.2, no. 279 (found in the area of the Altar Court).

Inv. no. 54.157 = *Samothrace* 3.3, pl. LX, no. 2 (provenance unknown).

Inv. no. 56.26 = *Samothrace* 2.2, no. 281 (provenance unknown).

Tiles whose color is not given:

Inv. no. 55.74 = *Samothrace* 2.2, no. 280 (found east of the Hieron).

Inv. no. 53.102 = *Samothrace* 2.2, no. 282 (found east of the Hieron).

For commentary, see P. Lehmann, *Samothrace* 3.1, 36-37 n. 4 and n. 5.

[112] *Samothrace* 3.1, 81.

[113] In his discussion of inscribed and stamped roof tiles, *Samothrace* 2.2, 113-15, nos. 276-82, K. Lehmann describes seven tiles, but only five of these are of the group discussed by P. Lehmann.

[114] *supra*, note 111.

[115] The small round building on the eastern hill is too small for the tiles. For that building, see note 109, *supra*.

[116] For P. Lehmann's claim that the foundations were raised, see *Samothrace* 3.2, 54-56 and figs. 365-68. For the Hellenistic floor, see *Samothrace* 3.1, 122.

[117] For the description of the stepping stones, see *Samothrace* 3.2, 56. For the remodelling of the Hieron, see *Samothrace* 3.2, 124-25.

[118] *Hesperia* 48 (1979) 8-9.

[119] McCredie, "Recent Investigations," (*supra*, note 88) 94; *Hesperia* 37 (1968) 218, 222.

[120] *Guide*⁴, 66.

[121] *Samothrace* 4.1, 96, 110, 117. Clearly the date of this building will have to be reconsidered. Its position along the same axis as the Hieron suggests that the two buildings were either part of the same building program or that the Hall of Votive Gifts was later.

[122] For the original reports of the rock altars, see K. Lehmann, *Hesperia* 19 (1950) 8-10 with pl. 8, nos. 18-19; 20 (1951) 3-4, with pls. 1h, 3b, 4a. The so-called "Altar of Hekate," located between the Temenos and the Arsinoeion, is not an altar, but part of the terrace wall supporting the Temenos, as examination on the site confirms. For K. Lehmann's claims that it is an altar, see *Hesperia* 21 (1952) 33 with pl. 7b; 22 (1953) 22-23 with pl. 8e-f. K. Lehmann claims that there is also an Archaic rock altar and drain beneath the Altar Court, *Samothrace* 4.2, 110-16, but the claim is disputable.

[123] For the shaft near the entrance of the Arsinoeion, see *Guide*⁴, 56.

¹²⁴ P. Lehmann, *Skopas in Samothrace* (Northampton 1974) 8-14; the precinct contained statues by Skopas in the fourth century. A. F. Stewart, *Skopas of Paros* (Park Ridge, New Jersey 1977) 108, suggests a slightly later date, but concedes that the propylon was finished by 330-320 B.C.

¹²⁵ *ibid.*, 36 n. 93. For a summary of Macedonian involvement at Samothrace, see A. K. Babritsas, "Σχέσεις τῆς Μακεδονίας μὲ τὴν Θράκην καὶ ἰδιῶς τὴν Σαμοθράκην κατὰ τὴν Ἑλληνιστικὴν Ἐποχήν," *Ancient Macedonia* (Thessalonike 1970) 109-14.

¹²⁶ Altar Court: K. Lehmann, *Samothrace* 4.2, 117-18. Doric building on the eastern hill: McCredie, *Hesperia* 37 (1968) 220-30. For dedicatory inscription, see pl. I(b).

¹²⁷ *Alex.* 2.2. The Athenian custom that respectable women be secluded from men outside their families made it impossible for young lovers to meet or even become acquainted except at religious festivals or funerals, resulting in a literary cliché which persists at Athens and elsewhere. Cf. Eur. *Hipp.* 24-28; Lys. 1.8; Chariton, *Chaer. et Call.* 1.4-5; Luc. *DMeretr.* 309.

¹²⁸ Curt. Ruf. 8.1.26.

¹²⁹ *Skopas in Samothrace* 36 n. 93. Cf. Paus. 5.20.10; E. N. Gardiner, *Olympia; Its History and Remains* (Oxford 1925) 133-34. A. Momigliano, *Filippo il Macedone* (Florence 1934) 174-75, suggests that the building was originally a treasury. S. G. Miller, "The Philippeion and Macedonian Hellenistic Architecture," *MDAI(A)* 88 (1973) 189-218, shows that the building was designed by a Macedonian architect.

¹³⁰ *Hesperia* 37 (1968) 220, inv. no. 65.843, 323-316 B.C.

⟨⟩ Ἔδοξ]ε [τῆι β]ουλῆι· ἐπειδὴ Βασιλεὺς Λυσίμαχος φίλος ὢν καὶ εὔ-
νους διατελεῖ τῆι πόλει καὶ πρ[ό]-
τερόν [τ]ε εὐεργέτηκεν ἡμᾶς καὶ
5 νῦν κ[εχομί]σμεθα τὴν ἱερὰν χώρα-
[ν τῆς ἠπε]ί[ρο]υ ἣν οἱ βασιλεῖς Φί-
[λιππ]ος καὶ Ἀλέξανδρος ἐτεμένι-
[σαν το]ῖς Θεοῖς καὶ ἀνέθεσαν χαὶ
[.......]ια τοῦ τεμένους κατέχρ-
10 [ινεω τῶν .]ιονος παίδων ἀποδοῦ[ν]-
[αι........]ισα πάντα ἀφ' οὗ χρόν-
[ου........]σαι ἐγβαλόντες ἡμ-
[ᾶς..........]ι τὸ ἱερὸν ος[...]
[................]αι διατελ[..]
15 [....................]Τ Ο Ν[....]

For suggested supplements to the text, see T. Hadzisteliou Price, "An Enigma in Pella: the Tholos and Herakles Phylakos," *AJA* 77 (1973) 66-71; L. Robert, *REG* 86 (1973) 115, no. 275, does not accept them.

¹³¹ See Appendix I, no. 15 and pl. V(a).

¹³² Herodotus mentions Samothracian fortresses on the mainland of which he names Sale (7.59) and Mesambria (7.108). Until at least the 420's, the tribute assessment for Samothrace included some of these towns. For an account of the Samothracian *peraia* under the Delian League, see *ATL* I, 517, 544; III, 195. The Samothracian *peraia* continued to be a concern of Samothrace into the third century. See the decree in honor of Epinikos, published originally by A. Bakalakis and R. L. Scranton, "An Inscription from Samothrace," *AJPh* 60 (1939) 452-58; comments by P. Roussel, "La pérée samothracienne au IIIᵉ siècle avant J.-C.," *BCH* 63 (1939) 133-41.

¹³³ Philostr. *VA* 2.43.

¹³⁴ *SIG³* 251H, col. II 9.

¹³⁵ The problem of Alexander's finances has been much discussed. The literary accounts give the impression that at the beginning of his eastern campaign, military expenses outstripped resources: Plu. *Alex.* 15.1; *Mor.* 327d; Curt. Ruf. 10.2.24; Arr. *An.* 7.9.6. These are generally accepted by A. Andreades, "Les finances de guerre d'Alexandre le Grand," *Annales d'Histoire Économique et Sociale* 1.3 (1929) 321; W. W. Tarn, *Alexander the Great* (Cambridge 1948) I, 14; J. R. Hamilton, *Plutarch, Alexander* (Oxford 1969) 37, and rejected by A. R. Bellinger, *Essays on the Coinage of Alexander the Great* (New York 1963) 37 n. 15. J. R. Ellis, *Philip II and*

Macedonian Imperialism (London 1976) 305 n. 45, disagrees with Bellinger. G. T. Griffith, "The Macedonian Background," *G&R* 12 (1965) 127, says that Alexander's lack of cash meant only that his income had not kept up with his expenses. Clearly his military commitments would have left little surplus for extensive temple donations before his eastern conquests.

¹³⁶ Plb. 5.10.6-8.

¹³⁷ A. Piganiol, "Les Dionysies d'Alexandre," *REA* 42 (1940) 285-92.

¹³⁸ A. R. Bosworth, "Alexander and Ammon," *Greece and the Ancient Mediterranean in Ancient History and Prehistory*, ed. K. Kinzel (Berlin 1977) 51-75.

¹³⁹ Curt. Ruf. 3.12.27; 4.2.2, 17.

¹⁴⁰ Jos. *AJ* 11.313-24.

¹⁴¹ A. S. Shofman, "The Religious Policy of Alexander the Great," *VDI* 140 (1970) 111-20, with Eng. summary, argues that this met with Macedonian resistance. See also E. A. Fredricksmeyer, *The Religion of Alexander the Great* (Diss: University of Wisconsin 1958).

¹⁴² Str. 641c; cf. Arr. *An.* 1.17.7, where Alexander ordered a temple of Zeus built at Sardis.

¹⁴³ M. N. Tod, *Greek Historical Inscriptions* (Oxford 1947) II, 241-42, no. 184; A. J. Heisserer, *Alexander the Great and the Greeks, The Epigraphic Evidence* (Norman, Oklahoma 1980) 142-44.

¹⁴⁴ Arr. *An.* 3.16.4.

¹⁴⁵ D. S. 18.4.4.; cf. Plut. *Mor.* 343d.

¹⁴⁶ Str. 13.593c.

¹⁴⁷ W. W. Tarn, "Alexander's ὑπομνήματα and the World-Kingdom," *JHS* 21 (1921) 1-17; *Alexander the Great* (*supra*, note 135) II, 378-98, App. 24, argues that the plan was a Hellenistic forgery. His arguments have been criticized by F. Hampl, "Alexanders des Grossen *Hypomnemata* und letzte Pläne," *Studies Presented to D. M. Robinson* (St. Louis 1953) II, 816-29 and by F. Schachermeyer, "Die letzten Pläne Alexanders des Grossen, *JÖAI* 41 (1954) 118-40 (= *Forschungen und Betrachtungen zur griechischen und römischen Geschichte* (Vienna 1974) 292-314. Following Schachermeyer, E. Badian, "A King's Notebooks," *HSPh* 72 (1968) 183-204, concludes that while the plans as given by Diodoros may not be a complete account of Alexander's intentions, they were likely to have been a selection made by Perdiccas who selected precisely those issues which he felt the army would be bound to reject.

¹⁴⁸ *Hesperia* 37 (1968) 222; 48 (1979) 8: Βασιλεῖς Φιλιππος Ἀ[λέξανδρ]ο[ς Θεοῖς Μεγ]ά[λοις]. See pl. I(b).

¹⁴⁹ *Hesperia* 22 (1953) 18-20.

¹⁵⁰ *Samothrace* 2.1, no. 9; see L. Robert, *Gnomon* 35 (1963) 60-61.

¹⁵¹ J. and L. Robert, *REG* 67 (1954) 158-59, no. 207, object to the identification of the donor as Arrhidaios because on inscriptions he is called always Basileus Philippos or Philippos, but this dedication could have been made before Alexander's death before Arrhidaios took the name of Philippos.

¹⁵² *Samothrace* 4.2, 125.

¹⁵³ Terms similar to *koies* have appeared on two vases, one from Attica and the other from the Theban Kabeirion, discussed by K. Lehmann, *ibid.*, n. 61.

¹⁵⁴ O. Broneer, *AJA* 71 (1967) 96-98, does not accept Lehmann's attribution to this building of a large marble slab necessary to Lehmann's reconstruction of the altar and fundamental to his claim that the building was an unroofed altar court.

¹⁵⁵ H. Seyrig, "Un édifice et un rite de Samothrace," *CRAI* (1965) 105-10, says that what Lehmann reconstructs as an altar was in fact a *kline* and suggests that the building was used for *theoxenia*.

¹⁵⁶ Broneer (*supra*, note 154) 97. P. Lechmann, *AJA* 71 (1967) 429-32, stresses the violence of the earthquake in an attempt to defend K. Lechmann's association of the marble slab with the building, without apparently realizing the damage of this assumption to K. Lehmann's hypothesis about the order of the architrave blocks.

¹⁵⁷ For this reason, F. Eckstein, in his review of *Samothrace 4.2*, *Gnomon* 38 (1966) 817-23, prefers K. Lehmann's reconstruction. J. and L. Robert, however, still maintain that Fraser's reconstruction is the more correct, pointing out that Lehmann's spelling "Arrhadaios" is a form unknown in Macedonia. J. and L. Robert also object to using terms known only from Hesychius to restore an inscription. See *REG* 78 (1965) 149, no. 315.

[158] For a discussion of this name, see L. Robert, *Gnomon* 35 (1963) 60-61. For K. Lehmann's claim that only a member of the royal family could have his name inscribed on a building dedication, see *Samothrace* 4.1, 118-19.

[159] 10.7.2, discussed by K. Lehmann, *Samothrace* 4.2, 132.

[160] Plu. *Alex.* 2.5-6; A. Henrichs, "Greek Maenadism from Olympias to Messalina," *HSPh* 82 (1978) 143 calls her the earliest historical maenad.

[161] *SIG³*, no. 252.6-8 (331-329 B.C.).

[162] Hyp. *Eux.* 24-25.

[163] *Il.* 16.233-35; *Od.* 14.327-28; 19.296-97.

[164] 2.52.

[165] The archaeological evidence is summarized by H. W. Parke, *The Oracles of Zeus* (Oxford 1967) 96-100, 114-20.

[166] *ibid.*, 118-20.

[167] P. 7, no. 6. The function of this building is not known. See *infra*, 55-56.

[168] Several different dates have been suggested for the stoa. F. Salviat has suggested that it was constructed in the late fourth century B.C., *BCH* 86 (1962) 303-304. In an early paper J. R. McCredie suggested a late Hellenistic date, "The Stoa on Samothrace—Preliminary Report," *AJA* 67 (1963) 214, but in a later publication he says only "Hellenistic," *Hesperia* 37 (1968) 201. In *Guide⁴*, 82, the stoa is dated to the first half of the third century B.C.

[169] For the date of the theater, see F. Salviat, "Le théâtre de Samothrace," *BCH* 80 (1956) 145.

[170] For bibliography on the date of the Nike statue from Samothrace, generally attributed by art historians to Pythokritos of Rhodes, early second century B.C., see M. Bieber, *The Sculpture of the Hellenistic Age* (New York 1961) 125 n. 13. K. Lehmann has excavated the fountain where the statue originally stood on a base shaped like a ship. His date for the construction is late third century or early second century B.C., a date which accords with that established on stylistic grounds. For Lehmann's comments about the date, see "The Ship Fountain," *Samothracian Reflections*, 183.

[171] For the date, see *Samothrace* 3.2, 76-79. For a description of the porch, *Samothrace* 3.1, 212-35; for the pedimental sculpture, 253-328.

[172] Appendix I, no. 14.

[173] *Samothrace* 2.1, no. 22.

[174] *IG* XII (8), no. 150 = *SIG³*, no. 372. Fraser, *Samothrace* 2.1, 13 calls attention to the fact that the kings mentioned in the inscription are Lysimachos' Macedonian predecessors, responsible for many dedications in the sanctuary.

[175] An inscription from Samothrace, *Samothrace* 2.1, no. 12, may be from this altar. For the cult of Lysimachos, see C. Habicht, *Gottmenschentum und griechische Städte* (Munich 1970²) 39-40.

[176] *supra*, note 130.

[177] The dedicatory inscription from the Arsinoeion (*Samothrace* 2.1, no. 10) establishes that Arsinoë was at the time wife of a king, but whether that king was her first husband Lysimachos or her second husband Ptolemy II Philadelphos depends on the interpretation of the status of her father Ptolemy I Soter, also mentioned in the inscription. He is called "Soter," not "Theos Soter." Fraser, *Samothrace* 2.1, 50, takes this as evidence that he was still alive. The inscription could not, then, date from the period of Arsinoë's marriage to Ptolemy II Philadelphos, because by that time Soter was already dead, and Philadelphos was king. The missing name of her husband on this inscription must have been Lysimachos, and if so, the inscription must be dated to his reign. Conze, *Samothrake* I, 17, dated the dedication of the Arsinoeion to the years of Arsinoë's marriage to Ptolemy II (276-247 B.C.), and on the basis of this dating argued for a strong connection between Samothrace and Egypt during this period.

[178] Just. *Epit.* 24.3.9.

[179] The Samothracian sanctuary was a place of asylum and had the advantage of being recognized as an international cult center. Arsinoë sought asylum there in 280 B.C., Ptolemy Philometer in 170 B.C. (Plb. 28.2.1, 5), Perseus in 167 B.C. (Sall. *Hist.* fr. 69.7; Livy 42.50.8, etc.), and Romans after the battle of Philippi in 42 B.C. (Nep. *Att.* 11.2). For the legal status of ἀσυλία in the Hellenistic period, see T. Klauser, *Reallexikon für Antike und Christentum* (Stuttgart 1950) I, 838-40 s.v. "Asylrecht" (Wenger).

¹⁸⁰ *Samothrace* 2.1, no. 11.

¹⁸¹ *ibid.*, 6 n. 19.

¹⁸² K. Beloch, *Griechische Geschichte*² (Berlin and Leipzig 1912-27) IV.2, 347.

¹⁸³ Otto Kern's arguments for the appearance of the Samothracian cult in Egypt "Zu dem neuen Mysterieneide," *APF* 12 (1937) 66-67, inflate the available evidence. Cf. Hemberg, 232.

¹⁸⁴ Ptolemy I died in 283 B.C., Lysimachos in 281.

¹⁸⁵ For the Hippomedon decree, see *Samothrace* 2.1, Appendix I. For bibliography concerning the Epinikos decree, see L. Robert, *Gnomon* 35 (1963) 78 n. 3. Both of these decrees are concerned with the Samothracian *peraia*, which was under Ptolemaic control. Neither decree, as commonly argued (e.g., Fraser, *Samothrace* 2.1, 8-11) implies Ptolemaic control of the island. The Samothracian concern was to insure supplies of grain for the island, grain which was apparently grown on the mainland by Samothracian *clerouchoi* and *georgoi* (Hippomedon decree, B, line 20). The lack of arable land on the island itself apparently necessitated the development of land on the *peraia*.

¹⁸⁶ Plu. *Agis*, 6.3; Plb. 4.35.13; *Samothrace* 2.1, 9 n. 34. See also O. Kern, "Aus Samothrake," *MDAI (A)* 18 (1893) 351.

¹⁸⁷ H. Bengtson, *Die Strategie in der hellenistischen Zeit* (Munich 1937-52) III, 181.

¹⁸⁸ Originally pointed out by P. Roussel, *BCH* 63 (1939) 136, and insisted upon by L. Robert, *Gnomon* 35 (1963) 79.

¹⁸⁹ There are no Samothracian initiate lists surviving from this period, but one of the *theoroi* lists (*Samothrace* 2.1, no. 22) may be this early.

¹⁹⁰ P. M. Fraser, "Archaeology in Greece 1968-69," *AR* (1968-69) 30; J. R. McCredie, "Excavations in Samothrace," *AD* 24 (1969) 365 and pl. 372.

¹⁹¹ Fraser, *Samothrace* 2.1, 10-11.

¹⁹² The inscription on the statue base reads: Βασιλέα Φίλιππον Βασιλέως Δημητρίου/Μακεδόνες Θεοῖς Μεγάλοις.

¹⁹³ It is now clear from an inscription recording a letter of Philip V to the citizens of Lemnos that he had visited the Kabeirion on Lemnos in order to be initiated there. For the text of this inscription see S. Accame, "Una letera di Filippo V," *RFIC* 69 (1941) 179-93; P. M. Fraser and A. H. McDonald, "Philip V and Lemnos," *JRS* 42 (1952) 81-83. Philip was also interested in other sanctuaries, for which see F. W. Walbank, *Philip V of Macedon* (Cambridge 1940, reprinted 1967) 268-70 and W. A. Laidlaw, *A History of Delos* (Oxford 1933) 117-18.

¹⁹⁴ Appendix I, no. 18.

¹⁹⁵ As K. Lehmann points out, *Samothrace* 3.2., 7.

¹⁹⁶ *OGIS*, no. 225 = C. Bradford Welles, *Royal Correspondence in the Hellenistic Period* (New Haven 1934) no. 18.30: ἐν τῶι ἱερῶι τῶι ἐν Σαμοθράικηι.

¹⁹⁷ *ibid.*, 92 and 97.

¹⁹⁸ *IG* XII (8), 38.

¹⁹⁹ P. M. Fraser and G. E. Bean, *The Rhodian Peraea and Islands* (Oxford 1954) 157 n. 1.

²⁰⁰ *Samothrace* 2.1, 7 n. 21.

²⁰¹ *supra*, note 196, 99.

²⁰² A. Brückner in W. Dörpfeld, *Troja und Ilion* (Athens 1902, reprinted 1968) II, 448, no. 3 and Beilage 59: τὴν δὲ ἐν Σαμο-/θράικηι ἐν τῶι ἱερῶι τῶν θεῶν [τῶν] /[μ]εγάλων. For the new fragment, found in 1969, see Z. Taşliklioğlu and P. Frisch, "New Inscriptions from the Troad," *ZPE* 17 (1975) 101-06 and P. Frisch, *Inschriften Griechischer Städte aus Kleinasien III: Die Inschriften von Ilion* (Bonn 1975) 118-23, no. 50.

²⁰³ P. Frisch, *Die Inschriften von Ilion*, 150-54, no. 63.

²⁰⁴ The inscription from Samothrace will be published by David Jordan.

²⁰⁵ The inscription from Philippi has never been published, but is on display in the museum at Philippi, inv. no. Λ.25. I am indebted to Charles Edson for calling this inscription to my attention.

²⁰⁶ The inscription is not published, but is on display in the museum at Kavala. It is recorded on a stele which served as a gravestone of an Athenian, Isodoros Nikostratou, who had been initiated at Eleusis and at Samothrace. For a description, see D. Lazarides, Ὁδηγὸς Μουσείου Καβάλας (Athens 1969) 87-88, Λ70. I am indebted to Helmut Koester for this reference.

[207] The inscription was originally published by Ph. M. Petsas, "A Few Examples of Epigraphy from Pella," *Balkan Studies* 4 (1963) 159-60, no. 3 and pl. VIII.1 (= *SEG* 24 [1969] no. 540), and a second time by D. Papakonstantinou-Dimantourou, *Πέλλα* I (Athens 1971) 145, no. 257 and pl. 10γ, second century B.C. It is inscribed on a statue base on which once stood two figures, perhaps the same male figures portrayed in the Samothracian Anaktoron. The statue was dedicated at Pella by a man from Magnesia on the Maeander. The text reads: Κράτων Κρατέρου Μάγνης ἀπὸ Μαιάνδρου Θεοῖς Μεγάλοις εὐχήν. For a summary of the sources on the Kabeiroi at Pella, see W. Baege, *De Macedonum Sacris* (Dissertationes Philologicae Halenses 22, 1913) 176.

CHAPTER THREE

[208] J. R. McCredie, *Hesperia* 37 (1968) 216-19 and fig. 3. See pl. I(a).

[209] *ibid.*, 219.

[210] Livy 45.5.4.

[211] Isoc. 4.157; Suet. *Nero* 34.8; Lib. 13.19; D. Chr. 17.5; Celsus *ap.* Orig. *Cels.* 3.59.

[212] *Samothrace* 2.1, no. 62: ἀμύητον/μὴ εἰσιέναι/εἰς τὸ ἱερόν.

[213] *Samothrace* 2.1, no. 63: Deorum, sacra/qui non accepe-/runt non intrant./ἀμύητον μὴ εἰ-/σιέναι.

[214] *Samothrace* 3.2, 8-9.

[215] P. Roussel, "L'initiation préalable et le symbole éleusinien," *BCH* 54 (1930) 49-54; G. Mylonas, *Eleusis and the Eleusinian Mysteries* (Princeton 1961) 238-39.

[216] *Samothrace* 2.1, no. 36, with Fraser's comments.

[217] K. Lehmann believes, from Paus. 9.25.5, that an inscription at the door of the Kabeirion at Thebes read ἀτέλεστον μὴ εἰσιέναι, *Samothrace* 3.2, 8 n. 33. As Lehmann points out, initiates on Lemnos were called τετελεσμένοι; see S. Accame, *ASAA* 19-21 (1941-43) 76, no. 2 and 79, no. 3. However the term is never used at Samothrace. The only Samothracian inscriptions to refer to the mysteries except for the initiate lists calls them μυστήρια, not τελεταί, *Samothrace* 2.1, App. I.7: μετασχεῖν τῶν μυστ[ηρίων].

[218] Hdt. 2.51; D.S. 5.48.4, 49.5, 77.3; D.H. 1.68.3; Clem. Al. *Protr.* 2.13.3; Him. *Or.* 9.12. For the possible range of meanings of these terms, see C. Zijderveld, *Τελετή, Bijdrage tot de kennis der religieuze terminologie in het Grieksch* (Purmerend 1934).

[219] K. Lehmann, *AJA* 44 (1940) 334 and *Guide*⁴, 51.

[220] K. Lehmann, *Hesperia* 19 (1950) 11-12, pl. 7, figs. 16. 21, 22; *Guide*⁴, 59. The top of the shaft was level with the floor of the Orthostate Structure.

[221] *De Ling. Lat.* 5.10.58.

[222] *Haer.* 5.8.9-10. For the suggestion that these statues stood before the double doors in the Anaktoron, see K. Lehmann, *AJA* 43 (1939) 139. For the suggestion that special revelations about death and resurrection in places guarded by ithyphallic statues, see C. Picard, "L'entrée de la salle absidale à l'Attideion d'Ostie," *RHR* 135 (1949) 129-42.

[223] Varro could have visited Samothrace when he traveled east with Pompey; see *De Re Rust.* II, praef. 6.

[224] 2.51.

[225] There is no specific evidence for the wearing of special clothing at Samothrace, but the casting off of old clothes and taking on new ones sees to have had a symbolic significance in other mystery celebrations. For robes in the mysteries of Isis, see Apul. *Met.* 11.24; J. Gwyn Griffiths, *The Isis-Book* (Leiden 1975) 308-14.

[226] Lamps were found in this chamber: K. Lehmann, *AJA* 44 (1940) 348. For evidence that the ceremonies took place at night, see Nonn. *D.* 3.171, 4.185, 13.402.

[227] *AJA* 44 (1940) 335, arguing that the new *mystes* was presented to the audience from this platform. Cf. Apul. *Met.* 11.24.

[228] A. D. Nock, "A Cabiric Rite," *AJA* 45 (1941) 577-81. For a relief showing the Korybantes and the *thronosis* of the infant Dionysos, see W. H. Roscher, *Ausführliches Lexikon* II, 1618, fig. 4.

[229] *Euthd.* 277d.

[230] K. Lehmann, *AJA* 43 (1939) 139-40.

[231] K. Lehmann, *AJA* 44 (1940) 353-55. The information about the kiln supports was communicated to me by J. R. McCredie, November 9, 1981.

[232] *Haer.* 5.8.9-10; cf. Eus. *PE* 2.1.39, 2.2.12 and D. M. Cosi, "Adamma: un problema e qualche proposta," *AAPat* n.s. 88 (1975-76) 153-56.

[233] *D.* 3.61-78. Hemberg, 117, suggests that Nonnos may have visited Samothrace, but he lived too late to have been there while the mysteries still flourished. Nevertheless, Nonnos was well-informed about Samothracian myths and the buildings in the sanctuary. He knew, for instance, of a round building and the two streams (*D.* 3.137-42, 164-66). He does, however, refer to the Samothracian divinities as Korybantes. Strabo, 10.466c, comments on the similarities between the Korybantes, Kouretes, Kabeiroi, Idaean Dactyls, and the Telchines and associates their characteristics with the Samothracian gods. See also, H. Jeanmaire, *Couroi et courètes* (Lille 1939) 593-616.

[234] *Schol. Par.* ad A.R. 1.918.

[235] *ibid.*, and *Schol. Laur.* ad A.R. 1.917-18.

[236] *Samothrace* 3.2, 26-27.

[237] *Samothrace* 2.1, no. 29, for which see *infra*, note 278.

[238] *Guide*⁴, 25, 32, 102, 131. J. R. McCredie has informed me by letter, November 9, 1981, that at least six new iron rings were found in the sanctuary in 1980.

[239] *Et. Mag.*, s.v. Μαγνῆτις.

[240] 6.1044-47: Exultare etiam Samothracia ferrea vidi/et ramenta simul ferri furere intus ahenis/in scaphiis, lapis hic magnes cum subditus esset;/usque adeo fugere a saxo gestire videtur.

[241] *NH* 33.1.23: Nec non et servitia iam ferrum auro cingunt, alia per sese mero auro decorant, cuius licentiae origo nomine ipso in Samothrace id institutum declarat.

[242] *Guide*⁴, 25. For bibliography on these rings and their meaning to the mysteries, see Hemberg, 110 n. 2.

[243] According to Aristotle, Thales attributed soul to a stone which had the power to move iron, *De An.* A2, 405a19. The image of the loadstone may have been used by Thales to demonstrate his theory that everything was full of gods, *ibid.*, A5, 411a7.

[244] *Ion* 533d. Socrates, discussing with Ion the rhapsodist's skill, says that it depends on a divine power (θεία δύναμις) which moves the rhapsodist just like the force in the loadstone which can make iron move.

[245] Cf. Hld. *Aeth.* 8.11.8, for a magic ring with power to protect against fire, described as τελετῆς, ὡς ἔοικε, θειοτέρας ἀνάμεστος. For rings as protection, see C. Bonner, *Studies in Magical Amulets* (Ann Arbor 1950) 4-7.

[246] Livy 45. 5.3-4.

[247] Ch. Champoiseau, "Note sur des antiquités trouvées dans l'île de Samothrace," *CRAI* 20 (1892) 22-25, with plate; See *infra*, Appendix I, no. 19 and pl. V(b).

[248] *Hesperia* 22 (1953) 14-15.

[249] *Samothrace* 3.2, 3-50.

[250] *ibid.*, 15, 24; but see A. D. Nock, "Early Gentile Christianity," *Essays* I, 54.

[251] *Samothrace* 3.2, 18-10 and fig. 348.

[252] Plutarch tells the story three times, once of Antalkidas at Samothrace (*Mor.* 217c-d), once of Lysander at Samothrace (*Mor.* 229d), and a third time of a Spartan general, with no mention of Samothrace (*Mor.* 236d). The problems associated with the authenticity of these accounts are summarized by F. Steinleitner, *Die Beicht im Zusammenhange mit der sakralen Rechtspflege in der Antike* (Leipzig 1913) 70-72. Because there is no evidence for an oracle at Samothrace, the second version is probably less accurate than the first, but Lehmann goes beyond the evidence when he emends the passage to refer specifically to the *bathra* outside the Samothracian Hieron. For his emendation, see *Samothrace* 1, no. 240, line 6, where Lewis follows Lehmann's κατάβηθι for the ms. κατάστηθι. For Lehmann's translation, see *Samothrace* 3.2, 20.

[253] 5.49.6, γίνεσθαι δέ φασι καὶ εὐσεβεστέρους καὶ δικαιοτέρους καὶ κατὰ πᾶν βελτίονας ἑαυτῶν τοὺς τῶν μυστηρίων κοινωνήσαντας.

[254] In Livy 45.5.4, Lucius Atilius demands why a possible murderer has been allowed to defile a sanctuary whose rites exclude murderers: "cur igitur...polluit eam (= insulam) homicida, sanguine regis Eumenis violavit, et, cum omnis praefatio sacrorum eos quibus non sint purae manus sacris arceat, vos penetralia vestra contaminari cruento latronis corpore sinetis?"

²⁵⁵ For exclusion of polluted people from sanctuaries, see *LSAM*, nos. 12, 18, 20, 29, 42, 51, 84; *LSCG Suppl.*, nos. 54, 56, 59, 63, 88, 89, 91, 115; *LSCG*, nos. 55, 68, 96, 99, 119, 124, 139, 151. *LSCG*, no. 124 explicitly forbids murderers. For restriction of murderers from the Eleusinian mysteries, see Isoc. 4.157; for the exclusion of the impious and wicked, see Suet. *Nero* 34.8.

²⁵⁶ *Iudicia*: Livy 45.5.7. For a priest of the Kabeiroi who purifies murderers: Hesych. s.v. χοίης. The purification of homicides may have been a rite distinct from initiation, but as with all occurrences of the term Kabeiroi in the literary sources, it is not clear whether the statement applies to Samothrace. Chapouthier, 161, thinks that it does and asserts on the basis of Hesychius that a *koies* was a priest of the Great Gods. Hemberg, 118 n. 4, however, quite rightly says that the connection between this passage and Samothrace is only an assumption. Lehmann believes that the function of the *koies* as a purifier of murderers was part of the Samothracian cult, but he does not think that it has anything to do with the rite which he calls "confession" and associates with the Samothracian *epopteia, Samothrace* 3.2, 19 n. 83. Steinleitner, (*supra*, note 252) 118-19, and Pettazzoni, "Confession of Sins and the Classics," *Essays on the History of Religions*, H. J. Rose, trans. (Leiden 1954) 55-67, both accept the passages from Plutarch as evidence for "confession" at Samothrace and both associate the role of the *koies* with initiation. Steinleitner is more cautious, limiting the purpose of "confession" to determining blood-guilt. Pettazzoni, however, believes that many initiates, especially soldiers, would have needed purification before partaking in the mysteries and claims that confession was originally associated with the purification of homicides.

²⁵⁷ Tert. *Apol.* 7.6, says that it was a matter of form in all the mysteries that the initiate give a promise for silence about the secrets learned. Val. Fl. *Arg.* 2.433, says that in Samothrace there were punishments for incautious tongues. In Livy 39.12-13 Hispala fears the angers of the gods if she divulges the secrets of the mysteries of the Bacchanalia. Cf. R. Reitzenstein, *Die hellenistischen Mysterienreligionen* (Berlin 1927) 194-96 (Eng. trans. by J. E. Steely [Pittsburgh 1978] 240-41).

²⁵⁸ Eur. *IT* 961-63; Arist. *Ath. Pol.* 7.1, 55.5; Paus. 1.28.5; see W. K. Pritchett, *The Greek State at War III. Religion* (Berkeley 1979) 66 n. 83 for oaths on stones.

²⁵⁹ For an oath sworn before entering a temple at Philadelphia, see *LSAM*, no. 20.

²⁶⁰ Pl. *Smp.* 318b. For the Eleusinian inscription, see K. Kourouniotes, *Eleusiniaka* (Athens 1932) I, 177 and 179, lines 16-17; N. J. Richardson, *The Homeric Hymn to Demeter* (Oxford 1974) 249-50.

²⁶¹ *Math.* 7.1.1.

²⁶² K. Lehmann, *Samothrace* 3.2, 20; P. Lehmann, *Samothrace* 3.1, 237-53, for the decoration of the ceiling.

²⁶³ This drain, discovered in the Austrian excavations in 1875, was carved in the euthynteria and stereobate levels, and a block with a channel cut into it must have led from the floor level above, *Samothrace* 3.1, 126-27 and figs. 81-84.

²⁶⁴ *Samothrace* 3.2, 23-25.

²⁶⁵ *supra*, note 255.

²⁶⁶ R. Ginouvès, *Balaneutiké* (Paris 1962) 378, 382, 396, 403. For a *periranterion* at the entrance to a sanctuary at Lindos, see *LSCG Suppl.*, 91.

²⁶⁷ Ginouvès, *ibid.*, 375-80 (Eleusis), 396-404 (oriental cults); Griffiths (*supra*, note 225) 286-87 (mysteries of Isis).

²⁶⁸ *CIMRM, passim* (Mithraea); K. Schefold, *Larisa am Hermos* (Berlin 1940) I, 80; W. M. Ramsay, *ABSA* 18 (1911-1912) 50-51 (Men at Antioch); P. Roussel, *Les cultes égyptiens de Délos* (Paris 1915-1916) 30-31 (Serapieion A), 36-45 (Serapieion B), 186, no. 175 (Serapieion C).

²⁶⁹ *Samothrace* 3.2, 24; cf. A. D. Nock, "Hellenistic Mysteries and Christian Sacraments," *Mnemosyne* Ser. 4, 5 (1952) 201 (= Nock, *Essays* II, 810): "Let me add that in pagan initiatory rites, washing was no more than a preliminary, and meals were meals, with no known special significance."

²⁷⁰ *Nub.* 498.

²⁷¹ *Samothrace* 3.2, 26.

²⁷² *Pax* 277-78. There is no reason to assume that Aristophanes had any special reticence about procedures associated with the Eleusinian mysteries. For the distinction between what was considered secret in the mysteries and what was not, see Richardson (*supra*, note 260) 304-308.

²⁷³ Albrecht Dieterich, "Ueber eine Scene der aristophanischen Wolken," *RhM* 48 (1893) 275-83 = *Kleine Schriften* (Leipzig and Berlin 1911) 117-24.

²⁷⁴ G. Roux, "Salles de banquets à Délos," *BCH* Supplement 1 (1973) 541-42, suggests that although the drain may have been used in ritual, it could easily have served for simply washing the floor.

²⁷⁵ *Samothrace* 3.1, 127, fig. 82. Inscriptions recording requirements for washing before entering temples or sacred precincts rarely demand a complete bath, but for a bath "from head downwards," see *LSCG*, no. 55 (cult of Men in Attica).

²⁷⁶ *supra*, notes 234-35.

²⁷⁷ *Samothrace* 2.1, no. 29.

²⁷⁸ I examined the inscription at Samothrace in 1976. A comparison of the lettering on the two extant fragments (*Samothrace* 2.1, pl. XV, a-b) shows that the name in the left hand wreath was a later addition. The Greek letters of the Kyzikene list below are evenly spaced and uniform in size while the letters in the wreath above are rough, jagged, and uneven in height and width. Further, although both the inscription below and the inscription within the circle have some characteristics in common (the *alpha* with broken cross bar and *sigma* with parallel horizontal bars), there are no traces of apices on the letters of the upper inscription, in contrast with the rather elegant lettering with definite apices of the inscription below. The name in the circle on the left, Andromachos Demetriou, looks as if it had been squeezed in after the circle was carved, by a stone cutter less competent than the person who inscribed the Kyzikene inscription below. The name of the *epoptes* on the right is known only from the manuscripts of Cyriacus, but it is unlikely that it was present on the original version of the stone. If only one of the original wreaths enclosed an inscription, the resulting asymmetry would certainly not be consistent with the careful balance of paired sets of decorative elements on the stone as a whole. There are many examples among Samothracian initiate lists of names added to earlier lists, see Chapter IV, 41-42, *infra*. Both Fraser and Lehmann agree that the Latin name below the wreath on the right is a later addition. See Lehmann, *Hesperia* 12 (1943) 120 and Fraser, *Samothrace* 2.1, 82 and pl. XV. The Latin lettering is larger, more irregular, and cut more deeply into the stone than the Greek letters of the Kyzikene inscription below. Neither Fraser nor Lehmann, however, entertain the possibility that the lettering in the inscription of the wreath on the left is not contemporary with the inscription below.

²⁷⁹ There is no independent evidence to support Lehmann's claim that a figure wearing a belt pictured on a Roman sarcophagus is actually a Samothracian *epoptes* wearing the *porphyris*. See *Samothrace* 3.2, 28, fig. 353. Likewise the inscription from Odessos, mentioned by Lehmann in note 124, although it includes the word *porphyris*, seems to be a document from a Bacchic cult having nothing to do with Samothrace. For this inscription, see now *IGBR* 1, no. 225 and *infra*, Ch. V, note 616. For robes in initiation scenes, see the Lovatelli urn and the Torre Nova sarcophagus, Mylonas (*supra*, note 215) figs. 83-84.

²⁸⁰ The oath is preserved twice: *PSI*, nos. 1162 and 1290.

²⁸¹ The text of no. 1290, lines 1-8, actually reads:

[...]φηχε[
[...] μεγάλη φωγ[ῆ..] .. [.......]
[... τ]ὸν μύστην π[ε]ριαγαγέτω [....]
[...]...ωντα ενφ[.].μω τεσσα[....]
[....]εδαη περὶ τὸν λείποντα [.....]
[....]αυτην, καὶ στησάτω μέσ[ον ...]
[...] διαθέματος καὶ ἐξορκούτω [διὰ]
[τοῦ] κήρυκος α.....[..]ντος.

²⁸² "Ein neuer orphischer Papyrustext," *APF* 13 (1939) 210-12.

²⁸³ The word is cited three times with this meaning: Sext. Emp. *M.* 5.53, Thrasyllos, *Catologus Codicum Astrologorum*, ed. F. Cumont (Brussels 1898) VIII (3) 101, and Vett. Val. (Kroll) 78, line 25. Sextus Empiricus, attacking the astrologer's method of ascertaining the position of the stars at a person's birth, uses the word in a definite astrological context. Thrasyllos makes clear the connection of this word with horoscopes and the zodiac.

[284] "Frammenti di un rituale d'iniziazione ai misteri," *ASNP* ser. 2, 6 (1937) 150.

[285] For a description of this floor and a diagram, see *TMMM* II, 243-45, no. 84 and fig. 77; *CIMRM* I, 120-21, no. 239 and fig. 71.

[286] *supra*, note 284, 150.

[287] *supra*, note 282, 211.

[288] *PSI* 12 (1951) 206: "...una raffigurazione concreta, un *simbolo astrale*, presso cui il μύστης dovesse pronunziare il giuramento."

[289] But see *CIMRM* I, 80-84, nos. 91-105 and G. Grimm, *Die Kunst der Ptolmäer-und Römerzeit im Ägyptischen Museum Kairo* (Mainz 1975) pl. 73, no. 38.

[290] Nilsson, *GRR* II, 695-96, suggests a cult of a "cosmic god." F. Cumont, "Un fragment de rituel d'initiation aux mystères," *HThR* 26 (1933) 157, argues for Mithraic connections.

[291] R. Merkelbach, "Der Eid der Isismysten," *ZPE* 1 (1967) 55-73. For oaths in mysteries of Isis, cf. Apul *Met.* 11, 15.

[292] *Samothrace* 3.1, 128-29 and fig. 85; *Samothrace* 3.2, 31 and fig. 354.

[293] P. Lehmann believes that the sculpture of the northern pediment of the Hieron represented the birth of Aetion. See *Samothrace* 3.1, 253-317. For the sacrifice of birds and chickens in the mysteries of Mithra, see M. Vermaseren, *The Excavations in the Mithraeum of the Church of Santa Prisca in Rome* (Leiden 1965) 127 and *CIMRM* II, nos. 1069, 1080, 1105, 1133, 1899, 1412, and 1679.

[294] *Samothrace* 3.1, 135-38; *Samothrace* 3.2, 34-39, especially 35-38 for K. Lehmann's comparison of the apse to a grotto or cave. There is no evidence from the excavation to suggest that the apse had this association. For his suggestion that the ceremonies performed here included the celebration of a divine child, a suggestion for which there is no literary evidence.

[295] *Samothrace* 3.1, 132, fig. 87.

[296] *ibid.*, 131-32.

[297] *Samothrace* 3.2, 44-49.

[298] *Guide*⁴, 27, fig. 9.

[299] *IPerg*, no. 554.

[300] R. Duthoy, *The Taurobolium* (Leiden 1969) 110, note 1.

[301] *Guide*⁴, 33.

[302] *Samothrace* 2.2, 24-25, 33-36, for inscribed cups and bowls found in the sanctuary; *AJA* 43 (1939) 140, for kantharoi, skyphoi, dishes, and iron knives found in the Anaktoron.

[303] *Hesperia* 48 (1979) 13-22.

[304] *ibid.*, 8, for rubble possibly from a dining chamber of the late sixth century B.C.

[305] *ibid.*, 10, fig. 3: L-M-N.

[306] *ibid.*, 18-19, for a description of these rooms.

[307] For washing, see G. Roux (*supra*, note 274) 551-52.

[308] *D.* 3.169-71.

[309] M. S. Goldstein, *The Setting of the Ritual Meal in Greek Sanctuaries: 600-300 B.C.* (Diss. Univ. of California 1978), for the archaeological evidence.

[310] For the meaning of the ritual meal, see J. P. Kane, "The Mithraic Cult Meal in its Greek and Roman Environment," *Mithraic Studies* ed. J. R. Hinnells (Manchester 1975) 321-29.

[311] P. R. Arbesmann, *Das Fasten bei den Griechen und Römern* (*RGVV* 21, Giessen 1929) 74-89, for fasting in the mysteries. See also N. J. Richardson, *The Homeric Hymn to Demeter*, 165-67.

CHAPTER FOUR

[312] D.S. 5.48.5-49.6. For a scholiast's comment that Agamemnon and Odysseus were Samothracian initiates, see the Laurentian and Parisian scholia to Apollonius of Rhodes, 1.918.

[313] 2.51-52.

[314] *Mor.* 217c-d, 229d, 236d; *supra*, note 252. Pettazzoni, "Confession of Sins and the Classics," 65, doubts the historical veracity of this incident.

³¹⁵ 10.472. From Strabo's remark that Demetrios claimed that no "mystic story of the Cabiri is told at Samothrace," it is clear that Demetrios must have been familiar with the mystic story which *was* told, something possible only through initiation. In addition to this evidence from Strabo, Macrobius, *Sat.* 3.4.7-9 says that a Tarquin, son of Demaratus of Corinth, was a Samothracian initiate.

³¹⁶ *Samothrace* 2.1, App. I; *supra*, note 217.

³¹⁷ *IG* XII (8), nos. 205, 215, 216; *Samothrace* 2.1, nos. 27, 31, 33, 39, 40, 41, 42, 51, 52, 55, 61.

³¹⁸ Several inscriptions are carved on stones with recessed edges. K. Lehmann suggests that these were shaped for insertion into a wall. Examples of these are *Samothrace* 2.1, nos. 47, 49, and 50, described by Lehmann when originally found, *AJA* 44 (1940) 345.

³¹⁹ *Samothrace* 2.1, nos. 53 and 53*bis*, parts of two separate inscriptions, apparently originally part of a larger series displayed on the walls of the Arsinoeion.

³²⁰ Samothracian decrees dated according to the *basileus*: *IG* XII (8), no. 155 and *Samothrace* 2.1, no. 6.

³²¹ 45.5.6.

³²² Lewis, *Samothrace* 1, 104, suggests that A.R. 1.915-21, describing the visit of the Argonauts to Samothrace, is an indication that by Apollonios' day initiation was available on demand. This interpretation of the passage is accepted by K. Lehmann, *Samothrace* 3.2, 11. F. Vian, Apollonius Rhodes, *Argonautiques* (Paris 1974) 19, commenting on the itinerary of the Argonauts, says that although the Argonauts were initiated on the night of their arrival, they may have stayed longer than one night.

³²³ *Samothrace* 2.1, no. 36. Cf. K. Lehmann, *Samothrace* 3.2, 12. Not everyone chose to partake of both rites on the same date. Cf. *Samothrace* 2.1, no. 29 and App. IV, for Asklepiades Attalou.

³²⁴ Hemberg, 108.

³²⁵ *April*: *Samothrace* 2.1, no. 51; *May*: *IG* XII (8), no. 215; Salviat, *BCH* 86 (1962) 279, no. 5; McCredie, *Hesperia* 34 (1965) 115; *June*: *CIL* III Suppl., no. 12321; *IG* XII (8), no. 173; *Samothrace* 2.1, nos. 28a, 34, 36; *July*: *CIL* I², no. 663; *August*: *IG* XII (8), no. 210; *September*: *IG* XII (8), no. 214; *Samothrace* 2.1, no. 40; *October*: *Samothrace* 2.1, no. 33; *November*: *Samothrace* 2.1, no. 53.

³²⁶ *Samothrace* 2.1, nos. 28a and 36.

³²⁷ The third list, *CIL* I², no. 665 (= *CIL* III, no. 12318) is not dated, although K. Lehmann, *Samothrace* 3.2, 10 n. 44, wrongly says that it is dated to June.

³²⁸ *IG* XII (8), no. 186b.

³²⁹ *IG* XII (8), no. 194. *Samothrace* 2.1, App IV, an inscription which discusses envoys from Kyzikos, but which may not be an initiate list, also carries the eponymous date according to the Kyzikene ἱππάρχας.

³³⁰ *Samothrace* 2.1, no. 27. The title is ἱερομνάμων. Fraser has suggested that the city could have been Byzantion, Perinthos, or Kalchedon. All that remains of the ethnic is -]ωνίου. The only surviving name on the list is a patronymic: Βε]νδιδώρο[υ], a name which Fraser points out is common is Macedonia, Thrace, and Thasos. L. Robert, however, maintains that theophoric names compounded from the divine name Bendis are widespread and make the identification of the city less precise. Robert also says that Perinthos is an unlikely choice because the Doric form ἱερομνάμων is an impossible form for that Ionian city. See *Gnomon* 35 (1963) 65-66.

³³¹ *IG* XII (8), no. 195 (= L. Robert, *Collection Froehner* [Paris 1936] no. 44) and *Samothrace* 2.1, no. 47. Initiates from Beroia occur on both lists. For references to discussions of the Macedonian era, see Fraser, *Samothrace* 2.1, 100 n. 1.

³³² For the difficulties in establishing the order of months in the original Macedonian calendar, see A. Samuel, *Greek and Roman Chronology* (Munich 1972) 139 and n. 1.

³³³ The inscription is published by J. R. McCredie, *Hesperia* 34 (1965) 115. Neither this month name, *Mounychion*, nor *Artemisios* is listed by Samuel as a Samothracian month, *ibid.*, 130. In the case of Artemisios, the inscription on which it occurs was not found at Samothrace, but is accepted as a Samothracian list by L. Robert, *Collection Froehner* (*supra*, note 331) 52-53.

³³⁴ Inscriptions with the *agoranomos* at the top of the stone with the *basileus*: *IG* XII (8), nos. 195, 221; *Samothrace* 2.1, nos. 57(?), 61, and App. IV. At the top without *basileus*: *Samothrace*

2.1, no. 34. *Agoranomos* at the end of initiate list: *IG* XII (8), nos. 184, 185, 186b, 199, 207, 224; *Samothrace* 2.1, nos. 36, 41.

[335] Robert lists *agoranomoi* connected with festivals at Ilion, Aktion, Erythrai, and Epidauros, *Gnomon* 35 (1963) 68-69.

[336] The terms εὐσεβής and *pius* also appear on inscriptions recording initiates of Mithra, for which see M. J. Vermaseren, *CIMRM* I, no. 15 (εὐσεβής) and II, nos. 1232 and 1234 (*pius*).

[337] *IG* XII (8), no. 216.

[338] *IG* XII (8), no. 205 and *Samothrace* 2.1, no. 28a.

[339] *Samothrace* 2.1, 75, commenting on no. 25. Fraser records three instances of single initiation records. There are more: *CIL* III Suppl., no. 7372; *IG* XII (8), nos. 193, 197b, 200(?), 202, 210; *Samothrace* 2.1, nos. 25, 56.

[340] McCredie, *Hesperia* 48 (1979) 17.

[341] *Samothrace* 2.1, no. 38.

[342] *IG* XII (8), no. 190.

[343] *Samothrace* 2.1, no. 33aII, 11-19.

[344] *IG* XII (8), nos. 189b and 190b.

[345] *IG* XII (8), no. 220, line 10.

[346] *IG* XII (8), no. 189c, see O. Rubensohn, *Die Mysterienheiligtümer in Eleusis und Samothrake* (Berlin 1892) 228 for an illustration of the layout.

[347] *Samothrace* 2.1, no. 34. Fraser thinks that this might be the eponymous dating, but can't explain why the name of the *basileus* would not be inscribed in Greek in the genitive case if this were so.

[348] *Samothrace* 2.1, no. 29a1; *supra*, note 278.

[349] *IG* XII (8), nos. 178, 5-7, and 220a, 5-7.

[350] *IG* XII (8), nos. 218 and 220a, 1.

[351] *Samothrace* 2.1, no. 33aII, 13-19.

[352] For a similar problem on another inscription where a man from Philippi is listed in a group called "Thasioi," see *Samothrace* 2.1, no. 59 and Fraser's commentary, 60.

[353] For a complete list of Samothracian *mystai* and *epoptai*, see Appendix III.

[354] *IG* XII (8), no. 216; Appendix I, no. 19, pl. V(b).

[355] See maps I-III.

[356] Thasos and Odessos can also be added to the list. Both appear as ethnics (together with Abydos) on an unpublished inscription at Samothrace, inv. no. 71.961. In addition, Hestiaios Pempidou of Thasos, who is praised for his *eusebeia* on a Samothracian proxeny decree found at Thasos, must also be an initiate. See *Études thasiennes* V, 18-20, no. 1169.

[357] Probably Aigai in Macedonia, mentioned immediately after Styberra.

[358] L. Robert believes that this is Alexandria in Egypt, and not Alexandria in the Troad. See *Monnaies antiques en Troade* (Paris 1966) 79 and *Gnomon* 35 (1963) 65 n. 7.

[359] L. Robert, "Sur quelques ethniques," *Hellenica* 2 (1946) 67, explains the ethnic Τρωαδεύς. Formerly used for the province, in the Imperial period it came to be used as the official ethnic of the citizens of Alexandria in the Troad.

[360] An inscription now in Kavala may record the name of a Samothracian initiate; *supra*, note 206.

[361] L. Robert identifies this town as Antioch on the Maeander; see *Gnomon* 35 (1963) 62.

[362] L. Robert identifies this town as Arsinoe, the former Patara; see *Hellenica* 11-12 (1960) 157 and *Gnomon* 35 (1963) 62.

[363] There are other lists which may list citizens from Byzantion. They are: *Samothrace* 2.1, nos. 27 and 55. L. Robert suggests that the *epoptai* listed on *Samothrace* 2.1, no. 28c were also from Byzantion. See *Gnomon* 35 (1963) 66-67.

[364] A Macedonian town near the Strymon River, north of Amphipolis. The exact location is debated. See L. Robert, *Gnomon* 35 (1963) 77 and N. G. L. Hammond and G. T. Griffith, *A History of Macedonia* (Oxford 1979) map 10.

[365] The name of the town is not given on the stone, but on the basis of the names listed, L. Robert suggests that the initiates were from Kos. For Robert's remarks, see F. Salviat, "Addenda samothraciens," *BCH* 86 (1962) 276-78.

[366] Fraser suggested that *Samothrace* 2.1, no. 27 may also list initiates from Perinthos, but

L. Robert has shown that the eponymous date from the home city of the initiates uses a Doric form impossible at Perinthos, an Ionic settlement. For Robert's analysis, see *Gnomon* 35 (1963) 65.

[367] Fraser is reluctant to identify this as the Macedonian town, but L. Robert points out that the initiate, Βοιωτός, has a rare name found there, *Gnomon* 35 (1963) 65 n. 7.

[368] L. Robert, *Études anatoliènnes; recherches sur les inscriptions grecques de l'Asie mineure* (Paris 1937, reprint 1970) 428-29, identifies this town as Tralles, near Miletos, and points out that the initiate's name, Ἀμάτοχος, a typically Thracian name, is unusual in this area.

[369] *Samothrace* 2.1, no. 29; *IG* XII (8), nos. 186a and 186b.

[370] *ibid.*, no. 186b.

[371] *ibid.*, no. 259; *infra*, note 375. Cf. *Hesperia* 48 (1979) 17, for titles of ship's officers.

[372] *ibid.*, no. 205.

[373] See Appendix I, nos. 33-39.

[374] For Kyzikene *theoroi*, see *infra*, p. 50.

[375] For four of the lists where Kyzikos is mentioned, see *supra*, p. 44. P. Lehmann, *Samothracian Reflections*, 30 n. 57, has pointed out that a fifth group of five names, printed as *IG* XII (8), no. 259, may have originally been inscribed on the stone copied by Cyriacus and now published as *Samothrace* 2.1, no. 29. In the Bodleian manuscript of Cyriacus' journal, the five men are called Κυζικηνῶν Εὐίεροι (*Samothracian Reflections* 26, fig. 19). The round building appears on *IG* XII (8), no. 189 (see *Samothracian Reflections*, 33, fig. 23) and also on *Samothrace* 2.1, no. 29 and App IV (*Samothracian Reflections*, fig. 25).

[376] *IG* XII (8), no. 190 (*Samothracian Reflections*, 33, fig. 24).

[377] *supra*, note 375, 36-44. For Kyzikene coins showing the building, see 37, figs. A-B. For the relief depicting the building, see 43, figs. 27-38.

[378] McCredie, *Hesperia* 48 (1979) 35-40 and figs. 9-15; McCredie compares this building with the building represented on the Kyzikene reliefs, but is unable, from the limited remains, to determine its function.

[379] *Samothrace* 2.1, no. 29, and *Samothrace* 2.1, App. IV, lines 8-9: Μῖκις Μνησισ[τρ]άτου, φύσει δ[ὲ] Ἀσκληπιάδης Ἀττάλου.

[380] ἀρχιτέκτων is the title of a magistrate at Kyzikos. For references, see Fraser, *Samothrace* 2.1, 115 and n. 16. P. Lehmann discusses the term in *Samothracian Reflections*, 41.

[381] F. Hazluck; *Cyzicus* (Cambridge 1910) 211-13, for references to inscriptions.

[382] K. Lehmann, *Samothrace* 3.2, 10 n. 43, considers sixteen of these documents. Not included are the initiate list published later by Salviat, *BCH* 86 (1962) 275-78, no. 4, and a new list found below the stoa, published by McCredie, *Hesperia* 48 (1979) 17. Another inscription from the recent excavations, inv. no. 68.354, also mentions *epoptai*. In addition to those lists which definitely record *epoptai*, there are at least eleven more where the word could be restored. As Lehmann points out in note 43, editors have preferred to restore μύσται instead of ἐπόπται wherever only the last letters of the word remained. Those inscriptions which could yield more names of *epoptai* if restored differently are: *IG* XII (8), nos. 184, 185, 189, 210, 215, 220; *Samothrace* 2.1, nos. 35, 42, 43, 49, 56.

[383] *IG* XII (8), nos. 186a, 215.20, 216; *Samothrace* 2.1, nos. 26, 28c, 29b, 41, 55, App. IV; *BCH* 86 (1962) 276-78, no. 4; *Hesperia* 48 (1979) 17; and an unpublished list, inv. no. 68.354.

[384] *CIL* III Suppl., no. 12318 (= I², no. 665), *IG* XII (8), no. 205; *Samothrace* 2.1, nos. 17b, 28a, 30, 31, 36.

[385] One of the men is a slave: Seleucus in *IG* XII (8), no. 205.6.

[386] Discrepancies between these figures and those of Lehmann, *Samothrace* 3.2, 14 n. 58, are due in part to the fact that he did not know of the list discovered by Chapouthier and Salač, but not published until 1962 by Salviat, *BCH* 86 (1962) 286-87, no. 4. Lehmann apparently does not count in his figures as initiates the names which occur in the longer lists without headings (e.g., *IG* XII (8), nos. 181, 182).

[387] Mylonas (*supra*, note 215) 237: the total cost of initiation for the Lesser and Greater Mysteries is estimated at fifteen drachmai.

[388] Fraser's comment, *Samothrace* 2.1, 77, that "the absence of '*mystes pius et*' before *epop[ta]* is striking" is clearly an exaggeration. It is more common to omit mention of the *epoptes' myesis*.

[389] *IG* XII (8), no. 186a; *CIL* III Suppl., no. 12318 (= I², no. 665); *Samothrace* 2.1, no. 55; *Hesperia* 48 (1979) 17.

[390] *Samothrace* 2.1, App. IV, line 7, of Asklepiades Attalou.

[391] *Samothrace* 2.1, no. 36.

[392] *ibid.*

[393] Greek inscriptions: *IG* XII (8), nos. 215, 216; *Samothrace* 2.1, nos. 26, 28c, 29b, 35 (?), 41; *BCH* 86 (1962) 276-78, no. 4.

Roman inscriptions: *IG* XII (8), no. 205; *Samothrace* 2.1, nos. 17b, 28a, 30, 31.

[394] *IG* XII (8), no. 205; *Samothrace* 2.1, nos. 28a, 31.

[395] *IG* XII (8), no. 216; *Samothrace* 2.1, nos. 26, 28c; *BCH* 86 (1962) 286-87, no. 4.

[396] *IG* XII (8), no. 215; *Samothrace* 2.1, no. 17b, 29a-b.

[397] *Samothrace* 2.1, no. 36. For Lehmann's remarks, see *Samothrace* 3.2, 14.

[398] *IG* XII (8), no. 205. Lehmann is mistaken about the names on this inscription (*Samothrace* 3.2, 12 n. 53); see *infra*, p. 96.

[399] *IG* XII (8), no. 186a.

[400] *IG* XII (8), no. 186b.

[401] *IG* XII (8), no. 216.

[402] *Samothrace* 2.1, nos. 26, 28c; *BCH* 86 (1962) 276-78, no. 4.

[403] L. Robert has suggested that the *epoptai* on *Samothrace* 2.1, no. 28c have names typical of Byzantion, see *Gnomon* 35 (1963) 66-67.

[404] *IG* XII (8), nos. 181, 182.

[405] P. Boesch, Θεωρός (Berlin 1908) 3. The etymology is disputed. L. Ziehen, *RE* VII A II, s.v. "Theoroi," 2243-44, prefers a compound etymology from the roots of both ὁράω and θεός.

[406] Boesch, *ibid.*, 5. For comments on the etymology of *theoros*, see G. Daux, "Théores et théarodoques," *REG* 80 (1967) 292-300.

[407] Plu. *Luc.* 13.1-2. The initiation ceremonies were separate from the public festival. Plutarch says that Voconius stopped at Samothrace to be initiated (μυούμενος) and to attend the public festival (πανηγυρίζων).

[408] *Guide*¹, 28. The inscription is *CIL* III, no. 720. It was Mommsen and Hirschfeld who originally maintained that the month was July. For comments, see Conze, *Samothrake* I, 39. F. Cumont believes these dates to be coincidental with the beginning of the Sothic year, "Les mystères de Samothrace et l'année cuniculaire," *RHR* 127 (1944) 55-60, but only one Samothracian initiate list is dated to this month. If July were the month of the festival, one would expect more of the initiate lists to be dated in July.

[409] *Schol.* Eur. *Ph.* 7.

[410] Hemberg, 107. For a reconstruction of the activities of the Samothracian festival, see F. Salviat, "Le théâtre de Samothrace," *BCH* 80 (1956) 142-45. Salviat believes that one of the major activities of the festival was the performance of plays in the theater in the Samothracian sanctuary. He maintains that the myth associated with Harmonia was one of several which were dramatized. The evidence for plays on Samothracian themes is found in inscriptions from Iasos and Priene; *infra*, notes 428-30. Salviat points out that one of the Samothracian *theoroi* lists includes two members from a κοινόν of theatrical performers, *IG* XII (8), no. 163c, 35-39: τοῦ κοινοῦ τῶν πε[ρὶ τον Διόνυσον]/τεχνειτῶν τῶν [ἀπὸ Ἰωνίας]/καὶ Ἑλλησπόντο[υ]. He also calls attention to the fact that one of the initiates on a Samothracian initiate list is called κιθαρίστρια, *IG* XII (8), no. 178, 6-8. From these two examples he concludes that theatrical performances must have included dramas and the singing of poetry and chants. Chapouthier, 174-75, maintains that the Samothracian legends were performed both as part of the secret initiation ceremony and in the public theater. There is no way to verify any of these suggestions.

[411] *Samothrace* 2.1, no. 22.

[412] There are no lists which are definitely from the first century A.D., but five could be as late as this. They are: *IG* XII (8), nos. 168, 171, 174-76.

[413] *Samothrace* 2.1, 14. For a map showing the cities which sent *theoroi* to Samothrace, see *infra*, map II.

[414] *Samothrace* 2.1, no. 22.

[415] The Roman names recorded on *IG* XII (8), nos. 173 and 174 are probably not part of the *theoroi* groups from Dardanos.

[416] Fraser's map, *Samothrace* 2.1, after page 12, showing the sites which sent *theoroi* to Samothrace, gives forty-five sites. He has omitted Astypalaia, probably the town of that name on the island near Kos, named on *IG* XII (8), no. 168b. The omission is pointed out by L. Robert, *Gnomon* 35 (1963) 61 n. 2. Fraser identifies Aigai of *IG* XII (8), no. 162 as the Lydian Aigai; the *theoroi* from Aigai appear between those of Dardanos and Myrina. See *supra*, note 357, for the Macedonian Aigai on *IG* XII (8) 206.

[417] The reading is doubtful. See L. Robert, *Gnomon* 35 (1963) 52.

[418] Myrina on the Ionic coast, named with other sites from the area.

[419] Myrina on the island of Lemnos, named with other island sites. There are, however, problems with this identification because the rest of the inscription may have been inscribed at a different time.

[420] L. Robert, *Gnomon* 35 (1963) 63, reads ['Ροδ]ίων in *Samothrace* 2.1, no. 22.26, arguing that the names which follow are Rhodian names.

[421] *IG* XII (8), no. 171.23 was originally read by Fredrich as Σανίων, but L. Robert, on the basis of the names listed, confirmed by examination of the stone itself, has decided that these *theoroi* were from Samos. He does not think that either of the towns called Sane had an independent existence. For his remarks, see "Inscriptions de Lesbos et Samos," *BCH* 59 (1935) 487-88; *Gnomon* 35 (1963) 62.

[422] L. Robert, *Villes d'Asie mineure* (Paris 1935) 43 n. 5, identifies this as the Carian Stratonikeia because one of the names in *Samothrace* 2.1, no. 24 is definitely a Carian name.

[423] *BCH* 86 (1962) 275-76, no. 4.

[424] *IG* XII (8), no. 172.2-4.

[425] Such a list is *IG* XII (8), no. 181. The name Sokles occurs in line 6 of this inscription, a name known from Pliny, *NH* 11.37.167, to have been a Samothracian name. A man named Sokles also appears as the proposer of a Samothracian decree, *Samothrace* 2.1, no. 1.

[426] For a detailed discussion of these sites, *infra*, Ch. V.

[427] *BMI* III, no. 444; L. Robert, "Notes épigraphiques," *RA* (1926) 173-74; *Tragicorum Graecorum Fragmenta*, vol. I, ed. B. Snell (Göttingen 1971) 130 T 1 C.

[428] *IPrien*, nos. 68-70; L. Robert, *RA* 24 (1926) 174-76. For further bibliography, see L. Robert, *Gnomon* 35 (1963) 59.

[429] *BMI* III, no. 444.31-32.

[430] *IPrien*, no. 68.10-11.

[431] P. Boesch, Θεωρός (*supra*, note 405), 28. See also L. Robert, *Gnomon* 35 (1963) 61, and n. 2.

[432] Fredrich, *IG* XII (8), 47; Livy, 42.25.6, with comments by N. Lewis, *Samothrace* 1, 46.

[433] Kyzikos: *IG* XII (8), no. 194; *Samothrace* 2.1, no. 29. Rhodes: *IG* XII (8), nos. 186a and 186b.

[434] *IG* XII (8), no. 163b, 16-18.

[435] *Samothrace* 2.1, no. 29.

[436] *IG* XII (8), nos. 186a and 186b.

[437] L. Robert, *Gnomon* 35 (1963) 67, believes that the *hieropoioi* did not serve a separate function, but that *hieropoioi* were *theoroi*. Fraser, *Samothrace* 2.1, 116 n. 20, commenting on the Kyzikine *hieropoioi*, suggests that "the title was bestowed on theoroi to external cult centers." *Hieropoioi* may have technically served as *theoroi*, but not all *theoroi* were *hieropoioi*. The office of *hieropoios* is a civic office at Athens, Delos, Kos, Kamiros, and Rhodes, but is not an office known in all cities which sent *theoroi* to Samothrace. At Kamiros *hieropoioi* served a variety of functions involved with sacrifices, the setting up of inscriptions in sanctuaries, and representing the city on missions to oracles. At Rhodes, where it was the *hierothytai* who served these functions, *hieropoioi* do not appear except as emissaries to Samothrace. See D. R. Smith, "Hieropoioi and Hierothytai on Rhodes," *AC* 41 (1972) 532-39. Smith accepts Rubensohn's reading of *IG* XII (1), no. 701.14 and says that the inscription records the duties of a *hieropoios* sent to Samothrace, Lemnos, and Didyma, but Rubensohn's suggestion of Samothrace for the lacuna in that line is not generally accepted. See *TitCam*, no. 78.

[438] *Samothrace* 2.1, no. 13, a small round altar dedicated by two *theoroi* from Paros. Cf. *Hesperia* 48 (1979) 26, inv. no. 70.456 for another dedication by Parian *theoroi*.

[439] *IG* XII (8), nos. 164, 165, 168, 170(d-e), 171; *Samothrace* 2.1, no. 23. There are also several extant Samothracian decrees awarding *proxenia* to citizens from various towns. Some of the *proxenoi* may have been *theoroi*. The towns mentioned are Mesata in Aetolia and Oitaia (*IG* XII [8], no. 151); Kalchedon (no. 152); Rhodes (no. 153); Zone (no. 155); Gortynia (no. 157); Maroneia (*Samothrace* 2.1, no. 6); and Rhoiteion (*BCH* 86 [1962] 270-74, no. 2). A Thasian who received *proxenia* at Samothrace seems to have received the award for something more substantial than serving as *theoros*; see *Études thasiennes* V, 18-20, no. 169, a Samothracian *proxeny* decree found at Thasos.

[440] *Samothrace* 2.1, 62.

[441] *Samothrace* 2.1, no. 23.

[442] *IG* XII (8), no. 170c.

[443] Twenty lists: *IG* XII (8), nos. 160a, 161, 162, 163, 164, 165, 166, 167, 168, 169, 170a-b, 170c, 170d-e-f, 171, 172; *Samothrace* 2.1, nos. 22, 23, 24, App. IIIA; *BCH* 86 (1962) 274-75, no. 3.

[444] Six lists: *IG* XII (8), nos. 160b, 173, 174, 175, 176, 177b.

[445] Benndorf, *Samothrake* II, 97-101, noticed that on a small group of lists the *theoroi* were called *mystai*, and he used this as evidence that the group as a whole was late. He did not notice that the formal lists seem to be official lists, whereas the *theoroi-mystai* lists seem to be private ones.

[446] *IG* XII (8), no. 160b.16-22.

[447] *IG* XII (8), no. 177b (the line where the *theoroi* would be expected to be called *mystai* is illegible).

[448] *IG* XII (8), no. 175.

[449] *IG* XII (8), no. 176.

[450] *Samothrace* 2.1, App. IIIA, probably found at Samothrace in the nineteenth century, now in the museum at Istanbul, is considered by Fraser and L. Robert to be a fragment of a Samothracian *theoroi* list.

[451] Ten carry official lists: *IG* XII (8), nos. 160a.1-b.15, 161, 162, 163, 164, 169, 170, 171; *Samothrace* 2.1, nos. 23, 24. Two are inscribed with names of initiated *theoroi* from Dardanos: *IG* XII (8), nos. 173, 174. The others are private lists inscribed on stones of various sizes. Of the other official lists, one is a stele (*Samothrace* 2.1, no. 22), two are copied by Cyriacus with, of course, no dimensions (*IG* XII [8], nos. 165, 172), four are too fragmentary to deduce the original dimensions, and the last one (*BCH* 86 [1962] 174-75, no. 3) is carved on a block of dimensions different from the uniform group.

[452] *Samothrake* II, 99.

[453] Fraser, *Samothrace* 2.1, 62-63.

[454] *Samothrace* 2.1, no. 22.

[455] *IG* XII (8), no. 176. See Salviat, *BCH* 86 (1962) 275.

[456] *Guide*⁴, 80.

[457] Dated by the dedicatory inscription on the architrave; *IG* XII (8), no. 229 and *Samothrace* 2.1, no. 72.

[458] Fraser, *Samothrace* 2.1, 127 n. 4, for attempts to identify her.

[459] Salviat, *BCH* 86 (1962) 281-90; McCredie, *Hesperia* 37 (1968) 208-209.

CHAPTER FIVE

[460] Except for the decree which implies that the Ptolemaic general Hippomedon was initiated (*Samothrace* 2.1, App. I = *IG* XII (8), no. 156) and the earliest known *theoroi* list (*Samothrace* 2.1, no. 22), there are at Samothrace no inscriptions earlier than the second century B.C. which actually mention *theoroi* or *mystai*.

[461] For a summary of the Samothracian gods in literature, see Roscher, *Ausführliches Lexikon* IV, 306-307, s.v. "Samothrakes, -thrakioi" (Höfer).

[462] 2.51.

⁴⁶³ *Pax* 276-79:

ὦνδρες τί πεισόμεσθα; νῦν ἀγὼν μέγας.
ἀλλ' εἴ τις ὑμῶν ἐν Σαμοθράκῃ τυγχάνει
μεμυημένος, νῦν ἐστιν εὔξασθαι καλὸν
ἀποστραφῆναι τοῦ μετιόντος τὼ πόδε.

⁴⁶⁴ Frg. 178 (Kock), dated 350-30 B.C., quoted by Athenaios, 10.421d. The passage implies that there were specific Samothracian charms or prayers which initiates could utter when in danger with hope of avoiding disaster:

...δειπνεῖ δ' ἄφωνος Τήλεφος, νεύων μόνον
πρὸς τοὺς ἐπερωτῶντάς τι, ὥστε πολλάκις
αὐτὸν ὁ κεκληκὼς τὰ Σαμοθρᾴκι' εὔχεται
λῆξαι πνέοντα καὶ γαληνίσαι ποτέ·
χείμων ὁ μειρακίσκος ἐστὶ τοῖς φίλοις.

⁴⁶⁵ *SP* III, no. 61.14-16:

...τῶν κάλων τις ἥψατο
[θοἰστίον] τ' ἐσκέψαθ', ἕτερος τοῖς Σαμόθραιξιν εὔχεται
[τῶι κυβερνή]τηι βοη[θεῖν], τοὺς πόδας προσέλκεται

See G. Vitelli, "Frammenti della 'commedia nuova'," *SIFC* n.s. 7 (1929) 235-42. Vitelli thinks that the fragment might be by Menander or some poet of the fourth or third century B.C. Objections have been raised against this attribution and date. Republishing the fragment with many corrections, A. Körte, *APF* 10 (1931-1932) 56-61, argues on stylistic, metrical, and contextual grounds that the date of composition is contemporary with the fragment's transcription (first century A.D.) and suggests that it was composed in Egypt by an imitator of Menander. Hemberg, 212, accepts the attribution of the fragment to Menander, but Menander would then be the earliest writer to use the expression οἱ Σαμόθρακες to refer to the Samothracian gods, a use which does not appear on inscriptions until the third century B.C. For a situation similar to the one in the fragment, however, cf. Thphr. *Char.* 25.2: καὶ κλυδωνίου γενομένου ἐρωτᾶν εἴ τις μεμύηται τῶν πλεόντων.

⁴⁶⁶ 47 (Pfeiffer):

τὴν ἁλίην Εὔδημος, ἐφ' ἧς ἅλα λιτὸν ἐπέσθων
  χειμῶνας μεγάλους ἐξέφυγεν δανέων,
θῆκε θεοῖς Σαμόθραξι, λέγων ὅτι τήνδε κατ' εὐχήν,
  ὦ λαοί, σωθεὶς ἐξ ἁλὸς ὧδ' ἔθετο.

⁴⁶⁷ Similar dedications to the Samothracian gods are known from Apameia Kibotos and Koptos; see Appendix I, nos. 54 and 57. For references to such dedications to other gods, see P. M. Fraser, *Ptolemaic Alexandria* (Oxford 1972) II, 834.

⁴⁶⁸ J. Bousquet, *RA* 29-30 (1948) 111, claims that Kallimachos must have travelled to Samothrace with Arsinoe and that the epigram shows that he was a Samothracian initiate, but the popularity of the Samothracian gods outside Samothrace in the third century B.C. shows that Kallimachos could certainly have been familiar with such dedications elsewhere. K. Lehmann, *Samothrace* 4.2, 168, 179, and fig. 73 (cf. I. Love, *Samothrace* 3.2, 214-15 and n. 13) translates ἁλίη as "saltcellar" and believes that tiny bowls found at Samothrace are such, but A. S. F. Gow and D. L. Page, *The Greek Anthology* (Cambridge 1965) II, 185, argue that the word means "salt tub" (for pounding) or "salt cask" (for storage).

⁴⁶⁹ Appendix I, no. 14.

⁴⁷⁰ Black Sea area: Olbia, Istros, Tomis, Kallatis, Bizone, Dionysopolis, Odessos. Northern Greece and Thrace: Seuthopolis, Alexandroupolis, Philippi, Amphipolis, Dion. Aegean islands: Samothrace, Methymna (Lesbos), Delos, Kythnos, Thera, Rhodes, Lindos, Karpathos, Syme. Asia Minor: Kalchedon, Gökçeören, Ilion, Teos, Ephesos, Mylasa, Stratonikeia, Aulai, Apameia, Fasilar. Egypt: Kyrene, Koptos. See map III.

⁴⁷¹ Ephesos, Kalchedon, Methymna (Lesbos), Mylasa, Rhodes, Samothrace, Stratonikeia, Teos.

⁴⁷² Amphipolis, Ephesos, Ilion, Philippi, Rhodes, Tomis.

⁴⁷³ Ephesos, Rhodes.

⁴⁷⁴ *IG* XII (8), no. 216, but see *supra*, note 206.

⁴⁷⁵ Hemberg divides his discussion according to the title by which the gods were called, distinguishing three main groups: Theoi Megaloi, Kabeiroi, and Theoi Samothrakes. Sometimes these titles are used interchangeably, sometimes they refer to mutually exclusive groups. Because the title Kabeiroi is not used at Samothrace and because the Samothracian title Theoi Megaloi is often used to refer to gods other than the Samothracian gods, I have omitted from this discussion inscriptions mentioning Kabeiroi and Theoi Megaloi unless the epithet Samothrakes is included. Hemberg lists as sites where inscriptions mention Theoi Megaloi or Theos Megas the following: Anaphe, Andania, Argos, Çaltillar, Erythrai, Imbros, Kalin Ağil, Karthaia (Keos), Keramos, Kierion, Magdola (Fayum), Megalopolis, Methana, Peiraieus, Setis (Egypt), Termessos, Thasos, Thera, Thessalonike, Tymandos. To these can be added the following: Alaşehir, *SEG* 20.14; Anapa, *CIRB*, no. 1202; Athens, *SEG* 21.536, IG II², nos. 1006-1008; Attalea (Pamphylia), *SEG* 17.592; Bağla (Caria), *SEG* 16.683; Bouga (Messenia), *SEG* 11.984; Gortys (Arcadia), *SEG* 15.234; Halonnesos, *IG* XII (8), no. 45; Istros, *SEG* 18.296; Karanis (Egypt), *SEG* 20.649; Kestros (Cilicia), *SEG* 20.105; Kyrene, *SEG* 9.7; Pella, *SEG* 24.540; Thebes (Egypt), *SEG* 8.761. Hemberg lists as sites where inscriptions mention Kabeiroi as follows: Chios, Delos, Didyma, Larisa, Lemnos, Miletos, Olynthos, Paros, Pella, Pergamon, Tanagra, Thebes, Thessalonika, Tlos. Add Naxos, *SEG* 25.939. Hemberg omits from his discussion of the Theoi Samothrakes the following sites: Alexandroupolis, Dion, Ephesos, and Kalchedon. Inscriptions from the following have been published since 1950: Bizone, Gökçeören, Kyrene, Seuthopolis, Aulai. From the sites which he discusses I have deleted Lartos (*IG* XII (1), no. 913) and Kamiros (*IG* XII (1), no. 701) because the inscriptions do not actually mention the Samothracian gods.

⁴⁷⁶ *IG* XII (8), no. 216.

⁴⁷⁷ Appendix I, no. 15, from the Samothracian *peraia*.

⁴⁷⁸ For instance, the Egyptian gods are often called Theoi Megaloi; see E. Bernand, *Inscriptions métriques de l'Égypte gréco-romaine* (Paris 1969) 634-35, no. 175, III.35; *Recueil des inscriptions grecques du Fayoum* (Leiden 1975) I, 174, no. 84; Vidman, *Sylloge*, nos. 39, 41, 350.

⁴⁷⁹ At Delos the Samothracian gods are identified with the Dioskouroi and the Kabeiroi, Appendix I, nos. 25-28. At Fasilar they are associated with the Dioskouroi, Appendix I, no. 55.

⁴⁸⁰ Appendix I, nos. 3, 5, 7, 9, 12, 13.

⁴⁸¹ Appendix I, no. 14, described in detail by D. P. Dimitrov, "Neuentdeckte epigraphische Denkmäler über die Religion der Thraker in der frühhellenistischen Epoche," *Latomus* 28 (1957) 181-93.

⁴⁸² J. and L. Robert, *REG* 72 (1959) 209-10, no. 225, believe that the inscription indicates earlier Hellenization of the Thracian interior than had formerly been believed.

⁴⁸³ *supra*, note 481, 190; see also D. Dimitrov and M. Čičikova, *The Thracian City of Seuthopolis* (BAR Supplementary Series 38, London 1978) 45.

⁴⁸⁴ Samothrace is described as a place of asylum by the following: D. S. 3.55.9; Livy, 45.4.3, 5.8; Plu. *Aem.* 23.11, 26.1, *Pomp.* 24.6; Vell. Pat. 1.9.4-5; *supra*, Ch. II, note 179.

⁴⁸⁵ Appendix I, no. 18. A new small piece of this inscription has been found in recent excavations at Dion and will be published by Demetrios Pantermalis of the University of Thessalonike.

⁴⁸⁶ G. Oikonomos, Ἐπιγραφαὶ τῆς Μακεδονίας (Athens 1915) 3; E. Bikerman, "La cité grecque dans les monarchies hellénistiques," *RPh* 65 (1939) 349; H. Schmitt, *Die Staatsverträge des Altertums* (Munich 1969) III, 308-12.

⁴⁸⁷ 15.23.9; 18.3.11.

⁴⁸⁸ L. Robert, "Monument de Lysimacheia," *Hellenica* 10 (1955) 269-71 and pl. 35.

⁴⁸⁹ Plb. 18.44.1-7; F. W. Walbank, *A Historical Commentary on Polybius* (Oxford 1967) II, 478-79, points out that Lysimacheia fell to the Thracians after Philip's withdrawal.

⁴⁹⁰ Appendix I, no. 32.

⁴⁹¹ *Thera* III, 89-102. See pl. IV(a-b).

⁴⁹² *IG* XII (3), no. 1345.

⁴⁹³ *Thera* III, 91 and figs. 73-74.

⁴⁹⁴ *ibid.*, 98, fig. 79 and pl. 5. For Apollo and lion on coins, see *Sylloge Nummorum Graecorum* (London 1933) Great Britain II, Lloyd Collection: 686-709; 1053-65.

⁴⁹⁵ See frontispiece.

⁴⁹⁶ U. Wilamowitz, *Der Glaube der Hellenen* (Berlin 1932) II, 388, says that Artemidoros left his portrait so that he would not be forgotten.

497 *Thera* III, 100.

498 An inscription found in a temple of Pan in Egypt was once thought to record the name of this Artemidoros, and on the basis of this inscription (*OGIS* I, no. 70) Hiller and others thought that Artemidoros had served Ptolemy I in Egypt. The inscription has now been re-examined and discussed by A. Bernand, *Le Paneion d'El-Kanaïs: Les inscriptions grecques* (Leiden 1972) 109-12, no. 43, who has determined that the name on the stone is not Artemidoros, but Melanias.

499 *IG* XII (3), no. 464. In his note to the inscription Hiller interprets it to mean that Artemidoros dedicated shrines to the first three Ptolemies at Thera, stating that Artemidoros spent all three reigns there. The inscription implies, however, that only the dedication to the third Ptolemy was made at Thera. The inscription is located near the *temenos*.

500 *IG* XII (3) Suppl., no. 1344 and note. Because Artemidoros drops the ethnic "Pergaios" in the inscriptions to the Olympian figures, Hiller thinks that he actually became a citizen of Thera, *Thera* III, 96.

501 *Thera* III, 96 and 90, fig. 73.

502 Wilamowitz (*supra*, note 496) II, 387, suggests that Artemidoros had learned about the Samothracian gods during a stay in Egypt, but the inscription on which this suggestion relies was incorrectly read (*supra*, note 498). Artemidoros did make a contribution to a temple of the Egyptian gods on Thera (*IG* XII (3), no. 463 = Suppl., no. 1388), but he would not have had to travel to Egypt to be acquainted with these gods. For the inscription and admonitions about its restoration, see Vidman, *Sylloge*, no. 139.

503 *IG* XII (3), no. 422.

504 Appendix I, no. 32 and pl. IV(a). The term ἐπήχοος appears often on inscriptions as an epithet of various gods. O. Weinreich, "Θεοὶ Ἐπήχοοι," *MDAI* (*A*) 37 (1912) 1-68 (= *Ausgewählte Schriften* I (Amsterdam 1969) 131-95, quotes 138 examples. The idea of a god who listens appears to not have been originally a Greek idea, but to have been imported from the east. Weinreich's examples are primarily from the islands, Thrace, and Asia Minor. P. Bruneau, *Recherches sur les cultes de Délos à l'époque hellénistique et l'époque impériale* (Paris 1970) 167-68, connects the appearance of the epithet on Delian dedications with eastern, non-Greek worshippers of the Egyptian gods and Apollo. This point of view is developed by J. Teixidor, *The Pagan God* (Princeton 1977) 7-10, where Teixidor shows that the term is used of gods of Phoenicia, Syria, and Palmyra. It is unusual for the epithet to be applied to anything but a god. Hiller, *Thera* III, 94-95, thinks that Artemidoros is simply clumsy, but Weinreich, 30, suggests that Artemidoros, who comes from the east, is influenced by Syrian practice. Weinreich cites an altar from from Syria inscribed Ζεὺς Βωμὸς Ἐπήχοος. Cf. *CMRDM* III, 78-79.

505 *Thera* III, 65-73; 107-109.

506 *IG* XII (3), no. 494. For Artemis of Perge, see R. Fleischer, *Artemis von Ephesos* (Leiden 1973) 233-54 and pls. 96-106a; S. Onurkan, "Artemis Pergaia," *MDAI(I)* 19-20 (1969-1970) 290-96.

507 *IG* XII (3) Suppl., no. 1388 = Vidman, *Sylloge*, no. 139, for which see F. Dunand, *Le culte d'Isis dans le bassin oriental de la Méditerranée* (Leiden 1973) II, 124-25. Artemidoros did not found the temple, but contributed to its repair.

508 For the expansion of the Egyptian cult in the Aegean in the early third century B.C., see P. Roussel, *Les cultes égyptiens à Délos du IIIe au Ier siècle av. J.-C.* (Paris-Nancy 1916) 71-83, no. 1 (= Vidman, *Sylloge*, 63, CE no. 1); T. A. Brady, *The Reception of Egyptian Cults by the Greeks* (University of Missouri Studies 10.1, Columbia Missouri 1935) 20-22; P. M. Fraser, "Two Studies on the Cult of Sarapis in the Hellenistic World," *OAth* 1 (1960) 22, 27, etc.; Dunand (*supra*, note 507) II, 4, 21, 85, 87.

509 H. Herter, *De Priapo* (*RGVV* 23, Giessen 1932) 12-24, 39-42, 313-14. Priapos is mentioned as one of the gods included in the *pompe* of Ptolemy II, Athen. 5.201d. Herter, *RE* XXII.II, 1914-42, s.v. "Priapos," leaves open the possibility that Artemidoros learned of Priapos in Egypt, but see *supra*, note 498.

510 *IG* XII (3), no. 421c. For Priapos at Lampsakos, see P. Frisch, *Die Inschriften von Lampsakos* (Bonn 1978) 44, no. 7, where Priapos is eponymous *prytanis*.

511 *IG* XII (3), no. 421b. Cf. Eur. *Hel.* 569; Ar. *Th.* 858; *IG* XII (1), no. 914 (Lartos). See also T. Kraus, *Hekate* (Heidelberg 1960) 11 (Miletos and Didyma), 28, 78, 85, 88. For Hekate and Priapos worshipped together at Tralles, see *BCH* 4 (1880) 337.

512 For Kybele, see J. Ferguson, *The Religions of the Roman Empire* (London 1970) 27 and M. J. Vermaseren, *Cybele and Attis* (London 1977) 41. For Artemis of Perge, see Fleischer (*supra*, note 506) 251.

513 *IG* XII (3) Suppl., no. 1338; see T. Dohrn, *Die Tyche von Antiochia* (Berlin 1960) 53-59, for cities, including Perge, where Tyche was city goddess; cf., however, Pind. *Ol.* 12.1-2.

514 *GGR* II, 190.

515 *IG* XII (3) Suppl., no. 1335d.

516 *ibid.*, no. 1350.

517 *ibid.*, no. 1349.

518 *Thera* III, 102.

519 Appendix I, no. 57.

520 The term "Red Sea" in early writers, including Herodotus, refers to the Indian Ocean, but includes the Red Sea. Dittenberger, *OGIS* I, 122, thinks that in this inscription it is the modern Red Sea which is intended.

521 Appendix I, no. 46.

522 H. G. Lolling, "Altar aus Sestos," *MDAI(A)* 6 (1881) 210.

523 *Études* IV, 317 n. 3.

524 Hemberg, 237.

525 Fraser, *Samothrace* 2.1, 9 n. 37.

526 *REG* 77 (1964) 188-90, no. 272.

527 Appendix I, no. 47, line 28.

528 A woman and her slave from Kassandreia are listed alone at Samothrace, *IG* XII (8), no. 178. Women from Ainos are listed independently twice, *ibid.*, nos. 218 and 221. Only three other women besides Aristarche are mentioned on the inscriptions associated with the Samothracian gods found outside the sanctuary. See Appendix I, nos. 37, 53.

529 Appendix I, no. 40; cf. the dedication by a priest at Rhodes, Appendix I, no. 39 and V. Kontorini's description of the unpublished section of the inscription, "L'autonomie de Ptolémaïs-Akko," *RN* ser. 6, 21 (1979) 39.

530 Probably the leader of the *hierothytai* at Lindos, for which see D. R. Smith, "Hieropoioi and Hierothytai on Rhodes," *AC* 41 (1972) 532.

531 Appendix I, no. 54.

532 *supra*, notes 466-68.

533 *De Nat. Deor.* 3.37.89; cf. D.L. 6.2.59.

534 Appendix I, no. 55.

535 The arrangement of the figures on this relief is similar to other representations of the Dioskouroi. Cf. Chapouthier, 23-96, especially nos. 37-39.

536 *Samothrace* 3.1, 252-53.

537 *Denkmäler*, 18.

538 The attempt by Swoboda, *ibid.*, 19, to explain the epithet ἀδαμεῖ[ς] by comparing it to ἀδάμνα, defined by Hesychius as a Phrygian word for "friend" (s.v. ἀδαμνεῖν) and Ἄδαμνα, the name which Hippolytos, *Haer.* 5.9.7, says the Samothracians call Attis, is out of place. The word on the inscription is spelled differently and is more likely to be related to ἀδάμας meaning "unconquerable".

539 Appendix I, no. 17.

540 F. Poland, *Geschichte des griechischen Vereinswesens* (Leipzig 1909) 122.

541 W. Baege, *De Macedonum Sacris* (Dissertationes Philologicae Halenses 22, Halle 1913) 180.

542 Hemberg, 217-18; see also S. Düll, *Die Götterkulte Nordmakedoniens* (Munich 1977) 96, for the association of this inscription with Hermes.

543 P. Collart and P. Devambez, "Voyage dans la region du Strymon," *BCH* 55 (1931) 180. The caduceus is also found on the bilingual inscription from Samothrace, *Samothrace* 2.1, no. 63, and on ceramics from the sanctuary, *Samothrace* 2.2, 121, no. 296, 124, no. 306a; *Samothrace* 3.2, 232, no. 148.

544 *IG* XII (8), no. 195, *infra*, note 559.

545 Appendix I, no. 56.

[546] P. M. Fraser, "Two Dedications from Cyrenaica," *ABSA* 57 (1962) 25-27, no. 2; J. and L. Robert concur, *REG* 77 (1964) 243, no. 561.

[547] *ibid.*, 26. The inscription, however, is not included in Vidman, *Sylloge*, 335-38, s.v. "Cyrenaica," nor is it mentioned by S. Applebaum, *Jews and Greeks in Ancient Cyrene* (Leiden 1979).

[548] *CMRDM* I, no. 83; III, 79.

[549] A. T. Kraabel, "῞Υψιστος and the Synagogue at Sardis," *GRBS* 10 (1969) 87-93; M. Simon, "Theos Hypsistos," *Ex Orbe Religionum*, Studia G. Widengren (Leiden 1972) I, 372-85; P. Boyancé, "Le dieu tres haut chez Philon," *Mélanges d'histoire des religions offerts* à Henri-Charles Puech (Paris 1974) 139-49.

[550] Appendix I, no. 55.

[551] *supra*, note 546, 27.

[552] Appendix I, no. 45.

[553] *ibid.*, no. 10.

[554] *ibid.*, no. 31.

[555] Hemberg, 220, following Hiller's note to *IG* XII (5), no. 1057 (= Appendix I, no. 31).

[556] L. Ross, *Archäologische Aufsätze* (Leipzig 1861) II, 671. Ross is responsible for the speculation about the early date.

[557] Appendix I, no. 16. Charles Edson has shared with me his notes on this inscription. I saw the inscription at Philippi in 1976.

[558] *Mystai* of the Samothracian gods are mentioned otherwise only at Tomis, Appendix I, no. 6, Dionysopolis, *ibid.*, no. 11, and Rhodes, *ibid.*, no. 38a.

[559] The only inscription at Samothrace where the gods are addressed in the dative as "Samothracian" is *IG* XII (8), no. 216, a list definitely set up in the sanctuary (see pl. V(b)). The inscription at Philippi refers to the gods as "those in Samothrace," a designation impossible on the island itself. In this respect the inscription differs from another Samothracian initiate list which was apparently taken from Samothrace in modern times, *IG* XII (8), no. 195. This list, found near the Dardanelles, giving names of people from Thessalonike and Amphipolis, is accepted by L. Robert, *Collection Froehner* (Paris 1936) 52-53, no. 44, as being originally from Samothrace.

[560] The inscription from Lindos is dedicated by a group of priests and therefore seems to belong to a different class. The inscriptions from Bizone, Gökçeören, and Kythnos are too fragmentary to be used for comparison. The inscriptions from Kyrene and Fasilar do not preserve the name of the dedicant and seem to be dedicated to deities who are the product of syncretism.

[561] *Pax* 277-78.

[562] 4.43.1.

[563] 4.49.2-3. The land of King Byzas is Byzantion. Diodoros, describing an altar erected by the Argonauts at Byzantion, says that sailors in his day still honored it. Hemberg takes this as evidence for altars of the Samothracian gods at Byzantion, 218-19, but there is no epigraphical or archaeological evidence for such altars. Diodoros' source is Dionysios Skytobrachion, the Alexandrian mythographer (*FGrHist* 32 F14), but because Dionysios is not a local source, he would have known about such altars only by hearsay. Dionysios wrote in the third century B.C.; the date is now is established by a papyrus. See J. S. Rusten, *Dionysius Scytobrachion* (Opladen, in press).

[564] D.S. 4.49.8. Apollonios of Rhodes, 1.915-21, has the Argonauts stop off at Samothrace for initiation before going to Kolchis. The events associated with the Samothracian gods, including the dedications at Samothrace, as related by Diodoros, occur on the way back from Kolchis. It is possible that these stories had their source in dedications at Samothrace claimed to have been made by the Argonauts themselves.

[565] Appendix I, nos. 6, 11, 38a.

[566] Appendix I, nos. 26-28, 42, 50, 51.

[567] Appendix I, nos. 4, 6, 11.

[568] Appendix I, nos. 50-51.

[569] L. Robert, *Le sanctuaire de Sinuri près de Mylasa* (Mémoires de l'institut français d'archéologie de Stamboul 7, Paris 1945) 12.

⁵⁷⁰ *Hyperberetaios* is one of the months of the Macedonian calendar used in Asia Minor after the death of Alexander, but the name is not fixed to a particular time of the year. At Ephesos it corresponds to early September and at Sidon it corresponds to December. See A. Samuel, *Greek and Roman Chronology* (Munich 1972) 174-75.

⁵⁷¹ L. Robert (*supra*, note 569) 83.

⁵⁷² Hemberg, 221.

⁵⁷³ *IG* XII (8), no. 169.

⁵⁷⁴ *supra*, note 569, 22. Robert calls the Samothracian gods "Kabeiroi" although the Kabeiroi are not mentioned at Mylasa.

⁵⁷⁵ *supra*, note 569, pl. IV, top center.

⁵⁷⁶ Hemberg, 221.

⁵⁷⁷ Appendix I, no. 42. F. Hiller von Gaertringen, "Die Samothrakischen Götter in Rhodos und Karpathos," *MDAI(A)* 18 (1893) 391-94, says that there were forty names on the list.

⁵⁷⁸ *IG* XII (1), no. 1034, note.

⁵⁷⁹ The priests associated with the Samothrakion at Delos are known only from the Athenian period after 166 B.C. A list of available names is found in Bruneau (*supra*, note 504) 397.

⁵⁸⁰ Appendix I, nos. 4, 6, 11.

⁵⁸¹ *ibid.*, no. 6. See P. Roussel, "Remarques sur quelques règlements religieux," *BCH* 50 (1926) 314 and I. Stoian, *Tomitana* (Bucharest 1962) 75-79. I exclude from the discussion an inscription included by Hemberg: G. Točilescu, "Neue Inschriften aus der Dobrudscha," *AEMÖ* 14 (1891) 22-26, no. 50, because it does not mention the Samothracian gods.

⁵⁸² *Apatoureon* is equivalent to Attic *Pyanepsion*, approximately October-November.

⁵⁸³ *supra*, note 581, 315, offering in support a similar formula from an inscription from Kallatis.

⁵⁸⁴ *AEMÖ* 6 (1882) 9. This interpretation was followed by: H. Herbrecht, *De sacerdotii apud Graecos emptione venditione* (Dissertationes Philologicae Argentoratenses 10, 1885) 45, no. 2; H. Hepding, *Attis, seine Mythen und sein Kult* (*RGVV* 1 Giessen 1903) 185; A. Dieterich, *Eine Mithrasliturgie* (Leipzig 1903) 104; L. Farnell, *Cults of the Greek States* (Oxford 1896-1909) III, 195; it is rejected by B. M. Metzger, "Methodology in the Study of the Mystery Religions and Early Christianity," *Historical and Literary Studies* (Grand Rapids, Michigan 1968) 15. A. D. Nock, "Early Gentile Christianity," *Essays* I, 110, says "The restoration is attractive, but conjectural, and once more we do not know what was implied; possibly again it is a typical reception of the fruits of the earth." Cf., however, an inscription from Thessalonike recording celebrations of a group of *mystai* of Dionysos Gongylos where a banquet of bread is part of the ceremony (first century A.D.): *IG* X (2.1), no. 259. See G. Daux, "Trois inscriptions de la Grèce du nord," *CRAI* (1972) 478-87.

⁵⁸⁵ *Schol.* Pl. *Grg.* 497c; cf. Eus. *PE* 2.3.18.

⁵⁸⁶ *supra*, note 581, 314; Hemberg, 222-23. Roussel's interpretation is consistent with the inscription from Dionysopolis, Appendix I, no. 11, where the duties of the priest include processions and sacrifices.

⁵⁸⁷ Appendix I, no. 4.

⁵⁸⁸ The word βωμόν is a conjecture for the missing letters at the end of line 29. The faint, but certain, traces of the preposition παρά in that line seem to demand the word βωμόν instead of ἱερόν. If it were a temple which was mentioned as the place for display of the inscription, the expression would be ἐν τῷ ἱερῷ. D. M. Pippidi, "Le temple du Θεὸς Μέγας à Istros, *BCH* 83 (1959) 463, originally read ἱερόν, but discarded this reading in favor of βωμόν in "Inscriptions d'Istros. Décret inédit du IIᵉ siècle," *Dacia* n.s. 5 (1961) 308. See also J. and L. Robert, *REG* 76 (1963) 156-57, no. 169.

⁵⁸⁹ Appendix I, nos. 3, 5.

⁵⁹⁰ This would be a good reason for doubting that the small marble temple in honor of Theos Megas, dated to the first quarter of the third century B.C., was the temple referred to as the Samothrakion. Pippidi, *BCH* 83 (1959) 464, thinks there were two separate buildings.

⁵⁹¹ *supra*, note 588, 157, suggesting that Dionysios was a shipowner.

⁵⁹² Pippidi, *Dacia* n.s. 5 (1961) 308, thinks the name should be read Διονύσιον ["Ισ]τρου, Θεῶν [Μεγάλων ἱε/ρέα], but L. Robert, *Les stèles funéraires de Byzance gréco-romaine* (Paris 1964) 184, reads Διονύσιον Στρουθίων[ος τοῦ --/---]ς following T. Oziol. See also *REG* 79 (1966) 401, no. 273.

Pippidi, "Decrete elenistice din Histria," *StudClas* 7 (1965) 187-88, does not agree. For the change from private to public cult, see W. S. Ferguson, "Orgeonika," *Hesperia* Suppl. 8 (1949) 130-63.

[593] Appendix I, no. 11.

[594] *Mystai* from Dionysopolis do not appear on the Samothracian initiate lists, but the decree from Odessos erected at Samothrace, *Samothrace* 2.1, no. 6, indicates that people from the Black Sea area traveled to Samothrace for initiation. See *infra*, notes 611-12.

[595] Hemberg, 225.

[596] Appendix I, nos. 1, 33, 34, 44.

[597] Appendix I, no 1. Symbols of the Dioskouroi are known from another Olbian inscription, *IAOSPE* I², no. 33. Hemberg, 231, thinks it unlikely that at this distance there would have been separate cults for the Dioskouroi and the Samothracian gods. See also G. M. Hirst, "The Cults of Olbia," *JHS* 23 (1903) 44 and E. Bellin de Ballu, *Olbia* (Leiden 1972) 140. There is, however, no evidence for such syncretism.

[598] Appendix I, no. 44. Sokolowski, *LSAM*, 14, says that D.S. 4.48.5 gives evidence for a cult of the Samothracian gods at Kalchedon, but the passage refers to Byzantion. Kalchedon does appear on a *theoroi* list at Samothrace, *Samothrace* 2.1, no. 22.

[599] Appendix I, nos. 33, 34, 41.

[600] Chapouthier, 181.

[601] Appendix I, nos. 7, 9.

[602] *ibid.*, nos. 12-13.

[603] *ibid.*, nos. 3, 5.

[604] *ibid.*, no. 4.

[605] *ibid.*, nos. 7, 8, 9.

[606] *ibid.*, nos. 3, 5.

[607] *ibid.*, no. 4.

[608] G. Bordenache and D. M. Pippidi, "Le temple du Theos Megas à Istros," *BCH* 83 (1959) 455-65.

[609] If it were a public temple and if the Samothracian gods were identified with Theos Megas at Istros, it seems strange that the decree appointing a permanent priest of the Samothracian gods, Appendix I, no. 4, was not erected in this building.

[610] Appendix I, nos. 12, 13. These two decrees of proxeny were once thought to be the same inscription. See J. Mordtmann, *MDAI (A)* 10 (1885) 315 n. 4. Kalinka's suggestion, *Antike Denkmäler*, no. 93, that these were two separate inscriptions is tentatively accepted by Mihailov, *IGBR* I, no. 41.

[611] *Samothrace* 2.1, no. 6; see Pippidi, *Dacia* n.s. 5 (1961) 399 and L. Robert, *Gnomon* 35 (1963) 57 for corrections to the date and text.

[612] An unpublished Samothracian initiate list includes an initiate from Odessos, inv. no. 71.961.

[613] The Samothrakion was not the only building used for the display of decrees at Odessos. Of the ten extant decrees from that city, only three include the final portion of the decree where the place of display is described. Two of these are Appendix I, nos. 12-13. The third, *IGBR* I, no. 43, was erected in the temple of Apollo. A fourth, *IGBR* I, no. 45, does not preserve the place of display, but seems to mention Dionysos in line 34.

[614] On a coin of Odessos (125-11 B.C.) he appears in a portrait as a bearded figure wearing a headband. On the reverse, the same figure is shown standing, wearing a long robe and headband, holding a *kalathos*. See B. Pick, *Die antiken Münzen Nord-Griechenlands* (Berlin 1898) I, no. 2214 (pl. IV.2). A similar figure appears on horseback on a coin of the third century B.C. (no. 2200, pl. 4.13). The second century coin is inscribed "Theou Megalou," and is similar to an uninscribed coin of the fourth century B.C., indicating that this is a traditional type. Originally the rider god was a separate figure, but during the third century B.C. some of the chthonic features of Theos Megas were incorporated into the rider figure who was later identified with the Greek Dioskouroi. See Pick, "Thrakische Münzbilder," *JDAI* 13 (1898) 160-67.

[615] Hemberg, 223-231. On a coin of the late second or early first century B.C. (Pick, no. 2218, pl. IV.17) Demeter with stalk of wheat and veil is coupled with Kore. Demeter is also found with stalks of wheat on coins of Kallatis, Tomis, and Dionysopolis, but never on the same coin as

Theos Megas. Except for a late example from Kallatis (Pick, no. 281, pl. II.9) where the Dioskouroi are found on the reverse of a coin showing Demeter on the obverse, there is no evidence from the coins that Demeter was associated with any of the local gods who may have been identified with the Samothracian gods at these sites.

[616] K. Lehmann, *Samothrace* 3.2, 27-28 and n. 124, believes that an inscription from Odessos (now published as *IGBR* I, no. 225) may be related to the Samothracian mysteries because it mentions some kind of purple garment. The inscription is probably from a gravestone, and it records various honors accorded one individual. L. Robert, *REG* 61 (1948) 180, no. 157, describes this person as a priest of Dionysos, but Lehmann believes that the three symbols mentioned on the stone, a purple (garment), a golden (crown?), and an ivy (wreath?) refer to three different mystery rites. However, the term *telete*, used in the text, is in the singular. It is therefore likely that all three symbols refer to a single rite associated with Dionysos and not connected with either Theos Megas or the Samothracian gods.

[617] Appendix I, no. 11.

[618] *Hesperia* 48 (1979) 26, inv. no. 70.348, a small marble base for a little statue.

[619] These inscriptions are listed by Bruneau (*supra*, note 504) 379-81, 390-91.

[620] I follow the terminology established by Bruneau in referring to these buildings. GD 123 is the building numbered 123 in P. Bruneau and J. Ducat, *Guide de Délos* (Paris 1966).

[621] F. Robert, *Trois sanctuaires sur le rivage occidental. EAD* XX (Paris 1952) 5-50. This identification has been questioned by Bruneau (*supra*, note 504) 388.

[622] F. Chapouthier, *Le santuaire des dieux de Samothrace. EAD* XVI (Paris 1935). For the dedications, see Appendix I, nos. 25-30. For the building, see pl. III(b).

[623] The only inscription to mention the Kabeirion calls it the Kabeirion τὸ εἰς Κύνθον (*IG* XI (2), no. 144A, line 90, about 297 B.C.). Because of doubts about how this phrase should be translated, some commentators believe that there were on Delos two Kabeirions, one on the Inopos and the other on Mt. Kynthos. See O. Rubensohn, *AA* 46 (1931) 375-79; Chapouthier (*supra*, note 622) 80; K. Lehmann, *Samothrace* 3.2, 36 and n. 164. Hemberg, 146-49, is not convinced. Bruneau (*supra*, note 504) 388, shows that the phrase Kabeirion τὸ εἰς Κύνθον cannot mean "Kabeirion on Mt. Kynthos," but rather "Kabeirion facing Mt. Kynthos" and is therefore applicable to GD 93 which faces the small mountain. There is therefore no need to assume that there were two buildings called Kabeirion.

[624] For plans, see *EAD* XVI, figs. 55 and 82.

[625] The chronological development of the building has been described by Chapouthier (*supra*, note 622) 77-83, summarized by Hemberg, 140-43.

[626] This building is similar in shape to a building (which may also have been a Kabeirion) at Larisa on the Hermes. See J. Boehlau and K. Schefold, *Larisa am Hermos* (Berlin 1940) I, 77-80, esp. 78, fig. 13.

[627] The architrave inscription has been restored by Chapouthier (*supra*, note 622) 35. The interior walls and facade were decorated with portrait busts in relief, of officers and friends of Mithridates. In the building itself was a statue of Mithridates (fig. 50) who, according to the inscription, was worshipped here as Dionysos.

[628] *EAD* XVI, 53-56. On the basis of a scholion to Eur. *Ph.* 274 Chapouthier calls this construction an *eschara*, but in shape it is similar to the well altars known from Akragas in Sicily, for which see P. Marconi, *Agrigento Arcaica* (Rome 1933) pl. XX. The strange feature of the Delian example is its height: 1.70m. There is, however, a possible parallel at Eleusis where an altar, identified as a *bothros*, found in a late Geometric building, has a similar height. See Mylonas, *Eleusis and the Eleusinian Mysteries*, 59.

[629] One complicating factor in tracing the origins of the Kabeiroi cult on Delos is a small, crude sanctuary located on Mt. Kynthos itself. The sanctuary is in the form of an artificial cave with a circular monument, possibly for libations, in front. Rubensohn, Chapouthier, and Lehmann (*supra*, note 623) believe this to be a second Kabeirion. The structure has been described by A. Plassart, *Les sanctuaires et les cultes du Monte Cynthe. EAD* XI (Paris 1928) 228-55. Plassart says that none of the pottery in the cave sanctuary is earlier than the Hellenistic period, and Bruneau (*supra*, note 504) 401-403, suggests that the cave was built as a Herakleion in that period.

[630] *EAD* XX, 45. For pottery, see 40, fig. 35. For sculpture, see 34-35, figs. 27-29.

[631] Bruneau (*supra*, note 504) 379.

[632] F. Robert, *EAD* XX, 44, summarizing an earlier article, "Inscription métrique trouvée au Dioscurion délien," *BCH* 58 (1934) 184-202. Hemberg, 143-45, concurs.

[633] I omit a discussion of *ID*, no. 2548, which F. Robert interprets as evidence for a second renewal of the Dioskouroi cult in the first century B.C. Bruneau (*supra*, note 504) 384-85 and 393-94, has pointed out that this inscription was not found in the temple known as the Dioskourion and dates it a century earlier. Athenians were not necessarily hostile to the Dioskouroi. They often used the theophoric name Dioskourides and even made private dedications to the Dioskouroi in GD 93.

[634] *ID*, no. 1498.

[635] *ID*, no. 1898.

[636] *ID*, no. 2605; cf. nos. 1899 (132/1 B.C.), 1900 (128/7 B.C.), 1901 (114/3 B.C.), and 1574 (102/1 B.C.).

[637] *ID*, nos. 1562, 1581, 1582, 1902 (102/1 B.C.). See Appendix I, nos. 25-28.

[638] Hemberg, 145.

[639] Chapouthier, 182.

[640] Bruneau (*supra*, note 504) 395, describes the process as assimilation and syncretism.

[641] P. Roussel, *Délos, colonie athénienne* (Paris 1916) 16; W. A. Laidlaw, *A History of Delos* (Oxford 1933) 169.

[642] The inscriptions recording priests include the Attic *demos* of each priest.

[643] *ID*, no. 1400, line 41. This inscription cannot be dated exactly, but is believed to be one of the early acts of the second Athenian administration. See *ID*, III, 3.

[644] Appendix I, nos. 22-24.

[645] G. Roux, "Salles de banquets à Délos," *Études déliennes, BCH Suppl.* 1 (1973) 551-52.

[646] Appendix I, 22-23.

[647] M. S. Goldstein, *The Setting of the Ritual Meal in Greek Sanctuaries* (Diss. Univ. of California 1978) 280.

[648] For pieces of sculpture, see *EAD* XVI, 70-72; for inscribed statue bases, 75-77. For dedications, see Appendix I, nos. 22-24.

[649] *EAD* XVI, 83.

[650] *ibid.*, 81. For the position of the altar base, see 9, fig. 11, no. 2. The two altar bases are shown on the same page, figs. 13-14.

[651] In spite of his insistence that there were rites of *myesis* in the Delian precinct of the Kabeiroi-Megaloi Theoi-Dioskouroi, Chapouthier himself has shown that the only literary source which might have supported his hypothesis cannot be used as evidence because of a manuscript error. See "La prétendue initiation de Pythagore à Délos," *REG* 48 (1935) 414-23, on Iamb. *VP.* 28.151, about mysteries at Eleusis, Imbros, Samothrace, and another site for which the manuscript has Delos, but for which Chapouthier reads Lemnos. Bruneau prints Chapouthier's translation (*supra*, note 504) 390, but does not mention Chapouthier's correction until 396, where he declines to accept it. N. Lewis, *Samothrace* 1, 95, no. 210, accepts it.

[652] Appendix I, no. 49.

[653] LeBas and Waddington, no. 527. See Appendix I, no. 52.

[654] Hemberg, 237-38.

[655] A. Wilhelm, *Beiträge zur griechischen Inschriftenkunde* (Vienna 1909) 183-87.

[656] L. Robert, *Études anatoliennes; recherches sur les inscriptions grecques de l'Asie mineure* (Paris 1937) 529-31.

[657] *IG* XII (8), no. 170e, lines 72-75, *theoroi* from Stratonikeia mentioned just before the envoys of King Attalos. L. Robert, *Gnomon* 35 (1963) 63-64, says that this must be the Carian Stratonikeia because one of the *theoroi* has a definite Carian name. Stratonikeian *theoroi* are also listed on *Samothrace* 2.1, no. 24b, lines 12-14, second century B.C.

[658] Appendix II, no. 1.

[659] Hemberg, 231-33.

[660] E. Visser, *Götter und Kulte im Ptolemäischen Alexandrien* (Amsterdam 1938) 19; H. I. Bell, "Popular Religion in Graeco-Roman Religion," *JEA* 34 (1948) 85, and *Cults and Creeds in Graeco-Roman Egypt* (Liverpool 1937) 17.

[661] Visser, *ibid.*, 19.

[662] For example, D.S. 4.43.1-2.

⁶⁶³ Delos and Fasilar, Appendix I, nos. 26-28, 55.

⁶⁶⁴ For the Dioskouroi in Egypt, see Visser (*supra*, note 660) 17-18, 83-84; Bell, *Cults and Creeds*, 17. Cf. E. Bernard, *Recueil des inscriptions grecques du Fayoum* (Leiden 1975) 145-48, no. 74.

⁶⁶⁵ *IG* XII (8), no. 206 (11 B.C.-A.D. 46). L. Robert, *Gnomon* 35 (1963) 65 n. 7, says that the four Alexandrians on this inscriptions have typical Egyptian names. The Samothracian initiate from Arsinoe on *IG* XII (8), no. 184, is probably from Lycia. See Robert, "Arsinoè de Kéos," *Hellenica* 11-12 (1960) 157.

⁶⁶⁶ Fraser, *Samothrace* 3.2, 10 n. 39.

⁶⁶⁷ T. Rönne and P. M. Fraser, "A Hadra-vase in the Ashmolean Museum," *JEA* 39 (1953) 88-89, distinguishing between *theoros* (religious envoy) and *presbutes* (political envoy).

⁶⁶⁸ "Zu dem neuen Mysterieneide," *APF* 12 (1934-37) 66-67.

⁶⁶⁹ Hemberg, 232 n. 6.

⁶⁷⁰ Appendix I, nos. 20-21 (Methymna), 35-38 (Rhodes), 43 (Syme), 48 (Teos), 53 (Rhodian *peraia*). I exclude two inscriptions which Hemberg associates with the worship of the Samothracian gods in the area of Rhodes, *IG* XII (1), nos. 162 and 913, because neither actually mentions the Samothracian gods or Samothrakiastai. See also *RE* V (Suppl.) 834, unpublished.

⁶⁷¹ Appendix I, no. 48.

⁶⁷² Hemberg, 238.

⁶⁷³ Appendix I, no. 20.

⁶⁷⁴ *ibid.*, no. 21.

⁶⁷⁵ Poland (*supra*, note 540) 456.

⁶⁷⁶ Appendix I, nos. 35-38, 43, 53. See *supra*, note 670.

⁶⁷⁷ Appendix I, 33-34, 40-42.

⁶⁷⁸ Poland (*supra*, note 540) 521.

⁶⁷⁹ Hemberg, 236.

⁶⁸⁰ Appendix I, no. 35.

⁶⁸¹ O. Rubensohn, *Die Mysterienheiligtümer in Eleusis und Samothrake*, 235; Appendix I, no. 38a.

⁶⁸² Poland (*supra*, note 540) 7, 74, does not commit himself to either interpretation. Hemberg, 236, does not follow Rubensohn. A. Maiuri, *Nuova silloge epigrafica di Rodi e Cos* (Florence 1925) 53, does. Cf. Appendix I, no. 38a, for sailors.

⁶⁸³ F. Hiller von Gaertringen, "Die Samothrakischen Götter in Rhodos und Karpathos," *MDAI (A)* 18 (1893) 386.

⁶⁸⁴ Appendix I, no. 36.

⁶⁸⁵ *ibid.*, no. 37.

⁶⁸⁶ *ibid.*, no. 38.

⁶⁸⁷ *ibid.*, no. 43.

⁶⁸⁸ *ibid.*, no. 53; P. M. Fraser and G. E. Bean, *The Rhodian Peraia and Islands* (Oxford 1954) 62-63.

CHAPTER SIX

⁶⁸⁹ Plu. *Marc.* 30.6.

⁶⁹⁰ Fraser, *Samothrace* 2.1, 15, commenting on the passage from Plutarch, says, "although the truth of this statement need not be doubted, the event which it records may well have been isolated, and no great significance should be attached to it."

⁶⁹¹ Livy 45.5.1-6.2.

⁶⁹² Plb. 29.8.8.

⁶⁹³ Livy 45.5.5-6.

⁶⁹⁴ *ibid.*, 45.5.3: sacram hanc insulam et augusti totam atque inviolati soli esse.

⁶⁹⁵ *ibid.*, 45.5.4; *supra*, note 254.

⁶⁹⁶ Hemberg, 119.

⁶⁹⁷ The earliest known Latin inscription from the sanctuary records the initiation of one of the Iuventii Thalnae, a family of some prominence in Rome in the first half of the second century B.C., *Samothrace* 2.1, no. 25. Fraser reads the name as Ḷ. Iu(v)entius. M. [fil.] Thalna. I saw the stone in 1976. It is cracked precisely where the vertical hasta of L would have to be. Charles

Edson, in an unpublished paper, suggests that the first initial should be read as P and that the initial of the father's name should be read as M', identifying the initiate as P. Iuventius Thalna who was sent to Macedonia in 148 B.C. to put down the insurrection of Andriskos. Given the poor condition of the stone, it is impossible to determine, however, the initial, and therefore impossible to confirm the identification.

⁶⁹⁸ J. Hatzfeld, *Les trafiquants italiens dans l'Orient hellénique* (Paris 1919) 60-62 and 248.

⁶⁹⁹ Fraser, *Samothrace* 2.1, 12, 15-16.

⁷⁰⁰ Lib. *Or.* 4.356 (Reiske); Mylonas, *Eleusis and the Eleusinian Mysteries*, 247.

⁷⁰¹ *Samothrace* 2.1, no. 63.

⁷⁰² *IG* XII (8), no. 232, where he is called ἀνθύπατος Μακεδονίας. See also *MP*, 63, no. 584; *RAEM* I, 67-69; cf. *MRR* II, 17 and 19 n. 2.

⁷⁰³ *IG* XII (8), no. 241, where he is called στρατηγὸς ἀνθύπατος Ῥωμαῖος; for this expression as the Greek translation for "proconsul", see H. J. Mason, *Greek Terms for Roman Institutions* (American Studies in Papyrology 13; Toronto 1974) 106, 160-61.

⁷⁰⁴ Cf. Lysimachos, *IG* XII (8), no. 150; Hippomedon, *Samothrace* 2.1, App. I.

⁷⁰⁵ *Samothrace* 2.1, no. 18; *RAEM* I, 103-21; *MP* 73, no. 677; *MRR* II, 201-202.

⁷⁰⁶ H. Bloch, "L. Calpurnius Piso Caesoninus in Samothrace and Herculaneum," *AJA* 44 (1940) 487.

⁷⁰⁷ Cic. *Pis.* 89.

⁷⁰⁸ *supra*, note 706, 488.

⁷⁰⁹ *Samothrace* 2.1, 57.

⁷¹⁰ Varro is the ultimate source: Tert. *Nat.* 1.10.17, *Apol.* 6.8; Arn. 2.73.

⁷¹¹ *Samothrace* 2.1, no. 34, recording the initiation of two freedmen, is the only exception.

⁷¹² R. Pettazzoni, "Una rappresentazione romana dei Kabiri di Samotracia," *Ausonia* 3 (1908) 79-90, suggested that a relief showing four gods, from the monument of the Haterii in Rome, represents the Samothracian gods. His proposal is treated with some reservation by P. Lehmann, *Samothrace* 3.1, 325-27, but accepted by U. Bianchi, *The Greek Mysteries* (Leiden 1976) 30, no. 58. Even if this identification can eventually be sustained, the existence of such a monument does not imply that the Samothracian gods were worshipped as such in Italy. The relief indicates the interest of but a single individual or a single family. There are similar problems with a relief from a Roman sarcophagus which K. Lehmann illustrates in *Samothrace* 3.2, 28, fig. 353. For other negative evidence, see Kern, *RE* X, s.v. "Kabeiros und Kabeiroi," 1449.

⁷¹³ *infra*, 100-103.

⁷¹⁴ R. Syme, *The Roman Revolution* (Oxford 1960) 135, 149.

⁷¹⁵ *IG* XII (8), no. 214; *MP*, 143, no. 1281; *RAEM* II, 155-56.

⁷¹⁶ *CIL* VI, no. 1524; *PIR*¹ III, 237, no. 470; Fluss, *RE* II 4, s.v. "P. Sextius Lippinus Tarquitianus," 2049, no. 28.

⁷¹⁷ The enigmatic *popiis* in line 6 of Cyriacus' transcription, read as *p[r]o piis* by Fredrich, is taken by Dessau, *ILS*, no. 4055, to be *[e]pop[te]s*.

⁷¹⁸ *Samothrace* 2.1, no. 50; Fraser, 102, suggests that the inscription is "probably not later than Hadrianic."

⁷¹⁹ There is a mistake in Fraser's transcription of the names on the stone. Line 4 should read: C. Modius Asclepeades, a name which is clear in the photograph. This error was noticed in reviews by F. R. Walton, *AJPh* 84 (1963) 99 and T. B. Mitford, *JHS* 82 (1962) 77.

⁷²⁰ *Samothrace* 2.1, no. 51. Unfortunately only the top part of the stone survives, so Fraser's conjecture that this official was in fact from Macedonia cannot be tested; see *RAEM* II, 160.

⁷²¹ *PIR*¹ III, 80, no. 566; *RAEM* II, 160-61.

⁷²² *Samothrace* 2.1, no. 53, where he appears as [Q. Pla]nius Sardus Varius Ambibulus.

⁷²³ *ILS*, no. 9486, where the name is read: Q. Planio Sardo...../ Ambibulo. Groag, *PIR*², III, 68, no. 5, thinks that this inscription refers to the man on the Samothracian inscription. See also *RAEM* II, 80-81.

⁷²⁴ J. R. McCredie, *Hesperia* 34 (1965) 114-15.

⁷²⁵ *Samothrace* 2.1, no. 53*bis*.

⁷²⁶ *Mith.* 63.

⁷²⁷ Plu. *Sull.* 26.

⁷²⁸ Plu. *Luc.* 13.1-2.

[729] For Varro's trip to the Aegean, see *De Re Rust.* 2, praef. 6; Bloch (*supra*, note 706) 489.

[730] Nep. *Att.* 11.2.

[731] For a Roman dedication at Delos to the Samothracian gods, see Appendix I, no. 29.

[732] *CII* III, no. 713 = *CIL* I², no. 663.

[733] *IG* XII (8), no. 206.

[734] *ibid.*, no. 207; *Samothrace* 2.1, nos. 31, 33(a)II, 36.

[735] *Samothrace* 2.1, no. 34.

[736] For Greek female initiates unaccompanied by men: *IG* XII (8), nos. 178, 218. 220a.1, 220a.4-7.

[737] *Samothrace* 2.1, no. 28a.

[738] The family of the Cornelii Lentuli was very prominent in Roman politics in the first two centuries B.C. This particular individual, son of Lucius, does not seem to be early enough to be identified with L. Cornelius L. f. n. Lentulus, consul in 199 B.C. See A. Samuel, *Greek and Roman Chronology*, 263. Another member of this family appears on a new list found at Samothrace in 1971. See J. M. McCredie, *Hesperia* 48 (1979) 17, where his name is wrongly read as Qu. M. Cn. Lentul[us]. The inscription should be read: mystae piei/qum Cn. Lentul[o], taking *qum* for *quom*. For the family, see G. V. Sumner, *The Orators in Cicero's Brutus: Prosopography and Chronology* (Toronto 1973) 143.

[739] *Samothrace* 2.1, no. 31 (99 or 44 B.C.); *CIL* III, no. 713 = I², no. 663 (92 B.C.); *Samothrace* 2.1, no. 32 (76 B.C.); *IG* XII (8), no. 173 (66 B.C.); *CIL* III, no. 12320 = I², no. 669 (50 or 49 B.C.); *Samothrace* 2.1, no. 33 (46 B.C.); *Samothrace* 2.1, no. 34 (35 B.C.). The eighth inscription, *IG* XII (8), no. 207, is dated according to the consulship of Julius Caesar and could therefore be from 59, 48, 46, 45, or 44 B.C.

[740] *Samothrace* 2.1, no. 31 (99 or 44 B.C.).

[741] *ibid.*, no. 33(a)II.

[742] *ibid.*, 87.

[743] Cic. *Att.* 4.16.1; D. R. Shackleton Bailey, *Cicero's Letters to Atticus* (Cambridge 1965) II, 200, suggests that Paccius had been the guest of Atticus on his way back to Italy.

[744] *IG* XII (8), nos. 178, 220; *supra*, 41-42.

[745] *IG* XII (8), no. 207 = *ILLRP* I, no. 212.

[746] The name of Ofatulena is known from an inscription from Foruli, *CIL* IX, no. 4417.

[747] The woman named Antonia in Samothrace 2.1, no. 31, is apparently a *liberta*.

[748] These names do not appear to be later insertions. Perhaps the Greeks were among the crew which brought the family to Samothrace.

[749] *Samothrace* 2.1, no. 36.

[750] *CIL* III, no. 713 = I², no. 663 = *ILLRP*, no. 210. For the business enterprises of the Lucceii in Rome, Rhegium and on Delos, see J. D'Arms, *Commerce and Social Standing in Ancient Rome* (Cambridge, Mass. 1981) 64.

[751] Degrassi, *ILLRP*, 137.

[752] J. Hatzfeld (*supra*, note 698) 60.

[753] *Samothrace* 2.1, no. 32; see Fraser, 85.

[754] *Att.* 1.1.2.; cf. *RE* XXX, s.v. "Minucius," no. 60.

[755] *RE, ibid.*, no. 66.

[756] *ibid.*, no. 67; *MMR* II, 115, 238.

[757] *CIL* I², no. 1339.

[758] *ID*, no. 1687.

[759] *Samothrace* 2.1, no. 34; Walton (*supra*, note 719) 99, points out that Fraser's square brackets in the first name, line 6, should be deleted.

[760] *Samothrace* 2.1, no. 16.

[761] *IG* XII (8), no. 205.

[762] For the term Ῥωμαῖος used indiscriminately for all residents of Italy, see Hatzfeld (*supra*, note 698) 245-46.

[763] *Samothrace* 3.2, 12 n. 53.

[764] *SIG*³, no. 1053 n. 5.

[765] Cf. [Dem.] 59.21 for an owner paying a slave's initiation fee at Eleusis.

[766] *CIL* III, no. 721.

[767] J. Hatzfeld, "Les italiens résidant à Délos," *BCH* 36 (1912) 60 and *supra*, note 698, 61.

[768] *IG* XII (8), no. 190a.5.

[769] *BCH* 23 (1899) 65; W. Schulze, *Zu Geschichte lateinischer Eigennamen* (Berlin 1904) 132. According to Hatzfeld (*supra*, note 698) 386, the family also appears at Naxos, Paros, Amorgos, Athens, and Gortyn.

[770] *CIL* III, no. 12318 = I², no. 665.

[771] P. Foucart, "Inscriptions du Pirée," *BCH* 6 (1882) 279, no. 3.

[772] *IG* XII (8), no. 189c. Rubensohn, *Die Mysterienheiligtümer in Eleusis und Samothrake*, 227-31, shows how Cestius' named was inscribed.

[773] *Flac.* 31.

[774] *IPrien*, no. 112; cf. Hatzfeld (*supra*, note 698) 62.

[775] *Att.* 5.13.1.

[776] *Samothrace* 2.1, no. 29.

[777] *CIL* X, no. 545; *Samothrace* 2.1, 82.

[778] For a summary of important Roman dedications in Greece in the second century B.C., see M. Guarducci, "Le offerte dei conquistatori Romani ai santuari della Grecia," *RPAA* 13 (1937) 41-58.

[779] *Trist.* 1.10.19-22.

[780] Tac. *Ann.* 2.54.

[781] *ibid.*, 15.50 and 71.

[782] F. Salviat, "Addenda samothraciens," *BCH* 86 (1962) 278-79.

[783] First century A.D.: *IG* XII (8), no. 214 (A.D. 14); *Samothrace* 2.1, no. 36 (A.D. 19); *CIL* III, no. 12321 (A.D. 48); *IG* XII (8), no. 215 (A.D. 65); *BCH* 86 (1962) 278-79, no. 5 (A.D. 65); *Samothrace* 2.1, no. 40 (A.D. 66 or 77).
Second century A.D.: *Samothrace* 2.1, no. 51 (A.D. 116); *Samothrace* 2.1, no. 53 (A.D. 124); *Samothrace* 2.1, no. 54 (A.D. 131); *CIL* III, no. 720 (A.D. 136); *Hesperia* 34 (1965) 114-15 (A.D. 165 or 166).

[784] *CIL* III, Suppl., no. 7370 (= *IG* XII (8), no. 210), dated before 8 B.C. because it gives the numerical name for the month of August, changed from Sextilis to Augustus in that year; see Samuel (*supra*, note 738) 155 n. 6. The inscription could be from the Republican period, the date 8 B.C. being simply a *terminus ante quem*. The other inscription is *IG* XII (8), no. 206, dated between 11 B.C. and A.D. 46.

[785] First century A.D.: *Samothrace* 2.1, nos. 38 (lines 1-4), 39, 44. Second century A.D.: *Samothrace* 2.1, nos. 50, 52, 53*bis*.

[786] *Samothrace* 2.1, no. 36.

[787] *IG* XII (8), no. 207.

[788] *ibid.*, no. 216.

[789] *AJA* 44 (1940) 356-57.

[790] *Samothrace* 2.1, 91.

[791] *IG* XII (8), no. 173.

[792] *ibid.*, no. 206.

[793] His position toward the end of the list is consistent with *IG* XII (8), no. 205 where the ship's commander is listed after the other initiates. Because people had to arrive by boat, it must have been common for passengers on the same boat to be initiated together. One fragmentary inscription, *Samothrace* 2.1, no. 19, seems to have been erected by passengers from one boat. Fraser believes it to be a dedication, but Walton, (*supra*, note 719) 99, suggests that it is an initiate list.

[794] Rhoimetalkes is also mentioned on an unpublished initiate list at Samothrace, inv. no. 71.961.

[795] Hatzfeld (*supra*, note 698) 61.

[796] E. Kornemann, *Kaiser Hadrian* (Leipzig 1905) 49-50.

[797] *HA, Had.* 13.1.

[798] *IG* XII (8), no. 243.

[799] *supra*, note 797, 13.1.

[800] *Samothrace* 2.1, no. 53 = *CIL* III Suppl., no. 7371.

[801] Fredrich, *IG* XII (8), 39; Hemberg, 72 n. 2. Even before the discovery of the new fragment, T. Mommsen, *CIL* III Suppl., 1329, questioned the association of Hadrian with this inscription,

suggesting *regibus Iov[e et Iunone]* for Hirschfeld's *regibus Iov[e et Aug(usto)]*; Mommsen's
reading is accepted by B. W. Henderson, *Life and Principate of the Emperor Hadrian* (London
1923) 289-90.

[802] Roman interest in Delphi probably goes back to the early fourth century B.C. See H. W.
Parke and D. E. W. Wormell, *A History of the Delphic Oracle* (Oxford 1956) 267-68. Romans
appear occasionally in Delphic inscriptions of the third century B.C. and regularly among Delphic
proxenoi of the second century B.C. See G. Daux, *Delphes au IIᵉ et au Iᵉʳ siècle* (Paris 1936)
586-89. A Roman receives *proxenia* at Delos between 241 and 232 B.C., *IG* XI (4), no. 642. The
earliest Latin dedication in a Greek sanctuary is a dedication to Athena at Lindos, *ILind*, no. 92
(*ca.* 250 B.C.).

[803] Guarducci (*supra*, note 778), 41-58.

[804] For the myth of the Penates, see G. Wissowa, "Die Überlieferung über die römischen
Penaten," *Hermes* 22 (1886) 29-57 (= *Gesammelte Abhandlungen zur römischen Religions- und
Stadtgeschichte* [Munich 1904] 95-128); J. Perret, *Les origines de la légende troyenne de Rome*
(Paris 1942); A. J. Kleywegt, *Varro über die Penaten und die „Grossen Götter"* (Amsterdam
1972).

[805] *FGrHist* 4 F 23.

[806] D.H. 1.68.2-4.

[807] F. Jacoby, *RE* X, 1748, s.v. Kallistratos, no. 39, suggests that the Kallistratos mentioned by
Dionysios is the Greek freedman, Domitius Callistratus who had been captured in 7 B.C. in one
of the campaigns against Mithridates, taken to Rome, and later freed.

[808] *FGrHist* 4 F 31 (Hellanikos).

[809] Mac. *Sat.* 3.4.7; see Wissowa (*supra*, note 804) 107.

[810] Mac., ibid; Serv. *in Aen.* 1.378.

[811] *Cam.* 20.6.7.

[812] 1.69.3-4.

[813] The two traditions were originally distinguished by Wissowa (*supra*, note 804) 105-108.

[814] Serv. *in Aen.* 1.378 = *HRR* I, 99-100, no. 6.

[815] Schol. Ver. *in Aen.* 2.717 = *HRR* I, 99, no. 5.

[816] Serv. *in Aen.* 3.287.

[817] Verg. *Aen.* 3.12, etc.

[818] Kleywegt (*supra*, note 804) 22.

[819] D.H. 1.68.2; Serv. *in Aen.* 3.12.

[820] *De Ling. Lat.* 5.10.58.

[821] Kleywegt (*supra*, note 804) 38-45.

[822] *De Civ. Dei* 7.28.

[823] Serv. *in Aen.* 3.12, 3.264, 8.679; Serv. Dan. *in Aen.* 2.196.

[824] Serv. *in Aen.* 3.264 and 8.679, with no reference to an earlier source.

[825] *supra*, notes 800-801.

[826] J. Oliver, "Latin Inscription from Samothrace," *AJA* 43 (1939) 465.

[827] *IG* XII (8), nos. 156A.21 (= *Samothrace* 2.1, Appendix 1A.21), 158.15, 153.11.

[828] Livy 45.5.6.

[829] *Samothrace* 2.1, 16.

[830] But see the tombstones erected for their children by a freedman and freedwoman, husband
and wife, apparently Samothracian initiates, *CIL* VI, nos. 5527-28.

[831] *Samothrace* 2.1, nos. 36 (twenty slaves), 44 (at least ten slaves), 53*bis* (at least sixteen
slaves); *CIL* III Suppl., no. 7373 (possibly twenty names, apparently slaves).

[832] It may have been considered advantageous to have others who travelled as passengers on the
same ship be initiated.

[833] Cornelius Lentulus, *legatus, Samothrace* 2.1, no. 28a.

APPENDIX I

INSCRIPTIONS WHICH MENTION Θεοὶ Σαμόθρακες, Θεοὶ οἱ ἐν Σαμοθράκῃ, Σαμοθράκια, or Σαμοθρακιασταί.

1. OLBIA

Statue base of dun-colored marble. H: 0.35m. W: 0.71m. Dated by letter forms to the second century B.C.
IAOSPE IV¹ (1901) no. 27.

> Εὐβίοτος ᾿Αρίστωνος
> ᾿Επικράτη<ν> Νικηράτου
> τὸν θεῖον
> θεοῖς τοῖς ἐν Σαμοθράικη[ι]
> ἱερησάμενον.

2. OLBIA

Three fragments of a white marble disk. Inscription carved along the edge, 0.017m. in height. Height of letters, 0.01-0.12m. Third century B.C. Found in Olbia in 1924 at excavation A, temple of Apollo. Preserved in the Nikolaevsky Provincial Museum of Regional Studies.

Blavatskaja, *MIA* 103 (1962) 252, no. 2; *IOlb*, no. 67.

> [᾿Ανθεσ?]τήριος θεοῖ[ς ἐ]ν Σα[μοθράικηι].

3. ISTROS

Fragment of a marble stele. H: 0.145m. W: 0.12m. Found at Istros, now lost. Dated to the end of the third or beginning of the second century B.C. (Pârvan).

Pârvan, *Histria* 4 (*Analele Academiei Romana* 38, 1915-16) 543-45, no. 4; Pippidi, *Histria* 1 (1954) 494-95; *Studii şi Cercetari* 5 (1954) 431-47, no. 186; *Contribuţii la Istoria veche a Romîniei* (1958) 49-50; *SEG* 16 (1959) no. 430.

> - - - - - - - - - - - - -
> καὶ ε[ὐνοίας τῆς εἰς τὸν]
> [δ]ῆμον· [ἀναγράψαι δὲ τόδε τὸ]
> ψήφισμα [εἰς στήλην τοὺς]
> ἡγεμόνας [καὶ ἀναθεῖναι]
> 5 ἐν τῶι Σαμο[θρακίωι]·
> [τ]ὸ ἐσόμενον [ἀνάλωμα δο]-

[ῡν]αι δὲ τοὺ[ς οἰκονόμους· πέμ]-
[ψαι] δὲ αὐ[τῶι καὶ ξένια τοὺς]
[οἰκονόμους - - - - - - - - -]

4. ISTROS

Two fragments of a marble stele. H: 0.75m. W: 0.43m. D: 0.16m. Second century B.C. Location: Museum at Histria (Romania), inv. no. 325.

Pippidi, *Dacia* n.s. 5 (1961) 308 and fig. 1; Robert, *REG* 76 (1963) 156-57, no. 169; Pippidi, *StudClas* 7 (1965) 186-91, no. 5 and pl. 3; Robert, *REG* 79 (1966) 401-02, no. 273; Pippidi, *Contribuţii la Istoria veche a Romîniei*[2] (1967) 242-59 and fig. 9; *SEG* 24 (1969) no. 1099; Pippidi, *Scythia Minora* (Bucharest 1975) 111-20.

- -
[.τῆ]ι πόλει ΕΙΑ.ΣΑΙ τὸν εὐεργέ[την· ἐφ'οἷς αὐ]-
[τὸ]ν ἐτίμησεν ὁ δῆμος τιμαῖς [ταῖς καθηκού]-
[σ]αις· νυνί τε χρείαν ἐχούσης τ[ῆς πόλεως χρ]-
[η]μάτων, ὅπως ὑπάρξηι σίτ[ου παράθεσις εἰς τρο]-
5 [φὴ]ν καὶ σωτηρία[ν] τοῦ δήμου, ἐπε[λθὼν ἐπὶ τὴ]-
[ν β]ουλὴν καὶ τὴν ἐκλη[σ]ί[α]ν [ἐ]πηγ[γείλατο]
[χρ]υσοῦς χιλίους εἰς ἐνιαυτόν, ἐπιδ[οὺς καὶ τὸν]
[τ]όκον τὸν γινόμενον τῶι δήμωι ε[ἰς ἐπευω]-
[ν]ισμὸν τοῦ σίτου [τ]οῦ ἀγορασθη[σομένου δι]-
10 [ὰ] τῆς ἐπαγγελίας· δεδόχθαι τῶ[ι δήμωι ἐ]-
παινέσαι Διονύσιον Στρουθίων[ος τοῦ...]
[...]ς, καὶ ἀναγράψαι εὐεργέτην τοῦ [δήμου]·
[στ]ῆσαι δὲ αὐτοῦ καὶ εἰκόνα χαλκῆ[ν ἐν τῆι]
[ἀγο]ρᾶι παρὰ τὸν Δῆμον καὶ τὰς εἰκόν[ας τὰς]
15 [τῶν...]ΥΣΑ...ΤΩ[.· τὸ] δὲ ἀνάλ[ωμα δοῦναι]
[μὲν τὸν οἰκονόμο]ν, [μερίσα]ι δ[ὲ τ]οὺς μερ[ιστάς].
- - - - - - - - - - - - - - - - - -ΙΟ- - - - -
- - -ΟΣ- - - - - - - -ΑΣΙΝ- - - - -Α[- - - αὐτ]-
ῶι ἀρετῆς ἕνεκεν καὶ εὐνο[ία]ς τῆς [εἰς τὸν δ]-
20 ῆμον· δεδόσθαι δὲ αὐτῶι καὶ ἐκγόν[οις ἀεὶ]
[τῶ]ι πρεσβυτάτ[ω]ι τῶν ὄντων ἱερωσύ[νην δη]-
[μ]οσίαι θεῶν τῶν ἐν Σαμοθράικηι καὶ στε[φανη]-
φορίαν καθάπερ καὶ τοῖς ἄλλοις ἱερεῦ[σιν, ὅπως]
καὶ οἱ λοιποὶ φι[λ]οτιμό[τεροι] γ[ίν]ωνται εἰδό[τες]
25 ὅτι ὁ δῆ[μος] τιμᾶι [τ]οὺ[ς ἀγ]αθοὺς τῶν ἀν[δρῶν],
ἀποδιδ[οὺ]ς χάριτ[ας ἀξία]ς τῶν εὐεργ[ετημά]-
των· ἀναγράψαι δ[ὲ τ]οὺς ἡ[γ]εμόνας [τὸ ψήφισ]-
μα τόδε ἐπὶ μὲν τοῦ παρ[ό]ν[τ]ος εἰς [τελαμῶ]-
να λευκοῦ λίθου καὶ [στ]ῆσα[ι] παρὰ τὸ[ν βωμὸν]

30 [τ]ῶν θε[ῶν] τῶν ἐν Σα[μ]οθ[ρά]ικηι· σταθ[έντος δὲ]
[τ]οῦ ἀνδριάν[τ]ος καὶ εἰς τὴν [β]άσιν το[ῦ ἀνδριάν]-
[το]ς· ἀν[αγορεῦσα]ι τὸ ψήφισμα καὶ Ε - - - - - - - -
- - - - - - - - - - - ΟΝΟΕ- - - - - καὶ· - - - - - - - -
- -

5. Istros

Two pieces of a stele. H: (together) 0.44m. W: (upper piece) 0.29m., (lower piece) 0.31m. Found at Istros, now in museum. Inv. nos. B147 and B268. Second century B.C.

Lambrino, *Istros* I (1934) 122-23, with plate; Robert, *REG* 68 (1955) 241, no. 163.

[- - - - - - - - -παρ]ε̣χόμενος
[- - - - - - - -]νῦν [....] πάλιν
[- - - - - - -] ΣΙ χρήματα [γι]νομ[έ]-
[να........] ο̣ς [.] τοῖς ἀπ᾽ ἀρχῆς ὑφ᾽ ἑα[υ]τ̣οῦ
5 [- - - - - - -] ὅπως αἱ φυλαὶ γίνωνται
[- - - - - κατ᾽] ἐνιαυτὸν ἡμέραν ἐπώ-
[νυμον αὐτο]ῦ̣ τὴν συναγωγὴν ποιουμέ-
[ναι ἀπὸ τῶν γ]ινομένων προσόδων ἐκ
[- - - - - - τ]ῶν δεδομένων ὑπ᾽ αὐτοῦ δι-
10 [αφόρων· τ]ύ[χ]ηι ἀγαθῆι· δεδόχθαι ταῖς φυ-
[λαῖς· ἐπα]ιν[έσ]αι μὲν ἐπὶ τούτοις Μένισ-
[χον.....] ἄ[ν]δρα καλὸν καὶ ἀγαθὸν γεγε-
[νημένο]ν κ[αὶ] παρ᾽ ὅλον τὸν βίον εὐεργε-
[σίας π]αρ[εχό]μενον πρὸς τοὺς πολίτ-
15 [ας]· ἄγε[ιν] δ[ὲ] αὐτοῦ καὶ ἡμέραν καθ᾽ ἕκασ-
[τ]ο[ν] ἐνια[υ]τὸ[ν], μηνὸς Ἀνθεστηριῶνος
[δ]ωδεκά[τ]η[ν, ἐν] ἧ θύσαντες τοῖς θεοῖς ἀ-
[γ]ουσιν τὴν [σ]ύνοδον ἀπὸ τῶν μεμερισ-
[μ]ένων δ[ι]αφ[ό]ρων καὶ στεφανώσουσιν
20 [αὐτ]ὸν χρυσ[ῶ]ι στεφάνωι ἀρετῆς ἕνε-
χ̣εν καὶ εὐνο[ί]ας τῆς εἰς τὰς φυλὰς· ἐπιμε-
[λ]έσθαι δὲ τῆ[ς] συνόδου καὶ τῆς ἀναγο-
[ρε]ύσεως το[ῦ στεφ]άνο[υ τοὺς κ]α[τ᾽ ἔ]-
[τος αἱ]ρουμένους ἐπισκόπο[υ]ς, ἀποσ-
25 [.......]α̣ι̣ [δ]ὲ αὐτῶι καὶ τ[οῖς] ἀπογόνοις
[αὐ]τοῦ ἐν ταῖς σ[υνόδοις τ]αύταις τὰ γέρα
[κα]θάπερ καὶ τοῖς ἱερεῦσιν· ὅς δ᾽ ἄν εἴπη ἤ (ἐ)πιμη-
[νι]εύση τοῦ ἀρθῆναι τὴν σύνοδον ἤ μὴ ἐπιτε̣-
[λ]έσωσιν τά ἱερὰ οἱ ἐπίσκοποι ἤ μὴ στεφανώ-

30 [σωσ]ιν τὸν εὐεργέτην ἀποτεισάτωσα[ν]
   [ταῖς] φυλαῖς χρυσοῦς πέντε καὶ ἔστωσ[αν]
   [ἱερόσ]υλοι· τὸ δὲ ψήφισμα τόδε ἀναγραφῆ[ναι]
   [εἰς τ]ελαμῶνα λευκοῦ λίθου καὶ ἀνατ[εθῆ]-
   ναι ἐν τῶι Σαμοθρακίωι.

6. Tomis

Marble plaque, broken at top and on left side.

Gomperz and Točilescu, *AEMÖ* 6 (1883) 8-9; Herbrecht, *Dissertationes Philologicae Argentoratenses* 10 (1886) 45, no. 2; *Recueil*, no. 704; *LGS* II, 247-48, no. 84; Roussel, *BCH* 50 (1926) 313-17; Robert, *BCH* 59 (1935) 433; Stoian, *Tomitana* (1962) 75-79 and pl. xi; *LSCG*, 173-75, no. 87.

Column I

   - - - - - - - - - - - - - - - - - - -
   - - - - - - - - - - - - - - - - - - -
   - - - - - - - - - - - - - - - - - - -
   - - - - - - - - - - - - - - - - - - -
5 - - - - - - - - - - - - - - - - - - -
   - - - - - - - - - - - - - - - - - - -
   - - - - - - - - - - - - - - - - - - -
   [- - - - - - - -] ν ἐπὶ τ[ούτ]-
   [οις - - - - - - εἰκόνα χαλ]κῆν ἐν τῶι
10 [ἱερῶι - - - - - - - -]ν· ὁ δῆμος
   [- - - - - - - - - ἔπαι]νος, στεφά-
   [νωσις τῶν γραπτῶν εἰκόν]ων καθ' ἑκάσ-
   [την θυσίαν, ἃ αὐτῶι ὑπάρξ]ει καὶ μεταλ-
   [λάξαντι τὸν βίον· αὐτός] τε Διαγόρας
15 [- - - - - - - - - - - - - -]έαυτῶι

Column II

   [Αγαθῆ Τύχ]η· ὁ πριάμενος τὴν ἱερω-
   [σύνην τῶ]ν μυστῶν θεῶν τῶν ἐν
   [Σαμοθρά]κη ἱερήσεται διὰ βίο[υ καὶ]
   ['Απατου]ρεῶνος ἑβδόμη παρ[έξει]
5 [τὰ ξύλ]α σχίζας καὶ ἐγχέει [τὸν οἶ]-
   [νον τοῖ]ς μύσταις καὶ πομπε[ύσει]
   [...π]αρ' αὐτοῦ· στεφανωθήσεται
   [παρὰ] τῶν μυστῶν φιλοτιμίας ἕνε-
   [κε]ν τῆς εἰς ἑαυτούς, ἐν ᾗ ἱερᾶται ἡμέ-
10 ρᾳ· συνθύσει δὲ καὶ τοὺς λιβάνους ἐμ
   πάσαις ταῖς συνόδοις μετὰ τοῦ προ-

υπάρχοντος ἱέρεω τῶν μυστῶν καὶ
οἷς ἐπιβάλλει ἐκ τοῦ νόμου· ὑπάρχειν
δὲ αὐτῷ τὸν στέφανον εἰς τὸ κατ' [ἀΐδι]-
15 ον· ἐπρίατο τὴν ἱερωσύνην Τίμ[αιος]
Στράτωνος χρυσῶν ἑπτά, χαλ[κῶν]
ἑξήκοντα οὓς ἔδωκε παραχρ[ῆμα].

7. KALLATIS

Marble fragment. Undated. Found in Mangalia; in museum in Bucharest (1891).
Točiliescu, *AEMÖ* 14 (1891) 35, no. 88; Robert, *RPh* 65 (1939) 152.

[τ]οὺς δὲ π[ροβούλους τοὺς προ]-
βουλεύοντ[ας τὸν μῆνα τὸν Δι]-
ονύσιον ἀ[ποδεῖξαι τόπον]
ἐν τῶι Σαμο[θραικίωι εἰς ὃν ἂν]-
ατεθήσεται - - - - - - - - - -

8. KALLATIS

Marble fragment. Found in Mangalia; in museum in Bucharest (1891).
Točilescu, *AEMÖ* 19 (1896) 110, no. 67.

[μεγάλων θεῶν τῶ]ν ἐν Σαμοθράικηι.

9. KALLATIS

Marble stele, broken on all edges. H: 0.67m. W: 0.35m.
Jirecek-Szanto, *AEMÖ* 10 (1887) 197-200; *SGDI*, no. 3089; *Antike Denkmäler*, no. 94; Robert, *RPh* 65 (1939) 152 = *Opera Minora Selecta* II, 1305.

- -
- - - - - - - - - - - - - - - - - μ ε - - - - -
- - - - - - - - - - - - - - - ος ἀμῶ[ς γέ?]
[πως?]- - - - - - - - - - - - - αν καὶ εκτ[ε?]-
- - - - - - - - - - - - - -να τοῦ δ[άμου]
5 - - - - - - - - - -ὠλιγ]ωρημένων [τῶν ἰ]-
[δίων κοινὰν σωτηρία]ν ὑπερτιθέμ[ενος]
[οὔτε κίνδυνον οὔ]τε κακοπαθίαν [ἐκκλί]-
[νων.....τ]ῶ[ι] δ[ά]μωι τι τῶν ποτὶ - - -
- - - - - -[ἐκ]πονῆσαι, τοῦ τε βασ[ιλέος]
10 - - - -[ἀ]ξι[ωθ]έντος ὑπὸ Ασαβιθ- - - - -
- - - - - ων, ὅπως λύσῃ τὸν ποτὶ Σ- - - -

- - - - ἐνεστακότα πόλεμον, ἐξ ἀπο[κατα]-
[στάσιο?]ς ἐκτενῶς καὶ προθύμως καὶ με[τὰ]
[παρ]ρησίας ἐχρημάτιξεν περὶ τῶν [τᾶς]
15 [π]όλιος δικαίων· ὅπως οὖν καὶ ὁ δᾶ[μος]
[φ]αίνηται τοὺς εὐνοοῦντας ἑαυτῶι κα[ὶ κα]-
[λ]ο[ὺ]ς καὶ ἀγαθοὺς ἄνδρας τιμῶν καθη[κόν]-
[τ]ως, ἐπαινε[ῖσ]θαι μὲν ἐπὶ τούτοις τόν τε [δᾶ]-
[μ]ον τὸν Ἀ[πο]λλωνιατᾶν ἔχοντα τὸν προ[θύ]-
20 μως ἀντιλαμβανόμενον τᾶς Καλλατ[ια]-
νῶν σωτηρίας καὶ Στρατώνακτα Λυ[γδά]-
μι[ο]ς· δεδόχθαι τᾶι βουλᾶι καὶ τῶι δάμ[ωι]
[ἐ]παγγείλασθαι αὐτῶι, ὅτι ὁ δᾶμος ἀ[ποκα]-
[τ]ασταθέντων αὐτῶι τῶν πραγμά[των]
25 [ε]ἰς τὰν ἐξ ἀρχᾶς διάθεσιν καὶ τηροῦν[τος]
[α]ὐτοῦ τὰν αἵρεσιν, ἃν ἔχων διατελεῖ [ποτὶ]
[τ]ὰ κοινά, ἀξίως αὐτὸν ἐπιστραφησε[ῖσθαι]
[τ]ῶν γεγονότων εἰς αὐτὸν εὐεργε[τημά]-
[τ]ων· ἀποστεῖλαι δὲ τοὺς στρατα[γοὺς τὸ]
30 [ἀ]ντίγραφον τοῖς Ἀπολλωνιατᾶν ἄ[ρχουσι]
[κ]αὶ παρ[α]καλέσαι αὐτοὺς τὸν ἔπαι[νον τι]-
[θέ]μεν εἰς τὸ τοῦ Ἀπόλλωνος ἱερὸ[ν τό]-
πον ἐπιτάδειον ἐκλεξαμένο[υς· καλέ]-
[σα]ι δὲ αὐτὸν καὶ τὸν βασιλέα ε[ἰς πρυ]-
35 [τα]νεῖον· τοὺς δὲ προβούλους [τοὺς προ]-
[β]ουλεύοντας τὸν μῆνα τὸν [παρόντα]
[ἀπ]οδεῖξαι τόπον ἐν τ[ῶι Σαμοθραικίωι]
[εἰς] ὃν ἀνατεθησεῖται [τὸ ψάφισμα, εἰς]
[δὲ τελα]μῶν[α ἀναγράψαι καὶ τὸ εἰς]
40 [αὐτὸν] ἀποτε[λέσαι ἀνάλωμα τοὺς - - -]
- - - - - - - - - - - - - - - - - - -

³⁷ τ[ῶι Σαμοθραικίωι] Robert.

10. BIZONE

Marble fragment broken on all sides. H: 0.13m. W: 0.16m. Letters: 0.026m. Second century B.C.

IGBR I², no. 7*ter*.

- - - - - - - - - - -
- - - - - - - - ΧΙΟ -
- - - - - - μενος
[θε]οῖς
[τοῖς ἐν] Σαμοθράιχ[ηι].

11. Dionysopolis

Gray-white marble stele. H: 0.70m. W: 0.46m. Museum at Serdicense, inv. no. 1200.
Latyšev, *Journal Ministerstva narodnogo prosveštenija* (1896) 1-19; *SIG*[1-2], no. 342; *IGRR* I, no. 662; *Antike Denkmäler*, no. 95; *SIG*[3], no. 762; Holleaux *Études*, I, 285-87; *IGBR* I, no. 13; Vidman, *Sylloge*, no. 703.

```
- - - - - - - - - - - - - - αι παρα - - - - - - - - - - -
- - - - - - - - - - - - - - τὸμ ἀνέλαβε - - - - - - - - - -
- - - - - - - - - - - - - ος Θεόδωρον καὶ Ἐπι - - - - - -
- - - - - - - - - - - - - σαν τοῖς ἰδίοις δαπανήμασι[ν- - -]
5       - - - - - - - - - - - - - αιων συναποδ[η]μῶν ἀπή[ρ]ατ[ο- - -]
[- - - - - - - - - - - -εἰ]ς Αργεδαυον πρὸς τὸν πατέρα α[ὐτοῦ?]
[- - - - - - παραγε]νόμενος δὲ καὶ συντυχὼν ἅμα - - - - - -
- - - - - - - - - - - -ν τὴν ἀπ' αὐτοῦ κατεκτήσατο τῆ[ς δὲ]
[- - - - - - - ἀπέ]λυσεν τὸν δῆμον, ἱερεύς τε γενόμεν[ος]
10      [-? τοῦ Θεοῦ Μεγ]άλου τάς τε πομπὰς καὶ τὰς θυσίας [ἐ]-
[πετέλεσε λαμπρ]ῶς καὶ τοῖς πολίταις μετέδωκεν τ[ῶν]
[χρεῶν, τῷ τε Σαρ]άπει λαχὼν ἱερεὺς ὁμοίως τοῖς δαπ[ανή]-
[μασιν ἀνεστράφ]η καλῶς καὶ φιλαγάθως, τοῦ τε ἐπωνύ[μου]
[τῆς πόλεως Διον]ύσου οὐκ ἔχοντος ἱερῆ ἀφ' ἐτῶν πληόγ[ων]
15      [παρακληθεὶς ὑ]πὸ τῶν πολιτῶν ἐπέδωκεν ἑαυτὸν κ[αὶ κα]-
[τὰ τὴν Γαίου] Ἀντωνίου παραχειμασίαν ἀναλαβ[ὼν]
[τὸν στέφανο]ν τοῦ θεοῦ τάς τε πομπὰς καὶ θυσίας [ἐπε]-
[τέλεσε καλ]ῶς καὶ μεγαλομερῶς καὶ τοῖς πολίταις μ[ε]-
[τέδωκε κρε]ῶν ἀφθόνως, θεῶν τε τ[ῶ]ν ἐν Σαμοθράκ[η]
20      [στέφα]νον ἀνειληφὼς διὰ βίου τάς τε πομπὰς χ[αὶ]
[τὰς θυσία]ς ἐπιτελεῖ ὑπέρ τε τῶν μυστῶν καὶ τῆς π[ό]-
[λεως, νεωστ]εί τε τοῦ βασιλέως Βυρεβιστα πρώτου καὶ μ[ε]-
[γίστου γεγ]ονότος τῶν ἐπὶ Θράκης βασιλέων καὶ πᾶσα[ν]
[τὴν πέρ]αν τοῦ ποταμοῦ καὶ τὴν ἐπὶ τάδε κατεισχη-
25      [κότος γ]ενόμενος καὶ πρὸς τοῦτον ἐν τῇ πρώτῃ καὶ με-
[γίστῃ φ]ιλίᾳ τὰ βέλτιστα κατεργάζεται τῇ πατρίδι λέ-
[γων κα]ὶ συμβουλεύων τὰ κράτιστα καὶ τὴν εὔνοιαν τοῦ β[α]-
[σιλέ]ως πρὸς τὴν τῆς πόλεως σωτηρ[ί]αν προσπαραμ[υ]-
[θού]μενος ἔν τε τοῖς λοιποῖς ἅπασιν ἀφειδῶς ἑαυτὸν
30      [ἐν]διδοὺς καὶ τὰς τῆς πόλεως πρεσβήας καὶ κινδύνους ἐπ[ι]-
δεχόμενος [ἀ]όκνως πρὸς τὸ πάντως τι κατεργάζεσθα[ι]
τῇ πατρίδι συμφέρον, πρὸς τε Γναῖον Πομπήϊον Γναίου υ[ἱ]-
ὸν αὐτοκράτορα Ῥωμαῖον ἀποσταλεὶς ὑπὸ βασιλέως Βυραβε[ι]-
[σ]τα πρεσβευτὴς καὶ συντυχὼν αὐτῷ τῆς Μακεδονίας ἐν το[ῖς]
35      περ[ὶ Ἡρ]άκληαν τὴν ἐπὶ τοῦ Λύκου οὐ μόνον τοὺς ὑπὲρ τοῦ βα[σι]-
```

λέως χρηματισμοὺς διέθετο τὴν εὔνο[ι]αν τὴν Ῥωμαίων πα[ρ]-
αγόμενος τῷ βασιλεῖ, ἀ<λ>λὰ καὶ περὶ τῆς πατρίδος τοὺς καλλίστου[ς]
διέθετο χρηματισμούς, καθόλου δὲ κατὰ πᾶσ(α)ν περίστασιν κ[αι]-
[ρ]ῶν ψυχῇ καὶ σώματι παραβαλλόμενος καὶ δαπάναις χρώμ[ε]-

40 νος ταῖς ἐκ τοῦ βίου, τινὰ δὲ καὶ τῶν πολιτικῶν χορηγιῶν σωματ[ο]-
ποιῶν παρ' ἑαυτοῦ τὴν μεγίστην ἐνδείκνυτα[ι] σπουδὴν εἰς τὴν ὑ-
πὲρ τῆς πατρίδος σωτηρίαν· ἵνα οὖν καὶ ὁ δῆμος φαίνηται τιμῶν
τοὺς καλο[ὺ]ς καὶ ἀγαθοὺς ἄνδρας καὶ ἑαυτὸν εὐεργετοῦντας, δε[δό]-
[χθ]α[ι τῇ] βουλῇ καὶ τῷ δήμῳ ἐπῃνῆσθαι μὲν ἐπὶ τούτοις Ἀχορνίων[α]

45 Διον[υ]σίου καὶ στεφανωθῆναι αὐτὸν ἐν τοῖς Διονυσίοις χρυσ[ῷ]
στεφάνῳ καὶ εἰκόνι χαλκῇ, στεφανοῦσθαι δὲ αὐτὸν καὶ εἰς τὸν λ[οι]
[π]ὸν χρ[όν]ον καθ' ἕκαστον ἔτος ἐν τοῖς Διονυσίοις χρυσῷ στε[φά]-
[ν]ῳ, δε...σθαι δὲ αὐτῷ καὶ εἰς ἀνάστασιν ἀνδριάντος τόπον τὸν ἐπιφανέστατον τῆς ἀγορᾶς.

12. Odessos

Decree of Odessos, now lost. Ca. 100 B.C.
CIG II, no. 2056; Mordtmann, *MDAI (A)* 10 (1885) 315, no. 4; *Recueil*, no.
332; *IGBR* I, no. 41.

Ἔδοξε τῆι βουλῆι καὶ τῶι
δήμωι· Κρατισθένης Ζωΐλου
εἶπεν· ἐπειδὴ Ἑρμεῖος Ἀσκληπιοδώρου
Ἀντιοχεὺς διατρίβων παρὰ βασιλεῖ

5 Σκυθῶν Κανιται εὔνουν καὶ πρόθυμον
ἑαυτὸν τῶι δήμωι διατελεῖ [παρεχόμενος]
καὶ ἰδίαι τοῖς ἐντυγχάνουσιν αὐτῶι
τῶν πολιτῶν συμπαρίσταται
σπουδῆς οὐθὲν ἐπιλείπων ἐν πᾶσι

10 τοῖς ἀξιουμένοις· δεδόχθαι τῆι
βουλῆι καὶ τῶι δήμωι δεδόσθαι
αὐτῶι καὶ ἐκγόνοις προξενίαν,
πολιτείαν, προεδρίαν, ἀτέλειαν
χρημάτων πάντων, ὧν ἂν

15 εἰσάγωσι καὶ ἐξάγωσι ἐπὶ κτήσει
καὶ ἐγγείων ἔγκτησιν καὶ δίκας
προδίκους καὶ εἴσπλουν καὶ
ἔκπλουν καὶ πολέμου καὶ εἰρήνης
ἀσυλεὶ καὶ ἀσπονδεί· εἶναι δὲ

20 αὐτοῖς καὶ ἔφοδον ἐπὶ τὴν
βουλὴν καὶ τὸν δῆμον πρώτοις
μετὰ τὰ ἱερά· τὸν δὲ ἱεροποιὸν

ἀναγράψαι τὸ ψήφισμα τοῦτο
εἰς τελαμῶνα καὶ θεῖναι εἰς
25 τὸ ἱερόν [τὸ Σαμοθράκιον].

²⁵ τὸ Σαμοθράκιον Mordtmann.

13. ODESSOS

Marble stele, broken on all sides except lowest edge. H: 0.25m. W: 0.21m. Letters: 0.01m. Museum at Serdicense, inv. no. 3522.

Mordtmann, *MDAI (A)* 10 (1885) 315, no. 4; *Antike Denkmäler*, no. 93 and photo; *IGBR* I, no. 42 and Pl. 14.

- -

[δ]εδόσθαι δ[ὲ αὐτῶι καὶ ἐκγόνοις προξενίαν, πο]-
[λι]τείαν, προεδρίαν, ἰσοτέλ[ειαν χρημάτων πάν]-
[τω]ν, ὧν ἂν εἰσάγωσιν ἢ ἐξά[γωσιν - - - - - ἐ]-
[πὶ κτ]ήσει [καὶ ἐν]γείων ἔνκτη[σιν καὶ δίκας προδί]-
5 [κου]ς κα[ὶ εἴ]σπλουν καὶ ἔκπλου[ν καὶ πολέμου καὶ εἰρή]-
[νη]ς ἀσυλεὶ καὶ ἀσπονδεί· εἶ[ναι δὲ αὐτοῖς καὶ ἔφο]-
[δο]ν ἐπὶ τὴν βουλὴν καὶ τὸν δ[ῆμον πρώτοις μετὰ]
[τὰ ἱερ]ά· τὸν δὲ ἱεροποιὸν ἀν[αγράψαι τὸ ψήφισ]-
[μα τ]όδε εἰς τελαμῶν[α καὶ θεῖναι εἰς ἱερὸν]
10   Σαμοθράκιον.

14. SEUTHOPOLIS

Marble stele, broken in three pieces, containing a total of 37 lines, of which only 8 are published.

D. Dimitrov, *SA* 1 (1957) 202-203 (lines 1-26 and 34-37 in Latin translation), and fig. 2; *Latomus* 28 (1957) 184-93, no. 2 and pl. 31, fig. 1 (photo of lines 27-37); J. and L. Robert, *REG* 72 (1959) no. 255; Danov, *RE* suppl. IX, col. 1376 (German translation); *IGBR* III, no. 1731 (lines 1-26 and 34-37 in Latin translation); *SEG* 24 (1969) no. 937; Dimitrov and Čičikova, *BAR Supplementary Series* 38 (1978) 43 and fig. 31.

1-26 Bona fortuna. Iusiurandum (ὅρκος) a Berenica et filiis eius Epimeni datum. Cum Seutha salvus et sanus (ὑγιαίνων) Epimenem bonaque eius (τὰ ὑπάρχοντα) Spartoco tradidisset et Spartocus Epimeni de his rebus pignus fidei (τὰ πιστά) dedisset, Berenicae et filiis eius Ebryzelmi, Teri, Satoco et Sadalae et nepotibus, qui nascentur, placuit, (10) ut Epimenes bonaque eius tradita Spartoco in vita manerent et Epimenes Spartoco vel iis, quibus ei (= Epimeni Spartocus) iubeat, utilitatem praeberet quantum (maxime) possit. Berenicae filii Epimenem e templo Samothracum deorum educant ea conditione, ut eum nullo modo iniuria afficiant, (20) sed eum bonaque eius Spartoco tradant et si Epimenes eos nulla iniuria afficit, nihil bonorum eius auferant, si autem quid afficere manifestus erit, Spartocus arbiter esto.

27   τὸν δὲ ὅρκον τοῦτον γραφῆναι
     εἰστήλας λιθίνας καὶ ἀνατεθῆναι
     ἐμ μὲγ Καβύληι εἰς τὸ Φωσφόριον καὶ
30   εἰς τὴν ἀγορὰν παρὰ τὸμ βωμὸν τὸν
     τοῦ Ἀπόλλωνος, ἐν δὲ Σευθοπόλει εἰς τὸ
     ἱερὸν τῶν θεῶν τῶν Μεγάλων καὶ
     εἰς τὴν ἀγορὰν ἐν τῶι τοῦ Διονύσου ἱε[ρῶι]
34   παρὰ τὸν βωμόν.

34-37   Religiose iurantibus et iusiurandum conservantibus bonum faustumque sit et Berenica
        iusiurandum pristinum (i.e. a Seutha Epimeni datum) ratum habeat.

15. ALEXANDROUPOLIS (SAMOTHRACIAN PEREIA)

Marble boundary stone. H: 1.09m. W: 0.50m. Letters: 0.05-0.06m. First
century B.C. Found at Alexandroupolis (Dedéagatsch); now in Archaeological museum in Istanbul.
    Seure, *BCH* 24 (1900) 147 and 574; Abbott, *CR* 15 (1901) 84a; *IG* XII (8)
39-40; Roussel, *BCH* 63 (1939) 133-41; McCredie, *Hesperia* 37 (1968) 220-21.
    Plate V(a).

                     Ὅρος
                     ἱερᾶς
                     χώρας
                     Θεῶν
                     τῶν ἐν
                     Σαμο-
                     θράκη.

16. PHILIPPI

Unpublished inscription. Philippi Museum; inv. no. Λ25.
    Fragment of a stele, broken at the top. Local marble. Late third or early
second century B.C.
    List of four *mystai* of the gods in Samothrace.

17. AMPHIPOLIS

Marble votive bas-relief (now built into the wall of the church). H: 0.455m.
W: 0.28m.
    Perdrizet, *BCH* 19 (1895) 110; *SIG³*, no. 1140; Collart and Devambez, *BCH*
55 (1931) 179-80, no. 8.

                     Μ. Καικέλιος
                     Σωτᾶς ὁ χαλκεύς

ἀπὸ τῆς τέχνης
Θεοῖς Μεγάλοις
τοῖς ἐν Σαμοθράκηι.

18. DION

Two inscribed pieces of gray marble. a. H: 0.25m. W: 0.22m. b. H: 0.19m.
W: 0.305m. Letters: 0.011m. 202-197 B.C. Now in museum at Dion. (A new
fragment, discovered in recent excavation, will be published by Demetrios
Pantermalis.)

Oikonomos, Ἐπιγραφαὶ τῆς Μακεδονίας, no. 1; E. Bickerman, *RPh* 65
(1939) 349; Robert, *Hellenica* 10 (1955) 269-70; *Staatsverträge* III, 308-10, no.
549.

a.   - - - - - - - -

　　　　　 - - - - - - -εντω - - - - -

　　　　 - - - συνσφραγι]σάσθωσαν δ[ὲ τὰς ὁμολογίας - - -

　　　　 - - -οἱ] στρατηγοὶ καὶ οἱ - - -

5   - - - εὺς τοῖς δημοσί[οις δακτυλίοις καὶ τῶι ἰδίωι αὐτοῦ ἕκαστος? - - - -

　　　　 - - - - βασιλέα Φίλιππον τ- - - -

　　　　 - - ἀναγραψ]άτω αὐτὴν εἰς τὰ δ[ημόσια γράμματα - -

　　　　 - - τῆι σ]υνθήκηι μήτε Λυσιμαχ[εῖς συμμαχίαν - - -

　　 - - -ποιείσθωσαν] ἐναντίαν τῆι πρὸς βασ[ιλέα Φίλιππον γεγενημένηι? - - -

10   　 - - -μήτε βασιλ]εὺς Φίλιππος συμμαχία[ν ποιείσθω ἐναντίαν τῆι πρὸς

　　　　　　　　　　　　　　　　　　　　　　　　　Λυσιμαχέας - - -

　　　　 - - -γεγενημ]ένηι μένηι· ὅπως δὲ κα[ὶ - - -

　　　　　 - - -ι καὶ τὰ φρούρια καὶ τ[ὰ τείχη? - - -

　　　　　　 - - -θωσαν κοινῆι - - -

　　　　 - - -ἐπαν]ορθοῦν π[άντα? - - -

　　　　　 - - - - - - - -

b.   - - - - - - - -

[- - - - - - - -πε]ρὶ ὅσων κοι[νῆι βουλευ- (?) - - - - - - - - - - - - - - - -]

- - - - - - - -ν Λυσιμαχεῖς- - - - - - - - - - - - - - - - - - -

[- - ὑπὸ] βασιλέως Φιλίππου. βασιλ[ε -]

[πεμφθέντων] πρεσβευτῶν ὑπὸ Λυσιμαχέων. ὀμό[σαι δὲ Λυσιμαχέων μὲν - - -
　　　 - - - -]

5   [τόνδε τὸν ὅρ]κον· ᵛ ὅρκος Λυσιμαχέων· ὀμνύω Δί[α Γῆν Ἥλιον Ἄρην
　　　 Ἀθηνᾶν Ἀρείαν καὶ τὴν Ταυροπόλον?]

- - - - - καὶ τοὺς θεοὺς τοὺς ἐν Σαμοθράι[κηι καὶ τοὺς ἄλλους θεοὺς πάντας
　　　 καὶ πάσας καὶ τὴν τοῦ βασιλέως Φιλίππου Τύχην?·]

[ἐμμενῶ ἐν τ]ῆ φιλίαι καὶ συμμαχίαι ἣν πεπο[ίημαι πρὸς βασιλέα Φίλιππον εἰς
　　　 ἅπαντα τὸν χρόνον καὶ οὐ ποιήσομαι συμμαχίαν ἐναντίαν τῆι πρὸς
　　　 βασιλέα]

[Φίλιππον?] καθότι ἐπισυντέθειμαι ὀμόσα[ι- - - - - - - -καὶ οὐθὲν παραβήσομαι τῶν]

[κατὰ τὴν συμ]μαχίαν τρόπωι οὐθενί· καὶ ἐάν τ[ι- - - - - - - - - - - - - - οὐκ]

10 [ἐπιτρέψω κατὰ δύναμιν τ]ὴν ἐμαυτοῦ· εὐορκοῦντι μ[έν μοι εὖ εἴη, ἐφιορκοῦντι δὲ ἐξώλεια καὶ αὐτῶι καὶ γένει τῶι ἐξ ἐμοῦ· ὀμόσαι δὲ καὶ βασιλέα Φίλιππον]

[τόνδε τὸν ὅρκον· ὅρκος Φιλίππου·] ὀμνύω Δ[ία Γῆν Ἥλιον κτλ.- - - - - - - - - -]

19. Samothrace

Marble stele. H: 0.85m. W: 0.38-0.44m. Letters: 0.012-0.016m. Dated A.D. 160-180.

Champoiseau, *CRAI* 20 (1892) 22, with plate; Reinach, *REG* 5 (1892) 201; Kern, *MDAI (A)* 18 (1893) 372; *IG* XII (8), no. 216.

Plate V(b)

       Θεοί
βασιλεύοντος Σαβείνου οἵδε
᾽Αθηναίων ἐμυήθησαν·
ὁ ἀπ᾽ ἄστεως στρατηγὸς ᾽Αθηναίων τῶν
5 ἐν Ἴμβρῳ Σωκράτης ᾽Αρχελάου Πειραι-
 εύς
Φιλοκράτης ὁ καὶ Εἰσίδωρος Φιλο-
   κράτους ᾽Οῆθεν
᾽Ασκληπιάδης Μηνοδώρου Φλυεύς,
10 Εὐσχήμων Χρυσέρωτος Πειραιεύς
Κορνήλιος ᾽Αδείμαντος ᾽Αναφλύστιος
Κορνηλία ᾽Αλεξάνδρα Κορ(νηλίου) ᾽Αδειμάντου θυ(γάτηρ)
Κορνηλία Φιλότροφον ἐξ ᾽Αζηνιέων
Σωτᾶς Βότρυος Δαιδαλίδης
15   ἐπόπται
Πό(πλιος) Ἑρέννιος Λεοντεὺς ᾽Αζηνιεύς
Κλᾶρος Κλάρου Αἰξωνηεύς
᾽Ιούλιος Ἕρμιππος
     Θεοῖς
     Μεγάλοις
     Σαμοθρᾳ-
     ξι.

20. Methymna (Lesbos)

Fragment of a white marble stele. Letters: 0.01m. Second century B.C. *CIG*, no. 2167b; *IG* XII (2), no. 506.

- - [ε]ἰκό[να χαλκῆν καὶ ἀναθεῖναι ἐν]
[τῷ τεμ]ένει, ἐπι[γράψαι δὲ τὸ κοινὸν τὸ]
Σαμοθρᾳκι[αστῶν Ἰόλλαν.....]
πόλεως ἀρετῆ[ς ἕνεκα καὶ εὐνοίας]
5 [τ]ῆς εἰς αὐτού[ς · στεφανῶσαι δὲ αὐ]-
[τὸ]ν καὶ μετὰ [τὰς σπονδὰς ἀνακη]-
[ρύσ]σοντας ὅτ[ι στεφανοῦσιν οἱ Σα]-
[μο]θρᾳκιασταὶ Ἰόλ[λαν τὰς θυσίας συν]-
[τ]ελέσαντα καὶ τ[- - - - - - - - -
10 .ον ἐπιμεληθέ[ντα - - - - - - - - -
ὑπάρχειν δὲ αὐ[τῶ ...... τοὺς ἐπαί]-
[ν]ους τούτους κ[αθ᾽ ἑκάστην σύνοδον δι]-
[ὰ] βίου τοῦ ἑαυτο[ῦ· ἐπιμελεῖσθαι δὲ]
τῶν κηρυγμάτω[ν - - - - - τοὺς ἐπιμηνί]-
15 ους τοὺς ἐνεστη[κότας μετὰ τοῦ γραμμα]-
[τ]έως. Ἀναγράψαι [δὲ τοῦτο τὸ ψήφισμα]
εἰς στήλην λιθ[ίνην καὶ στῆσαι εἰς τὸ]
τέμενος· ἀνα - - - - - - - - - - - -
- - - - - - - - - - - - - - - - - -

21. Methymna (Lesbos)

Fragment of a stele. Letters: 0.008m. Second century B.C.
IG XII (2), no. 207.

- - - - - - - - - - - - - - - φ]ιλο[δοσίας]
[κ]αὶ χορη[γίας οὐδὲν ἐλλείπ]οντες, ἐνδε[ικνύ]-
μενοι τὴν ε[ὔν]οιαν ἣν ἔχουσιν πρὸς [τοὺς]
Σαμοθρᾳκιαστάς· ὅπως οὖν ᾖ πᾶσι φ[ανε]-
5 ρὸν ὅτι τὸ κοινὸν τῶν Σαμοθρᾳκιαστ[ῶν τι]-
μᾷ τοὺς φιλοτιμουμένους εἰς αὐτο[ύς,]
ἀγαθῇ τύχῃ ἐφη[φ]ίσθαι· ἐπαινέσ[αι αὐ]-
τοὺς ἐπί τε τῇ πρὸς τοὺς θεοὺς εὐσεβ[είᾳ καὶ]
ἐπὶ τῇ πρὸς τοὺς Σαμοθρᾳκιαστὰς φι[λοδοσί]-
10 ᾳ καὶ στεφανοῦν αὐτοὺς καθ᾽ ἑκά[στην]
σύνοδον διὰ βίου τοῦ ἑαυτῶν· ὅτ[αν δὲ ἡ πομ]-
[π]ὴ τῶν Σαμοθρᾳκιαστῶν παραπ[έμπηται ἐκ]
[το]ῦ πρυτανείου εἰς τὸ ἱερὸ[ν - - -]
- - - - - - - - - - - - - - - - - -

22. Delos

Stele of blueish marble. 156/155 B.C. Museum of Delos, inv. no. Γ679α-χ.
ID, no. 1412A, lines 24-33 (from a temple inventory).

ΕΝ ΤΩΙ ΣΑΜΟΘΡΑΚΕΙΩΙ·

- - - - - - - - - ἀνδ[ρι]αντίδιον - - -

25 [- - - - - - - - - κανοῦν - - - ἔχον - - - ὡς] ἕν· στέφαν[ον ἀργυροῦν ὄν] ἔχει ὁ
Ἡρακλῆς, ἀ[νάθεμ]α Μάρκου, [ὁλκὴ Η· πῖλοι ἀργυροῖ δύο, ἀνάθεμα]
Μαάρκου Ῥωμαίου, ὦ[ν]
[ὁλκὴ - - - - - ·ª ἀγάλματα ξύλι]να ἐφ' [ἵππων. ΕΝ Τ]ΩΙ ΠΡΟΣΤΟΩ[Ι·
ἀνδριαντίδι]ον λίθινον ἐπὶ βάσεως λιθίνης, ἀνάθεμα Ἀντιδό[του Τυρίου·
τράπεζα λι]θίν[η ἐφ'] ἧς πῖλοι λ[ίθ]ινοι δύο. ΕΝ Τ[ΕΙ]
[ΑΥΛΕΙ· - - - - - ·Ἡρακλῆ? ἐπὶ βάσεως λιθίν]ης. ΕΝ Τ[ΩΙ ΠΡΟΣΤΟ]ΩΙ·
κλεῖναι ξύ[λιναι Γ καὶ] ἄλλαι κατεαγ[εῖαι] τέτταρες· ἄγκυρα ξυλίνη
δίβολος· [σκυτάλ]ιον ἐβέν[ινον ἄλυσιν ἔχον σιδηρᾶν ...]
[- - - - - - - - πελέκι]ον καὶ ἀπ' [ἀγκύρας] σιδήριον κ[ίρκον ἔχ]ον κα[ὶ
ἄγκυρ]α ξυλίνη τ[ὸν? ......]η μόλυβδον ἀποκεκομμένη· λύχνον χαλκοῦν
τὸ
ἄνω[θεν] οὐκ ἔχον.

23. Delos

Marble stele. 156/155 B.C. Museum of Delos, inv. no. Γ308.
ID, no. 1417A, col. 1, lines 155-67 (from a temple inventory).

155 ΕΝ ΤΩΙ ΣΑΜΟΘΡΑΚΙΩΙ· Ἡρακλῆ χαλκοῦν· ἄλλο ἀνδριαντίδιον, τὸ ἀριστερὸν σκέλος κατεαγὸς καὶ τὴν ἀριστερὰν· κανοῦν πόδα ἕνα ἔχον καὶ
ὡς ἕν· στέφανον ἀργυροῦν ὄν <ἔ>χει ὁ Ἡρακλῆς, ἀνάθεμα Μάρκου, ὁλκὴ Η·
πῖλοι ἀρ-
γυροῖ δύο, ἀνάθεμα Μάρκου Ῥωμαίου, ὦν ὁλκὴ Η· ναΐδιον ξύλ(ι)νον (ἐν)
ὧι τὰ τῶν θεῶν ἀγάλματα ξύλινα ἐφ' ἵππων. ΕΝ ΤΩΙ ΠΡΟΣΤΟΩΙ· ἀν-
160 δριαντίδιον λίθινον ἐπὶ βάσεως λιθίνης, ἀνάθεμα Ἀντιδότου Τυρίου·
τράπεζα λιθίνη ἐφ' ἧς πῖλοι λίθινοι δύο. ΕΝ ΤΕΙ ΑΥΛΕΙ· ἀνδριαντίδιον χαλκοῦν· Ἡρακλῆ ἐπὶ βάσεως λιθίνης. ΕΝ ΤΩΙ ΠΡΟΣΤΟΙΩΙ· κλῖναι
ξύλιναι Γ κα<ὶ> ἄλλα<ι> κατεαγεῖαι τέτταρες· ἄγκυρα ξυλίνη δίβολος· σκυ-
τάλιον ἐβένινον, ἄλυσιν ἔχον σιδηρᾶν. Καὶ τάδε· τρίαιναν ἐντελῆ· πελέ-
165 κιον καὶ ἀπ' ἀγκύρας σιδήριον κίρκον ἔχον καὶ ἄγκυραν ξυλίνην
τοῦ μολύβδου ἀποκεκομμένην· λύχνον χαλκοῦν τὸ ἄνωθεν οὐκ ἔχον-
τα· ἄγκυραν σιδηρᾶν ἐντελῆ.

24. Delos

Marble stele. Dated after 156/155 B.C. Museum of Delos, inv. no. Γ529.
ID, no. 1423Ba, col. II, lines 8-17 (from a temple inventory).

ΕΝ ΤΩΙ ΣΑΜ[Ο]-
[ΘΡΑΚΕΙΩΙ· - - - - - ἀνδριαντίδι]ον τὸ ἀριστερὸν {πτερον} σκέλος κατεαγὸς
καὶ τὴν ἀρισ-

10 [τερὰν χεῖρα· - - - - - -· στέφανον] ἀργυροῦν ὅν ἔχει ὁ Ἡρακλῆς, ἀνάθημα
Μααρχου, ὁλκὴ Η· πῖλ[οι]

[ἀργυροῖ δύο - - - - - - - - - - -] ὧν ὁλκὴ Ⱶ· ναΐδιον ξύλινον ἐν ὧι τὰ τῶν θεῶν
ἀγάλματα ξύλιν[α]

[- - - - - - - - ἀνδρι]αντίδιον λίθινον ἐπὶ βάσεως, ἀνάθημα Ἀντιδότου Τυρίου·
τρά-

[πεζαν - - - -. ΕΝ Τ]ΕΙ ΑΥΛΕΙ· ἀνδριαντίδιον Ἡρακλῆν χαλκοῦν ἐπὶ βάσεως
λιθίνης

[- - - - - - - -κλίνα?]ς λιθίνας ΙΙΙ καὶ ἄλλας κατεαγείας ΙΙ· ἄγκυρα ξυλίνη
δίβολος· σ[κυτάλιο]ν ἐβέν[ι]-

15 [νον - - - -·]τρίαιναν ἐντελῆ καὶ πελέκιον καὶ ἀπ' ἀγκύρας σιδήριον κίρκον ἔχον καὶ
ἄγκυ-

[ραν ξυλίνην, τ]ὸ μόλυβδον ἀποκεκομμένον· λύχνον χαλκοῦν τὸ ἄνωθεν οὐκ
ἔχοντα· ἄγκυραν σιδη-

[ρᾶν ἐντελῆ

25. Delos

Part of an epistyle block of building dedicated by Helianax. 102/101 B.C.
Museum of Delos, inv. no. E 483.
Chapouthier, *EAD* XVI, fig. 42; *ID*, no. 1562.

1 ['Ο ἱερεὺς Ἡλιάναξ Ἀσκληπιοδ]ώρου Ἀθηναῖος, ὁ διὰ βίου ἱερεὺς Πο[σειδῶνος
Αἰσίου, γενόμενο]ς καὶ θεῶν Με[γάλων Σαμο]θράκων Διοσκούρων
[Καβείρων]

2 [ὑπὲρ τοῦ δήμου τοῦ Ἀθηναίων καὶ τ]οῦ δήμου τοῦ Ῥωμαίων τὸν ναὸν [καὶ τὰ ἐν
αὐτῶι ἀγάλματα καὶ τ]ὰ ὅπλα θεοῖς οἷς ἱερά[τευσε καὶ βασιλ]εῖ Μιθραδάτηι
Εὐπάτορι Διονύσωι,

3 [ἐπὶ ἐπιμελητοῦ] τῆς νήσου Θεοδότου τοῦ Διοδώρου Σουνιέως.

26. Delos

Block of the wall of the building dedicated by Helianax. Museum of Delos,
inv. no. E 490. 102/101 B.C.
Reinach, *BCH* 7 (1883) 349, no. 8; *OGIS*, no. 430; Chapouthier, *EAD* XVI,
33, no. 10 and fig. 36; *ID*, no. 1581.

ΔΟΡ - - - - - - ράτην τῶν πρώτων φίλων
βασιλέως βασιλέων μεγάλου Ἀρσάκου,
ὁ ἱερεὺς Ἡλιάναξ Ἀσκληπιοδώρου Ἀθηναῖος
ὁ διὰ βίου ἱερεὺς Ποσειδῶνος Αἰσίου, γενόμενος [δὲ]
5 καὶ Θεῶν Μεγάλων Σαμοθράκων Διοσκούρων Καβε[ίρων],
Θεοῖς

27. Delos

Inscribed on two blocks from the wall of the building dedicated by Helianax. Museum of Delos, inv. no. E 548. 102/101 B.C.
Chapouthier, *EAD* XVI, 33, no. 9; *ID*, no. 1582.

['Ηλι]άναξ 'Α[σκληπιοδώρου 'Αθηναῖος]
[ὁ] δι[ὰ βίου] ἱερεὺς [Ποσειδῶνος Αἰσίου]
γενόμενος   δὲ   κ[αὶ θεῶν Μεγάλων]
Σαμοθράκων   Δι[οσκούρων Καβείρων]
5 Μιθραδάτην   Εὐ[- - τὸν σύντροφον?]
βασιλέως   'Αρσά[κου - - - - - - -]
καὶ ἐπὶ   τῶν Γ- - - - - - -

28. Delos

Statue base of white marble. H: 0.65m. W: 0.50m. Museum of Delos, inv. no. E 715.
Chapouthier, *EAD* XVI, 39 and fig. 51; *ID*, no. 1902.

Ήλ[ι]άναξ 'Ασκληπιοδώρου
'Αθηναῖος ὁ διὰ βίου ἱερεὺς
Ποσειδῶνος Αἰσίου, γενόμενος
δὲ καὶ ἱερεὺς Θεῶν Μεγάλων
5 Σαμοθράκων Διοσκούρων Καβείρων
ἐν τῶι ἐπὶ 'Εχεκράτου ἄρχοντος
ἐνιαυτῶι... ἱδρύσατο.

29. Delos

Small marble base. H: 0.07m. W: 0.115m. Found in the Inopos, east of GD 93. Museum of Delos, inv. no. A 1777.
Hatzfeld, *BCH* 36 (1912) 202, no. 11; Chapouthier, *EAD* XVI, 88 and fig. 114; *ID*, no. 2441.

Δέκμος
Στλάκκιος
Θεοῖς Σαμό-
θραξιν, εὐχήν.

30. Delos

Small marble block. H: 0.095m. W: 0.145m.
Chapouthier, *EAD* XVI, 88 and fig. 113; *ID*, no. 2481.

Θεῶν Με-
γάλων

Σαμοθ[ρ]ά-
χων Καβε[ί]-
ρων

31. KYTHNOS

Long tablet of white marble.
Ross, *Archäologische Aufsätze* II, 671; *IG* XII (5), no. 1057.

[Σαμ]οθραικίων θεῶν.

32. THERA

Carved into the natural rock face in the *temenos* of Artemidoros, to the left
of the altar of Homonoia. Middle of the third century B.C.
Hiller von Gaertringen, *Thera* III, 94 (in German) and fig. 81; *IG* XII (3)
Suppl. no. 1337; Geffeken, *Griechische Epigramme*, no. 172.
Plate IV(a-b).

Θεῶν Σαμοθράικων.
Ἀρτεμίδωρος
Ἀπολλωνίου Περγαῖος.
Βωμὸν ἀγήρατον Σαμοθρᾶιξι θεοῖσιν ἔτευξεν
Περγαῖος Ἀρτεμίδωρος ἐπήκοον εὐχομένοισιν.

33. RHODES

Fragment of a marble stele. H: 0.20m. W: 0.18m. Letters, with apices,
dated second or first century B.C.
Maiuri, *ASAA* 8-9 (1925-26) 320, no. 3.

- - - - - - - - - - - - - - -
    Δι[ονύσου?],
[Ἀ]γεφῶν - - - - - - - - - -
   Ἀσκλ[απιοῦ],
  [Κ]λεταῖος Ξενο[τίμου?]
5   Ἡρακλεῦ[ς],
  [Ε]ὐφράνωρ Σωσιχρά[τευς]
   Διοσκ[ούρων],
[Ἀρ]ιστομαχίδας Ἀρισ[τομάχου]
   Θεῶν Σαμο[θράκων],
10 [Ἵπ]παρχος Ἐργ[ιάδευς]
- - - - - - - - Λ - - - - - -

34. RHODES

Piece of reddish stone built into the walls of a fort, broken on top, bottom, and right edge.

Hiller, *MDAI (A)* 18 (1893) 386, no. 2; *IG* XII (1), no. 8; Vidman, *Sylloge*, no. 174.

[ἱερεῖς....Σαρ]άπιος· Στρά[τι]ππος ’Ασ - - -
[’Απο]λλόδοτος β ’Ιστά(νιος). Ἡρακλεῦ[ς] - - -
[x]αθ’ ὑ(οθεσίαν δὲ) Δαΐφρονος. ’Αριστομ[ένευς] - -
[....]ς β τοῦ Μοιωνίδ[ευς] - - - - - - - - - - -
5 [.....]ίτας. Κορυβα[ν]τω[ν] - - - - - - - - - -
[Θεῶν Σ]αμ[ο]θράκω[ν] - - - - - - - - - - - -

35. RHODES

Rectangular marble base.

Foucart, *RA* 11 (1865) 218; Hiller von Gaertringen, *MDAI (A)* (1893) 385; Rubensohn, *Die Mysterienheiligtümer von Eleusis und Samothrake*, 234-35; *IG* XII (1), no. 43.

- - - - - - - - - - - - - - - - - -
στρατευσάμενον κατὰ πό[λεμον]
ἔν τε ταῖς καταφράκτοις ναυσί
καὶ ἐν τριημιολίαις καὶ τιμαθέντα
5 ὑπὸ ἁλικιωτᾶν τοῦ κοινοῦ θαλλοῦ
στεφάνωι καὶ χρυσέωι ἀρετᾶς
ἕνεκα καὶ εὐνοίας τᾶς εἰς αὐτούς·
καὶ στρατευσάμενον ὑπὸ ἄρχοντα
’Αντίοχον καὶ τιμαθέντα ὑπὸ
10 Σαμοθραικιαστᾶν μεσονέων τοῦ
κοινοῦ χρυσέωι στεφάνωι ἀρετᾶς
ἕνεκα καὶ εὐνοίας καὶ φιλοδοξίας
ἂν ἔχων διατελεῖ εἰς τὸ Σαμοθραικιαστᾶν μεσονέων κοινόν· καὶ
15 τοὶ συμστρατευσάμενοι ἐτίμασαν
Σαμοθραικιαστᾶν καὶ Λημνιαστᾶν
τὸ κοινὸν ἐπαίνωι χρυσέωι στεφάνωι
ἀρετᾶς ἕνεκα καὶ εὐνοίας καὶ φιλοδοξίας
ἂν ἔχων διατελεῖ εἰς τὸ Σαμοθρακιαστᾶν
20 καὶ Λημνιαστᾶν τῶν συνστρατευσαμένων
κοινόν· καὶ πρωρατεύσαντα τριηρέων
καὶ ἄρξαντα ἀφράκτων
καὶ ἐπιστάταν γενόμενον τῶν παίδων
καὶ ἱεροθυτήσαντα

25   καὶ πρυτανεύσαντα. θεοῖς.

Ἐπίχαρμος Σολεύς, ὧι ἁ ἐπιδαμία δέδοται,

καὶ Ἐπίχαρμος Ἐπιχάρμου Ῥόδιος ἐποίησαν.

36. Rhodes

Tablet, top part broken away. H: 0.40m. W: 0.285m. Decorated with five olive wreaths and parts of two others.

Hiller von Gaertringen, *MDAI (A)* 18 (1893) 389, no. 3; *IG* XII (1), no. 163.

τὸ κοι-

νόν. Σαμοθραικιαστᾶν Σωτηριαστᾶν

Ἀριστοβουλιαστᾶν. Ἀπολλωνιαστᾶν Θεαι{αι}δηττείων

Ἀστυμηδείων.

37. Rhodes

Dark stone. H: 0.32m. W: 0.63m. First century B.C.

Hiller von Gaertringen and Saridakis, *MDAI (A)* 25 (1900) 109, no. 108.

- -

-χευς, Εὐστράτα Μεθυμναία καὶ Ἀριάδνη τὰν ἀ[νεφιάν, τιμαθεῖσαν μὲν]

ἐν ταῖς συνόδοις καὶ ἐν ταῖς ἄλλαις καθ᾽ [ἔτος παναγύρεσι εὐσεβείας]

καὶ ἀρετᾶς ἕνεκα καὶ εὐνοίας καὶ φιλοδοξίας [ἇς ἔχουσα διατελεῖ ἐς τὸ]

Ἀσκλαπιαστᾶν Νικασιωνείων Ὀλυμπιαστᾶν [κοινόν, τιμαθεῖσαν δὲ]

5   καὶ ὑπὸ Σαμοθρακιαστᾶν Ἀφροδι<σια>στᾶν [κοινοῦ

- -

- -

συνθυτᾶν -

- -

10   -

εὐεργεσίας [τᾶς ἐς τὰν πάτρα]ν τὰν Ἐρατιδᾶν - - -

[τιμαθεῖσαν δὲ καὶ] χρυσέωι στεφάνωι καὶ [εἰκόνι] - - -

- -

38. Rhodes

Rectangular base with hole for insertion of a funereal stele. Local marble. H: 0.14m. W: 0.29m. First century B.C.

Maiuri, *Nuova silloge epigrafica di Rodi e Cos*, no. 43.

Τὸ κοινὸν τὸ Σαμοθραικιαστᾶν

ἐτίμασε Μοσχίωνα

Φασηλίταν χρυσέωι

στεφάνωι καὶ ὑπὸ

5   Παναθηναϊστᾶν
      θαλλίνωι καὶ ὑπὸ
      Ἀφροδισιαστᾶν θαλλίνωι.

38a. RHODES

Fragment of a base, found in the excavation of the *tetrapylon*. First century B.C.

G. Pugliese Carratelli, *ASAA* n.s. 1-2 (1942) 153, no. 13 and pl. xi. 2; D. Morelli, *I culti in Rodi* (Studi Classici e Orientali 8, Pisa 1959) 57.

- - - - - - - - - - - α[......] Φίλωνος
[τὸ κοινὸ]ν τὸ Σαμοθρα[ι]κιαστᾶν
[Νικο?σ]τρατείων συνμυστᾶν
[συνστρα]τευσαμένων ὑπὸ τριήραρχον
5   - - - -ωνᾳ [Φίλ]ωνος

39. RHODES

V. Kontorini, *RN* Ser. 6, 21 (1979) 39, first century B.C., published in part.

- - - - - - - - - - - - - - - καὶ
στεφανωθέντα ὑπὸ
Πτολεμαιέων τᾶς ἱερᾶς
καὶ ἀσύλου καὶ αὐτονόμου
χρυσέωι στεφάνωι καὶ
λαβὼν πολιτείαν
παρὰ τᾶς πόλιος αὐτῶν·
καὶ διασώσας τριήρη
τῶν κατὰ Λιβύαν τόπων·
Θεοῖς τοῖς ἐν Σαμοθράκᾳ
χαριστήριον.

40. LINDOS

Bottom part of a rectangular altar. H: 0.34m. W: 0.35m. Third century B.C. (?).

Loewy, *AEMÖ* 7 (1883) 136, no. 72; Hiller, *MDAI (A)* 18 (1893) 390, no. 4; *IG* XII (1), no. 788; Vidman, *Sylloge*, mo. 203.

. . . .
- - - - Ἱπποκράτε[υς] - - -
[Ἀπ]όλλωνος Πυθαέ[ως]·
[Ἀ]ριστόμαχος Ἀλ[εξ]ά[νδρου]
5   ἀρχιεροθύτας,
      Ἀριστοκράτης Πολυξένου

ἱερεὺς Σαράπιος·
Δαμωφέλ[η]ς Πεισύλου
Θεοῖς τοῖς ἐν Σαμοθράιχαι
10   χαριστήριον.

41. LINDOS

Rectangular pillar, broken on bottom. Marble from Lartos. About 215 B.C. H: 0.85m. W: 0.414-0.431m. D: 0.38m.
ILind, no. 134; Vidman, *Sylloge*, no. 202.

Ἱερεὺς Ἁλίου
Ἀρχοκράτης Ἀρχιπόλιος
καθ᾽ ὑοθεσίαν δὲ Λυσιστράτου
Ἀθανᾶς Πολιάδος
5   καὶ Διὸς Πολιέως
Πεισίλοχος Ἀριστοφύλου
Ποτειδᾶνος Ἱππίου
Τιμαχράτης Ἀγεμάχου
Ἀπόλλωνος Πυθίου
10   Ἀπολλόδοτος Εὐχρατίνου
Ἀφροδίτας
Εὐσθένης Ἱεροχλεῦς
Μουσᾶν
Ἀριστόπολις Εὐφανίσχου
Διονύσου
Τιμοκράτης Τιμαινέτου
Ἀσχλαπιοῦ
Σώδαμος Τιμαγόρα
καθ᾽ ὑοθεσίαν δὲ Εὑίστωρος
[Ἡ]ρ[α]χλεῦς
Ἀρίστων Κλεωνύμου
Διοσχόρων
Κράτων Κράτωνος
θε[ῶ]ν Σαμοθράιχων
Δαμοχ[ρά]της [......]λου
Σαρά[πιος]
- - η - [Ἀν]αξιλάου
- - - - α - ερ - -
- - - - - αγ - του

42. KARPATHOS

Local stone, built into a wall. H: 0.67m. W: 0.51m. Early second century B.C.

Hiller von Gaertringen, *MDAI* (*A*) 18 (1893) 391, no. 6; *IG* XII (1), no. 1034.

[Θ]εῶν Σαμοθράικων ἱερεῖς

- - - - - - - - - - - - - -

.....ς Κα[λλιάν]ακτος
'Αγορα.....Κρατιστόλα
5 'Α[ρ]χιάδης Σιμιάδα
Στρ[α]τίων Εὐμάχου
Κρέων Δαμοκρέωνος
[Μ]ενεκράτης Τελέσωνος
'Αρκεσίλας 'Αρχιμβρότου
10 [Θ]α[ρ]σαγό[ρας] Στ[ασ]ιμβ[ρό]του
Φιλτατίων 'Αγησάνδρου
Μόσχος Μοσχίωνος
[Π]ολύμναστος Πολυγνώτου
Φιλίσκος Κλείνου
15 ['Αρ]ιστολαΐδας Πραταγόρα
Διογένης Διογνήτου
[Ν]ίκαρχος 'Ι[φ]ιδάμου(?)
[Λά]μαχος Μαχάονος
'Α[ρ]χέμαχος 'Αρχεκράτευς
20 Φιλίσκος Τιμασιδίκου
[Π]όλλις Νευπόλιος
[Φ]ιλήρατος Κλειν[ί]α
[Πο]λ[υκ]λῆς Πολυ[κ]λ[εῦς]
Δαμόχαρ[ι]ς Στασικλεῦς
25 Θέρσι[ππ]ος Θερσαγ[όρα]
Ξενο[γ]είτω[ν] Διοκ[λεῦς]
'Αντιοχίδας [τοῦ δεῖνος]
..ων - - - - - - - - - -
[Ε]ὐκλ[ῆς τοῦ δεῖνος]
30 'Επιπ[- - τοῦ δεῖνος]
Πολ - - - - - - - - -
.ο - - - - - - - - - - -

Νικήρατος Αἰσχίλου
Χαρμάδας 'Επικλεῦ[ς]
35 Καλλικράτης 'Αναξικλείτου
'Αριστομένης 'Αντισίμου
'Ασκλαπιάδας Κλευκράτευς
Φε[ρέ]πο[ν]ος(?) [Π]αντακλεῦς
Νικάνωρ Πολιμνάστου
40 'Αριστοκράτης Ταχίστ[ου]
Χορόνικος Πραξί[π]-
που, καθ' ἰοθεσίαν δὲ
Δεξανδρίδα.

43. SYME

Tablet of limestone built into the outside wall of a church. Letters not earlier than first century B.C.

IG XII (3), no. 6.

[Τ]ὸ κοινὸν Σαμοθρακι[α]στᾶν 'Α[φ]ρο[δισιασ]-
[τ]ᾶν Βορβοριτᾶν ὑπὲρ Ε[ὐ]φροσύνο[υ]
'Ιδυμέως μετοίκου [εὐ]εργέτα

[τ]οῦ κοινοῦ· ἐπαιν[εῖ] καὶ στεφανοῖ χρ[υ]-
5 [σέ]ῳ στεφάνῳ [ἀρε]τᾶς ἕνεκα καὶ
[εὐ]νοίας ἂν ἔχων διετέλ[ε]ι ΄ς ἀμὲ τὸ[ν]
[ἄπ]αν<τα> χρόνον· καὶ ἐστεφανωμένο[ν]
   [χ]ρυσέοις [στ]εφάνοις ὑπ᾿ ἀμῶν τὸ τ[ρίτον sive -έταρτον]
[καὶ] ἐσταφανωμένον ὑπὸ ᾿Α[δ]ωνιασ[τᾶν ᾿Αφροδισιασ]-
10 [τᾶν(?)] ᾿Ασκλαπιαστᾶν Σύρων [χρ]υσ[έῳ στεφάνῳ]
[καὶ] ὑπὸ τᾶς κτοίνας τᾶς - ΗΛΛ - - -
     χρυσέῳ στεφάνῳ καὶ ὑπὸ τᾶς κτο[ί]-
[ν]ας τᾶς ᾿Επι[β]ωμοῦς(?) χρυσέῳ στε-
[φ]άνῳ καλοκἀγαθίας ἕνεκα ἂν ἔ-
15 [χ]ων [δ]ι[ε]τέ[λει] ΄ς [τὸ κ]οινὸ[ν]
     θεοῖς.

44. Kalchedon

Marble stele.

B. Latyšev, *Journal Ministerstva narodnogo prosvestenija* (1885) 312-18; *SGDI*, no. 3052; *Recueil*, no. 733; *SIG*[3], no. 1011; *LSAM*, no. 3.

   [- -]ταν δαμοσιο[ργίαν- - - - -]
   [-ἑκάστωι] τῶν ἱερείων ἐν τῶ[ι αὐτῶι] χρόνωι· ἱε[ρεῖ]
   [.......ἀ]πὸ τᾶς μνᾶς Τ· ἱερεῖ ᾿Ερμᾶ ἀπὸ τᾶς μνᾶς [Τ]
   [ἱερεῖ ῎Α]μμωνος ἀπὸ τᾶς μνᾶς Τ· ἱερεῖ ῾Ηρακλεῖος
5 [ἀπὸ τᾶ]ς μνᾶς CΙΙ::ἱερεῖ θεῶν Σαμοθραικίων
   [ἀπὸ τ]ᾶς μνᾶς CCCΙΙ· ἱερεῖ Διὸς Βουλαίου ἀπὸ τᾶς
   [.....] είας CCΤΙ. τοῦ δὲ λοιποῦ τὸ ἥμισον τοῦ Μα-
   [χανεί]ου, τὸ δὲ λοιπὸν τοῦ ᾿Απελλαίου τοῦ ἐπὶ ᾿Ολυμπι-
   [οδώρου]. ἀφελέσθαι δὲ μηθενὶ ἐξεῖμεν τὰν ἱερωτείαν·
10 [ὅς δέ κ]α εἴπῃ ἢ προαισιμνάσῃι ἢ ἐν [β]ουλᾶι ἢ ἐν δάμωι, ὀ-
   [φειλέτω] δραχμὰς Μ ἱερὰς τοῦ ῾Ηρακλεῖος, καὶ τὰ
   [προαισ]ιμναθέντα ἢ ῥηθέντα ἄκυρα ἔστω. ἀναθέ-
   [τω δὲ α]ὐτὸν ὁ βασιλεὺς ἐπεί κα τὰν τιμὰν δῶι, τὸ δὲ
   [ἀνάλω]μα δωσεῖ ὁ πριάμενος τὰν ἱερωτείαν. γρά-
15 [ψαι δὲ κ]αὶ εἰς σανίδα κοῖλα γράμματα καὶ ε[ἰ]στάλαν
   [καὶ στᾶσα]ι τὰν μὲν στάλαν πρὸ τοῦ ἱεροῦ, τὰν δὲ σα-
   [νίδα εἰς] τὸ βουλεῖον. ἀρξεῖ δὲ αὐτῶι τὰς ποθόδου
   [ἀφ᾿ οὗ ὁ πρ]ότερον ἱερεὺς οὐκ ἐλάζετο.
   [ἐπρία]το τὰν ἱερωτείαν Μενέμ[αχος- -]
20 [- -]λου δραχμᾶν ΓΧ[ΧΓ⁼].
   [τριακο]στά· ΗΗΨ. δυοκαιεβδομη[κοστὰ καὶ]
   [μυρ]ιασταὶ τρεῖς· ΗΓΟΙΙ. διακοσιοστά·]
   [ΔΔΔΓCCΤ]. χαρύκειον· CCΤ[Ι- - -

45. Gökçeören (Near Nikomedeia)

Limestone base. H: 0.74m. W: 0.31m. D: 0.31m. Letters: 0.03m.

Şahin, *Neufunde von antiken Inschriften in Nikomedeia*, no. 82; *TAM* IV, no. 88.

```
- - - - - - - - - - -
καὶ Στρενπαν[ῶν]
[κ]αὶ Βα<ι> τηνῶν [καὶ]
Παιξιαιτηνῶ[ν]
καὶ ΟΛΗΣ- - - - -
5   .ας Σωσ[ίπα]τρο[ς]
...ερου τὸν βω-
[μ]ὸν ἀνέστησεν
[θ]εοῖς Σομοθρᾳξιν (sic)
[ἐ]κ τῶν ἰδίων.
```

46. Ilion

Round altar. H: 1.10m. D: 0.60m. Found near Sestos, originally from Ilion.

Lolling, *MDAI (A)* 6 (1881) 209-14; *OGIS* I, no. 88; Holleaux, *Études* III, 317 no. 3; Robert, *REG* 77 (1964) no. 272; Frisch, *Die Inschriften von Ilion*, no. 44.

```
Ὑπὲρ βασιλέως Πτολεμαίου καὶ βασιλίσσης
Ἀρσινόης θεῶν φιλοπατόρω[ν]
καὶ τοῦ υἱοῦ αὐτῶν Πτολεμαί[ο]υ,
θεοῖς τοῖς ἐν Σαμοθράικηι
5   Ἀριστάρχη Μικύθου Περγαμηνή.
```

47. Ilion

Three fragments of a stele. a. H: 0.17m. W: 0.26m. b. H: 0.18m. W: 0.26m. a-b found in Çiplak, now in Paris (Louvre). c. Found on Akropolis in Ilion, now lost.

a-b: Osann, *SIAGL*, nos. 22, 32; *CIG*, no. 3597; c: Schliemann, *Trojanische Altertümer*, no. 316 = *Ilios*, no. 711; a-c: Frisch, *Die Inschriften von Ilion*, no. 63.

```
a.    [Ὁ]μολογία Ἰλιέων        [καὶ Σκαμανδρέων]
      [ἐ]πὶ ἱερέως Ἀριστονόμου τοῦ Ν [- - μηνὸς - - ἀπ]-
      [ι]όντος, ὡς δὲ Σκαμανδρεῖς ἄ[γουσιν ἐπὶ - - - μη]-
      [νὸς Πανή]μου τετράδι ἀπιόντος [- - - - - - - -]
5     [- - - - - - -] οἱ κατοικοῦντες Σ[καμανδρέων - -]
      [- - - - - - - - - -]ι τῶν ἐν Σκα[μάνδροις οἰκούντων]
      [- - - - - - ἐν Σκαμ]άνδροις ανε [- - - - - - - -]
```

[- - - - - - - - - -]απενφ[- - - - - - - - -]

[- - - - - - - - - -ἐ]φηβε [ὑσαντες - - - - -]

b. 10 [- - ἑκάστης] ἡμέρας ὀβολοὺς δύο καὶ πυρῶν χοίνικ[ας -

[- - - - ἡμι]ωβέλιον· τὸν δὲ ὑπηρέτην λειτουργεῖ[ν - -

[- - - - χρη]μάτων εἰς τὴν πόλιν· αἱρεῖσθαι δὲ καὶ α[- - ἐκ τῶν οἰ]-

[κούντων ἐν Σκαμ]άνδροις· τὸν δὲ αὐτὸν καὶ γυναικονομεῖν[- -

[- - - - ὤνη]σιν καὶ πρᾶσιν, καθότι προεψήφισται· αἱρεῖσθα[ι - -

15 [- - - - - τ]ῶι δὲ αἱρεθέντι δίδοσθαι εἰς τὴν εὐ[- - -

[- - αἱρεῖσθα]ι δὲ καὶ ἱερονόμον τῶν οἰκούντων ἐ[ν Σκαμάνδροις - -

[- - - -]θαι πάντα αὐτοῖς ἐξ ἀρχῆς δίδο[σθαι - -

[- - - δ]ραχμὰς ἑκατὸν καὶ πεντ[ήκοντα - -

[- - -] κατ’ ἐνιαυτὸν ἕως δραχ[μῶν - - -

20 [- - -] τῆς Ἰλιέων χώρας [- - - -

c.   [- - -]σα[- - - - - - - - - - -

[- - -]εσαι[- - - - -]νου[- - -

[- - τ]ὰ βουκόλ[ια - - Π]έτραν φ[- -

[-]ς κατὰ πλῆθος εἰς οινιστρα[- - -

25 [-]των ἐψηφίσθαι Σκα(μαν)δρεῖς ο[- -

[-]ς ἄνδρας τούς συνθησομέν[ους - - - - καθάπερ]

[- πρότ]ερον ὑπῆρχεν, καὶ στήλω[σιν τῆς ὁμολογίας εἶναι - -

[- - -κα]ὶ ἐν τῷ τῶν Σαμοθράκ[ων θεῶν ἱερῷ - - -

[- - -το]ῖς ἀποκαθισταμένο[ις - - -

30 [- - - - -]ενους τὴν σύνθεσιν [- - -

[- - - - ὁ]μολογίας τὸ ἀντίγρα[φον - -

[- - - δι]οικήσοντες ἡρέθησ[αν - -

[- - - Δι]οπείθου, Μιλήσιος [- - -

[- - - -]θου, Διοπείθης Β[- - -

35 [- - - Ἀν]τιφάνης Ἀπ[ελλοῦς - -

48. Teos

Square block of blue marble. Middle of the second century B.C. There are fourteen wreaths, each encircling an inscription, but only seven of the inscriptions are legible. Found in a Turkish cemetery at Séghedjik.

Pottier and Hauvette-Besnault, *BCH* 4 (1880) 164; Recueil, no. 1307.

Οἱ συν-	Ὀ[ργ]-	Οἱ	Οἱ σὺν
άρχοντες	[ε]ῶνες	σὺν	- - - -
οἱ σὺν Μη-	οἱ σὺν Ἀ-	- - -	- - - -
τροδώρωι	θηνοδό-	Παραπρυτάνεις - - -	
Μητροδώ-	τωι Μη-	- - -	
ρου.	τροδώ-	οἱ σὺν	Σαμο-
	ρου.	Μητρο-	θραχια-
ὁ θία-		δώρωι	σταὶ οἱ σὺν Μύσται Ἀττα-
σος ὁ		Ὀνησίμου	Ἀθηνοδό- οἱ σὺν Ἀ- λισταὶ

10　　[Σι]μαλ[ί-]　　　　τοῦ Ἀνα-　　τωι Μη-　　θηνοδότωι　　οἱ σὺν Κρά-
　　　　[ων]ος　　　　　ξιβίου　　　τροδώ-　　Μητροδώρου　τωνι Ζωτί-
　　　　　　　　　　　　　　　　　ρου.　　　　　　　　　　χου.

49. EPHESOS

Marble stele, over 2m. in height; inscribed on the front and on the right
side. Found by chance, partially buried, near the harbor. A.D. 54-59.
　　J. Keil, *JÖAIBeibl* 26 (1930) 52-54; H. Wankel, *Die Inschriften von
Ephesos* Ia, 122-28, no. 20A.

- - - - ΦΙΣΙ - - -

[Ν]έρ[ω]νι Κλαυδίωι Καίσ[α]ρι Σε[βα]στῶι
Γερμανικῶι τῷ αὐτοκράτορι κ[αὶ Ἰουλίᾳ]
Ἀγριππείνῃ Σεβαστῆι τῇ μητρὶ αὐτ[οῦ]
5　καὶ Ὀκταουίᾳ τῇ γυναικὶ τοῦ αὐτοκράτορος
καὶ τῶι δήμωι τῶι Ῥωμαίων καὶ τῶι δήμω[ι]
Ἐφεσίων οἱ ἁλιεῖς καὶ ὀψαριοπῶλαι τὸν
τόπον λαβόντες ψηφίσματι ἀπὸ τῆς πόλεως
τὸ τελωνῖον τῆς ἰχθυϊκῆς κατασκευάσαν-
10　τες ἐκ τῶν ἰδίων ἀνέθηκαν. Οἵδε προσκατή-
νενκαν εἰς τὸ ἔργον κατὰ τειμήν·

Πόπλιος Ὀρδεώνιος　　　　　Ἕσπερος Δημητρί- δη(νάρια) κε'
Λολλιανὸς σὺν γυναικὶ　　　ου μετὰ τῶν υἱῶν
καὶ τοῖς τέκνοις κίον(ας) δ'　Κό(ϊντος) Λαβέριος Νίγερ δη(νάρια) κε'
15　Πόπλιος Κορνήλιος　　　　μετὰ τοῦ υἱοῦ
Ἀλέξανδρος τοῦ ὑπαί-　　　Εἰσᾶς Ἑρμοχάρεως δη(νάρια) κε'
θρου στρῶσαι λίθωι　　　　μετὰ τῶν υἱῶν
Φωκαϊκῶι πήχεις ρ'　　　　Γάϊ(ος) Φούριος μετὰ δη(νάρια) κε'
Τιβ(έριος) Κλαύδιος Μητρόδω-　τοῦ υἱοῦ
20　ρος σὺν γυναικὶ καὶ τοῖς　Μᾶρ(κος) Οὐαλέριος Φρόν- δη(νάρια) κε'
τέκνοις κείονας γ'　　　　των μετὰ θυγατρός
καὶ στρῶσαι τὸ τετράσ-　　Ἀρτεμίσιος Λεσβίου δη(νάρια) κε'
τυλον τὸ παρὰ τὴν στή-　　Πό(πλιος) Σαβίδιος Ἀμέθυσ- δη(νάρια)
　　　　　　　　　　　　　κε'
λην λίθωι Φωκαϊκῶι　　　τος μετὰ τῶν υἱῶν
25　Πό(πλιος) Γερελλανὸς Μελλεῖ-　Ἱέραξ Ἑρμοκράτου δη(νάρια) κε'
τος κείονας β'　　　　　　σὺν γυναικί
Εὔπορος Ἀρτεμιδώρου　　Δίδυμος Θευδᾶ δη(νάρια) κε'
κείονα α' καὶ δην(άρια) ιβ'　Δημήτριος Δημη- δη(νάρια) κε'
Φιλοκράτης Ἀπελλᾶ　　　τρίου Κηναρτᾶς
30　σὺν τοῖς τέκνοις　　　　Ξάνθος Πυθίωνος ,β
κείονα α' καὶ δην(άρια) ιβ'　πλίνθους

Λεύ(κιος) Ὀκτάουιος Μάχερ
μετὰ τῶν ἀδελφῶν
κείονα α᾿

35 Πό(πλιος) Ἀνθέστιος Ποπλίου
υἱ[ὸς] κείονα α᾿
Ὀνήσιμος Ἀπολλωνίου
καὶ Διονύσιος Χαρει-
σίου κείονα ποίκιλον

40 Πό(πλιος) Κορνήλιος Φῆλιξ
σὺν Κορηλίᾳ Εἰσίωι
κείονα α᾿
Σεπτούμιος Τρόφιμος
μετὰ τῶν τέκνων κίονα

45 Ἡρακλείδης Ἡρακλίδου
τοῦ Ἡρακλείδου δην(άρια)
Ἐπαφρᾶς Τρυφωνᾶ με-
τὰ τοῦ υἱοῦ κεραμίδας τ᾿
Πό(πλιος) Ναίουιος Νίγερ μετὰ

50 τῶν τέκνων δην(άρια) ν᾿
Πό(πλιος) Οὐήδιος Οὐῆρος
μετὰ τοῦ υἱοῦ δην(άρια) ν᾿
Λεύ(κιος) Φαβρίκιος Τοσίδης
μετὰ τοῦ υἱοῦ δην(άρια) ν᾿

55 Πό(πλιος) Κορνήλιος Φιλισ-
τίων μετὰ τοῦ υἱοῦ δη(νάρια) ν᾿
Λε(ύκιος) Ὀκτ[άο]υιος Ῥοῦφος
μετὰ τῶν υἱῶν δην(άρια) ν᾿
Τρύφων Ἀρτεμιδώρου

60 δηνάρια λζ᾿
Εἰσᾶς Ἀρτεμιδώρου δη(νάρια) λζ᾿
Ἄτταλος Χαριξένου
Ἀμαξᾶς μετὰ τοῦ υἱοῦ
δη(νάρια) λ᾿

65 Ἐπικράτης Ἀντιόχου δη(ναρια) λ᾿
Κρουκρᾶς μετὰ τῶν υἱῶν
Ἰσᾶς Ἰσιδώρου δη(νάρια) λ᾿

Φόρβος παραφύλαξ ‚α
πλίνθους
Σεκοῦνδος παραφύλαξ ‚α
πλίνθους
Μᾶρ(κος) Ἀντώνιος Βάσσος
μετὰ τῆς θυγατρὸς τῶν
στοῶν τὰς ὀλένας πάσας
Συνέρως Κλεάνα- δη(νάρια) κ᾿
κτος μετὰ τοῦ υἱοῦ
Οὐετλῆνος Πρῖ- δη(νάρια) κ᾿
μος μετὰ τοῦ υἱοῦ
Γν(αῖος) Κορνήλιος Εὔ- δη(νάρια) ιε᾿
νους μετὰ παιδίου
Ἄτταλος Ἀττάλου δη(νάρια) ιε᾿
τοῦ Κασιάδου
Διογένης Διογέ- δη(νάρια) ιε᾿
νου μετὰ τοῦ υἱοῦ
Οὐεττίδιος Νεί- δη(νάρια) ιε᾿
κανδρος σὺν υἱοῖς
Γάϊος Ῥωσκίλιος δη(νάρια) ιε᾿
Ζώσιμος Γαΐου Φουρίου δη(νάρια) ιε᾿
Βάκχιος Εὐφροσύ- δη(νάρια) ιε᾿
νου μετὰ τῆς μητρός
Λού(κιος) Οὐιτέλλιος δη(νάρια) ιε᾿
μετὰ τοῦ υἱοῦ
Λού(κιος) Κώνσιος Ἐπα- δη(νάρια) ιε᾿
φρόδειτος
Ἀριστέας Ἀριστο- δη(νάρια) ιε᾿
βούλου μετὰ τοῦ υἱοῦ
Ῥουφίκιος Φαῦστος δη(νάρια) ιε᾿
Πό(πλιος) Λείουιος δη(νάρια) ιε᾿
Ἀντίοχος Ψυχᾶς δη(νάρια) ιε᾿
μετὰ τοῦ υἱοῦ
Χάρης Χάρητος δη(νάρια) ιε᾿
μετὰ τῶν υἱῶν

Ἐργεπιστατήσαντος καὶ ἐξευρόντος τὴν κατασκευὴν
τοῦ ἔργου Λευκίου Φαβρικίου Οὐιταλίου τοῦ καὶ ἀνα-
70 θέντος ἐκ τῶν ἰδίων μετὰ τῆς ἰδίας γυναικὸς
καὶ τῶν ἰδίων θρεπτῶν κείονας β᾿ τοὺς παρὰ τὸ Σα-
μοθράκιν σὺν τοῖς ὑποκειμένοις βωμοῖς.

50. MYLASA

Inscribed on a block of white marble. H: 0.71m. W: 0.305m.

Robert, *Le sanctuaire de Sinuri près de Mylasa*, no. 47a and plate 14.

['Επι στεφανηφόρου - - - τοῦ - - ἱερέως Θ]εῶν Σα[μ]οθράικων,

[μηνὸς - - - -ἑκτῇ· αἱρεθέντες κατὰ ψήφισμα κ]τηματῶναι

[ὁ δεῖνα - - - - - - - - - - - - -Διόδο]τος Ταυρίσκου, κατὰ

[δὲ υἱοθεσίαν Λέοντος τοῦ 'Επαινέτου, Δημήτριος Λ]έοντος τοῦ Μυός.

5 [.. ωνίδης Λέοντος τοῦ Μυωνίδου, Παμμένης 'Ερ]μογένου Ταρχονδαρεῖς

[- - - - - - - - - - - - - - - - - - - -'Αρ]ιστέου τοῦ Μιννίωνος

[ἐκτηματώνησαν παρὰ τοῦ δεῖνος - - γέας τὰς] ἐν 'Υσαρβιδοις τὰς τε ὀνο-

[μαζομένας- - - - - - - - - - σὺν τοῖς δένδρ]εσι πᾶσι καὶ ταῖς ἐνούσαις

[ἀμπέλοις - - - - - - - - - - - - καὶ ὁ ποταμὸς καὶ πέρα[ν] τοῦ

10 [ποταμοῦ - - - - - - - - - - - πέρα]ν τῆς ὁδοῦ τῆς ἐφ' 'Ιερᾶς Κώμης

[φερούσης - - - - - - - -αἷς ὁμοροῦσιν] Αἰνέας 'Ιάσονος τοῦ 'Απολλωνίου

[- - - - - - - - - - - - - - - - - - 'Απο]λλωνίου Κοσητιος, Μέλας

[- - - - - καὶ ἄλλην - - - - - - - - - -] Σ ἐν ᾗ πέφυκεν ἡ συκάμινος

- - - - - - - - - - - - - - - - - - - -τῆι αἱμασιᾶι ταύτηι οἷς ὁμο-

15 [ροῦσιν ὁ δεῖνα κτλ.]

51. MYLASA

Three fragments of a marble block.

Robert, *Le sanctuaire de Sinuri près de Mylasa*, no. 49 and plates 7b-c.

['Επὶ στεφανηφόρου τοῦ δεῖνος τοῦ δεῖνος ἱερέως Θεῶν Σαμο]θράικων μη[νὸς

'Υπερβερε]ταίου ἑκτῃ·

[- -Τ]αρχονδαρ[- - Παρ?]μένους κτη-

[ματῶναι - - - - - - - - - - - - - - - -Διό]δοτον Τ[αυρίσκου, κατὰ δὲ]

ὑοθεσίαν

4 [Λέοντος τοῦ 'Επαινέτου, Δημήτριον Λέοντος τοῦ Μυός, ..]ωνίδην [Λέοντος τοῦ

Μυωνίδου - -]

52. STRATONIKEIA

LeBas and Waddington, no. 527; Wilhelm, *Beiträge zur griechischen Inschriftenkunde* 183-87; Robert, *Études anatoliennes* 530-31.

Δεύτερος [π]ύρ[γ]ος. <συν-

αθροίζεσθαι πρὸς> τῶι

'Ηρακλείωι καὶ τῶι ἐχο-

μένωι φυλα[κ]είωι. ἄμφο-

δα τὸ Σαμοθράικιον καὶ τὸ

5 ἐχόμενον ἕως τοῦ πο-

ταμοῦ. ἐπίσημον

ρόπαλον.

53. Aulai (Rhodian Peraia, Bay of Kyr-Vassili)

Rectangular base of reddish marble. H: 0.42m. W: 0.72m. Letters of the Roman period, probably first century A.D.

Wescher, *RA* (1864) 471; *SGDI*, no. 4274; Poland, *Geschichte des griechischen Vereinswesens*, 566, no. 304; Maiuri, *ASAA* 4-5 (1921-22) 481-82, no. 36; *SEG* 4 (1929) no. 168.

> Ἀλεξάνδρου Κεφαλλᾶνος τειμαθέν[τος]
> ὑπὸ Ἀδωνιαστᾶν Ἀφροδεισιαστᾶν
> Ἀσκλαπιαστᾶν τῶν ἐν Αὐλαῖς
> χρυσέῳ στεφάνῳ
> 5 καὶ τᾶς γυναικὸς αὐτοῦ Νύσας Κώας
> καὶ Ἐπαφροδείτου Κώου, τιμ[α]-
> θέντος ὑπὸ Ἡροειστᾶν Σα[μο]-
> θρᾳκιαστᾶν χρυσέῳ στε[φά]-
> νῳ καὶ τᾶς γυναικὸς αὐ[τοῦ]
> 10   Τρυφέρας Ἐφεσ[ίας].

54. Apameia Kibotos

CIG, no. 3961; Ramsay, *The Cities and Bishoprics of Phrygia* 1.2, no. 289.

> Στράτων Ἄρχοντος σωθεὶς
> κατὰ θάλ[ασ]σαν Θεοῖς [Μ]ε[γ]άλοις Σα[μ]όθρ[α]ξιν χαιρεστήριον.

55. Fasilar

Rock-cut relief with inscription. Undated.

Sterrett, *Papers of the American School of Classical Studies at Athens* 3 (1884-85) 169, no. 277; Cronin, *JHS* 22 (1922) 112; *Denkmäler*, 17-18, no. 16 and fig. 4, no. 4; P. Lehmann, *Samothrace* 3.1, 252, fig. 210.

> Διόσκοροι
> Σαμοθρά-
> κων ἐπιφα-
> νεῖς θεοὶ
> 5 ἀδαμεῖ-
> [ς ἀ]εί.

56. Kyrene

Slab of white marble. Broken below. H: 0.125m. W: 0.155m. Th: 0.555m. Letters: 0.010-0.017m.

Fraser, *BSA* 57 (1962) 25-27 and pl. 1(b); Pugliese Carratelli, *ASAA* n.s. 23-24 (1961-62) 317, no. 168; *SEG* 20 (1964) 183, no. 724.

Πατρὶ
θεῶι
Σαμοθρᾶκι
ἀθανάτωι
5   ὑψίσ[τωι]
- - - - - ?

57. Κορτος

Inscription carved on a stone of yellow limestone.

Miller, *RA* 3rd ser. 2 (1883) 179, no. 3; *OGIS* I, no. 69; Holleaux, *Études* III, 93; Robert, *REG* 64 (1951) 132.

Θεοῖς μεγάλοις Σαμοθρᾳξι
᾿Απολλώνιος Σωσιβίου
Θηραῖος, ἡγεμὼν τῶν
ἔξω τάξεων, σωθεὶς
5   ἐκ μεγάλων κινδύνων, ἐκ-
πλεύσας ἐκ τῆς ᾿Ερυθρᾶς
θαλάσσης εὐχήν.

APPENDIX II

PAPYRI

1. PHILADELPHIA

Papyrus fragment, dated 250 B.C.
PCZ II (1926), no. 59296, lines 30-33.

30   καὶ ὥστε Ἐριεῖ λα[τόμωι
     τῶν σταθεισῶν [
     Σαμοθράικων καὶ φια[λῶν
     εἰς σπονδὴν [

APPENDIX III

SAMOTHRACIAN *MYSTAI* AND *EPOPTAI*

In this appendix the following abbreviations have been used:

IG = IG XII (8)

Sam 2.1 = P. M. Fraser, *Samothrace* 2.1, *The Inscriptions on Stone*

A. SAMOTHRACIAN MYSTAI

Ἀβαῖος Ἀντιδώρου, *IG*, no. 181.16.

Abascantus, *Hesperia* 34, 115, line 32, slave of proconsul.

Ἀγαθ{ε}ος Ἀγάθου, *IG*, no. 182.15.

Ἀγάνθιος Εὐ[βούλου], *Hesperia* 48, 17, line 6, τριήραρχος, Knidos.

Ἀγας____ _____, *IG*, no. 186a.15, συνέγδαμος, Rhodes.

Ἀγρεοφῶν Δι____, *IG*, no. 200.2.

Ἀδρι[ανό]ς? *IG*, no. 225.4.

Aesthreptio, *Hesperia* 34, 115, line 41, slave.

Ἀθαναίς, *IG*, no. 222.4, Kaunos.

Ἀθηνίων Βίθυος Βεροιαῖος, *IG*, no. 195.17, Beroia.

Αἰσχίνας Ἀ_____, *BCH* 86, no. 4.1, Kos?

Λεύχιος Ἄχαι[ο]ς Διοφάνους, *Sam.* 2.1, no. 33aI.15-16.

Ἀκέστωρ Εὐκτήμονος, *IG*, no. 182.14.

Q. Acorenus Q. 1. Alexsander, *IG*, no. 174.10.

Ἀλέξανδρος Ἀρτεμιδώρου, *IG*, no. 182.6.

Ἀλέξανδρος Αὐτοφῶντος, *BCH* 86, no. 4.7, Kos?

Ἀλέξανδρος Ἱκεσίου Μάγνης, *IG*, no. 206.9.

Ἄλυπος Λέοντος, *IG*, no. 195.21.

C. Amacil(ius) (??). Isinis (??), *Sam.* 2.1, no. 53*bis*.4, *lictor*.

Ἀμάτοχος [Δ]ημημτρί[ου], *IG*, no. 190b, Tralles.

[Ἀ]μφί<λ>οχο[ς], *Sam.* 2.1, no. 28b.13, ἀκόλουθος.

Ἀμφίων, *IG*, no. 224.1.

Ἀν_____, *Sam.* 2.1, no. 36.19.

Ἀναξικράτης Ἀναξικρατε[υς], *IG*, no. 186a.11, συνέγδαμος, Rhodes.

Ἀνδρόμαχος, *IG*, no. 222.6, Kaunos.

Ἀνδρόμαχος Δημητρίου, *Sam.* 2.1, no. 29aΙ. 1-4.

[Ἀ]νδρόμαχ[ος][Κρ]ατέρου, *IG*, no. 190a.17-8.

Ἀνδρόνιχος Ἀπολλωνίου, *IG*, no. 183.9, Abydos.

P. Aninius P. 1. Sai_____, *Hesperia* 48, 17, line 22.

Anthimus, *CIL* III Suppl., no. 7373.5, slave?

Ἄντανδρος Θεοδώρου, *IG*, no. 176.4, θεωρός, Elis.

Ἀντίγονος Τι[του?], *IG*, no. 207.14.

Ἀν[τί]μαχος Ν[εί]χωνος, *IG*, no. 183.7, from Abydos.

Antiochus Pac[ci], *Sam.* 2.1, no. 33aII.20.

Ἀντίοχος Σχοπίου, *IG*, no. 174.6, θεωρός, Dardanos.

P. Antipạ[...]ristis, *Hesperia* 34, 115, line 5, Proconsul from Macedonia.

Ἀντίπατ<ρ>ος [Ἀλε]ξάνδρου, *Sam.* 2.1, no. 37.3-4.

Ἀντιφάνης Ἀπολλωνίου Ἰλιεύς, *IG*, no. 206.4.

Ἀντιφάνης Διοσκουρ[ί]δου Στυβερραῖος, *IG*, no. 206. 11-12.

Ἀντίφιλος Ἀντιφίλου Βυζάντιος, *IG*, no. 206.5-6.

Antonia M. 1. _____, *Sam.* 2.1, no. 31.8.

M. Antonius Cn. f. _____, *Sam.* 2.1, no. 31.7.

Μᾶρκος Ἀντ[ών]ιος Ἡγησίας, *IG*, no. 206.12-13.

M. Ἀντώνιος Ὀπτᾶτος Φιλιπεύς, *Sam.* 2.1, no. 59.6, Philippi.

P. Antonius Cn. f. V___, *Sam.* 2.1, no. 31.6.

Ἀπολλόδωρος το[υ]___ου, *IG*, no. 220a.12, Maroneia.

Ἀπολλόδωρος Δεινοχλέους, *IG*, no. 173b.12, θεωρός, Dardanos.

[Ἀ]πολλόδωρος Εὐ___, *IG*, no. 181.21.

Ἀπολλοφάνης Διοδώρου, *IG*, no. 183.4, Abydos.

Ἀπολλωνίδης Ἀλεξιμάχου, *IG*, no. 173b.15, Dardanos.

Ἀπολλωνίδης Ζεύξιδος, *IG*, no. 182.4.

Ἀπολλώνιος Ἀντιφάνου Ἰλιεύς, *IG*, no. 206.5, Ilion.

Ἀπολλώνιος Ἀπολλωνίου, *IG*, no. 182.13.

Ἀπολλώνιος Γλαυκίου, *IG*, no. 195.15-16, ἀπελεύθερος, Amphipolis.

Ἀπολλ[ών]ιος Δη[μ]έου, *IG*, no. 183.8, Abydos.

Ἀπολλώνιος Διονυσίου, *IG*, no. 259.5.

Ἀπολλώνιος Εὐδα[ί]μονος, *IG*, no. 182.11.

Ἀπολλών[ιος]Μηνοφάν[ους], *IG*, no. 190a.19-20.

[Ἀπ]ολλὼς [Δι]οδότ[ου], *Sam.* 2.1, no. 28c.9-10.

M. Aranplius? *IG*, no. 215.11.

Ἀρισ... Παντέ[ως], *IG*, no. 201c.13-14.

Ἀρισταγόρας Εἰσιδώρου, *Sam.* 2.1, no. 59.5, Thasos.

Ἀριστογένης Νιχομάχο[υ], *IG*, no. 186b.22, ἱεροποιός, Rhodes.

Ἀριστοχράτης Ἀντιφάνεος, *IG*, no. 176.5, θεωρός, Elis.

Ἀριστομένης Ἀριστομένους, καθ' ὑθεσίαν δὲ Δωροθέου, *IG*, no. 160b. 20-21, θεωρός, Keramos.

Ἀριστοφῶν _____, *IG*, no. 181.9.

Ἀρίστων Ἀριστοθε[ι]ου, *Sam.* 2.1, no. 33aI.13-14.

Ἀρριδαῖος Ἱμέρου, *BCH* 86, no. 4.5, Kos?

L. Arrunti[us _____magister], *Sam.* 2.1, no. 40.5.

Ἀρτεμίδωρος, *IG*, no. 173b.20, ἀχόλουθος, Dardanos.

Ἀρτεμίδορος Πυθέου, *IG*, no. 182.8.

Artemo Nearchi, *IG*, no. 173a.7.

Ἀρχέπολι[ς] Ἀρχεπόλεως, *IG*, no. 195.8-9, Thessalonike.

Ἀσκλαπίων Μητροδώρου, *IG*, no. 185.4.

Ἀσκλᾶς, *IG*, no. 204.10, ἀκόλουθος.

Ἀσκληπιάδης Ἀ<ττ>άλου, *Sam.* 2.1, no. 29a³.12, Kyzikos.

Ἀσκληπιάδη[ς] Διοκλεύς, *Hesperia*, 48, 17, lines 10-11, γραμματεύς, Knidos.

Ἀσκληπιάδης Διονυσίου, *IG*, no. 182.9.

Ἀσκληπιάδης Μηνοδώρου Φλυεύς, *IG*, no. 216.9, Attica.

Ἀσπασία, *IG*, no. 215.7, Maroneia.

Ἀτείριο[ς? Θεο]χρή[στου?], *IG*, no. 196.6, Epidamnos.

__. Aṭelḷi[us __ f. or 1.], *Sam.* 2.1, no. 17b.

Ἀττινᾶς Διογένου, *IG*, no. 190a.14-15, Alopekonnesos.

Auctus, *Sam.* 2.1, no. 53*bis*.9, slave.

M. Aur[el___] or Mauṛ[us (?)], *Sam.* 2.1, no. 39.4.

[Αὐ]τομέδων, *IG* XII Suppl., no. 344.4.

. Afini__ _____, *Sam.* 2.1, no. 39.3.

B_____ _____, *IG*, no. 199.2-3.

Babullius [P]amphilus M. 1. [A]stymeno[s], *IG*, no. 190a.4-5.

M. Baebius [_____Ofatuleni] Sabini, *IG*, no. 207.15.

Βαιβία Φρό[ντωνος?], *IG*, no. 220.1.

<B>άχχιος _____, *Sam.* 2.1, App. IV.24, Kyzikos.

Bato Batonis, *Sam.* 2.1, no. 50.5.

Beitus, *IG*, no. 207.18, slave.

Βῖθυς, *IG*, no. 177a.7.

Βῖθυς Γλαυκίου, *IG*, no. 195.14, Amphipolis.

Βῖ[θ]υς Λεόντιδος, *IG*, no. 183.14, Abydos.

Βοιωτὸς Βριαρέως Σειραῖος, *IG*, no. 206.8, Serrhai.

Γάμος, *IG*, no. 220b.21, ἀπελεύθερος.

Γηρους? _____, *IG*, no. 183.17, Abydos.

[Γ]λαυκί[ας] .όλωνος, *Sam.* 2.1, no. 28c.5.

Γλαυκίας Ἀπολλοδώρου, *IG*, no. 195.10, Amphipolis.

Γλαυκίας Γλαυκίου, *IG*, no. 195.12, Amphipolis.

Γλαφυρ[ί]δ[η]ς, *IG*, no. 220b.20, ἀπελεύθερος.

Γρόσφ[ος], *IG*, no. 224.6.

Δαλεῖνος, *IG* XII Suppl., no. 344.14.

Δαλιάδας Ἀντιπάτρου, *IG*, no. 186b.21, ἱεροποιός, Rhodes.

Δαμαγόρας Φιλίσκου, *IG*, no. 189b.19.

[Δ]αμᾶς, *IG*, no. 189a.6.

Δαμασα____ _____, *IG*, no. 186a.14, συνέγδαμος, Rhodes.

Δαμάτριος Ἀμφοτεροῦ, *IG*, no. 186a.8, ἱεροποιός, Rhodes.

Δᾶος, *IG*, no. 177a.5.

Δᾶφνος, *IG*, no. 224.3.

Daphnus, *CIL* III Suppl., no. 7374.3.

Δημ_____, *Sam.* 2.1, no. 33aII.2.

Δημήτριος Ἀπολλωνίου Ἀλεξανδρεύς, *IG*, no. 206.9-10, Alexandria.

Δημήτριος Ἀρτεμιδώρου, *IG*, no. 182.10.

Δημήτριος Δημητρίου, *IG*, no. 259.2, Kyzikos?

Δημοκράτ[η]ς Οὐλιάδου, *IG*, no. 182.1.

Διαγόρα[ς], *IG*, no. 199.1.

Δίδυμος Διδύμου Ἀλεξανδρεύς, *IG*, no. 206.6, Alexandria.

Διζάσσχος, *Sam.* 2.1, no. 33aΙ.12.

Δίναρχος Ἀγαθ__, *Sam.* 2.1, no. 33aΙ.21-2.

Διογένης _____, *IG*, no. 206.14, ἀπελεύθερος.

[Δι]ογένης Ἀττάλου, *IG*, no. 194.11, ἱεροποιός, Kyzikos.

[Δι]ογένης .ω.ν.ο[υ?], *IG*, no. 181.15.

Diodo[rus], *IG*, 207.18, slave.

[e.g., Διόδ]οτος [e.g., Ἀριστοδ]άμου, *Sam.* 2.1, no. 35.2-3.

Diodọ[t]us A[th]enogenis, *IG*, no. 173a.6.

Διοκλῆς Εὐάνδρου, *IG*, no. 189b.20.

[Di]onysides Chresimus, *CIL* III Suppl., no. 7373.4.

Διονύσιος, *IG*, no. 199.2.

Διονύσιος, *IG*, no. 225.10.

Διονύσιος, *IG*, no. 206.12, κυβερνήτης, Aigai.

Dionysius, *Hesperia* 34, 115, line 16, slave.

Διονύσιος Ἀρχεπόλεως, *IG*, no. 195.19-20.

Διονύσιος Διοδότου, *Sam.* 2.1, no. 33aΙ.19-20.

[Δ]ιον[ύσιος] [Δ]ιονυσ[ίου], *Sam.* 2.1, no. 28c.1-2.

Διονύσιος Διοδώρου, *IG*, no. 173b.17, Dardanos.

Διονύσιος Ἐφέσιος, *IG*, no. 186b.24, ναύτης, Ephesos.

Διονύσιος Μαντᾶς, *IG*, no. 195.13-14, Amphipolis.

Διονύσιος Σκοπίου, *IG*, no. 174.5, θεωρός, Dardanos.

Διονύσιος Τιμο[κλ]είους, *IG*, no. 182.3.

Dionysius L. se[r](vus), *IG*, no. 174.9, slave.

Διονυσοκλῆς Μητροδώρου, *Sam.* 2.1, no. 33aΙ. 10-11.

Διότιμος Διοτίμου, *BCH* 86, no. 4.3, Kos?

Dominịs, *Hesperia* 34, 115, line 26, slave.

Dorus, *CIL* III Suppl., no. 7373.8.

Δωσίθεος, *IG*, no. 177a.4-5.

Εἰρήνη, *IG*, no. 178.7, κιθαρίστρια, ἀκόλουθος, Kassandreia.

Εἰσίδωρος, *IG*, no. 220b.22, ἀπελεύθερος.

῞Ελενος _____χου, *Sam.* 2.1, no. 33aII.9.

[῎Ε]ṿδημος (?), *IG*, no. 190a.22.

Εος____, *Sam.* 2.1, no. 36.23, slave.

Ἐπαμινώνδας, *IG*, no. 177a.6.

Ἐπαφρᾶς, *IG*, no. 185.6, ἀοιδός.

Ἐπαφρόδε[ιτος], *IG*, no. 220b.23, ἀπελεύθερος.

Epaphroditus, *Sam*. 2.1, no. 52.4, slave.

Epaphus, *Sam*. 2.1, no. 36.26, slave.

Ἐπιγένης _____, *Sam*. 2.1, no. 33aI.23.

Ἐπίγονος Μενεστράτου, *IG*, no. 182.7.

Ἐπτ(?).....[Κρί]σπος, *Sam*. 2.1, no. 43.4.

[Her]mas, *Sam*. 2.1, no. 36.21, slave.

Hermes, *Sam*. 2.1, no. 53*bis*.8, slave.

[Ἑρ]μίας, *IG* XII Suppl., no. 344.6.

[Ἕ]ρμων Δημητρίου, *IG*, no. 183.11, Abydos.

Eros, *CIL* III Suppl., no. 7373.7.

[Eu]andrus [P]aramoni, *IG*, no. 215.6.

Εὐβούλα Διονυσίου, *IG*, no. 220a.13, Maroneia.

Εὔβουλος Ἀρχιπόλιος, *Hesperia*, 48, 17, lines 4-5, ναύαρχος, Knidos.

Εὔδωρος, *IG*, no. 173b.20 (*Sam*. 2.1, 73), ἀκόλουθος.

Εὐήμερος, *IG*, no. 177a.5.

Εὐήμερος Λεόν[τ]ιδος, *IG*, no. 183.13, Abydos.

Εὔηνος, *IG*, no. 224.6.

Ε[ὐ]μέν[ης](?), *Sam*. 2.1, no. 33aII.3.

[Ε]ὔνομος, *IG*. no. 181.11.

Εὐπορίων, *IG*, no. 185.6, ἀοιδός.

Euporus, *Sam*. 2.1, no. 53*bis*.8, slave.

Euprepe[s], *Sam*. 2.1, no. 53*bis*.9, slave.

[E]urus or [D]urus, *Sam*. 2.1, no. 38.8.

Εὐσύης Ἐφέσιος, *IG*, no. 186b.26, ναύτης, Ephesos.

Εὐσχήμων Χρυσέρωτος Πειραιεύς, *IG*, no. 216.10, Athens.

Eutyches, *Hesperia* 34, 115, line 38, slave.

[E]utyches, *CIL* III Suppl., no. 7373.2.

Eutychus, *Sam*. 2.1, no. 52.3, slave.

Zelotus, *Hesperia* 34, 115, line 18, slave.

Ζή< λω? >τος Ῥοδοκλήου Ῥόδων, *Sam*. 2.1, no. 29b¹.4-5, Rhodes.

Ζηνοδώρα _____σίου, *IG*, no. 199.3-4.

Ζήνων Ζήνωνος, *IG*, no. 259.4, Kyzikos?

Zoticus, *Hesperia* 34, 115, line 33, slave.

[Ζ]ώϊλος, *IG* XII Suppl., no. 344.5.

Ζωσίμη, *IG*, no. 220a.7, Thasos, femina.

Ἡλιόδωρ[ος], *Sam*. 2.1, no. 28b.11, ἀκόλουθος.

Ἡραῖος Ἀλεξάνδρου, *BCH* 86, no. 4.9, Kos?

[Ἡ]ρακλῆ[ς] [Ἡ]ρακλέ[ους], *Sam*. 2.1, no. 28c.3-4.

Ἥρων Ὑγιαίν[ο]υ[τος], *Sam*. 2.1, no. 60.3-4.

Θεογείτων Σατύρ[ου], *IG*, no. 181.10.

P. Theodosus, *Hesperia* 34, 115, line 8.

Θεόδωρος _____, *IG*, no. 181.7.

Θεο<ζ>ᾶ<ς> Μοιρα<γ>ό<ρ>ο<υ>, *Sam.* 2.1, no. 29b¹. 2-3.

[Θ]εόμνης Θεοδώρου, *IG*, no. 181.14.

Θεόξενος Μητροδώρου, *Sam.* 2.1, no. 33aI.6-7.

Θεότιμος 'Αριστοδάμου, *BCH* 86, no. 4.8.

Θέρσων 'Ηρογείτονος, *Sam.* 2.1, no. 29a³.13, Kyzikos.

Θεύδωρος 'Ηραγόρ[α], *IG*, no. 186a.12, συνέγδαμος, Rhodes.

Θεύδωρος Θευδώρου, *BCH* 86, no. 4.2, Kos?

Θέων Δνμητρίου, *IG*, no. 183.10, Abydos.

Θηβαΐς, *Sam.* 2.1, no. 47.13, slave, Beroia.

Θήρων Περίνθιος, *IG*, no. 186b.25, ναύτης, Perinthos.

Θρασύμαχος Πολυδ__, *IG*, no. 181.18.

<Θ>ράσων, *Sam.* 2.1, App. IV.23, Kyzikos.

'Ιεροκλῆς Δημητρίου τοῦ Μοσ____, *IG*, no. 160b.19, θεωρός, Keramos.

['Ι]ερόμαχο[ς] 'Ατ[τ]άλου, *Sam.* 2.1, no. 28b.6-7.

'Ικ[έ]σιος 'Αντιόχου, *IG*, no. 220a.10.

Εὐήμερος Λεόν[τ]ιδος, *IG*, no. 183.13, Abydos.

Εὔηνος, *IG*, no. 224.6.

Ε[ὐ]μέν[ης](?), *Sam.* 2.1, no. 33aII.3.

[Ε]ὔνομος, *IG*. no. 181.11.

Εὐπορίων, *IG*, no. 185.6, ἀοιδός.

Euporus, *Sam.* 2.1, no. 53*bis*.8, slave.

Euprepe[s], *Sam.* 2.1, no. 53*bis*.9, slave.

[E]urus or [D]urus, *Sam.* 2.1, no. 38.8.

Εὐσύης 'Εφέσιος, *IG*, no. 186b.26, ναύτης, Ephesos.

Εὐσχήμων Χρυσέρωτος Πειραιεύς, *IG*, no. 216.10, Athens.

Eutychẹs, *Hesperia* 34, 115, line 38, slave.

[E]utyches, CIL III Suppl., no. 7373.2.

Eutychus, *Sam.* 2.1, no. 52.3, slave.

Zẹlotus, *Hesperia* 34, 115, line 18, slave.

Ζή<λω?>τος 'Ροδοκλήου 'Ρόδων, *Sam.* 2.1, no. 29b¹.4-5, Rhodes.

Ζηνοδώρα _____σίου, *IG*, no. 199.3-4.

Ζήνων Ζήνωνος, *IG*, no. 259.4, Kyzikos?

Zoticus, *Hesperia* 34, 115, line 33, slave.

[Z]ώϊλος, *IG* XII Suppl., no. 344.5.

Ζωσίμη, *IG*, no. 220a.7, Thasos, femina.

'Ηλιόδωρ[ος], *Sam.* 2.1, no. 28b.11, ἀκόλουθος.

'Ηραῖος 'Αλεξάνδρου, *BCH* 86, no. 4.9, Kos?

['Η]ρακλῆ[ς] ['Η]ρακλέ[ους], *Sam.* 2.1, no. 28c.3-4.

῭Ηρων 'Υγιαίν[ο]ϙ[τος], *Sam.* 2.1, no. 60.3-4.

Θεογείτων Σατύρ[ου], *IG*, no. 181.10.

P. Ṭheodosus, *Hesperia* 34, 115, line 8.

Θεόδωρος _____, *IG*, no. 181.7.

Θεο<ζ>ᾶ<ς> Μοιρα<γ>ό<ρ>ο<υ>, *Sam.* 2.1, no. 29b¹. 2-3.

[Θ]εόμνης Θεοδώρου, *IG*, no. 181.14.

Θεόξενος Μητροδώρου, *Sam.* 2.1, no. 33aI.6-7.

Θεότιμος 'Αριστοδάμου, *BCH* 86, no. 4.8.

Θέρσων 'Ηρογείτονος, *Sam.* 2.1, no. 29a³.13, Kyzikos.

Θεύδωρος 'Ηραγόρ[α], *IG*, no. 186a.12, συνέγδαμος, Rhodes.

Θεύδωρος Θευδώρου, *BCH* 86, no. 4.2, Kos?

Θέων Δνμητρίου, *IG*, no. 183.10, Abydos.

Θηβαΐς, *Sam.* 2.1, no. 47.13, slave, Beroia.

Θήρων Περίνθιος, *IG*, no. 186b.25, ναύτης, Perinthos.

Θρασύμαχος Πολυδ__, *IG*, no. 181.18.

<Θ>ράσων, *Sam.* 2.1, App. IV.23, Kyzikos.

'Ιεροκλῆς Δημητρίου τοῦ Μοσ____, *IG*, no. 160b.19, θεωρός, Keramos.

['Ι]ερόμαχο[ς] 'Ατ[τ]άλου, *Sam.* 2.1, no. 28b.6-7.

'Ικ[έ]σιος 'Αντιόχου, *IG*, no. 220a.10.

['Ι]ουλία Γηπ[αι]πύρο[υ], *IG*, no. 218.4, Ainos.

['Ιουλ]ία Καλλικράτου, *IG*, no. 218.5, Ainos.

'Ιουλ[ι]ε[ῖς], *IG*, no. 223.7, Alexandria Troas.

Γ. 'Ιούλιος Αὐφιδιανός Τι(βερίου) ἀδε(λφός), *IG*, no. 219.3-4.

C. Iulius Augu[rinus], *BCH* 86, no. 5.6.

Γ. 'Ιούλιος Νίγερ, *IG*, no. 221.4-5.

L. Iulius Sp. f. Pap. Niger, *Sam.* 2.1, no. 36.8.

[Τιβέ]ριος 'Ιούλιος [Εὐφ]ρόσυνος, *IG*, no. 206.1.

Iunius, *Hesperia* 34, 115, line 27, slave.

Γάϊος 'Ιούνιος Λυσίμαχος, *IG*, no. 206.2.

'Ιππόδαμος 'Αναξάνδριδ[ος], *Hesperia* 48, 17, line 7, τριήραρχος, Knidos.

'Ισίδοτος _____, *IG*, no. 186a.13, συνέγδαμος, Rhodes.

'Ισίδω[ρ]ος, *IG*, no. 225.9.

Γα. 'Ιτύριος Πούδης, *Sam.* 2.1, no. 47.8, Beroia.

Ḷ. or Ṗ. Iu(v)entius M'. [fil.] Thalna, *Sam.* 2.1, no. 25.

Κάδμος Θάσιο[ς], *IG*, no. 206.4, Thasos.

Καλλικράτης Δαματρίου, *IG*, no. 186a.10, συνέγδαμος, Rhodes.

[Καλλιό?]πη Νίκωνος, *IG*, no. 218.6, Ainos.

Callistion, *Sam.* 2.1, no. 53*bis*.7, slave.

[Κ]άνθος Κυδί[μου], *IG*, no. 181.17.

Κάστωρ 'Επικράτ[ους], *Sam.* 2.1, no. 56. 2-3.

Cedruṣ, *Sam.* 2.1, no. 36.19, slave.

Κέρδων ['Α]ν[τ]ιμάχου, *IG*, no. 183.12, Abydos.

C. Cestius, *IG*, 189c.42.

Ciṃ_____, *Hesperia* 34, 115, line 28, slave.

Κλάρος Κλάρου Αἰξωνεύς, *IG*, 216.17, Athens.

Κλαύδιος Σύμφορος Θεσσαλονικεύς, *Sam.* 2.1, no. 58.4-5, Thessalonike.

Tị. Çḷ[audius____], *Sam.* 2.1, no. 40.8.

Ti. Claudius D____, *Sam.* 2.1, no. 40.7.

Τι. Κλαύδιος Εὔλαιος, *Sam.* 2.1, no. 47.5, Beroia.

Clenas, *Sam.* 2.1, no. 36.22, slave.

Κλεοπάτρα Θεοδότου, *IG*, no. 195.11, Amphipolis.

Κλευ____ Νικασιβούλου, *Hesperia* 48, 17, lines 8-9, τριήραρχος, Knidos.

Q. Clod(i)us Q. l. Agacles, *IG*, no. 173a.5.

Q. Clodius Longus, *IG*, no. 215.5.

Κόλλις Κόλλιδος ὁ καὶ Μάρεις, *IG*, no. 206.11.

Κομμέν[ι]ος (?), *IG*, no. 225.2-3.

Cor.. Maṭrod[orus], *Sam.* 2.1, no. 28a.10.

Κορνηλία Ἀλεξάνδρα Κορ(νηλίου) Ἀδειμάντου θυ(γάτηρ), *IG*, no. 216.12, Athens.

Κορνηλία Φιλότροφον ἐξ Ἀζηνιέων, *IG*, no. 216.13, Athens.

Κορνήλιος Ἀδείμαντος Ἀναφλύστιος, *IG*, no. 216.11, Athens.

Cn. (Cornelius) Lentuḷ(us), *Hesperia* 48, 17, line 20.

[L. C]ornelius L. l. Phil[o], *Sam.*, 2.1, no. 28a.6.

.....o. Corne[lius __. l.], *Sam.* 2.1, no. 28a.14.

....us Cornel[ius __. l.], *Sam.* 2.1, no. 28a.12.

Cosmeta, *CIL* III Suppl., no. 7373.8.

Κότυς Γλαυκίου, *IG*, no. 195.14-15, ἀπελεύθερος, Amphipolis.

[Κ]ροῖσος, *Sam.* 2.1, no. 28b.8.

Κρόν[ι]ος Ἡλιοδώρου Ἀλεξανδρεύς, *IG*, no. 206.6-7, Alexandria.

L. Q[uinctius?], *CIL* III, no. 714.1.

Κυϊντία Μίλωνος, *IG*, no. 218.3, Ainos.

Κῦρος, *IG*, no. 224.4.

P. Curtilius Commodus, *Sam.* 2.1, no. 53*bis*.2.

P. Curtius P.[l.] I____, *IG*, no. 207.13.

Lacon, *Sam.* 2.1, no. 53*bis*.9, slave.

Laetus, *Sam.* 2.1, no. 36.20, slave.

Lectis, *CIL* Suppl., no. 7373.7.

Ḷeontiscus [L]ẹon[t]ịsçị, *IG*, no. 215.7.

Τίτος Λέπιδος Νύ[μ]φιος, *IG*, no. 206.3-4.

Λεωνίδης [ἄρχων] ὑπερετικοῦ [πλοίου δη]μọσίου, *IG*, no. 205.11-13.

M. Ḷivius Pamplus, *IG*, no. 190a.2-3.

P. Livius M. l. Pal(atina), *CIL* III, no. 713.2.

C. L. Luccius C. f., *CIL*, no. 714.1.

Lycoṛịs, *Hesperia* 34, 115, line 17, slave.

[Λ]υκόφρον[ος], *Sam.* 2.1, no. 28b.9.

Λυσιμένης Ἀπολλωνίδου, *IG*, no. 173b.11, θεωρός, Dardanos.

Λυσίων Ε____, *IG*, no. 196.4, Epidamnos.

Lutaciu[s ____], *BCH* 86, no. 5.5.

L. Luuceius M. f. leg(atus), *CIL* III, no. 713.2.

M. Luuceius M. l. Artemidorus, *CIL* III, no. 713.3.

Μα_____ _____, *Sam.* 2.1, App. IV.22, Kyzikos.

Μαγιανός, *Sam.* 2.1, no. 59.9, slave, Thasos.

P. Magul[nius], *Sam.* 2.1, no. 32.8.

[P. M]allius P. l. Lict[avius?], *Sam.* 2.1, no. 28a.9.

[. M]anius Demetr[ius], *Sam.* 2.1, no. 28a.8.

Mappius, *Hesperia* 34, 115, line 15, slave.

C. Mari ____, *Sam.* 2.1, no. 30.3.

__ Marius Fructus, *Sam.* 2.1, no. 36.10.

Ç. Marius L. f. Ste. Schinas, *Sam.* 2.1, no. 36.5.

Μάρχιος Μυρισμὸς Θεσσαλονεικεύς, *Sam.* 2.1, no. 58.6-7, Thessalonike.

Marcius Felix Vic[____], *Hesperia* 34, 115, line 9.

[M]arone[ys], *IG*, no. 189a.8.

Μελάνιππος, *IG*, no. 189b.21.

Menan[de]r, *Hesperia* 34, 115, line 24, slave.

[Me]nander Chius, *Sam.* 2.1, no. 36.12.

Μένανδρος, *IG*, no. 178.2, ἀκόλουθος, Azoros.

[Μέ?]γανδρος _____, *IG*, no. 181.3.

Μενέδημος Μενεδήμου, *IG*, no. 183.5, Abydos.

Μενέμαχος Μητροδώρου Βυζάντιος, *IG*, no. 206.7-8, Byzantion.

Μέντωρ, *IG*, no. 189b.22.

Μένυλλα Ἱπποστράτου Κασσανδρεῖτις, *IG*, no. 178.5, Kassandreia.

Μηνόδωρος Τέχνωνος, *IG*, no. 182.2.

Μηνόφαντος Φιλοκράτους, *IG*, no. 173b.18, Dardanos.

Μηνόφιλο<ς>, χυβερνήτης, *Sam.* 2.1, no. 29a³.13, Kyzikos.

Μηνόφιλος Φιλίππου, *Sam.* 2.1, no. 33aI.8-9.

Μητρόδωρ[ος], *IG* XII Suppl., no. 344.15.

Μητρόδωρος Βίθυος, *IG*, no. 195.16.

Μητρόφάν[ης] (or Μητρόφαν[τος]), *IG*, no. 181.4.

Μητρῶναξ _____, *IG*, no. 181.8.

Μίχα Θάσιος, *IG*, no. 184.11, Thasos.

Μίνναρος, *Sam.* 2.1, no. 26b.2.

Q. Minuc[ius ____?] Thermus, *Sam.* 2.1, no. 32.6-7.

C. Mispius, *CIL* III, no. 714.2.

C. Modius Asclepiades, *Sam.* 2.1, no. 50.4a.

[Μοι]ραγένης, *IG*, no. 189b.23.

Moschus, *Hesperia* 34, 115, line 22, slave.

Μόσχος Μενεχράτου, *IG*, no. 259.3.

Mydus, *Hesperia* 34, 115, line 29, slave.

Μυσίλας (?) τριήραρχος, *IG* 259.1.

......r. Muti(us). C. 1. ... *Sam.* 2.1, no. 28a.13.

[C.] Mutius C. 1. Erun____, *Sam.* 2.1, no. 28a.7.

L. Ne.ius, *IG*, no. 173.4.

Νεικόλαος Ὀλίου Αἴνιος, *IG*, no. 221.6, Ainos.

Νεικόστ[ρ]ατο[ς], *IG*, no. 220b.19, ἀπελεύθερος.

Nicephorus, *Sam.* 2.1, no. 53*bis*.7, slave.

Νικησίλ<ης> Σωτέλους, *IG*, no. 201b.9-11.

Νικήφορος, *IG*, no. 177a.3.

Ν[ικο?]λαος, *IG*, no. 225.5-6.

Νικόστρατο[ς], *IG*, no. 224.2.

Numenius, *Hesperia* 34, 115, line 25, slave.

[Ν]υμφικός, *Sam.* 2.1, no. 59.11, Thasos.

[Ν]υμφόδωρος _____, *IG*, no. 181.5.

Νυμφόδορος Νυμφοδ[ώρου], *IG*, no. 209.7-9, Chios.

O..... Λέοντος, *IG*, no. 195.20.

T. Ofatulenus _____, *IG*, no. 207.9.

T. Ofatulenu[s _____], *IG*, no. 207.11.

T. Ofatulen[us _____] Sabinus, *IG*, no. 207.5-6.

T. Ofatulenus S[abinus? ____], *IG*, no. 207.12.

Γάος Ὀκταύιος Βάσος, *IG*, no. 206.3.

Ὅμιλος, *IG*, no. 174.7, ἀκόλουθος, Dardanos.

Onesimus Virin[__?] Dec[__?], *Hesperia* 34, 115, lines 36-37, slave.

M. Oppius Nepos, *CIL* III, no. 721.

Opt[atus], *Sam.* 2.1, no. 36.21.

Ὀπ[τ]ης? Μενίσκου, *IG*, no. 183.16, Abydos.

Q. Hortensius M. l. Archelaos, *CIL* III, no. 713.4.

M. Ὀρφίδιος Ἀργησίλαος, *Sam.* 2.1, no. 58.2-3, Herakleia apo Strymonos.

[Ὀ]τρύας Στησικλέους, *IG*, no. 181.20.

Valeries, *IG*, no. 209.4.

L. Veneilus L. f. Pollion, *IG*, no. 174.9.

Asc[..]us Vennus Ϝις_____, *Hesperia* 34, 115, line 10.

A. Vereius Felix, *Sam.* 2.1, no. 50.4b.

Vilius, *Sam.* 2.1, no. 38.7, slave?

Q. Visellius L. f., *Sam.* 2.1, no. 29a¹.5.

Οὐλπία Ἀλεξάνδρα, *Sam.* 2.1, no. 47.6, Beroia.

Pa____, *Sam.* 2.1, no. 36.28, slave.

Paideros, *Sam.* 2.1, no. 36.27, slave.

C. Pacciu[s] C. l. Apollonides, *Sam.* 2.1, no. 33aII.15-16.

M. Paccius P. f., Fal. Rufus, *Sam.* 2.1, no. 33aII.14-15.

Παλ__ _____, *IG*. no. 220b.17.

Παλαίστριχος Διοκλεῦς, *BCH* 86, no. 4.6, Kos?

Sex. Palp[e]llius Candidus Tullittianus, *Sam.* 2.1, no. 50.2-3.

Paneros, *Sam.* 2.1, no. 36.25, slave.

[Pa]ntonicus, *CIL* III Suppl., no. 7374.4.

Παράμονος, *Sam.* 2.1, no. 47.12, slave, Beroia.

Παράμονος Ζωίλου Σιρραῖος, *Sam.* 2.1, no. 46. 8-10, Serrhai.

Parthenopae[us], *Hesperia* 34, 115, line 31, slave.

Παρμενίσκος Ἀριστέω[ς], *Sam.* 2.1, no. 29a³.10, ἱεροποιός, Kyzikos.

Παρμενίσσκος, *IG*, no. 178.2, στρατηγός, ὁπλοφόρος, Azoros.

Pasiphilus, *Hesperia* 34, 115, line 40, slave.

Πάτριχος, *IG*, no. 173b.15 (*Sam.* 2.1, 73), slave, Dardanos.

Παυσανίας Διφίλου, *IG*, no. 174.4, θεωρός, Dardanos.

Πειθ____, *IG*, no. 206.14, ἀπελεύθερος of King Rhoimetalkes.

Πεισικράτης Τιμαράτου, *IG*, no. 186a.7, ἱεροποιός, Rhodes.

Περδίκας, *IG*, no. 222.5, Kaunos.

Περιγένης Φιλοχάρους, *Sam.* 2.1, no. 33aI.17-18.

Πέρσας Μενάνδρου, *IG*, no. 195.18-19.

[Σπό]ριος Πέρσιος Κοΐντου [Ῥω]μαῖος, *IG*, no. 205.10-11.

[Q. Pla]ṇius Sardus Varius Ambibulus, *Sam.* 2.1, no. 53.6.
Procos. [provinci]ae Mac[e]doniae.

Πο_____, *Sam.* 2.1, no. 26b.1.

[Π]ολύδωρος Ἀπολλ____, *IG*, no. 181.13.

Πολύχαρμος Χάρμου, *IG*, no. 182.5.

L. Pomponius Maximus Flavius [Sil]yanus, *Sam.* 2.1, no. 51. 6-7, Q. propr.
[prov. Maced.].

Ποσίδεος Λεόντιδος, *IG*, no. 183.15, Abydos.

Ποσιδώνιος, *IG*, no. 215.14, Maroneia.

[Πρ]άξων, *IG*, no. 209.1.

Πρεῖμος Ἀπολλωνίου Ἀλεξανδρε[ύς], *IG*, no. 206.10.

Pretiosus, *Sam.* 2.1, no. 53*bis*.6, slave.

[Pr?]iamus, *CIL* III Suppl., no. 7373.5.

Πρόκλος, *Sam.* 2.1, no. 33aII.5.

Ἀ. Προύσιος, *IG*, no. 221.6, Ainos?

Πρῶτος, *IG*, no. 185.6, ἀοιδός.

[Π]τολεμᾶς or [Π]τολεμα[ῖος], *Sam.* 2.1, no. 28b.12, ἀκόλουθος.

[Π]τολλᾶ[ς] [Ἡρ]ακλέους, *Sam.* 2.1, no. 28c.7-8.

Πυθ_____, *IG*, no. 207.8.

Πυθαγόρας, *IG*, no. 189b.40-41.

Πυθίων Ἀριστοκλείους, *Sam.* 2.1, no. 33aI.4-5.

Purpurio, *Sam.* 2.1, no. 50.6, slave.

Restitutu[s], *Sam.* 2.1, no. 53*bis*. 10, slave.

T. Ῥουτειλίου Ποτείτου Οἰκονόμος, *IG*, no. 221.5, Ainos?

_____ Rufus, *CIL* III Suppl., no. 7372, Praetorius.

[Ῥ]οῦφος Ἑρμ...ιας, *Sam.* 2.1, no. 41.8.

[R]upịlia Q. f. Quinta, *Sam.* 2.1, no. 36.6, femina.

Ῥῶς Βίθυος, *IG*, no. 195, margin, Thessalonike.

[_____] Σαλλούστιος Ῥοῦφος, *IG*, no. 206.1-2.

Σάτυρος Σκαμάνδρου, *IG* XII Suppl., no. 344.12-13.

Sc_____, *Sam.* 2.1, no. 36.22, slave.

Σει[ληνὶς] Διονυσικλείου, *IG*, no. 220a.13-14, femina, Maroneia.

Seleysys, *IG*, no. 189a.9.

Septimius Tigrines, *Hesperia* 34, 115, line 7.

[M. S]e[rvilius?] M. l. Pamp[hilus], *Sam.* 2.1, no. 34.7.

M. Servilius M. l. Philo, *Sam.* 2.1, no. 34.6.

P. Sextius Lippinus Tarquitianus, *IG*, no. 214.5, quaestor of Macedonia.

Σι..τας, *Sam.* 2.1, no. 33aII.4.

Siger[us], *Sam.* 2.1, no. 52.3 *AJPh* 84, 99.

Αὖλος Σικίνιος Λευκίου Ῥωμαῖος Ἀθηνίων, *IG*, no. 205.8-9.

Σκο_____, *IG*, no. 206.15, ἀπελεύθερος of King Rhoimetalkes.

Sp_____, *Sam.* 2.1, no. 36.27, slave.

Στατ[ίλιος], *IG*, no. 225.8.

Στάχυς, *Sam.* 2.1, no. 47.11, slave, Beroia.

Στρατονείκη, *IG*, no. 215.15, femina, Maroneia.

Στράτων Ἐπικράτων, *IG*, no. 182.12.

Σωκλῆς _____, *IG*, no. 181.6.

Σωκλῆς Οἰᾳ _____, *IG*, no. 181.19.

Σωκλῆς Ὀλυμπιοδώρου, *IG*, no. 173b.13-14 (*Sam.* 2.1, 73), Dardanos.

Σωκράτης Ἀρχελάου Πειραιεύς, *IG*, no. 216.4-6, Athens.

Σώσαρχος, *Sam.* 2.1, no. 28b.14, ἀκόλουθος.

[Σ]ωσίβιος Πολυκλέου, *IG*, no. 181.22.

Σωσικλῆς Εὐκράτευς, *IG*, no. 186a.6, ἱεροποιός, Rhodes.

Σωσί[λα]ος Παρμενίῳ[νος], *IG*, no. 196.5, Epidamnos.

[Σ]ώστρατο[ς] Προκλείου, *Sam.* 2.1, no. 28b.3-4.

Σωτᾶς Βότρυος Δαιδαλίδης, *IG*, no. 216.14, Athens.

T[...]eacranis, *Hesperia* 34, 115, line 39, slave.

T. l. = T(iti) l., *IG*, no. 209.3.

Τ.υ, *Sam.* 2.1, no. 39.5.

Ταλο[ύ]ρας, *IG*, no. 177a.6.

Tarula, *Sam.* 2.1, no. 36.28, slave.

Crassupes P. Teidius P. f. Pom(ptina), *CIL* III Suppl., no. 12318.

Tertia. Dom_____, *IG*, no. 207.7.

Τιθύτα Ἐντίμου, *IG*, no. 220a.14-15, Maroneia.

Τιμαγόρας Θεοκλείδου, *IG*, no. 201b.7-8.

[Τ]ίμαρχος, *IG* XII Suppl., no. 344.9.

To_____, *Sam.* 2.1, no. 36.23, slave.

[Τύ?]ννων, *IG* XII Suppl., no. 344.7.

Tyranni[o], *Sam.* 2.1, no. 52.5, slave.

[U]rsus, *Sam.* 2.1, no. 38.7.

C. Fadius Endymion, *Sam.* 2.1, no. 53*bis*.3, lictor.

Φανέας Σημ____, *IG*, no. 201c.16-17.

Felix, *Sam.* 2.1, no. 36.29, slave.

Felix Aucustor Verna, *Hesperia* 34, 115, lines 34-35, slave.

Φιλ____, *Sam.* 2.1, no. 33aII.1.

Φιλάργυρο[ς], *IG*, no. 222.7, Kaunos.

Phileus, *Hesperia* 34, 115, line 19, slave.

Φιλῖνος Φιλίνου νεώτερος, *IG*, no. 183.6, Abydos.

[Φ]ιλιππεύς, *IG*, no. 209.2.

Philippus, *CIL* III, no. 12321.

Philo____eus, *Hesperia* 34, 115, line 21.

Philodamus[Pac]ci, *Sam.* 2.1, no. 33aII.17, slave.

Φιλοκράτης ὁ καὶ Εἰσίδωρος Φιλοκράτους 'Οῆθεν, *IG*, no. 216.7-8, Athens.

Φιλοκτα, *Sam.* 2.1, no. 26b.3.

Philomusus, *IG*, no. 207.17, slave.

[Φιλό]ξενος Φιλοξένου, *Sam.* 2.1, no. 29a³.11, ἱεροποιός, Kyzikos.

Φιλόστοργος, *Sam.* 2.1, no. 59.10, slave, Thasos.

Φιλόστρατος, *IG*, no. 177a.4.

[Φιλο]τειμία Παραμόνου, *IG*, no. 220a.6, Thasos.

Φιλούμενος, *Sam.* 2.1, no. 59.8, slave, Thasos.

Φίλων ['Αδρ]άστ[ου?], *IG*, no. 196.3, Epidamnos.

[Κόϊν]τος Φλάυιος, *Sam.* 2.1, no. 41.7.

Pho[e]bus, *Sam.* 2.1, no. 36.24, slave.

Φοῖβος, *IG*, no. 225.5.

Fortuna[tus], *CIL* III Suppl., no. 7373.9.

L. Fourius L. f. Ouf(entia), *CIL* III, suppl., no. 12318.

A. Furius ____, *IG*, no. 207.10.

Χαρίδημος Χαριδήμου, *IG*, no. 182.16.

[Χ]ρήσιμος, *Sam.* 2.1, no. 41.10, slave.

Χρήσιμ[ος], *IG*, no. 225.6.

Xy[stus], *Sam.* 2.1, no. 36.29, slave.

'Ωπηνεύ[ς] 'Αριστοκλείους, *Sam.* 2.1, no. 33aI. 2-3.

'Ωρομέδων Σαίνοντος, *BCH* 86, no. 4.4, Kos?

Names for which only the patronymic survives:

____λδόρης 'Αντιδώρου, *IG*, no. 181.12.

____ρέτη 'Αντιόχου, *IG*, no. 179.2.

____ιον ['Α]ντιφῶν[τος], *IG*, no. 218.7, Ainos.

____δοτος 'Απολλωνίου, *IG*, no. 220a.8.

____ς 'Απολλω[νίου], *IG*, no. 180.8.

____ς 'Αριστοδάμο[υ] ["Α]ρσινοεύς, *IG*, no. 184.12-13, Arsinoe.

___ας Ἀρίστωνος, *IG*, no. 180.2.

_____['Ασκλη]πιάδου, *IG*, no. 197b.8.

___ας Ἀσκληπιάδου, *Sam*. 2.1, App. IV.20, Kyzikos.

_____ος Ἀφροδισίου Ἀντιοχεύς, *IG*, no. 184.4, Antioch.

_____[Βε]νδιδώρο[υ], *Sam*. 2.1, no. 27.5.

_____[Δ]ημητρίο[υ], *Sam*. 2.1, no. 42.5, Ainos.

_____ος Δημητρίου, *IG*, no. 202.2.

_____ς Διογένους Πριαπηνός, *IG*, no. 184.5, Priapos.

_____Διονυσίου, *IG*, no. 180.1.

_____[Δ]ιονυσίου, *IG*, no. 180.6.

___ιον Διονυσίου, *IG*, no. 218.8, Ainos.

_____Ἡρακλείδα, *IG*, no. 180.7.

_____ος Θεοχάρου, *IG*, no. 194.12, ἱεροποιός, Kyzikos.

_____ς Ἱέρωνος Ἀντιοχεύς, *IG*, no. 184.3, Antioch.

...νος Ἰσίω[νος], *IG* XII Suppl., no. 344.3.

_____Μενάνδρου, *IG*, no. 180.4.

___ιων Μίκα, *IG*, no. 184.9.

_____[Ξε]νακῶντος, *IG*, no. 180.3.

___Ὀβρίμου, *IG*, no. 189b.1.

_____ος Ὀλυμπιαδώρου, *IG*, no. 180.5.

_____['Ρο?]ύφου, *IG*, no. 217.4, Ainos.

_____ς Στρατοκλέους, *IG*, no. 184.8.

_____κλῆς Φιλάργου 'Ρόδ[ιος], *IG*, no. 184.2, Rhodes.

[___ Φ]ιλώτου, *Sam*. 2.1, no. 42.4, Ainos.

Alphabetized by cognomina:

[Λ]ούκιος .θ?_____ Ἀθηνίων, *Sam*. 2.1, no. 41.5-6.

N(umerius) ....ni[us N.] l. Ep[hor]us? *IG*, no. 173a.3.

___. I[...]us Lupercianus, *Hesperia* 34, 115, line 6.

_____alis Peregrinus, *Sam*. 2.1, no. 53*bis*.4, lictor.

_____asidius Stephaniu[s], *Sam*. 2.1, no. 36.9.

Alphabetized by ethnic:

___ος Θεσσαλονεικεύς, *Sam*. 2.1, no. 58.1, Thessalonike.

___y.rus Pergamenus, *Sam*. 2.1, no. 36.11, Pergamon.

Broken names:

[..]aberi[us]_____, *Sam*. 2.1, no. 32.9.

___all[i]a Paro.nilici, *Sam*. 2.1, no. 38.5.

[.]AM[..]SS[- - -], *Hesperia* 34, 115, line 20, slave.

_____ανίας, *IG*, no. 189b.29.

_____ _____ανιος, *Sam*. 2.1, no. 35.9.

_____.asperȩṣ M.._____, *Sam.* 2.1, no. 52.1.

_____ _____ἄτωνος, *IG*, no. 189b.21.

____αχος, *IG*, no. 189b.25.

....c.....ṇμ....., *Sam.* 2.1, no. 28a.11.

____dnsis Syr____, *IG*, no. 213.4.

____ ____δώρου, *Sam.* 2.1, no. 35.8.

_____erȩus, *Hesperia* 34, 115, line 42.

____hes, *Sam.* 2.1, no. 53*bis*.7, slave.

____ __ηνος, *Sam.* 2.1, no. 42.6, Ainos.

..θόδημο[ς], *Sam.* 2.1, no. 28b.5.

____ιαδα, *IG*, no. 220b.16.

____ιϰλῆς, *IG*, no. 189b.31.

____ __ιοντος, *IG*, no. 189b.20.

____ίου, *IG*, no. 206.15, ἀπελεύθερος of King Rhoimetalkes.

____ις, *Sam.* 2.1, no. 59.13.

..ίων, *IG* XII Suppl., no. 344.11.

____ __χίου, *IG*, no. 189b.2.

____ϰλῆς, *IG*, no. 189b.28.

...χος τοῦ Ἰμ..., *IG*, no. 190a.24.

____χράτης, *IG*, no. 189b.24.

__χῶιος?.....νίου, *IG* XII Suppl., no. 344.1-2.

_____l_____, *Sam.* 2.1, no. 34.8.

____λε__, *Sam.* 2.1, no. 33aII.9.

____.λησσ____, *Sam.* 2.1, no. 41.10, slave.

____ΛΙ____, *Sam.* 2.1, no. 33aII.6.

__λης Ἀχ_____ [ϰαθ' υἰοθεσία]ν δὲ Δημον[ίϰου], *IG*, no. 213.2.

[_____?]l.usius, *Sam.* 2.1, no. 36.13.

____μαχος, *IG*, no. 189b.26.

____my____, *Sam.* 2.1, no. 33aII.19.

____νδρος, *IG*, 189b.27.

_____νιχος, *IG*, no. 206.14, ἀπελεύθερος of King Rhoimetalkes.

_____ _____νος, *Sam.* 2.1, no. 35.7.

_____ ____όδας, *IG*, no. 189b.3.

_____one, *Sam.* 2.1, no. 33aII.10.

____-ονος, *Sam.* 2.1, App. IV.19, Kyzikos.

____orus, *Sam.* 2.1, no. 53*bis*.6, slave.

_____ος, *IG*, no. 184.7.

_____ __οσί[ου], *IG*, no. 217.5, Ainos.

_____ _____ου, *Sam.* 2.1, no. 35.6.

_____ _____ου, *Sam.* 2.1, no. 27.6.

_____ ____ους, *Sam.* 2.1, no. 27.7.

_____ρ, *Sam.* 2.1, no. 59.12, slave.

_____ς, *IG*, no. 189b.32.

____σιανός____γορέως, *Sam.* 2.1, no. 37.5-6.

___stator, *CIL* III Suppl., no. 7373.9.

_____ _____ _____τianianus, *Sam.* 2.1, no. 50.1, Q(uaestor) prov. Ṃ[ac](edoniae).

____tion, *Sam.* 2.1, no. 53*bis*.10, slave.

____τόμαχος, *IG*, no. 184.6.

_____us, *Sam.* 2.1, no. 53*bis*.8, slave.

_____us, *Sam.* 2.1, no. 53.8, leg. [p]ro pr. pr̥ov. eiusdem (i.e., Macedoniae).

_____ων, *IG*, no. 189b.30.

_____ ...ωνέως, *Sam.* 2.1, no. 33aI.1.

B. Samothracian Eροptai

A..____, *Sam.* 2.1, no. 26b.8.

Ἀγάθινος Εὐβ[ούλου], *Hesperia* 48, 17, line 6, τριήραρχος, Knidos.

Ἀγας__ _____, *IG*, no. 186a.15, συνέγδαμος, Rhodes.

Ἀλέξανδρος Ἰκάρου, *BCH* 86, no. 4.13, Kos?

Ἀναξικράτης Ἀναξικράτε̣[υς], *IG*, no. 186a.11, συνέγδαμος, Rhodes.

[Ἀ]πολλόδωρος B_____, *Sam.* 2.1, no. 26a.5.

Ἀσκληπ_____, *Sam.* 2.1, no. 26b.9.

Ἀσκληπιάδη[ς] Διοκλεύς, *Hesperia* 48, 17, lines 10-11, γραμματεύς, Knidos.

Γεράνιος, *BCH* 86, no. 4.14.

[Γλα]υκίας [Λέο]ντος, *Sam.* 2.1, no. 28c.16-17.

Δαμασα__ _____, *IG*, no. 186a.14, συνέγδαμος, Rhodes.

Δαμάτριος Ἀμφοτεροῦ, *IG*, no. 186a.8, ἱεροποιός, Rhodes.

Διον_____, *Sam.* 2.1, no. 26b.7.

Διοφάνης, *Sam.* 2.1, no. 26b.5.

Εὔβουλος Ἀρχιπόλιος, *Hesperia* 48, 17, 4-5, ναύαρχος, Knidos.

Θεύδο̣[το]ς, *Sam.* 2.1, no. 26b.4.

Θεύδωρος Ἡραγόρ̣[α], *IG*, no. 186a.12, συνέγδαμος, Rhodes.

Ἰούλιος Ἕρμιππος, *IG*, no. 216.18, Athens.

Ἱππίας Αἰσχυλίνου, *BCH* 86, no. 4.11.

Ἱππόδαμος Ἀναξάνδριδ̣[ος], *Hesperia* 48, 17, line 7, τριήραρχος, Knidos.

Ἰσίδοτος _____, *IG*, no. 186.13, συνέγδαμος, Rhodes.

Καλλικράτης Δαματρίου, *IG*, no. 186.10, συνέγδαμος, Rhodes.

Κλευ__ Νικασιβούλου, *Hesperia* 48, 17, lines 8-9, τριήραρχος, Knidos.

Κόνων, *Sam.* 2.1, no. 26b.6.

[.] C̣ornelius L. f. Lent[ulus], *Sam.* 2.1, no. 28a.3.

[Λ]έων or [Κλ]έων [Βο]σπορίχο[υ], *Sam.* 2.1, no. 28c.14-15.

Q. Luccius Q. [f.], *Sam.* 2.1, no. 31.4.

C. Mari__, *Sam.* 2.1, no. 30.

____ Marius Fructus, *Sam.* 2.1, no. 36.17.

[C.] Marius L. f. Ste. Schinas, *Sam.* 2.1, no. 36.15.

Μῖκις Μνησισ[τρ]άτου φύσει δ[ε] Ἀσκληπιάδης Ἀττάλου, *Sam.* 2.1, App. IV.8-9, Kyzikos.

Πεισικράτης Τιμαράτου, *IG*, no. 186a.7, ἱεροποιός, Rhodes.

Πό(πλιος) Ἐρέννιος Λεοντεὺς Ἀζηνιεύς, *IG*, no. 216.16, Athens.

Πυθίων Πυθίωνος, *BCH* 86, no. 4.12, Kos?

Πυθόδωρος Δημοσ[τράτ]ου, *IG*, no. 215.19-20.

[Rupili]a Q. f. Quinta, *Sam.* 2.1, no. 36.16.

Σέλευκος, *IG*, no. 205.6, ἀκόλουθος.

Λεύκιος Σικίνιος Μαάρκου Ῥωμαῖος, *IG*, no. 205.4-5.

____ Σόσσιος _____, *Sam.* 2.1, no. 41.3.

Σωσθένης Θευ___, *Hesperia* 48, 17, line 9, τριήραρχος, Knidos.

Σωσικλῆς Εὐκράτευς, *IG*, no. 186a.6, ἱεροποιός, Rhodes.

P. Teidius P. f. Pom__, *CIL* III Suppl., no. 12318.

L. Fourius L. f. Ou[f](entia?) Crassupes, *CIL* III Suppl., no. 12318.

[Χα]ρίδαμος [Χα]ρίδαμος or [Ἀ]ρίδαμος [Ἀ]ρίδαμος, *Sam.* 2.1, no. 28c.12-13.

Broken names:

...ειο..., *Sam.* 2.1, no. 28c.20.

____ε.ν____, *Sam.* 2.1, no. 26a.7.

__επ.......α, *Sam.* 2.1, no. 26a.3.

...nio.ni____, *Sam.* 2.1, no. 17b.2.

____όδοτος, *Sam.* 2.1, no. 26a.4.

[..σ]θένης [Φα]έννο[υ], *Sam.* 2.1, no. 28c.18-19.

____υπ____, *Sam.* 2.1, no. 26a.2.

PLATES-ACKNOWLEDGEMENTS

Frontispiece, I-IV: Photographs taken by the author, July, 1976.

V(a). Istanbul, Archaeological Museum.

V(b). CRAI 20 (1892) 22.

INDEX

I. Greek Men and Women

Agis IV (Sparta), 22

Akornion Dionysiou (Dionysopolis), 73

Alexander III (the Great), 5, 16-21
  finances, 110-11, n. 135
  hypomnemata, 111 n. 147
  religious policy of, 17-18

Alexander IV (son of Alexander the Great), 16, 18, 26

Alexandros (Kephallenia), 86

Andriskos, 135 n. 697

Andromachos Demetriou (Samothracian initiate), 117 n. 278

Antalkidas (Sparta), 38

Antiochos II (Theos), 24

Antiochos III (the Great), 24

Apollonios of Thera, 64-5

Aristarche Mikythou (Pergamon), 65

Arrhidaios, see Philip III (Arrhidaios)

Arsinoë II, 22, 38, 81, 82, 112 ns. 177 and 179

Arsinoë III, 65

Artemidoros Apolloniou Pergaios, 61-64, 126 n. 496, 127 ns. 498-500, 502, 509; see frontispiece

Asklepiades Attalou, Samothracian initiate, 45

Attalos (Pergamon), 133 n. 657

Diagoras (Melos), 65-66

Dionysios Strouthionos (Istros), 72-73

Epaphrodeitos (Kos), 86

Epikrates Nikeratou (Olbia), 74

Epimenes (Seuthopolis), 60

Epinikos (Ptolemaic governor of Thrace), 22, 110 n. 132

Erieus (stone-cutter, Philadelphia), 81

Eubiotos Aristonos (Olbia), 74

Eumenes (Pergamon), 88

Euphrosynos Idymeos (Syme), 85

Evander, 88

Helianax Asklepiodoros Athenaios (Delos), 77

Hestiaios Pempidou (Thasos), 120 n. 356

Hippomedon (Ptolemaic general), 22-23, 38

Isodoros Nikostratou (Samothracian initiate), 113 n. 206

Laodike (wife of Antiochos II), 24

Lysander (Sparta), 38

Lysimachos, 21, 22, 38, 60, 81, 112 ns. 175 and 177, 113 n. 184

Mithridates VI, Eupator Dionysos (the Great), 77, 93, 95, 132 n. 627, 138 n. 807

Moschion Thaselitas (Rhodes), 85

Nysa (Kos), 86

Olympias (wife of Philip II), 17, 19, 38, 42

Parmeniskos Aristeos (*hieropoios* from Kyzikos), 53

Perdiccas, 18, 111 n. 147

Perseus, 23, 53, 87-89, 102, 112 n. 179

Philip II, 16-18, 38

Philip III (Arrhidaios), 16, 18-20, 26, 38, 111 ns. 151 and 157

Philip V, 23, 38, 60, 89, 113 n. 193

Philoxenos Philoxenou (*hieropoios* from Kyzikos), 53

Ptolemy I (Soter), 22, 112 n. 177, 113 n. 184, 127 n. 498

Ptolemy II (Philadelphos), 22, 24, 38, 81, 112 n. 177

Ptolemy III (Euergetes), 22

Ptolemy IV (Philopator), 65

Ptolemy V (Epiphanes), 65

Ptolemy Keraunos, 22

Pyrrhos of Epiros, 20

Rhoimetalkes, 99, 137 n. 794

Seuthes III (Seuthopolis), 59

Skopas, 110 n. 124

Sokles (Samothrace), 123 n. 425

Theondas (Alexandria), 82

Theondas (*basileus* at Samothrace), 39

Tryphera (Ephesos), 86

II. Roman Men and Women

Agrippina, 80

Alexandros Babullius F. l., 96

Lucius Atilius, 88

M. Aufidius M. l., 96

Augustus, 91, 100

Babullius Pamphilus M. l. Astymenos, 96-97

M. Caecilius Sotas, 66-67

L. Calpurnius Piso, 90-91

C. Cestius, 97

M. Claudius Marcellus, 87

Cornelius Lentulus, 93

Cn. (Cornelius) Lentulus, 136 n. 738

L. Cornelius Sulla, 96

L. Furius L. f. Crassupes (*sic*), 96

Germanicus, (Julius Caesar), 97

Hadrian, 100, 102, 137 n. 801

Hilarus Prim[us], 42

C. Julius Augurinus, 98

C. Julius Caesar, 90, 94

L. Julius Caesar, 90

III. Index Locurum

IV. Gods and Heroes

PLATE I

a) Samothrace: Paved circular area on the eastern hill.

b) Samothrace: Architrave block from the building dedicated by Philip III and Alexander IV.

PLATE II

a) Samothrace: Anaktoron and Arsinoeion.

b) Samothrace: Interior of the Hieron.

PLATE III

a) Samothrace: Stoa on the western hill.

b) Delos: Samothrakion.

PLATE IV

a) Thera: *Temenos* of Artemidoros; altar of the Samothracian gods (left) and altar of Homonoia (right).

b) Thera: *Temenos* of Artemidoros, inscription on altar of Samothracian gods.

PLATE V

b) Samothrace: Appendix I, no. 19.

a) Alexandroupolis: Appendix I, no. 15.

I. Sites from which Mystai came to Samothrace

II. Sites from which Theoroi came to Samothrace

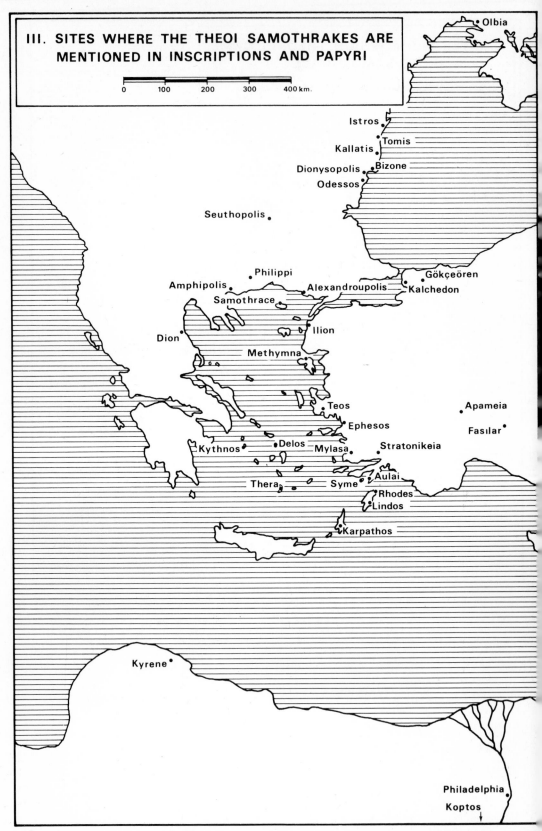

III. Sites where the Theoi Samothrakes are mentioned in Inscriptions and Papyri